I0027274

ANSON COUNTY, NORTH CAROLINA

Deed Abstracts, 1749-1766

Abstracts of Wills & Estates, 1749-1795

By

BRENT H. HOLCOMB, C.A.L.S.

CLEARFIELD

Copyright © 1974, 1975
Brent H. Holcomb

Copyright © transferred to
Genealogical Publishing Co., Inc.
Baltimore, Maryland
1979
All Rights Reserved

Originally published in three volumes
Clinton, South Carolina
1974-1975

Consolidated, repaged, and reprinted
with a new index and table of contents by
Genealogical Publishing Co., Inc.
Baltimore, Maryland
1980, 1991

Reprinted for Clearfield Company by
Genealogical Publishing Company
Baltimore, Maryland
2010

Library of Congress Catalogue Card Number 79-67870
ISBN 978-0-8063-0871-5

Made in the United States of America

CONTENTS

INTRODUCTION

Anson County was formed in 1748 or 1749 from Bladen County. At its formation it included a vast territory, having as its northern border the Virginia line until the formation of Rowan County in 1753, having no western boundary until the formation of Mecklenburg County, February 1, 1763, and having an indeterminate southern boundary until the survey of the South Carolina line, September 24, 1764. Before the Mecklenburg County and the S.C. border surveys, Anson County included all or parts of the South Carolina counties of Marlboro, Chesterfield, Lancaster, York, Chester, Cherokee, Union, Spartanburg, Greenville, Laurens, and Newberry. The records abstracted in this volume include the period when Anson County was at its largest.

The Anson County deed books now extant are copies made by a later Anson County clerk from the original books. Notice the deed on page 23 referring to a deed recorded in Volume A, pp. 24-25. The copy now extant shows this deed in Volume A. page 19. Obviously the scribe on the copies now extant had his problems with old handwriting as he recorded Henry Summaral as Henry Lummaral. Some of these deeds have incomplete grant references. For some, I have attempted to provide more complete data by checking in the Land Grant Office. References to the file numbers, etc. are given. All of the deed books are abstracted in their entirety as now extant, except Volume 7, where it is explained. Volume 1 commences with page 123. Perhaps the first 122 pages were destroyed in a court house fire. Only some of the later deeds have recording dates. All those given have been included. There exist presently two copies of these deed books, the "originals" at Archives and the Wadesboro copies. I have found the Wadesboro copies to be remarkably free of error. The page numbers vary, and the pagination used here is that of the Wadesboro copies since those are the page numbers in the deed index. The only discrepancy inthe Wadesboro copies is the marks of the signers. The Wadesboro copies have mostly x's, while the originals have varying marks. I have copied the marks from the originals and put them with my abstracts. In addition the 1763 tax list has been transcribed and included. Although incomplete, it is the first extant tax list from Anson County. It was made after the formation of Mecklenburg County, but before the South Carolina border survey. For later information on many persons found in these deeds, see my Mecklenburg County, North Carolina Deed Abstracts 1763-1779 and my Deed Abstracts of Tryon, Lincoln & Rutherford Counties, North Carolina 1769-1786 Tryon County Wills & Estates.

The probate records of Anson County have suffered some severe losses by Court House fires. Those extant for the period 1749-1795 are found in one volume (C. R. 005.801.1) at North Carolina Archives. These appear to have been copied from loose papers, as neither the wills nor the estates papers are in any logical order. Included here are also Anson County wills, inventories, administration bonds, and returns of probates of wills and estates (1766-1772) from the Secretary of the Province papers. Before 1760, all such proceedings were kept by the Secretary of the Province. Unfortunately, the only original wills wills from Anson County for this early period are those of the Secretary of the Province. The inventories and administration bonds often show no county designation; therefore, if a search is made for an individual who may have died prior to 1760, a check should be made in those papers. The returns of probates and administrations are valuable, as there are no court minutes extant from Anson County except from 1771-1777, and these returns contain information on some wills and estates no longer extant (e. g., Violet Primrose and Charles Cox). The second volume of Anson County wills (C. R. 005.801.2) overlaps this time period slightly, beginning in 1790. The second volume should be checked if a person is known to have died before 1795 and is not found here.

Brent H. Holcomb, C. A. L. S.
Columbia, South Carolina

Page 1: THOMAS TOMKINS of "Hanson" Co., planter, for ₺300 money of S. C.
to WILLIAM FORBES of same, planter, 200 A on S side Pee Dee between
WILLIAM DINKINS and JOHN WILLIAMS...granted to TOMKINS 22 May 1741...dated
25 March 1749...THOMAS TOMKINS (SEAL), MARY TOMKINS (SEAL), Wit: PATRICK
SHEALS, FRANCES CHAPPEL (₣-her mark).

Pp. 2-3: 28 March 1749, JOHN ASHLEY of Anson Co., planter, to SAMUEL ARNELL
of same, planter, for ₺15 money of Va.,...100 A on N side of Great
Pee Dee at the mouth of Little River...granted to sd. ASHLEY at Newbern 174-...
JOHN ASHLEY (Q) (SEAL), Wit: J. D. PHILLIP, THOS JONES.
                    [JOHN ASHLEY obtained a grant of 500 A, north side of Great Pee
                    Dee, 22 Nov 1746, File #950, Book 10, p. 113.]

Page 4: 20 Dec 1749, PHILIP HINSON of Anson Co., planter, to BENJAMIN DEUMER
of Louisa Co., Va., for ₺20 proc. money...50 A on N side Great Pee
Dee, part of a 600 A tract granted to sd. HINSON...PHILIP HINSON (SEAL), Wit:
JOHN DENNEN, WM. BEDINFIELD, HENRY BEDINGFIELD.

Page 5:Blank.

Pp. 6-7: 6 Sept 1749, JAMES COWARD of Anson Co., planter, to HENRY SOMMERLIN of
same, planter, for ₺150 money of S. C....194 A adj. land where HENRY
SOMMERLIN now lives on NE side Great Pee Dee...granted to JAMES COWARD...
JAMES COWARD (SEAL), Wit: WILLIAM FORBES, CHARITY FORBES.

Pp. 7-8: 4 Dec 1749, JOHN HORNBACK, planter, to ANDREW MOREMAN, planter, for
₺50 proc. money...land on E side of Great Pee Dee, the upper corner
of a tract of 213 A laid out for WILLIAM ATKINS, out of the same tract of 640
A granted to SOLOMON HEWS 22 May 1741, conveyed by sd. HEWS to JOHN LEE by
deed 27 Aug 1746, and from sd. LEE to JOHN HORNBACK by deed 2 March 1747...JOHN
HORNBACK (SEAL), Wit: EDMD CARTLIDGE, ELIZABETH CARTLIDGE.

Pp. 9-10: 27 Feb 1748, JOHN HICKS of Anson Co., planter, to HENRY SOMMERLIN of
Johnson, planter, for ₺20 money of Va.,...200 A on NE side of Great
Pee Dee...PHILIP HENSONs line...plantation where JOHN GOODIN formerly dwelt...
granted to JOHN HICKS ____ 1743...JOHN HICKS (SEAL), Wit: EDMUND IRBY, WM.
FORBES.

Pp. 11-12: 4 Dec 1749, JOHN HORNBACK of Anson Co.,planter, to CHARLES MOORMAN
and BENJAMIN MOORMAN of same, for ₺50 proc. money...land on S side
Great Pee Dee...mouth of Walkers gut...Rockey River...400 A granted to sd. HORN-
BACK 21 June 1746...JOHN HORNBACK (SEAL), Wit: EDMD CARTLIDGE, ELIZABETH CART-
LIDGE.

Pp. 12-13: JOHN BERRY, late of Bladen Co., planter, for ₺60 S. C. currency
pd. by EDMUND IRBY "now of same county" carpenter, land in Anson
Co. on NE side of Pee Dee...adj. tract granted to GEORGE LENIOR...200 A
granted to JOHN BERRY...dated 10 Jan 1748...JOHN BERRY (X) (SEAL), Wit:
WILLIAM BEDINGFIELD, WILLIAM HICKS.

Pp. 14-15: 26 Sept 1749, WILLIAM KEMP of Anson Co., to ANDREW COX of same,
for ₺8 proc. money...150 A, part of a 400 A tract surveyed for sd.
KEMP on S side Pee Dee on Mill Creek...including plantation ANDREW COX now
lives on...WILLIAM KEMP (X) (SEAL), Wit: JOHN KEMP, JOHN CONAWAY.

Pp. 16-17: 26 Sept 1749, JAMES JONES of Craven Co., S. C., planter, to ANDREW
HAMTON of Anson Co., planter, for ₺500 proc. money...640 A granted
to sd. JONES 22 May 1741...on S side P. D.... Beech Creek... JAMES JONES (ꟻ)
(SEAL), Wit: WM. BEDINGFIELD, WM KEMP (X), JO STAFFARD.

Pp. 17-18: 13 Feb 1748, ROBERT HUMPHRIS of Anson Co., to DUNCAN GRANT of same,
for ₺10 Va. currency...100 A on N side of Great Pee Dee, S side of
Little River...below WILLIAM STONEs now dwelling place...half of 200 A granted
to ROBERT MILLS 24 March 1747...confirmed by MILLS to WILLIAM STONE by deed...
then to ROBERT HUMPHRIS...ROBERT HUMPHRIS (RH) (SEAL), Wit: CHARLES ROBINSON,
BENJAMIN B. VINES.

Page 19: 28 June 1750, SAMUEL DAVIS of Anson Co., to JOSEPH TOOPS, planter of
same, for ₺30 Va. money...539 A on NE side Yadkin, granted to SAMUEL
DAVIS by my Lord Granville's deed...SAM. DAVIS (SEAL), Wit: JOHN DUNN, ANTHONY
HUTCHINS.

Pp. 20-21: 3 March 1748, NICHOLAS SMITH of Bladen Co., planter, to NATHANIEL
HILLEN of Anson Co., planter, for ₺50...land on N side Great Pee
Dee, half of a tract of 400 A, granted to sd. SMITH, 5 Oct 1743...NICHOLAS
SMITH (X) (SEAL), Wit: C. ROBINSON, CHAS ROBINSON JUNR.

Page 22: 8 March 1750/1, Anson Co., N. C., JOHN WILLIS for 50 pistols money
of Va. pd. by THOMAS HARRINGTON, do sell one negroe York...JOHN
WILLIS JUNR., Wit: JOHN McCOY (ꟻ), CALEB HOWELL, E. CARTLIDGE.

Pp. 23-24: 12 Nov 1750, JOHN WILLIAMS of Anson Co., planter, to WILLIAM FORBES of
same, planter, for ₺22 s2, Va. currency, 108 A on S side Great Pee
Dee, adj. land conveyed from JOHN WILLIAMS to WILLIAM FORBES, land formerly
property of JOHN RODES...JOHN WILLIAMS (SEAL), Wit: HENRY LUMMARAL (H), PHILIP
HERNDON. N. B. sd. JOHN WILLIAMS to make above tract clear of Quitrents to 12
April 1751.

Pp. 24-25: 27 July, 1750, JOHN CLARK of Anson Co., labourer, to BENJAMIN DUMAS,
of same, labourer, for ₺50 proc. money...land on S side Great Pee
Dee and N side Rockey River...opposite ANDREW MOORMANs land...400 A granted to
JOHN CLARK 13 Apr 1749...JOHN CLARK (SEAL), Wit: CHARLES MOREMAN, ANTHONY
HUTCHINS, JOHN GREGG (ꟻ).

Pp. 26-27: 20 Oct 1750, JOHN CLARK of Anson Co., to NATHANIEL HILLEN of same,
for ₺100 proc. money...land on NE side of Great Pee Dee above mouth
of Little River...at NICHOLAS SMITHs corner...JACOB COLLSONs line...400 A
granted to JOHN COLLSON 26 Nov 1749...JOHN CLARK (SEAL), Wit: WILLIAM OVERALL,
SAMUEL BEESON.

Pp. 28-29: 18 July 1751, ROWLAND WILLIAMS, of Anson Co., planter, to JOHN GAMBRIL
of same, planter, for ₺8 proc money of America...land on S side Great
Pee Dee... SE side of Browns Creek, 6 or 7 miles above the mouth...150 A
granted to SAMUEL HOUGH 7 Apr 1750, and sold by him to sd. WILLIAMS 16 July 1751...
ROWLAND WILLIAMS (W) (SEAL), Wit: CHARLES ROBINSON JUNR, ANTHONY HUTCHINS.

Pp. 29-30: 13 Oct 1750, WILLIAM TURNER of Beckly Co., S. C. planter, to SAMUEL
DAVIS of Anson Co, planter, for Ⱡ390 current Bills of S. C. ...land
on N side Great Pee Dee...upper corner of land laid out for GEORGE LENIOR...400
A sold to WILLIAM TURNER by SOLOMON HEWS 13 Sept 1746...WILLIAM TURNER (SEAL),
Wit: BENJAMIN BOWCHER, ISSACHAR WILLCOCKS.

Page 31: 20 Oct 1750, JOHN CLARK of Anson Co., for Ⱡ100 Va. money pd. by
JOSEPH WHITE of same, Gent., sell negroes Jack, Phillis, Ben, Charles,
Jack...JOHN CLARK (SEAL), Wit: EDMD CARTLIDGE, ANTHONY HUTCHINS.

Page 32: 10 Nov 1750, WILLIAM DINKINS of Anson Co., planter, to WILLIAM FORBES
of same, planter for Ⱡ70 Va. money...300 A on S side Pee Dee...granted
to sd. DINKINS 22 May 1741....WILLIAM DINKINS (ↄ) (SEAL), Wit: MAR. KIMBROUGH,
HENRY SUMMARAL (H).

Page 33: 17 Apr 1751, JOHN FITZGERALD and HUGH WILLSON, planter to ISAAC
FALKINBOURGH for Ⱡ40 proc. money...200 A on S side Pee Dee called
Pleasant Hill...granted to sd. FITZGARRALD 30 Sept 1748...since then sd.
FITZGARRALD sold HUGH WILLSON 100 A for Ⱡ8 Va. money, June 1750...JOHN
FITZGARRALD (SEAL), HUGH WILLSON (SEAL), Wit: CALEB HOWELL, JOHN BERRYMAN, ANDREW
FALKENBOUGH (A).

Page 34: 22 June 1751, JOHN KEMP of Anson Co., planter, for Ⱡ30 wherein I stand
justly indebted to ELIZABETH KEMP...do sell her 200 A adj. where sd.
ELIZABETH KEMP now lives, one gray mare with young colt, two cows and calves,
etc....JOHN KEMP (SEAL), Wit: GEORGE KING, JOSEPH KEMP (K).

Pp. 35-36: 15 Jan 1750, EDMUND CARTLIDGE of Anson Co., yeoman, to JOHN McKAY of
same, planter, for Ⱡ5 proc. money, 100 A on S side Great Pee Dee...
granted to sd. CARTLIDGE 17 Apr 1745...E. CARTLIDGE (SEAL), Wit: JOHN HAMER,
JOHN BRANDON, JAS MACKILWEAN.

Page 37: 13 Jan 1750, JOHN HICKS of Anson Co., to WILLIAM HICKS of same, for
Ⱡ3 sterling...200 A on N side Pee Dee, part of 400 A granted to
GEORGE SENIOR   25 July 1743...JOHN HICKS (SEAL), Wit: WILLIAM ELLIS, WILLIAM
BARROWS (W).

Page 38: 15 Oct 1750, CATHERINE LEE of Anson Co., widow, to her son JOSHUA
STROWD of same, for love good wills & affection...all my goods and
chattels...CATHARINE LEE (X) , Wit: THOS MOORMAN, JOHN HORNBACK.

Page 39: 16 Oct 1750, JEREMIAH SWAN of Anson Co., planter, to PETER PRESLAR of
same, planter, for Ⱡ30 Va. money...200 A on S side of Rockey River...
granted to sd. SWAN 8 Oct 1747...JEREMIAH SWAN (SEAL), Wit: WILLIAM PHILLIPS,
JAMES HUTCHINS.

Pp. 40-41: 11 June 1750, NICHOLAS SMITH of Bladen Co., planter , to ROBINSON
TOWNSEND of Anson Co., planter, for Ⱡ20 Va. money...200 A on S
side of Great Pee Dee and above Little River...granted 13 Oct 1749 to sd.
SMITH...NICHOLAS SMITH (N) (SEAL), Wit: CHAS ROBINSON SENR, CHAS. ROBINSON JUNR.

Pp. 42-43: 25 June 1750, CHARLES ROBINSON SENR. of Anson Co., planter, to
CHARLES ROBINSON JUNR of same, for s5 money of Va...200 A on
E side of Little River of Great Pee Dee...granted to CHARLES ROBINSON SENR
22 Nov 1746...CHARLES ROBINSON (SEAL), Wit: THOMAS RODGAMAN, LUKE BLAKELY.

Pp. 43-44: 15 July 1751, JOHN McKAY of Anson Co., yeoman, to CHARLES ROBINSON,
Esqr., for ₺30s10 Va. money...300 A on N side Great Pee Dee...E
side of Little River...granted 20 June 1746 to sd. McKAY...JOHN McKAY (₤)
(SEAL), Wit: ANTHONY HUTCHINS, M. BROWN.

Pp. 45-46: 29 Oct 1748, JOHN CLARK of Anson Co., to BENJAMIN DUMAS of Louisa
Co., Va., for ₺200 proc. money...land in Bladen Co. on N side of
Great Pee Dee called Buffaloe Island, granted 20 June 1746...JOHN CLARK (SEAL),
Wit: JOSEPH WHITE, JOHN COLEMAN, SAML FRENCH, DAVID P.

Page 46: TYREE HARRIS of Va. , appoints BENJAMIN DUMAS of Anson Co., Gent,
lawful attorney to sell my lands in Anson Co...21 Apr 1752...
TYREE HARRIS (SEAL).

Pp. 47-48: 24 Oct 1748, JOHN GILES of Johnston Co, to HENRY WALKER of Bladen
Co., for ₺25 money of Va., land on S side Great Pee Dee beg. at
corner of ROB PARKINS on Walkers Island, 300 A granted to GILES 26 Nov 1746...
JOHN GILES (SEAL), Wit: WM. KEMP (K), ABRA BOYD, HENRY GARRETT.

Page 49: 13 Sept 1750, JOHN GILES of Johnston Co., planter, to HENRY WALKER of
Anson Co., planter, for ₺26 proc. money...300 A S side Pee Dee...near
ROBERT PARK'S...granted to sd. GILES 3 Dec 1746... JOHN GILES (SEAL), Wit:
SAML. DONALDSON, WILLIAM HARRISON.

Page 50: Blank

Pp. 51-53: South Carolina (Lease and release). 25 March 1749, JASPER KING
of Prince Frederick Parish, Craven Co., S. C., planter, to JOHN
WILLIAMS of same (lease price, s5, release price ₺150 S. C. money), 400 A
in Bladen Co., N. C. on SW side Pee Dee, Rockey Creek...JOHN WESTFIELDS
upper line...granted 22 May 1741...JASPER KING (SEAL), Wit: FRANCISS FUTHY,
ROBERT FUTHY, JOHN GLEN, C. ROBINSON.

Pp. 54-55: 23 Oct 1750, JOHN WILLIAMS of Craven Co., S. C., to WILLIAM RODES,
a minor of same, for s5 proc. money...300 A, part of a tract of 400
A sold to WILLIAMS by JASPER KING...opposite PHILIP HENSON's...should sd.
WILLIAM RODES expire, land shall fall to his four sisters, MARTHA, ANNE,
SUSANNAH and ELIZABETH...JOHN WILLIAMS (SEAL), Wit: JOHN KEMP. ANTHONY HUTCHINS.

Pp. 56-57: 22 July 1750, JACOB COLLSON of Anson Co., to THOMAS HARRINGTON of same,
planter, for ₺20 Va. currency...200 A on N side Great Pee Dee...
above the waggon ford road at JOHN COLLSON's upper corner...granted to sd.
JACOB COLLSON 26 Nov 1746...JACOB COLLSON (SEAL), Wit: JOHN CHEEK (₤), JOHN
COLLSON.

Pp. 58-59₺ 28 June 1750, JOHN COLLSON of Anson Co., planter, to JOHN CHEEK of
same, for ₺50 proc. money...200 A on N side Great Pee Dee above mouth
of Brown Creek at JOHN CLARKs lower corner...granted to JOHN COLLSON 26 Nov
1746...JOHN COLLSON (SEAL), Wit: JOHN DUNN, ANTHONY HUTCHINS.

Pp. 59=60: 23 May 1750, THOMAS HOPPER of Anson Co., planter, to JOHN SMITH
of same, planter, for ₺10...5 A on lower side of Little River of
Pee Dee & near the mouth of Thickety Creek, part of a tract formerly conveyed
to THOMAS HOLMES by patent & then to THOMAS HOPPER...THOMAS HOPPER (SEAL), Wit:
JONATHAN HOLMES (H), BENJAMIN HORNE (B).

4

Pp. 61-62: 3 March 1748, NICHOLAS SMITH of Bladen Co., planter, to WILLIAM
            PHILLIPS of Anson Co., for ₤30 Va. currency...land on N side of
Great Pee Dee at lower end of tract where LEEs Cabbin was...granted to sd.
NICHOLAS SMITH 1748, 200 A...NICHOLAS SMITH (N) (SEAL), Wit: C. ROBINSON,
NATHANIEL HILLEN.

Page 63: 22 June 1750, JAMES DENSON, SENR. of Anson Co., planter to WILLIAM
            DOWNS of same, planter, for ₤10 Va. money...land on N side Great
Pee Dee, granted to sd. DENSON 22 Nov 1746...100 A...JAMES DENSON (+) (SEAL),
Wit: THOMAS RIDGE, LUKE BLAKELY, SAML ARMSTRONG.

Pp. 64-65: 21 June 1750, JAMES DENSON SENR of Anson Co., planter, to JAMES
            DENSON JUNR of same, planter, for s5 Va. money...100 A on N side
Great Pee Dee, granted to JAMES DENSON SENR 22 Nov 1746...JAMES DENSON (+),
Wit: WILLIAM DOWNS, LUKE BLAKELY.

Pp. 66-67: 20 June 1750, GEORGE CLEMMONS of Anson Co., planter, to JONATHAN
            HELMS of same, planter, for ₤6 Va. money, 50 A on N side Great
Pee Dee, granted to GEORGE CLEMANS, 7 April 1750...GEORGE CLEMANS (+) (SEAL),
Wit: C. ROBINSON, SAML DAVIS.

Pp. 67-68: 19 Sept 1750, THOMAS GEORGE of Anson Co., planter, to JOHN COLLSON
            of same, planter, for ₤12 Va. Money...100 A on S side Pee Dee,
granted to THOMAS GEORGE 4 Apr 1750...THOMAS GEORGE (SEAL), Wit: THOMAS
HARRINGTON (T), JOHN CHEEKS (I).

Page 69: 17 Oct 1750, JOHN COLLSON to ELIZABETH,AGNES, and WHITMILL HARRINGTON,
            2 daughters and son of my wife MARY by her former husband MR. JOHN
HARRINGTON, for natural love and affection...negroes and cattle...and JOHN
& MARY COLLSON to our son WILLIAM COLLSON...all are minors...shall be kept until
WHITMILL the youngest, shall arrive at 21, which shall be 20 Feb 1768...JOHN
COLLSON (SEAL), MARY COLLSON (M) (SEAL), Wit: None.

Pp. 69-70: 20 Apr 1752, JAMES CRAFFORD of Anson Co., planter, to JOHN COLLSON
            of same planter, for ₤30 proc. money...land in fork of Great Pee
Dee and Rockey River...granted to JOHN COLLSON 26 Nov 1746, sold to JAMES BARTON
17 Apr 1751, and by BARTON to JAMES CRAFFORD 27 Apr 1751, 200 A...JAMES CRAFFORD,
Wit: ANTHONY HUTCHINS, CALEB TOUCHSTONE.

Pp. 71-72: 16 July 1751, THOMAS HARRINGTON of Anson Co., planter, to SAMUEL
            HOUGH of same, planter, for ₤40 proc. money...land on N side ef
Great Pee Dee above mouth of dry creek...JACOB COLLSONs line...320 A...granted
to JAMES BENTLEY 26 Nov 1746, and sold to sd. HARRINGTON 26 Apr 1748...THOMAS
HARRINGTON (T) (SEAL), Wit: JOS. TOOPS, JOHN PHILLIPS, CHAS. ROBINSON JUNR.

Pp. 73-74: 30 Nov 1751, JOHN KEMP of Anson Co., planter, to CHRISTOPHER and
            BENJAMIN CLARK of Louisa Co., Va., for ₤60 money of Va....land on
W side Pee Dee near an Indian Grave...240 A...granted to WM. KEMP 21 Jan 1746...
JOHN KEMP (SEAL), Wit: ANDREW MOORMAN JUNR., ANDREW MOORMAN (A).

Page 75: 5 June 1750, JOHN HITCHCOCK of Craven Co., S. C. , planter to THOMAS
            MOORMAN of Anson Co., for ₤64 proc. money...land on E side Pee Dee,
Hitchcock Creek...200 A, part of 300 A granted to sd. HITCHCOCK 22 May 1741...
(later gives amount as 250 A)...JOHN HITCHCOCK (SEAL), Wit: JOSEPH HALL, THOMAS
JONES.

Page 76: 16 July, 1751, EPHRAIM LILES of Anson Co., laborer, to JOHN MOORMAN
of same, laborer, for ₤30 proc. money...200 A on N side Pee Dee below
mouth of Lake Creek...granted to LILES 28 Mar 1751...EPHRAIM LILES (E) (SEAL),
Wit: WM. TERRY, C. CARTLIDGE.

Pp. 77-78: 26 Apr 1748, JAMES BENTLEY of Bladen Co., to THOMAS HARRINGTON of
same, planter, for ₤50 proc money...land on NE side Pee Dee above mouth
of Dry Creek...JACOB COLLSONs line...granted to BENTLEY 26 Nov 1746, 320 A...
JAMES BENTLEY (SEAL), Wit: JOSEPH WHITE, JOHN CLARK, JOHN COLLSON.

Pp. 79-80: 23 Jan 1751, WILLIAM STONE of Anson Co., planter to ANDREW MOORMAN
of same, planter, for ₤30 Va. money...land on E side Great Pee Dee,
adj. SOLOMON HEWS land & JOHN HITCHCOCK's land, 200 A granted to STONE 20
Apr 1745...WILLIAM STONE (W) (SEAL), Wit: BURLINGHAM RUDD, CALEB HOWELL.

Pp. 80-81: 21 Apr 1752, WILLIAM KEMP of Anson Co., planter, to FRANCIS CLARK
of Colony of Va., planter, for ₤46s6 Va. currency...land on E side
Great Pee Dee, 213 A granted to SOLOMON HEWS 22 May 1741...WILLIAM KEMP (SEAL),
Wit: HENRY DOWNS, M. BROWN.

Pp. 82-83: 13 July 1750, JOHN CLARK of Anson Co., planter, to JOSEPH WHITE of
same, Esqr., for ₤100 of Va., land on S side Great Pee Dee, granted to
CLARK 28 Sept 1745, 300 A, including the island...JOHN CLARK (SEAL), Wit: JAMES
HUTCHINS, ANTHONY HUTCHINS.

Pp. 83-84: 26 Sept 1749, JAMES JEWERS of Anson Co. to JOHN ASHLEY JUNR of same
for ₤10 proc. money...200 A, part of 400 A granted to JEWERS 7 Apr
1749...on N side Great Pee Dee, known by the name of Buffaloe...JAMES JEWERS
(I) (SEAL), Wit: WILLIAM PHILLIPS, JOHN GAMBRILL (G).

Pp. 85-86: 11 Feb 1751, RICHARD JONES of Craven Co., S. C. planter, to JOHN
MARK of Beauford Co., N. C., cooper, for ₤100 proc money, land on
E side Pee Dee...corner of tract laid out for MATTHEW CREED, 320 A granted to
RICHARD JONES, 174-, ...RICHARD JONES (SEAL), Wit: JACOB PAUL, SAML BURTON.
          [Richard Jones obtained a grant of 320 A, N side P. D., 22 May
          1741, File #342, Book 5, p. 381.]

Pp. 87-88: 12 Apr 1749, THOMAS JONES of Bladen Co., surveyor, to EDMUND CARTLIDGE
of same, planter, for ₤16, proc. money...land on E side Pee Dee, 200
A...THOMAS JONES (SEAL), Wit: WM. PHILLIPS, ALEX OSBURN.

Pp. 88-89: 7 Sept 1751, ANDREW HAMPTON of Anson Co., to AMBROSE STILLE of same,
trader, for ₤150 Va. currency...640 A on SW side of Pee Dee above
Buch Creek...granted to JAMES JONES 22 May 1741....ANDREW HAMPTON (SEAL), Wit:
M. BROWN, JOHN HAMER, JACOB FORKENBROUG.

Pp. 89-90: 1 May 1750, CALEB HOWELL of Anson Co., planter to ANDREW FALKINBURGH
of same, planter, for ₤15 Va. money...200 A on S side Great Pee Dee...
about half a mile above Mount Pleasant, half of a grant to CALEB HOWELL 14 Mar
1745...CALEB HOWELL (SEAL), Wit: HENDRICK VALKENBURY, ISAAC FALKINBURGH (I),
JOHN BERRYMAN.

Pp. 90-91: 6 July 1749, FRANCIS MACKELWEAN of Anson Co., surveyor, to SAMUEL
FRENCH of same, planter, for ₺30 Va. money...200 A granted to sd.
MACKELWEAN 11 Apr 1749 on S side Pee Dee, on both sides Cedar Creek...
FRANCIS MACKELWEAN (SEAL), Test: JAS. MACKELWEAN, JOSEPH WHITE.

Pp. 92-93: 1 Feb 1750, JOHN CLARK of Anson Co., planter, to GEORGE SKIPPER, of
same, planter, for ₺50 Va. currency....200 A on N side Pee Dee,
granted to JOHN CLARK 7 Apr 1749...JOHN CLARK (SEAL), Wit: HENRY BEDINGFIELD,
JOHN KIMBROUGH, ALEX. GORDON.

Pp. 93-94: 8 Aug 1747, THOMAS TOMPKINS planter and MARY "his wife Spinster"
of Bladen Co., to MATTHEW CREED of Craven Co., S. C, carpenter, for
₺100 of S. C. , 200 A, half of a 400 A grant to sd. TOMPKINS 22 May 1741, on
Pee Dee, adj. WILLIAM DINKINS land...THOMAS TOMPKINS (SEAL), MARY TOMPKINS
(X) (SEAL), Wit: FRANCIS AWBREY, JOHN LOYD, WILLIAM DINKINS (∂), [Plat included
in deed.]

Pp. 95-96: 20 June 1750, HUGH LORRIMER of Craven Co., N. C., to SAMUEL MARTIN
of Anson Co., planter, 300 A granted 14 March 1745...on S side Pee
Dee above mouth of Little River...DENSONs land...HUGH LORRIMER (SEAL), Wit:
JOHN JENKINS, JACOB JENKINS,

Pp. 97-98: 29 Oct 1748, JOHN CLARK of Anson Co., to BENJAMIN DUMAS of Louisa
Co., Va., for ₺50 proc. money...land granted 4 Oct 1748...250 A
on N side Great Pee Dee, adj. CLARKs corner, WIDOW HERRINGTONs line...JOHN CLARK
(SEAL), Wit: JOSEPH WHITE, SAML FRENCH, DAVID PROVENDER.

Pp. 99-100: 19 Sept 1749, JOHN STAFFORD of Anson Co., to WILLIAM KEMP of same,
for ₺50 proc money...land on S side Pee Dee ...from deed of convey-
ance from JOHN READ 1745, 213 A...JNO STAFFORD (SEAL), Wit: ABRA BOYD, JOHN
McCOY (Ⅎ), JACOB DENKENS (Ⱦ).

Pp. 101-102: 28 July 1749, SOLOMON HEWS of Anson Co., to MARMADUEK KIMBROUGH,
for ₺60 Va. money...200 A on S side Pee Dee, granted to sd. HEWS
20 Apr 1745...SOLOMON HEWS (SEAL), Wit: JOHN CRAFFORD, JOHN DENEN, ALEX. GORDON.

Page 103: 1 May 1752, WILLIAM SHERRILL to his son ABBENTON SHERRILL...cattle
other half to son in law JAMES ROBINSON...WILLIAM SHERRILL (X) (SEAL),
Wit: JOHN WODSON, JOHN CLARK, JAMES HUTCHINS.

Pp. 104-105: 29 Oct 1748, JOHN CLARK of Anson Co., to BENJAMIN DUMAS of Louisa
Co., Va., for ₺100 Proc. money...500 A on N side Great Pee Dee...
corner of SOLOMON HEWS...corner of PHILIP HENSONs...granted 4 Oct 1748...
including an Island...JOHN CLARK (SEAL), Wit: JOSEPH WHITE, SAML.FRENCH., JOHN
COLEMAN, DAVID PROVENDER.

Pp. 105-106: 26 June 1750, JOHN FITZGERALD of Anson Co., planter, to HUGH WILSON
of same, planter, for ₺8 Va. money...100 A on S side Great Pee
Dee...granted to sd. FITZGERALD 13 Sept 1748...JOHN FITZGERALD (SEAL), Wit:
JOHN DUNN, THOS JONES.

Pp. 107-108: 26 Dec 1749, THOMAS HOLMS of Anson Co., to THOMAS COLEMAN, for ₺20
proc money..land on N side Pee Dee...JOHN FRANCIS corner... 100 A...
THOMAS HOLMS (T) (SEAL), Wit: JOHN HAMER, WILLIAM COLEMAN, JOHN JURDIN (Ⱦ).

Page 109: 27 June 1750, JOHN HITCHCOCK of Craven Co., S. C. to JOSEPH HALL,
        for Ⱡ7 proc. money...land on E side Pee Dee..corner of THOMAS MOOR-
MAN...50 A, part of 300 A granted to JOHN HITCHCOCK 22 May 1741...JOHN HITCH-
COCK (SEAL), Wit: THOMAS MOORMAN, THOMAS JONES.

Page 110: 15 Apr 1751, JAMES STEWART of Anson, planter, to BURLINGHAM RUDD of
        same, planter, for Ⱡ20 proc. money...300 A on S side Great Pee Dee...
Jones' Creek...granted to sd. BURLINGHAM RUDD 11 Apr 1749...JAMES STEWARD (Ⱡ)
(SEAL) , Wit: BENJ. JACKSON, JOHN ASHELY (A), CALEB HOWELL.

Page 111: 12 Oct 1750, BURLINGHAM RUDD of Anson Co., planter to JOHN RED of same,
        planter, 300 A granted 11 Apr 1749...Jones' Creek, for Ⱡ40 proc money
...BURLINGHAM RUDD (SEAL), Wit: JOSEPH SLOAN, JOSEPH NOBLES (Ⱡ).

Page 112: 1750, JOHN READ of Anson Co., planter, to JAMES STEWARD of same,
        planter, for Ⱡ40 proc. money...300 A on S side Great Pee Dee granted
to BURLINGHAM RUDD 11 Apr 1749...JOHN READ (SEAL), Wit: BURLINGHAM RUDD, WILLIAM
OWENS (WO).

Pp. 113-114: 15 Oct 1750, JOHN CLARK of Anson Co., to SAMUEL WILKINS of same,
        for Ⱡ150 Va. money...2 tracts on N side of Clarks River below
S fork of Cataba... JAMES ROBINSONs line...213 A and another tract of 300 A
granted 7 Oct 1749...JOHN CLARK (SEAL), Wit: GEORGE RIDICK, JAMES HUTCHINS,
JOHN DUNN.

Pp. 115-116: 16 July 1750, JOHN CLARK of Anson Co., to JAMES ROBINSON of same,
        for Ⱡ60 proc money...487 A on N side Clarks River...granted to sd.
CLARK 7 Oct 1749...JOHN CLARK (SEAL), Wit: JONLD WOODSON, WM SHERILL (W).

Pp. 117=118: 12 Apr 1751, JOHN COLLSON of Anson Co., planter, to SAMUEL FRENCH,
        of same, planter, for Ⱡ15 Va. money...land on S side PEE Dee bought
of THOMAS GEORGE, 100 A...granted to THOMAS GEORGE 4   Apr 1750...JOHN COLLSON
(SEAL), Wit: M. BROWN, THOMAS MOORMAN.

Pp. 118-119, Jan. 1751, THOMAS HARRINGTON of Anson Co., to HENRY WALKER of
        same, for Ⱡ60 Va. money...195 A on S side Great Pee Dee above mouth
of Turkey Creek, granted to JOHN CLARK 20 June 1746...sd. HENRY WALKER JUNR...
THOMAS HARRINGTON (X) (SEAL), Wit: JOHN HEAMER , JAMES HUTCHINS.

Pp. 120-121: 21 Aug 1750, SAMUEL GOODMAN of _____Co., N. C. to JOHN JENKINS of
        Anson Co., for Ⱡ32 Va. money...200 A on W side Pee Dee, adj.
JOHN HORNBACKs...SAMUEL GOODMAN (SEAL), Wit: JOHN TOMPKINS, THOMAS TOMPKINS.

Pp. 121-122: 20 Oct 1750, JOHN COLLSON of Anson Co., to JOHN CLARK of same,
        Gent., for Ⱡ500...land on N side Great Pee Dee above mouth of
Little River at NICHOLAS SMITHs corner...400 A...JACOB COLLSONs line...granted
to JOHN COLSON 26 Nov 1746...JOHN COLLSON (SEAL), Wit: WILLIAM OVERALT, NATHANIEL
HILLEN.

                    End Book A, No. 1
                    Containing all Conveyances to 1751

Pp. 123-124: 10 Nov 1754, JOHN WILSON of Rowan Co., to the Rev. Mr. JOSEPH
TATE of Lancaster Co., Pa., for ₺20 Va. money...432 A above
JAMES MITCHELL's and the fall of big creek of Little River...JOHN WILSON
(SEAL), Wit: WALTER CARRUTH, JNO. BRALY, ROB'T McPHERSON.
Acknowledged by JOHN WILSON before PETER HENLY CJ, 22 May 1756.
[This land now in S. C.]

Pp. 125-127: 9 & 10 Nov 1754, JOHN WILSON of Rowan Co., to the Revd. Mr.
JOSEPH TATE of Lancaster Co., Pa., (lease s5, release ₺30 Va.
money)...600 A above ARTHUR McCLURE's entry on Big Creek of Little River or
fairforest, waters of Broad River...JOHN WILSON (SEAL), WIT: WALTER CARRUTH,
JNO. BRALEY, ROBERT McPHERSON. Acknowledged by JOHN WILSON before PETER
HENLY CJ, 26 May 1756.   [This land now in S.C.]

Page 128: Repeat of lease on page 123.

Pp. 129-131: 15 & 16 Oct 1755, GEORGE COWIN & his wife [not named] of
Granvill Co., S.C., slaymaker, to JOHN HITCHCOCK, planter, of
Anson Co., (lease s5, release ₺20 sterling)...400 A on N side Broad River...
GEORGE COWIN (SEAL), Wit: JOHN McTACET, JOHN TOWNSEND Deed, HENRY HARDAN (H).

Pp. 132-134: 28 & 29 Apr 1756, HENRY FALKENBOROUGH of Anson Co., to JACOB
FALKENBOROUGH of same, (lease s5, release ₺100 proc. money)...
134 A on S side great Pee Dee...HENRY FALKENBOROUGH (SEAL), Wit: JOHN LEETH,
ISAAC FALKENBOROUGH (/).

Page 135: 2 Mar 1756, JOHN LEETH of Anson Co., planter to TARANCE CARRELL,
for ₺40 Va. money, 80 A granted to HENRY FALKENBOROUGH 6 Apr 1750...
conveyed by sd. HENRY Jan. 1754, on N side great Pee Dee, near Naked Creek...
JNO. LEETH (SEAL), Wit: JNO. DUNN, JAS. ARMOR.

Pp. 136-137: 6 Jan 1756, JOHN HORNBACK of Anson Co., planter, to MARSHALL
DEGGE, planter, for ₺10 Va. money...100 A on S side great Pee
Dee, nigh to a Spring...on Island Creek, upper part of land laid out for
JNO. NEWBERRY, granted 7 Oct 1747....JOHN HORNBACK (SEAL), Wit: JAS. MACKELLROY,
(+++), FRANCIS PARKER.

Page 138: 28 Dec 1755, MATTHEW FLOID of Anson Co., planter, to WILLIAM HILL-
HOUSE of same, planter, for ₺18 proc. money..450 A on N side Broad
River, adj. JAMES FANNINGs line, JOHN ELIOTs line...MATTHEW FLOID (SEAL),
Wit: NARCUS STOKES, JOHN HITCHCOCK, HENRY HARDAN (H).

Page 139: 12 Mar 1756, TOWNSEND ROBINSON, Esqr., of ANSON Co., to WILLIAM
TERRY, Esqr., of same, for ₺50 proc. money...300 A on S side great
Pee Dee above the mouth of Little River, opp. a bluff in DENSONs land...
TOWNSEND ROBINSON (SEAL), Wit: JOHN COLLSON, WM. DOWNS, THOS. PRESTWOOD.

Page 140: 24 Apr 1756, ROBERT DAVIS of Anson Co., to ALEXANDER CROCKET,
"orphan and son of ROBERT CROCKET decd in Augusta in V irginia"
..."for natural love and affection," 202 A on N branch of Waxaw Creek...
ROBT. DAVIS (SEAL), Wit: ROBERT RAMSEY, JOHN CROCKET, REPENTANCE TOWNSEND.

Pp. 141-142: 19 Apr 1756, RICHARD BRADFORD of Anson Co., planter, to WILLIAM
              TERRY, Esqr., of same, for ₤25 proc. money...300 A on N side Pee
Dee, adj. THOMAS STAFFORD WILLIAMS, on Hitchcock Creek, granted to BRADFORD
15 Mar 1756...RICHARD BRADFORD (SEAL), Wit: E. CARTLIDGE, JAS GORDON, THOMAS
STAFFORD WILLIAMS (ᴛ).

Page 143: 5 Jan 1756, THOMAS KEMP, now or lately of Anson Co., to JOHN PERSONS
            of same, carptr., for ₤15 Va. money...150 A on W side great Pee Dee
...on both sides Mill Creek, part of 400 A granted to WM. KEMP, 22 Apr.
1749...adj. THOMAS TOMPKINS, THOMAS COIL, granted to THOS. KEMP by power
of attorney from ELIZABETH & JOHN KEMP, 2 June 1754....THOMAS KEMP (ᴛ) (SEAL),
Wit: HEZ. RUSS, JOHN AFCIE, July 6, 1756.

Page 144: 27 Apr 1756, WILLIAM STONE of Anson Co., to SAMUEL PARSONS of same,
            for ₤20 proc. money...100 A part of a grant of 200 A to WILLIAM
STONE, 3 Oct 1755, near a long branch on N side Little River...WILLIAM STONE
(W) (SEAL), Wit: WILLIAM DOWNS, JOHN SMITH July 7, 1756.

Pp. 145-146: 20 Jan 1756, BENJAMIN DUMAS, planter, of Anson Co., to EDMUND
              & SARAH LILLY of same, for ₤100 proc. money...400 A on S side
Pee Dee on N side Rockey River, opp. to ANDREW MOORMAN's land, granted to
JOHN CLARK 13 Apr 1749, sold to sd. DUMAS 10 July 1750...BENJ. DUMAS (SEAL),
Wit: JEREMIAH DUMAS, ZECHARIAH SMITH,JNO. COLLSON, July 7, 1756.

Page 147: 26 Apr 1756, EDMUND LILLY to BENJAMIN DUMAS, for ₤100 proc. money...
            390 A on N side great Pee Dee, adj. JOHN LILLY's corner, including
Buffaloe Island...granted to EDMUND LILLY 1753...EDMUND LILLY (SEAL), SARAH
LILLY (SEAL), Wit: JEREMIAH DUMAS, ZECHARIAH SMITH, BETTY PRESTWOOD.

Page 148: 26 Apr 1756, WILLIAM TERRY, Gent., of Anson Co., to JOHN JAMES, planter,
            of same, for ₤20 proc. money...100 A on a branch of Hitchcocks Creek...
WM. TERRY (SEAL), Wit: CHARLES ROBINSON, E. CARTLIDGE, July 8.

Page 149: 27 Apr 1756, JOHN HITCHCOCK of Anson Co., to HENRY HARDEN of same,
            planter, for ₤10...470 A on W side Broad River, on Sugar Creek, a
branch of Fairforest Creek...JOHN HITCHCOCK (SEAL), Wit: ALEXR. GORDON, GEORGE
CATHEY.
                    [This land now in S. C.]

Pp. 150-151: 5 Nov 1755, LEONARD DYSON of Edgcomb Co., planter, to THOMAS
              ARMSTRONG of Cumberland Co., for ₤40 proc. money...300 A on
NE side great Pee Dee...great bluff on SW side Little River...conveyed to
LEONARD DYSON by deed from NICHOLAS DYSON 6 Feb 1747...LEONARD DYSON (SEAL)
Wit: JOHN VERRELL, WILLIAM LANE. Proved by JOHN VERRELL 6 Nov 1755, JAS.
HASELL C.J.

Pp. 152-153: 17 Dec 1755, JOHN HORNBACK of Anson Co., planter, to WILLIAM
              HOGGATT of Rowan Co., planter, for ₤20 Va. money...100 A on
S side Great Pee Dee, adj. STONE's Island, Island Creek...part of a grant to
JOHN NEWBERRY 17 Oct 1747, 500 A...JOHN HORNBACK (SEAL), Wit: THOMAS MOORMAN,
NATHL. CHAMBERS.

Pp. 153-154: 22 Apr 1756, BENJAMIN DUMAS of Anson Co., to JOHN COLLSON of
same, for ₤50 ... on S side Great Pee Dee, adj. JOHN HALL,
granted 27 Feb 1756...BENJAMIN DUMAS (SEAL), MARTHA DUMAS (X) (SEAL), Wit:
JEREMIAH DUMAS, ZECHARIAH SMITH, EDMUND LILLY.

Page 155: 3 Jan 1755, DAVID HILDRETH of Anson Co., planter, to JAMES HILDRETH,
for ₤20 proc. money...300 A, part of 600 A granted to HOPKIN HOWELL
11 Oct 1749, conveyed by him to DAVID HILDRETH 4 Sept 1755...DAVID HILDRETH
(SEAL), Wit: JNO TAMER, E. BROWN, BENTLEY GRANTLEY.

Pp. 156-159: 27 & 28 Apr 1756, ANDREW PRESLAR, black Smith, to PETER ARRANT,
Ordinary Keeper, (lease s5, release ₤60)...390 A on S side Yadkin
...both sides Buffaloe Creek, adj. JOHN BRANDON's land...ANDREW PRESLAR (SEAL),
Wit: HENRY DOWNS, JNO. DUNN.

Pp. 160-162: 1 Jan 1756, JOHN BETTY & ELIZABETH his wife of Anson Co., to
THOMAS BETTY of same, planter, (lease s5, release ₤100 proc.
money)...land on N side Catawba, including part of an Island, 300 A granted
to JOHN BETTY Jan 1754...JOHN BETTY (SEAL), ELIZABETH BETTY (X) (SEAL), Wit:
WILLIAM LITTLE, JEAN THOMAS, JOHN THOMAS.

Pp. 163-165: 18 Feb 1756, TOWNSEND ROBINSON and his wife[not named], Sheriff,
to JOHN LEONARD, farmer (lease s5, release ₤40)...227 A on
S side Fishing Creek, adj. THOMAS STEELs, KILPATRICKs line, granted 1755...
TOWNSEND ROBINSON (SEAL), [Wife did not sign], Wit: JOHN BETTY, PATR. KER.

Page 166; Blank.

Pp. 167-170: 1 & 2 July, 1755, JOHN THOMAS & JEAN his wife, to JAMES ARMOR (lease
s5, release ₤20)...land on S side Catawba on a small creek between
Allison's & Crowder's Creek, adj. JAMES CAMPBELL's land, 600 A, granted to
JOHN THOMAS 28 Mar 1755...JOHN THOMAS (SEAL), JEAN THOMAS (SEAL), Wit: WILLIAM
HACKER, JOHN BUCHANNAN (B).

Pp. 171-174: 18 & 19 Mar 1756, JOHN LINN of Anson Co., to ROBERT McCORKELL
of same, (lease s5, release ₤22 Va. money)...321 A on N
side Catawba, adj. lines of sd. LINN & JOSEPH WHITE...JNO. LINN (SEAL),
Wit: HENRY WHITE, JAMES LINN.

Pp. 175-177: 26 & 27 Feb 1756, DAVID WHITE of Anson Co., to JOHN HOGGAN
(lease s5, release ₤18 N. C. money)...270 A on S side Twelve
Mile Creek...DAVID WHITE (SEAL), Wit: HENRY WHITE, JAS. LINN, STEPHEN WHITE.

Pp. 178-181: 12 & 13 Apr 1756, THOMAS GORDON & ELIZABETH his wife of Anson
Co., Prov. of S. C, to WILLIAM GORDON of same (lease s5, release
₤50 proc. money)...land on S side Tyger River, adj. THOMAS GORDON's line...
460 A, and the sd. THOMAS GORDON, son to MR. JOHN GORDON, decd...patented
27 May 1754...THOMAS GORDON (SEAL), ELIZABETH GORDON (O) (SEAL), Wit: ADAM
McCOOLL, GABL. BROWN, EDWD. MUSGROVE.
[This land now in S. C.]

Pp. 182-184: 9 & 10 July 1755, JAMES KUYKENDALL & SARAH his wife of Anson
Co., to HUGH KELLY of same (lease s5, release Ł10 Va. money)...
278 A on main fork of Kings Creek, adj. JNO MOOREs line, granted to sd.
KUYKENDALL 21 Sept 1754...JAMES KUYKENDALL (SEAL), SARAH KUYKENDALL (ł)
(SEAL), Wit: ETON McCODY, JAMES ARMOR, JOHN McDOWELL
"The within Plantation Exposed to Sale and Sold according to the Just order
and Directions of the law made and provided for the same on pound Proc.
money I say pr. me PATR. KER D. S. December 27th 1755"

Pp. 185-188: 12 & 19 Apr 1756, THOMAS GORDON & FLIZABETH His wife to BENJAMIN
GORDON, brother of sd. THOMAS (lease s5, release Ł50 proc. money)
...300 A on S side Tyger River, including an improvement where "auld Mr.
TYMMINGS now lives, claimed by STEPHEN HOULSTON" patent 3 Aug 1753...THOMAS
GORDON (SEAL), ELIZABETH GORDON (0) (SEAL), Wit: ADAM McCOOL, GABL. BROWN,
EDWARD MUSGROVE.

Pp. 189-191: 10 & 11 Dec 1755, JOHN HITCHCOCK Planter of Anson Co., to JOHN
McCOPIN, planter of same, (lease s5, release Ł20 Va. money)...
200 A on N Side of Brod River, N fork of Sandy River...JOHN HITCHCOCK (SEAL),
Wit: JOHN LOVELESS, MARCUS STOKES, HENRY HARDIN (H).

Pp. 192-194: 12 & 13 Apr 1756, THOMAS GORDON & ELIZABETH his wife to RUTH
GORDON, mother of sd. THOMAS GORDON, (lease s5, release Ł50)...
640 A[lease says 300 A], patented 24 Sept 1754, on head of little river, on
N side Broad River, on the dividing ridge...sd. THOMAS GORDON, son of JOHN
GORDON, decd...THOMAS GORDEN (SEAL), ELIZABETH GORDON (0) (SEAL), Wit: ADAM
McCOOLL, GABL. BROWN, EDWARD MUSGROVE.

Pp. 195-196: 24 & 25 Sept 1755, JOHN ARMSTRONG of Anson Co., to GEORGE
RUTLEDGE of same, for Ł10 Va. money...land on N side Broad
River, on main fork of Turkey Creek, 225 A, granted to sd. ARMSTRONG 31 Aug
1753...JOHN ARMSTRONG (SEAL), Wit: ANDREW BARRY, RICHARD BARRY, JANNET BARRY.

Pp. 197-200: 21 & 22 Jan 1756, AVINGTON SHERRILL of Anson Co., to WILLIAM
WILSH (lease s5, release s5)...170 A on S fork Catawba, adj.
JAS. SPRATS corner, JOSEPH MELEKINS, THOS. POTTS...AVINGTON SHERRILL (SEAL),
Per. SHANA SHERRILL (SEAL), Wit: WILLIAM MILLS (M), JOHN ALEXANDER.

Pp. 201-204: 17 & 18 Feb 1756, JOHN KELSO of Anson Co., to SAMUEL THOMPSON,
(lease s5, release Ł10)...on N side Catawba, S side Waxhaw
Creek, 345 A...JOHN KELSO (SEAL), Wit: ROBERT McCLENECHAN, HENRY WHITE,
PHILIP WALKER.

Pp. 205-208: 21 & 22 Apr 1756, WILLIAM MOORE & MARGARET his wife of Anson
Co., to JOHN HARVEY of same, (lease Ł2, release Ł40)...land
on N side Catawba, S side Cane Creek, 280 A...WILLIAM MOORE (SEAL), MARGARET
MOORE (⊬) (SEAL), Wit: ROBT. McCLENACHAN, ARCH. BERWICH.

Pp. 209-212: 29 & 30 Oct 1755, JOHN CLARK of Anson Co., to BLENNY MILLS (lease
s5, release Ł5)...200 A, part of 1000 A granted to JOHN CLARK,
bought of SAMUEL WILKINS, adj. JAMES ROBINSONs line...JNO. CLARK (SEAL), Wit:
ISRAEL ROBINSON, WILLIAM MILLS (M).

Pp. 213-215: 12 & 13 Apr 1756, THOMAS GORDON & ELIZABETH his wife, to JOHN
GORDON, brother to sd. THOMAS, (lease s5, release Ł50 proc.
money)...land patented 13 Aug 1753, 300 A on N side Tyger River on Beaver Dam
Creek...below JAMES OTERSONs...sd. THOMAS, son of JOHN GORDON, decd...
THOMAS GORDON (SEAL), ELIZABETH GORDON (0) (SEAL), Wit: ADAM McCOOLL, GABL.
BROWN, EDWD. MUSGROVE.
                [This land now in S.C.]

Pp. 216-218; 23 & 24 Apr 1756, WILLIAM BEARD of Anson Co., to ROBERT DAVIS
                (lease s5, release Ł 30 Va. money)...300 A on Waxaw Creek...
WILLIAM BEARD (SEAL), Wit: JOHN CROCKETT, ROBT. RAMSEY, REPENTANCE TOWNSEND.

Pp. 219-221: 12 & 13 Apr 1756, THOMAS GORDON & ELIZABETH His wife to BENJAMIN
                GORDON, (lease s5, release Ł50 proc. money)...300 A on S side
Tyger River, on a small creek called Fishing Creek, patented 25 Feb 1754...
THOMAS GORDON (SEAL), ELIZABETH GORDON (0) (SEAL), Wit: ADAM McCOOLL, GABL.
BROWN, EDWD. MUSGROVE.

Pp. 222-224: 23 & 24 1756, ROBERT RAMSEY of Anson Co., to MOSES DAVIS of
                same, (lease s5, release Ł35 Va. money)...380 A on Waxaw
Creek...ROBERT RAMSEY Wit: JOHN CROCKETT, REPENTANCE TOWNSEND, ARCHD.
CROCKETT.

Pp. 225-228: 22 & 23 Dec 1752, EDWARD GIVINS, planter, of Anson Co., to
                THOMAS GILLESPY of same, (lease s5, release Ł40 sterling)...
land on S side Catawba, below mouth of Davidsons Creek, 275 A...EDWARD
GIVINS (0) (SEAL), Wit: JAS. CARTER, ALEX. OSBORN, Proved. by JAMES CARTER
27 May 1756, PETER HENLY, C.J.

Pp. 229-232: 8 & 9 Sept 1756, WILLIAM ALEXANDER of Rowan Co., to WILLIAM
                STEVEN of same (lease s5, release Ł25)...two tracts on S
side Catawba, one granted to JAMES ARMOR 9 Sept 1750, conveyed by L. &. R.
to WILLIAM ALEXANDER 2 July 1755, 300 A...the other adj. it, 150 A granted
to GEORGE CATHEY 29 Mar 1753, conveyed to sd. ALEXANDER by L. &. R. , 17
July 1755...WILLIAM ALEXANDER (SEAL), Wit: JOHN DAVISON, HENRY HENDRY.

Pp. 233-234: 19 June 1756, WILLIAM MOUAT, attorney at law, to CHARLES ADAMS
                of Newbern, Merchr., for Ł40 proc. money...400 A on S side
Pee Dee on upper side Brown Creek, conveyed by THOMAS UNDERWOOD to PATRICK
KERR, and then to WILLIAM MOUAT...WILL MOUAT (SEAL), Wit: PAT. KENNEDY,
JOS. BRYANT.
        N. C., Newbern, Sept. Supreme Court, 1757, Present. The Honble RICHARD
SPAIGHT and EDWARD GRIFFETH, Esquires, Justices...deed proven by oath of
PATRICK KENNEDY. JNO. SMITH C L C.

Pp. 235-236: 20 Jan 1757, JAMES PICKETT to ANTHONY HUTCHINS, for Ł100 proc.
                money...200 A, part of 500 A granted to JOSEPH WHITE 26 Sept
1746, on S side Great Pee Dee, adj. JNO LEATHS land, conveyed by JOSEPH
WHITE to HENRY FALKENBOROUGH 2 Apr 1748, then to JAMES PICKETT 28 OCt 1755...
also 100 A where sd. PICKETT now lives, conveyed by ISAAC NORMAN to JAMES
PICKETT 15 July 1753...also land granted to NICHOLAS SMITH 13 Oct 1749, on S
side Pee Dee, above mouth of Little River, about half a mile above the wagon
ford road, 200 A conveyed to TOWNSEND ROBINSON then to sd. PICKETT...JAS.
PICKETT (SEAL), Wit: M. BROWN, WILLIAM ANDERSON FOWLER.

Pp. 237-239: 10 & 11 Jan 1757, FREDERICH HAMBURG (HAMBRIGHT) and SARAH his wife, to
CONROD SAYLER of same, (lease s5, release ₺ 8 proc. money)...202 A on
S side Catawba on Doctors Creek...granted to sd. HAMBRIGHT 24 Sept 1754.... FREDERICK
HAMBRIGHT (SEAL), SARAH HAMBRIGHT (SEAL), Wit: BENJAMIN HARDEN, JOSEPH HARDEN, JOHN
KUYKENDALL, BENJAMIN HARDEN.

Page 240: 1 Nov 1754, JAS MacMANUS of Anson Co., to JOHN CAMPBELL of Bertie Co., for
₺ 35 Va. money...300 A on S side Pee Dee, adj. WILLIAM KEMPs corner...JAMES
McMANUS (SEAL), Wit: THOMAS JONES, WILLM. LESTIE, JOHN DUNLAP. Proved by JOHN DUNLAP
23 Feb 1756. PETER HENLY, C. J.

Page 241: Blank

Pp. 242-243: 26 July 1756, JAMES DENSON SENR of Anson Co., to JAMES DENSON, JUNR. of
same, for ₺40, 150 A on N side great Pee Dee, at the Red Bluff, part of
a 500 A grant to DENSON SENR, 22 Nov 1746...JAMES DENSON (+) (SEAL), Wit: WILLIAM
DOWNS, OWEN REED, THOS. HARRINGTON (T).

Pp. 244-245: 26 Jan 1757, BURLINGHAM RUDD SENR to BURLINGHAM RUDD JUNR both of Anson
Co., for ₺20 sterling...200 A on Jones's Creek, granted to sd. RUDD SENR
11 Apr 1749...BURLINGHAM RUDD (SEAL), Wit: HENR. DOWNS, JNO. SMITH, JOHN FROHOCK.

Pp. 245-246: 12 Aug 1756, EPHRAIM LILES, Planter, of Anson Co., to AMBROSE STILLE, for
₺15, 200 A on Little River of Great Pee Dee, formerly belonging to ABRA-
HAM BOYD, adj. JOHN McCOYs tract, 300 A belonging to sd. BOYD and recovered by sd.
LILES in County Court of Anson, for a Debt due...EPHRAIM LILES (E) (SEAL), Wit: JAMES
LILES (₮), DAVID LILES (X).

Page 247: 28 Oct 1756, THOMAS PRESTWOOD of Anson Co., to ZECHARIAH SMITH of same, for
₺25 proc. money, 200 A on N side Great Pee Dee, granted to JOSEPH WHITE, adj.
JAMES DENSONs line...THOS. PRESTWOOD (SEAL), Wit: TOW. ROBINSON, ALEX. LEWIS.

Pp. 248-251: 8 & 9 May 1756, SAMUEL COBRUN & MARGARET his wife to MATHIAS CLAUS, (lease
s5, release ₺10 N. C. money)...400 A on S side Catawba River on Chigles Creek, about
half a mile above a fall, surveyed for PETER EPEACK...SAMUEL COBURN(X) (SEAL),
MARGARET COBURN (M) (SEAL), Wit: CHARLES BETTY, JOHN BLACK, JNO. THOMAS.

Page 252: Blank.

Pp. 253-256: 24 & 25 Sept 1756, ANDREW BARR, Esq. of Anson Co., to RICHARD BARRY of
same [lease says "Tanner"; release, "farmer"], (lease s5, release ₺3)...
540 A on N side Tanyard Branch, below the Tanhouse, adj. SAML. WILSONs line, where sd.
ANDREW now lives, granted to ANDREW BARRY, 23 Feb 1754...ANDW. BARRY (SEAL), Wit:
ALEX. OSBURN, MATH. TOOLE.

Pp. 257-258: 28 June 1756, DAVID JONES, Esqr., Sheriff of Rowan Co., to HENRY RAMSOUR of
Anson Co....whereas TYRE HARRIS of Louisa Co., Va., did sell 10 Apr 1752
to ANDREW LAMBERT of Rowan Co., land N side S fork Catawba, on lower end of Indian
field, 600 A, granted to sd. HARRIS 13 Sept 1749...the sd. LAMBERT being indebted to
CHARLES TURNBULL of Va., merchant, by due of law obtained Judgement for ₺338 sterling
against goods, chattles, etc. of sd. ANDREW LAMBERT "Enfield Edgecomb N. Hampton and
GRanville Counties"...sold to HENRY RAMSOUR for ₺15 s10 VA. money...DAIVD JONES Shf.
(SEAL), Wit: PHILIP RUDISILI [signed in German], FRANCIS BEATY.

Page 259: Blank.

Pp. 260-262: 28 & 29 Oct 1756, ROBERT McPHERSON, Schoolmaster, to FRANCIS
              BEATY, Register of Rowan Co. (lease s5, release ₺30 proc. money)
...600 A in two tracts, 300 A on both sides N fork of Sandy River, including
DUCKERs improvements, granted to sd. MCPHERSON 3 Oct 1755...300 A on S side
Catawba, adj. JEREMIAH POTTS, LEWIS's line...ROBT. McPHERSON (SEAL), Wit:
WALTER CARRUTH, JAMES CARRUTH.
N.B. the 300 A adj. POTTS was granted to sd. McPHERSON 13 Mar 1756. Acknow-
ledged by ROBERT McPHERSON 25 May 1757 before PETER HENLY C.J.

Page 263: Blank.

Pp. 264-266: 1 & 2 Dec 1755, THOMAS WALKER of Anson Co., to JAMES HENDERSON of
              Rowan Co., (lease s5, release ₺10)...land on S side Catawba River,
on N branch of Fishing Creek, adj. MATTHEW TOOLs survey, 356 A granted to
THOMAS WALKER (SEAL), Wit: ALEX. LEWIS, BENJ. LEWIS.

Pp. 267-268: 4 Aug 1757, ANDREW MOORMAN, planter, to JOHN COLLSON, planter, both
              of Anson Co., for ₺60 Va. money...part of a tract that was JOHN
HORNBACKS, on S side Great Pee Dee, on mouth of Walkers gut...200 A granted
to sd. HORNBACK 21 June 1746, conveyed to CHARLES MOORMAN & BENJAMIN, by them
to sd. ANDREW MOORMAN...ANDREW MOORMAN (SEAL), Wit: DAVID DUMAS, JEREMIAH DUMAS.

Pp. 269-270: 24 Jan 1758, CAPT. WILLIAM TERRY of Anson Co., to SAMUEL WILKINS,
              of same, yeoman, for ₺50...part of a tract granted to JAMES
DENSON 22 Nov 1746, 100 A...conveyed by him to WILLIAM DOWNS, weaver, 22 June
1750, by him to WILLIAM TERRY __ oct. 1757, also 100 A conveyed by JAMES
DENSON to JAMES DENSON JUNR. 21 June 1750, then to WILLIAM TERRY __ Oct 1757
... WILLIAM TERRY (SEAL), Wit: M. BROWN, AMBROSE STELLE, DANIEL HOLLADAY.

Pp. 271-272: 29 Oct 1757, JAMES DENSON JUNR of Anson Co., to WILLIAM TERRY of
              same, for ₺20 sterling...100 A on NE side Great Pee Dee, sold to
sd. DENSON by deed 21 June 1750...JAMES DENSON (SEAL), Wit: JOHN FROHOCK,
JAMES ROBINSON.

Pp. 273-275: 24 & 25 Oct 1755, EVAN LEWIS of Anson Co., & MARY his wife to
              JOHN MOORE for ₺30 Va. money...land on S side Catawba, S side
Indian Creek, 600 A granted to EVAN LEWIS 10 Apr 1752...EVAN LEWIS (SEAL),
MARY LEWIS (M) (SEAL), Wit: ALEX. LEWIS, DAVID JOHN.

Pp. 276-277: 26 July 1756, JOHN HALL of Anson Co., to HENRY STOKES for s30...
              150 A on both sides Rockey River..granted to JOHN HALL 25 Feb
1754...JOHN HALL (SEAL), Wit: MICAJAH STOKES, WM. FIELDEN.

Page 278: 25 Jan 1757, RICHD. YARBROUGH of Anson Co., to JOEL YARBROUGH of
           same, for ₺30 proc. money...100 A on E side Little River, adj.
CHARLES ROBINSON, and a tract surveyed for JOHN McCOY...granted to sd.
RICHARD YARBROUGH 20 Sept 1756...RICH'D YARBROUGH (SEAL), Wit: WM. DOWNS,
JONATHAN DOWNS, WILLIAM STONE.

Page 279: Blank.

Pp. 280-281: 28 Mar 1757, JOHN PICKENS Esqr., of Craven Co., S. C., to ROBT.
            McCLENACHAN of Anson Co., to Ƀ55 Va. money...500 A conveyed to sd.
PICKENS at Jany. Court of Anson 1755, Registered in book B folio 391 and 392...
bounded on the W by Catawba River, including ten mile branch...JOHN PICKENS
(SEAL), Wit: ANDREW PICKENS, ARCH. CROCKETT, WM. DAVIS.

Pp. 282-283: 7 Aug 1756, AMBROSE JOSHUA SMITH of Rowan Co., to BENJAMIN DUMAS
            of Anson Co., for Ƀ150 Va. money...2 tracts containing in the
whole 900 A... on S side great Pee Dee...1st tract, 400 A on NE side Walkers
Island, 2 miles below mouth of Rockey River...2nd tract, 500 A on lower end
of Youngs Island, above mouth of Brown Creek, granted to ROBERT PARK by two
patents, 28 Sept 1745 and 14 Mar 1745, made over to JOHN SPANN 14 Oct 1747
proved before the Chief Justice 14 Sept 1749, recorded in Bladen Co., Book C,
folio 126, 26 June 1750...sd. tracts with 300 A on Little River made over by
JOHN SPANN to AMBROSE SMITH 22 June 1756... A. J. SMITH (SEAL), Wit: JEREMIAH
DUMAS, FRANCIS SMITH, JAMES JOWERS.

Page 284: 4 Sept 1756, STEPHEN BROWN of Anson Co., to MORGAN BROWN, for Ƀ30
          proc. money, 170 A on N side Great Pee Dee, below mouth of Mountain
Creek, granted to JOHN TAMER 29 Sept 1750...S. BROWN (SEAL), Wit: JNO. TAMER,
SAML. FIRTH.

Pp. 285-286: 28 & 29 Oct 1756, JOHN STEVERIGHT of Anson Co., planter, to RICHARD
            YARBROUGH of same, (lease s5, release Ƀ30 proc. money)...100 A
on NE side Pee Dee, adj. lines of CHARLES ROBINSON, JOHN McCOY...granted to sd.
STEVERIGHT 7 Sept 1756...JOHN STEVERIGHT (SEAL), Wit: JNO LEETH, WM. DOWNS,
JAMES PICKET.

Page 287: Blank.

Page 288: 13 Sept 1756, PATRICK KER of Anson Co., to WILLIAM GUTTREY, for Ƀ14
          proc. money...105 A on N side Cane Creek on E side Catawba, granted
to KER 3 Oct 1755...[deed left incomplete].

Page 289: 12 June 1756, WILLIAM DINKINS of Anson Co., planter, to MATHEW CREED,
          late of sd. county, carpenter, for Ƀ15 Va. money, land on SW side
Great Pee Dee...patented to sd. DINKINS 16 Mar 1740/1...WILL DINKINS (C) (SEAL),
Wit: HEZEKIAH REEP, PHILIP HERNDON.

Pp. 290-293: 16 Nov 1756, GASPER SLIGER & ELIZABETH his wife, to ARCHIBALD ELIOT,
            for Ƀ10 NC money...land on W side Catawba, adj. lands of GASPER CULP,
half of tract where GEORGE NEALS now lives...768 A patented 25 Sept 1754...
GASPER SLIGER (SEAL), ELIZABETH SLIGER (ハ) (SEAL), Wit: ARCHIBALD CAIRNS,
JNO. STONE.

Pp. 294-296: 28 & 29 Dec 1755, JOHN CLEMENT & JUDETH his wife of Halifax Co.,
            Georgia, to SAMUEL COBURN of Anson Co., (lease s5, release Ƀ15)...
378 A on S side Catawba above SAML. COBRUNS land on the Tuckaseged path....
granted to JUDITH COBURN, now wife of JOHN CLEMENT, 30 Aug 1755...JOHN CLEMENT
(SEAL), JUDITH CLEMENT (SEAL), Wit: ALEX. LEWIS, JACOB COBURN, WM. CARD.

Page 297: Blank.

Pp. 298-300: 7 & 8 Mar 1757, JOHN BEATY of Anson Co., [lease says "Schoolmaster,"
            release, "farmer"] to EDWARD HOGAN of same, (lease s5, release Ƀ40)...
200 A on Doctors Creek, adj. two tracts of COBURNs by a schoolhouse branch...
JOHN BEATY (SEAL), Wit: ANDW. BARRY, HUGH BARRY, JEANET BARRY.

Page 301: 3 July 1758, SAMUEL McCLERRY of Anson Co., to JOHN FROHOCK of same,
for Ł20...400 A on 12 mile Creek, granted to sd. McCLERRY 31 Mar
1753...SAML. McCLERRY, (SEAL), Wit: JS. CUMMING, CHARLES ALEXANDER.

Pp. 302-304: 2 & 3 July 1758, WILLIAM BARNETT of Anson Co., to JOHN FROHOCK,
(lease s5, release Ł40)...land near mouth of 12 mile creek, formerly surveyed for JOHN DUDGIN, 400 A...WILLIAM BARNETT (SEAL), Wit: JS. CUMMING,
SAML. SPRAT.

Pp. 305-307: 2 & 3 July 1758, WILLIAM BARNETT to JOHN FROHOCK (lease s5, release
Ł40)...300 A on N side Catawba on the branch of Cane Creek, adj.
THOS MACKLEHENNYs survey...WILLIAM BARNETT (SEAL), Wit: JS. CUMMING, SAML. SPRAT.

Page 308: 4 July 1757, ANTHONY HUTCHINS of Anson Co., to JAMES PICKETT of same,
for Ł100...land where ISAAC NORMAN lived on mouth of Turkey Creek and
land where HENRY FALKENBOROUGH lived conveyed by sd. PICKETT to sd. ANTHONY by
deed...ANTHO. HUTCHINS (SEAL), Wit: M. BROWN, GEORGE ONEILL (✗).

Page 309: 26 July 1758, ARCHIBALD GRIMES of Anson Co., planter, for Ł20 Va.
money, to ALEXANDER GORDON ...land on N side Pee Dee, adj. WHITEs
corner...200 A...ARCHIBALD GRIMES (SEAL), Wit: NICHOLAS BOND, BENTLEY FRANKLYN.

Page 310: Blank.

Page 311: 28 Nov 1757, JAMES TERRY of Anson Co., to JAMES DOWNING, for Ł20
...tract granted to TERRY 26 Nov 1757, on N side Hitchcock Creek,
adj. JOHN WEBBS corner...JAMES TERRY(SEAL), Wit: M. BROWN, ISAAC DAVENPORT (∓).

Pp. 312-313; 27 Nov 1757, MORGAN BROWN, surveyor to WILLIAM SANDERS, carpenter,
for s5...land granted to sd. MORGAN 26 Nov 1757, on Woddy's
branch, intercepting a line between sd. WILLIAM & JOHN PELLAM...M.BROWN (SEAL),
Wit: JOHN FROHOCK, JAMES DOWNING.

Pp. 314-315: 29 Oct 1757, WILLIAM DOWNS, weaver, now of Anson Co., to WILLIAM
TERRY of same, for Ł20 sterling...land on N side Pee Dee, 100 A
confirmed to sd. DOWNS by deed 22 June 1750...WILLIAM DOWNS (SEAL), Wit: JOHN
FROHOCK, JAMES ROBINSON.

Page 316: __ Oct 1757, WILLIAM CRITENDEN of Anson Co., joiner, to JAMES HUTCHINS
JUNR., for Ł5...30 A, part of 75 A on NE side Pee Dee, on N side Little
River, granted to sd. CRITENDEN 25 May 1757...WILLIAM CRITENDEN (SEAL), Wit:
H. DOWNS, ANTHO. HUTCHINS.

Page 317: 24 July 1758, THOMAS DOWNER of proc. on NC, planter, to BENTLY FRANKLIN,
of same, for Ł10 proc. money..land on S side Pee Dee, lower side of
Island Creek...granted to JOHN HAMER 25 May 1757 and sold to THOMAS DOWNER...adj.
JOHN NEWBURY's land, 50 A...THOS. DOWNER, THOS PRESTWOOD, JAMES PICKETT.

Page 318: Blank.

Page 319: 26 June 1758, WILLIAM McCOY, planter, to ALEXANDER GORDEN, of Anson Co.,
for Ł40 proc. money, land on S side Great Pee Dee, 300 A...WILLIAM
McCOY (WILL)(SEAL), Wit: JAS. DOWNING, WILLIAM HICKS.

Page 320: 26 July 1757, MARMADUKE KIMBROUGH of Anson Co., to WILLIAM LITLE of same, for ₺100 proc. money...200 A on S side Pee Dee. opp. GEORGE SEMORS land... granted to SOLOMON HEWS 25 Apr 1745, conveyed to sd. KIMBROUGH...MAR. KIMBROUGH (SEAL), Wit: GEORGE LITTLE, ROBERT ABRAMS.

Page 321: Blank.

Page 322: 25 Jan 1758, WILLIAM HARRINGTON to THOMAS DAVIS, for ₺20 proc. money... 200 A on Clarks Creek, granted to sd. HARRINGTON 27 Sept 1756... WILLIAM HARRINGTON (+)(SEAL), Wit: EDMUND LILLY, JOSHUA WEAVER.

Page 323: Blank.

Pp. 324-325: 11 Mar 1758, EPHRAIM LILES of Anson Co., planter, to JOHN HAMER, of same, for ₺40 proc. money...100 A on S side Pee Dee, adj. JOHN NEWBERRY above Island Creek...EPHRAIM LILES (E) (SEAL), Wit: JOHN HUSBAND, VIOLET PRIMROSE, JAMES LILES (Ŧ).

P. 326-327: 25 July 1757, AMBROSE JOSHUA SMITH of Orange Co., N.C., to WILLIAM LITLE of Anson Co., for ₺20 Va. money...300 A on both sides of Dry Creek, lower side Little River, granted to ROBERT PARKS 25 Sept 1745, sold in Johnson & Bladen Counties to JOHN SPANN...sd. 300 A with 2 other tracts sold to sd. SMITH 22 June 1756...and registered in Anson Co., last April...A. J. SMITH (SEAL), Wit: GEORGE LITTLE, ROBERT ABRAMS.

Page 328: 5 Dec 1754, SAML. YOUNG to BENJAMIN HARDIN & JOHN HARDING for ₺20 Va.,money...320 A on E side Catawba, above ROBERT YOUNG's & CHAS. BEATY's lands., including place where sd. HARDINGS now live...SAML. YOUNG (SEAL), Wit: ALEX. GORDON, JAMES FURMIN.

Pp. 329-331: 27 & 28 Mar 1758, CHARLES BURNET of Anson Co., to JAMES GAMBLE of same (lease s5, release ₺36 proc. money)...300 A on N side Catawba, part of land purchased of THOMAS McELHONEY on the Rudy Creek...CHARLES BURNET (SEAL), ANNE BURNET (6) (SEAL), Wit: JNO. CROCKET, ROBT. McCLENACHAN.

Page 332: Blank.

Page 333: 20 June 1757, JACOB BROWN of Anson Co., to ANDREW CATHEY of same, for ₺24...1000 A granted to JOHN KILLION 30 Sept 1749, conveyed to JACOB BROWN 1 Jan 1754...JACOB BROWN (SEAL), Wit: GEORGE BROWN, JOHN HILL, JNO. THOMAS.

Pp. 334-336: 9 & 10 1756, JAMES COWARD of Anson Co., to ARCHIBALD GRAHAM of same, (lease s5, release ₺50)...108 A, part of 312 A on N side Pee Dee, granted 27 Sept 1756...JAMES COWARD (SEAL), Wit: AMBROSE STILLE, ELISHA PARKER (P), PHILIP HENSON.

Pp. 337-340: 13 & 14 Apr 1757, PETER ARRAND & CATHERINE his wife of Rowan Co., to BOSTON BOYS & JACOB COOK of Rowan Co., (lease s5, release ₺50) ...390 A on S side Yadkin, both sides Buffelow Creek, adj. JOHN BRANDON's land... PETER ARRAND, signed in German, CATHERINE ARRAND (+) (SEAL), Wit: WILLIAM HARRISON, JOHN WHITSITT.

Page 341: 10 June 1758, JAMES McELROY of Anson Co., to BENJAMIN MARTIN of same,
for ₺30 Va. money...150 A granted to JACOB FALKENBOROUGH 3 Mar 1754,
conveyed 27 Apr 1757...on N side Pee Dee...JAMES McELROY (-ⅎ₸⁻) (SEAL), Wit:
JOHN WEBB (-ⅎₜ-), WILLIAM BLEWET.

Page 342; Blank.

Page 343: 20 Jan 1758, FRANCIS DEVENPORT of Anson Co., to JOHN JAMES of same,
yeoman, for ₺20 proc. money...200 A granted to DEVENPORT 26 Nov 1758
...adj. EDMUND CARTLIDGE's line...cartlidge's Creek, on drain of Hitchcock Creek...
FRANCIS DEVENPORT (SEAL), Wit: JOHN COLE, M. BROWN.

Page 344; Blank.

Page 345: 13 Dec 1755, JOHN CRAFFORD of Craven Co., SC, to THOMAS BINGHAM of same,
for ₺20 "south Currency"...300 A on both sides Hitchcock Creek, granted
4 Apr 1750...JOHN CRAFFORD (SEAL), Wit: DURHAM HILLS, JOHN CRAFFORD JUNR., THOMAS
CRAFFORD.

Pp. 346-347: 10 July 1758, ENOS THOMAS Of Anson Co., Yeoman, to JAMES DOWNING,
for ₺30 proc. money...300 A on S branch of Cartlidge's Creek...
ENOS THOMAS (SEAL), Wit: ELIZ. BROWN, JNO. COLE, VIOLET PRIMROSE.

Ppge348-349: 3 May 1758, EDMUND CARTLIDGE, yeoman, TO JOHN CRAFFORD JUNR., for
₺100 proc. money...200 A granted to THOMAS JONES 10 Apr 1745...
conveyed to CARTLIDGE 11 Apr 1749...E. CARTLIDGE (SEAL), Wit: WILLIAM BLEWET,
JAMES DOWNING, CHARLES SPEADLING (ℰU), JOHN FREMAN (ꟷ).

Pp. 349-351: 10 & 11 Feb 1759, JAMES ALEXANDER & MARY his wife, of Anson Co.,
to JAMES DUNN of Rowan Co., (lease s5, release 10 pistoles)...
190 A granted to sd. ALEXANDER 4 Apr 1753, adj. JOHN CLARK's corner...JAMES
ALEXANDER (SEAL), MARY ALEXANDER (M) (SEAL), Wit: NATHL. ALEXANDER, ROBERT
HARRIS JUNR.

Pp. 352-353: 8 Sept 1758, WILLIAM HOCKER & JACOB FORNEY of Anson Co., planters,
to FRANCIS BEATY of Rowan Co., surveyor & Publick Register, for ₺10
proc. money...200 A granted to sd. HOCKER & FORNEY 26 Nov 1757 on W side Catawba
both sides of a fork of KILLIONs creek, below LEONARD SEALES land, above land
laid off for GEORGE RENICKS, including a small improvement made by CHRISTOPHER
GUISE...WILLIAM HOCKER (SEAL), JACOB FORNEY (SEAL), Wit: JOHN BEATY, THOMAS BEATY.

Page 354: 24 Apr 1759, EDWARD ELLERBEE of Anson Co., to WILLIAM BLACK JUNR., son
of DOLLE BLACK, daughter of GEORGE MEATHEM, merchant in Aberdeen, for
₺160 proc. money...96 1/2 A, part of 650 A granted to JOHN ELLERBEE 14 Mar
1745, adj. ALEXANDER GORDON, Esqr., & MARY LUCAS...EDW. ELLERBEE (SEAL), Wit:
WILLIAM HAMER, ALEX. GORDON.

Page 355: Blank.

Page 356: 9 Nov 1758, BENJAMIN VINES of Anson Co., to BENJAMIN DUMAS, SENR.,
of same, for ₺100 proc. money...200 A on N side Pee Dee, on S side
Clarks Creek...granted to sd. VINES 1757...BENJAMIN VINES (B) (SEAL), Wit:
JEREMH. DUMAS, ZECH. DUMAS., FRANCES DUMAS (F).

Pp. 357-359: 18 & 19 Jan 1758, JOHN BRAVARD Esqr.. of Rowan Co., to ZEBULUN
BRAVARD, planter, of Anson Co., (lease s5, release Ł40 sterling)...
450 A in Anson Co....JOHN BRAVARD (SEAL), Wit: JOHN FROHOCK, FRANCIS BEATY.

Page 360: Blank.

Pp. 361-362: 24 Oct 1758, THOMAS LAND to ROBT. MCCLENACHAN, for Ł30...427 A
on S side N fork Rockey Creek, adj. land of THOMAS BURNS...THOMAS
LAND (⊥) (SEAL), Wit: JAS. ROBINSON, REPENTANCE TOWNSEND.

Pp. 363-364: 20 Jan 1757, ANTHONY HUTCHINS, Planter, by two bonds, bound to
JOSEPH BROWN & WILLIAM DRAKEFORD of Georgetown, S. C., for
Ł5609 s2 d8 for the payment ofŁ 2084 s11 s4 before 25 Dec next 1758...do sell
to sd. BROWN & DRAKEFORD, 200 A on N side Pee Dee, conveyed from THOMAS HARRING-
TON to sd. HUTCHINS 1 Mar 1752 & another tract of 100 A on N side Pee Dee con-
veyed by WILLIAM GAMBRETT to HUTCHINS...& 60 A on N side Pee Dee conveyed by
SAMUEL HOUGH to HUTCHINS __ Dec 1754...and 200 A on E side Browns Creek,
conveyed from JACOB PAUL to HUTCHINS...and 200 A on N side Pee Dee, conveyed
from WILLIAM DOWNS to HUTCHINS 24 July 1756...ANTHO. HUTCHINS (SEAL), Wit: M.
BROWN, ELIZ. BROWN.

Page 365: Blank.

Pp. 366-367: 6 OCt 1758, THOMAS LAND of Anson Co., to GEORGE SLIGER, for Ł50...
193 A conveyed from ROBERT McCLENACHAN to sd. LAND...patented 25
Feb 1754...THOMAS LAND (I) (SEAL), ELINOR LAND (H) (SEAL), Wit: ROBT. McCLENACHAN,
WM. TAYLOR.

Pp. 368-369: 3 Feb 1759, WILLIAM TERRY to CORNELIUS ROBINSON, for Ł50 Va. money...
300 A on S side Pee Dee, opp. to land of JAMES DENSON, granted to
HUGH LARRIMOR 14 Mar 1745, by him sold to SAMUEL MARTIN, 10 June 1750, conveyed
to TOWNSEND ROBINSON, then to WILLIAM TERRY...WM. TERRY (SEAL), Wit: JAMES ALLEY,'
SHADRACK DENSON, CHAS. ROBINSON.

The End of Book No. 1.

Pp. 162-163: 13 Mar 1751, JOHN WESTFIELD of Craven Co., S. C., Black smith, to
JOHN KIMBROUGH of Anson Co., for ₺500 money of S. C., 640 A on
W side Greate Pee Dee...below Long Island...adj. lower corner of JOSEPH KING...
pattent dated 22 May 1741...JOHN WESTFIELD (SEAL), SARAH WESTFIELD (SEAL), Wit:
WILLIAM BEDINGFIELD, JOHN TOMKINS, JOHN JONES (X).

Pp. 164-165: 2 June 1750, SAMUEL ARNOLD of Anson Co., planter, to JOHN MacDANIEL
of same, for ₺20 proc. money, 100 A on N side Great Pee Dee at mouth
of Little River...sold to ARNOLD by JOHN ASHLEY, SENR., 28 Mar 1749...SAMUEL
ARNOLD (SEAL), Wit: ABSOLOM MacDANIEL, WILLIAM HALLAMS (Ⱦ).

Pp. 165-166: 1750, WILLIAM DINKINS of Anson Co., planter, to JOHN TOMKINS of
same, planter, for ₺10 proc. money, 240 A part of 640 A granted
to DINKINS, 1741, on SW side Pee Dee...WILLIAM DINKINS (Ə), Wit: THOMAS
TOMKINS, JOHN JENKINS, JAMES BABORE (X).

Pp. 166-167: 20[?] Aug 1750, SAMUEL GOODMAN of Prov. of N. C., Bartee, to JOHN
HORNBACK of Anson Co., for ₺32 of Va., 200 A on W side Pee Dee, adj.
JOHN GRADYs on E side Long Island...SAMUEL GOODMAN (SEAL), Wit: JOHN JENKINS,
MATTHEW CREED.

Pp. 168-169: 20 Apr 1752, TYREE HARRIS of Louisa Co.,,Va., planter, to ANDREW
LAMBERT of Anson Co., for ₺80 Va. money, 600 A on neare side of
S fork of Cataba..."lower end of an Engin old field..." granted to TYREE HARRIS
13 Sept 1749...TYREE HARRIS (SEAL), Wit: WALTER CARRUTH, ANTHONY HUTCHINS.

Pp. 169-171: 3 Apr 1752, THOMAS GLASPEE & NAOMI his wife of Anson Co., planter,
to HENRY CHAMBERS of same, planter, (lease s5, release ₺45 of Va.)
640 A in Parish of St. George, Anson Co., on N side of third creek at Buffalow
Branch...granted to GLASPEE by JOHN EARL GRANVILLE 24 June 1751...THOMAS GLASPEE
(SEAL), NAOMI GLASPEE (SEAL), Wit: GEORGE CATHEY, RICHARD HELLIER.

Pp. 171-174: 24 June 1741, RT. HONOURABLE JOHN EARL GRANVILLE viscount CARTERET
and BARRON CARTERET of Hawns in County of Bedford, Great Britain,
to THOMAS GLASPEE, for s3 proc. money...640 A in Anson Co., on N side third creek
at Buffalo Branch...THOMAS CHILD and FRANCIS CARBIN, attorneys for GRANVILLE...
GRANVILLE (SEAL), by THOMAS CHILD and FRANCIS CORBIN, Wit: BEN WHEATLEY, RICHARD
HOLLIER.

Pp. 174-176: 24 June 1750, JOHN EARL GRANVILLE to GEORGE CATHEY for s3 proc.
money...312 A in Parish of St. George, Anson Co., on N side of
JAMES CATHAYs...GRANVILLE (SEAL), by THOMAS CHILD and FRAS. CORBIN, Wit: BEN
WHEATLEY, RICHARD HELLIER.

Page 177: Blank

Pp. 178-180: 6 Feb 1752, GEORGE CATHEY & JANE his wife of Anson Co., planter to
JOHN LYNN of same, Gent. (lease s5, release ₺40), 312 A on N side
JAMES CATHEYs...granted by JOHN EARL GRANVILLE...GEORGE CARTHEY (SEAL), JANE
CARTHEY (Ɇ) (SEAL), Wit: EDWARD CUSICK, RICHARD HELLIER.

Pp. 181-182: 25 Dec 1751, THOMAS REDD, late of Bladen Co., labourer, to WILLIAM
TERREY of Anson Co., for ₺20 Va. money, 200 A on N side Greate Pee
Dee, THOMAS JONES' lower corner...granted 22 Nov 1746...THOMAS REDD (SEAL), Wit:
JOHN SCOFF, JOHN McCOY (𝍐), JOSEPH WHITE.

Pp. 183-184: 17 July 1752, THOMAS POTTS of Anson Co. to SAMUEL HAYWARD of same,
for ₺10 Va. money...land on S side Catabar R...FRANCIS MACKILWAINE
line...granted to POTTS 29 Sept 1750, 400 A...THOMAS POTTS (SEAL), Wit: WILLIAM
SHERIF JUR (W), ANTHONY HUTCHINS.

Pp. 185-186: 19 Apr 1751, JOHN McDANIEL, planter, to JACOB SUMMORLIN, planter for
₺50 proc money...land on N side Greate Pee Dee, beg. at mouth of
Little River, 100 A...JOHN McDANIEL (SEAL), Wit: JOHN DUNN, HENRY FALKINBURG (H).

Page 187: 15 July 1752, WILLIAM BLACK, March in Onslow Co., appoint my trusty
friend ALEX. GORDEN in Anson Co., marchant, my lawfull attorney to
receive from persons owing me in S. C. or Anson Co....WM BLACK, Wit: NOBLE
LADD, JAMES GRIFFIT.

PP. 188-189: 18 July 1752, JOSEPH WHITE of Anson Co., to HENRY TOUCHSTONE
of same, for ₺20 Va. money...land on N side Pee Dee beg. at
DENSONs line...granted to JOSEPH WHITE (SEAL), Wit: BURLINGHAM REED, JOHN LEATH.

Page 189: 28 July 1751, ABRAM PAUL of Craven Co., S. C. planter, to STEPHEN
JACKSON of Anson Co., planter, for ₺50 Va. money...200 A on S side
Thompson Creek...ABRAM. PAUL (SEAL), Wit: WILLIAM RUSHING, BENJAMIN JACKSON.

Page 190: Blank

Pp. 191-192: 19 July 1751, BENJAMIN HORN of Anson Co., planter, to JOHN McDANIEL
of same, planter, for ₺10 Va. money...land on S side Greate Pee Dee,
N side Jones Creek, 150 A granted to sd. HORN 11 Oct 1749...BENJAMIN HORNE (B),
Wit: M. BROWN, ROBT. BRAVARD.

Pp. 193-194: JOHN CROOKSHANK of Anson Co., to EDWARD COFFEY of same, for ₺35
Va. money...land on S side Greate Pee Dee, N side Jones Creek, 150 A...JOHN
CROOK 𝍐 (SEAL), Wit: JAS HUTCHINS, SCATTON DAVIS, JOHN RED.

Pp. 195-196: 11 Jan 1751, DUNKIN GRANT of Anson Co., planter, to HENRY DOWNS of
same, for ₺10 Va. money...land on N side Greate Pee Dee, on Little
River...100 A granted to ROBERT MILLS & conveyed to WILLIAM STONE 2 Aug 1748,
then to ROBERT HUMPHREYS...DUNKIN GRANT (𝒹) (SEAL), Wit: RICHARD YARBOROUGH,
WILLIAM STONE (X), JOHN SMITH.

Page 197: Blank

Pp. 198-199: 17 Oct 1751, THOMAS HOPPER of Anson Co., planter, to JOHN SMITH of
same, planter, for ₺35 Va. money...land on E. side of Little River
of Pee Dee below mouth of Thicketty Creek, 200 A...granted 6 Oct 1758...THOMAS
HOPPER (𝍐) (SEAL), Wit: HENRY DOWNS, GILBERT HAYES, WM. DOWNS.

Pp. 200-201: 7[?] Apr 1751, JOHN COLLSON of Anson Co., planter, to JAMES BARTEN
of same, planter, for ₺16 proc. money...200 A in fork of Greate
Pee Dee & Rockey Rivers...granted to COLLSON 6 Nov 1746...JOHN COLLSON (SEAL),
Wit: M. BROWN, THOS MORMAN.

Pp. 202-203: 3 Apr 1752, JOSEPH TOOPS of Anson Co., to EDWARD HUGHES of same,
  planter, for ₤37 Va. money...land on NE side Yadkin River...579 A
granted to SAMUEL DAVIS ESQR. from JOHN EARL GRANVILLE 20 Sept 1748...from sd.
DAVIS to TOOPS 28 June 174_[should read 1750, see Vol. A, p. 19]...recorded in
Anson Co., Book A., No. 1. fo. 24-25...JOSEPH TOOPS (SEAL), Wit: FRANCIS DAVIS,
WM. HARRISON.

Pp. 204-207: 26 Apr 1753, JAMES BARTON & ANNA his wife of Anson Co., to JAMES
  CRAFORD of Little Pee Dee in same Co., (lease s10 N. C. money,
release ₤200)...200 A granted to JOHN COLLSON in Bladen Co., fork of Greate Pee
Dee and Rockey Rivers...JAMES BARTON (SEAL), ANNA BARTON (P) (SEAL), Wit: JOHN
SMITH, WM. TERRELL.

Pp. 208-209: 19 Nov 1750, JOHN STONE of Anson Co., planter, to CHARLES ROBINSON of
  same, Gent., for ₤20 Va. money...land on W side of Little River of
Great Pee Dee, 100 A granted to CHARLES ROBINSON 22 Nov 1746...conveyed to sd.
STONE 2 Mar 1746/7...JOHN STONE (Ŧ) (SEAL), Wit: JOHN ASHLEY SENR. (⅂), TOWNCAN
ROBINSON, CHARLES ROBINSON.

Page 210: Blank

Pp. 211-212: 7 Jan 1750/1, SAMUEL FRENCH of Anson Co., to FRANCIS MACKILWAINE,
  surveyor, for ₤30 proc. money...land granted to sd. MACKILWAINE
Apr. 1749 on S side Pee Dee, both sides Ceader Creek [acreage not given]...
later sold to sd. FRENCH...SAMUEL FRENCH (SEAL), Wit: JNO DUNN, JAS MACKILWANE.

Pp. 213-214: 7 May 1751, SAMUEL DAVIS of Anson Co., to ABRAHAM ODUM of same,
  planter, for ₤100 Va. money. .land on NE side Greate Pee Dee...adj.
land laid out for GEORGE LENOR...400 A...granted to sd. DAVIS by deed 13 Oct
1750 ...SAML DAVIS (SEAL), Wit: HENRY SOMERLIN (H), WM. FORBES, HENRY BEDINGFIELD.

Page 215: Blank.

Pp. 216-217: 15 Apr 1752, THOMAS HARRINGTON of Anson Co., planter, to JAMES HUTCHINS
  of same, planter, for ₤___ proc. money...lower part of tract of 300
A granted to JOHN GILES 18 Oct 1747 and conveyed to sd. HARRINGTON by deed...100 A
above the mouth of Cedar Creek...THOMAS HARRINGTON (T), Wit: JOHN CHEEKS (Ŧ),
ANTHO. HUTCHINS.

Page 218: Blank

Pp. 219-220: 18 July 1752, JOSEPH WHITE & FRANCIS MACKILWANE of Anson Co., to
  THOMAS BERY of same, for ₤50 proc. money...land on S side Pee Dee
near SMITHs Creek...500 A granted to WHITE & MACKILWANE 30 Apr 1749...JOSEPH
WHITE (SEAL), FRANCES MACKILWANE (SEAL), Wit: JACOB SAMMARALL, ANTHONY HUTCHINS.

Pp. 221-222: 20 May 1752, SAMUEL HUGH of Anson Co., p nter, to ROWLAND WILLIAMS
  JUR. of same, planter, for ₤15 Va. money....160 A, part of a
grant to JAMES BARTLEY 26 Nov 1748, sold by BARTLEY to THOMAS HARRINGTON by deed
26 Apr 1748, conveyed by HARRINGTON to HUGH 16 July 1751, on N side Greate Pee
Dee, at mouth of Dry Creek...SAMUEL HOUGH (SEAL), Wit: JNO. HAMER, M. BROWN, JOHN
GAMBELL (EG).

Pp. 223-224: 21 Apr 1752, WILLIAM SMITH of Anson Co., Parish of ST. George, planter,
  to BENJAMIN SMITH of same Co. & parish, planter, for ₤35 proc. money...
land on S side Greate Pee Dee, 260 A granted to WM. SMITH 28 Sept 1750...WILLIAM
SMITH (3) (SEAL), Wit: M. BROWN, JOHN LEATH.

Page 225: Blank.

Pp. 226-227: 20 Jan 1750, JACOB PAUL of Anson Co, planter, to JAMES TERRY of
                same, planter, for ₤30 proc. money...land on N side Greate Pee
Dee above mouth of Hodgecock [sic] Creek...300 A granted to sd. PAUL 7 Oct 1748
...JACOB PAUL (SEAL), Wit: WM. TERREY, HENRY BEDINGFIELD.

Pp. 228=229: 2 Dec 1751, JOHN ASHLEY, JUR. of Anson Co., planter, to THOMAS WARD
                of same, planter, for ₤12 proc. money...part of a grant of 400 A
to JAMES TERRERS, 7 Apr 1749, conveyed to sd. ASHLEY 26 Sept 1749 by deed...N
side Great Pee Dee, on a branch of Little River, Bafilo Bog, 200 A...JOHN ASHLEY
JUR. (SEAL), Wit: JOHN ASHLEY (N), CHARLES ROBINSON JUR.

Page 230: Blank

Pp. 231=232: 25 Apr 1752, MATTHEW MILLS of Anson Co., planter, to HENRY DOWNS of
                same. planter, for s5 Va. money...land on W side Little River of
Greate Pee Dee to the Ford of Town Creek, 500 A granted to ROBT MILLS 22 Nov 1746
conveyed to sd. MATTHEW 20 June 1750...[later refers to 100 A]...MATTHEW MILLS
(X) (SEAL), Wit: WM. STONE (M), JOHN SMITH, E. CARTLEDGE.

Pp. 233-234: 25 Dec. 1750, THOMAS REDD, late of Bladen Co., laborer, to JOHN
                MOØRMAN of Anson Co., laborer, for ₤5 Va. money...land on N sƒde
Pee Dee, 100 A...patent of 200 A 22 Nov 1746 to THOMAS REDD...THOMAS REDD (SEAL),
Wit: JOHN SCOTT, JOHN McKOY (Ŧ), JOSEPH WHITE.

Pp. 235-236: 22 July 1752, HENRY DOWNS of Anson Co., Gent., to WILLIAM CRITTENDEN,
                of same, Joyner, for₤10 Va. money...land on N side Greate Pee Dee
100 A, lower part of a grant to ROBT. MILLS & later conveyed to WM STONE 2 Aug
1743...sold to DOWNS by DUNKIN GRANT 21 Feb 1752...HENRY DOWNS (SEAL), Wit: JOHN
LEETH, WM HARRISON.

Pp. 237-238: 20 May 1752, SAMUEL HOUGH of Anson Co., planter, to JOHN GAMBILL of
                same, planter, for ₤50 Va. money...100 A granted to JAMES BENTLY
26 Nov 1746, conveyed to THOMAS HARRINGTON 26 Apr 1748, conveyed by him to
SAMUEL HOUGH 16 July 1752, adj. COLLSON land...SAMUEL HOUGH (SEAL), Wit: JNO.
HAMER, M. BROWN, ROWLAND WILLIAMS (W).

Page 239: Blank

Pp. 240-241: 23 Apr 1742, JOSEPH WHITE of Anson Co., & MARGARET his wife to SAMUEL
                WILKINS of same, planter, for ₤20 Va. money...300 A in Parish of
St. George, on S side Greate Pee Dee, mouth of Savanah Creek...granted to JOSEPH
WHITE 22 Nov 1743...JOSEPH WHITE (SEAL), MARGARET WHITE (M) (SEAL), Wit: JOHN
DUNN, SAML DAVIS.

Page 242: Blank.

Pp. 243-244: 5 Mar 1752, THOMAS HARRINGTON of Anson Co., planter, to ANTHONY
                HUTCHINS of same, for ₤20 Va. money...200 A on N side Greate Pee
Dee, above the Waggon Ford at JOHN COLLSONs upper corner...granted to JACOB
COLLSON 26 Nov 1746, & conveyed to sd. HARRINGTON...THOMAS HARRINGTON (T) (SEAL),
Wit: JOHN CLARK (Ŧ), MARY HUTCHINS (M), German Signature [JOHANN ? SWYGATT?].

Pp. 245-246: 3 June 1752, JOHN HAMER of Anson Co., Yeoman, to WILLIAM NEWBERY of
               same, planter, for ₺20 Va. money...170 A on N side Greate Pee Dee
below mouth of Mountain Creek...granted to sd. HAMER 29 Sept 1750...JNO. HAMER
(SEAL), Wit: JOHN FRANCES, M. BROWN.

Pp. 247-248: 24 June 1752, JOHN MARKS of Anson Co., cooper, to JOHN NEWBERY of
               same, Mill wright, for ₺30 proc. money...land on E side Pee Dee, adj.
corner of MATHEW CREED, 320 A granted to RICHARD JONES, 22 May 1741, conveyed to
sd. MARKS 11 Feb 1751/2...JOHN MARKS (SEAL), Wit: WILLIAM BLEWET, EDWARD CARTLIDGE.

Pp. 249=250: 19 June 1752, JOHN NEWBERY of Anson Co., Millwright, to JOHN HAMER
               of same, for ₺100 Va. money...land granted to sd. NEWBERY 8 Oct
1747, 540 A...S side Mountain Creek, 200 A...JOHN NEWBERY (SEAL), ELIZABETH
NEWBERY (SEAL), Wit: M. BROWN, EDWARD CARTLIDGE, ISAAC VICK.

Page 251: Blank.

Pp. 252-253: 19 June 1752, JOHN NEWBERY of Anson Co., Mill wright to MORGAN BROWN
               of same, for ₺50 Va. money...part of 540 A grant made 8 Oct 1747...
on Pee Dee below the Grassy Island, includes Jordan Island, 180 A...JOHN NEWBERY
(SEAL), ELIZABETH NEWBERY (SEAL), Wit: E. CARTLIDGE, JNO. HAMER, ISAAC VICK.

Pp. 253-254: 10 June 1752, SAMUEL FRENCH of Anson Co., planter, to DANIEL TOUCHSTONE
               of same, planter, for ₺20 Va. money...100 A granted to THOMAS GEORGE
4 Apr 1750, conveyed to JOHN COLLSON 19 Sept 1750, to SAMUEL FRENCH 12 Apr 1751...
S side Greate Pee Dee...SAMUEL FRENCH (SEAL), Wit: M. BROWN, JNO. HAMER, JOHN
FRANCIES.

Pp. 255-256: 16 Oct 1752, WILLIAM SHERRILL JUR. of Anson Co., to JOHN ANDERSON JUR.
               of same, planter, for ₺50 proc. money...land on S fork Clark's Creek,
granted to SHERILL 16 Oct 1752 [acreage not given]...WM SHERILL (W) (SEAL), Wit:
M. BROWN, HENRY HENDRY.

Pp. 257-258: 20 Sept 1752, THOMAS KEMPT of Anson Co., planter, to BENJAMIN CLARK
               of Colleny of Virginia, planter, for ₺30 Va. money...land on S side
Greate PEe Dee...widow KEMPs Corn field...BENJAMIN & CHRISTOPHER CLARKs corner,
which they bought of JOHN KEMP...200 A...THOMAS KEMPT (T) (SEAL), Wit: WILLIAM
KEMPM., ARTHOR SKIPPER (O), BENJAMIN MENRS (▽).

Page 259: Blank.

Pp. 260-261: 16 June 1751, SAMUEL HOUGH of Anson Co., planter, to ROWLAND WILLIAMS
               of same, planter, for ₺20 proc. money...land on S side Greate Pee
Dee, E side Brown Creek, 6 or 7 miles above mouth of sd. creek...300 A granted to
sd. HOUGH 7 Apr 1750...SAML HOUGH (SEAL), Wit: THOMAS UNDERWOOD, BENJAMIN VINES,
CHAS. ROBINSON JUR.

Pp. 262-263: 8 Oct 1752, ANDREW MOOREMAN JUR. of Anson Co., planter, to ISAAC
               CLARK of Colleny of Virginia, planter, for ₺42s15 Va. money...land on
N side Greate Pee Dee, near bank of Solomon's Creek ,587 A granted to sd. MOORMAN
21 Apr 1750...ANDREW MOORMAN (SEAL), Wit: JOHN MOORMAN (B), ANTHO. HUTCHINS.

Page 263: 4 Oct 1752, WILLIAM SMITH of Anson Co., to PETER PRESLY for ₺20 Va.
           money...negro slave Juomany...WILLIAM SMITH ( ) (SEAL), Wit: WILLIAM
BLEWET, M. BROWN.

Page 264: 20 Oct 1752, PETER PRESLY of Anson Co., to ANTHONY HUTCHINS of same, for
£20 Va. money...negro slave Juomany...PETER PRESLER(P) (SEAL), Wit:
WILLIAM BLEWET, M. BROWN.

Pp. 264-265: 15 Aug 1752, EDWARD COFFEY of Anson Co., planter, to HENRY FALCON-
BOROUGH, of same, planter, for £26 Va. money...150 A on S side
Greate Pee Dee, NE side Jones Creek, 6 or 7 miles above mouth of sd. creek...
granted to JOHN RED 18 June 1746, sold to JOHN CROOKHANKS, then to EDWARD
COFFEY....EDWARD COFFEY (SEAL), Wit BURLINGHAM RUDD, JOHN McCOYE (£), ANDREW
FORKINBURG (A).

Pp. 266-269: 14 Apr 1752, PETER ELLET of Anson Co., to GEORGE RANECK of same,
(lease s5, release £30)...land on N side Catawba, about 2 miles
upon Ellet's Creek from Ye mouth granted to sd. ELLET 4 Apr 1750...300 A...
PETER ELLET (P) (SEAL), Wit: ANDW. BARRY, CHARLES MOORE, WILLIAM PRICE.

Pp. 270-271: 20 June 1750, ROBERT MILLS of Anson Co., planter, to MATTHEW MILLS, for
s5...at mouth of a certain branch, W side Great Pee Dee to the Ford
of Town Creek, 500 A granted to ROBERT MILLS ___ Nov 1746...ROBERT MILLS (X) (SEAL),
Wit: CHARLES ROBINSON, LUKE BLAKELY.

Pp. 272-274: "Begun here to register by me JOHN DUNN Pub. Reg. as Followethe"
20 March 1753, ALEXANDER OSBORNE, GENT., and AGNES his wife of Anson
Co., to JAMES DUNN of same, (lease s5, release £15)...half on 456 A tract, 256 A
adj. JAMES ROBINSONs, the other half of sd. tract, adj. ROBERT BRAVARDs corner...
ALEX. OSBORN (SEAL), AGNES OSBORN (SEAL), Wit: JOHN McWHORTER, HENRY HENDRY.

Pp. 275-277: 20 March 1753, ALEXANDER OSBORN and AGNES his wife to JAMES ROBINSON
(lease s5, release £15)...256 A, half of 456 A tract, adj. ROBERT
BRAVARD...ALEX OSBORN (SEAL), AGNES OSBORN (SEAL), Wit: JOHN McWHORTER, HENRY
HENDRY.

Pp. 278-280: 12 Jan. 1753, WILLIAM ALEXANDER of Anson Co., merchant, to JOSHUA
NICHOLS of same, planter, (lease s5, release £75)...land adj.
JOHN PATTERSON, SAML BLYTHE, 640 A...WILLIAM ALEXANDER (SEAL), Wit: JOHN
BRANDON, HENRY HENDRY.

Page 281: 14 Nov 1752, WILLIAM DICKINS to JOHN McNIGHT, for £48 Va. money...600
A S side Cataba, both sides Ellison's Creek, granted to DICKINS 27
Sept 1751...WILLIAM DICKINS (SEAL), Wit: JOHN DAVISON, HENRY HENDRY.

Pp. 282-284: 16 July 1752, ROBERT McCAPPEN & BARBARA his wife of ANson Co., to
JAMES ARMOUR of same, (lease s5, release £20 Va. money)...315 A
which the sd. ARMOUR now lives on...JOHN PRICE's corner...ALEX. CATHEYs corner...
granted to MCCAPPEN 4 Oct 1751....ROBERT McCAPPEN (SEAL), BARBARA McCAPPEN (SEAL),
Wit: ALEX. OSBORN, GEORGE RENICK.

Pp. 285-286: 16 Apr 1753, JACOB PAUL of Anson Co., planter, to THOMAS UNDERWOOD
of same, carpenter, for £30 Va. money...200 A granted to MATHEW
CREED 22 May 1741, conveyed to PAUL 26 June 1749...S side Greate Pee Dee, about 13
miles above the Great Cheraws...JACOB PAUL (SEAL), Wit: MORGAN BROWN, MORGAN
BROWN JUR.

Pp. 286-287: 4 Dec 1752, CAPT JOHN CLARK of Anson Co., planter, to BENJAMIN DUMAS
              of same, planter, for ₺50 Va. money...land on N side Greate PEe
Dee, 250 A adj. Widow HARRINGTON's line...also 810 A including Buffelow Island, the
first tract granted to CLARK 2 Oct 1751...the other 10 June 1746...JNO CLARK (SEAL),
Wit: DAVID DUMAS, WALTER GIPSON, GEORGE MICHIEL.

Pp. 287-288: 17 Apr 1753, THOMAS WARD of Anson Co., planter, to JOHN STONE of same,
              planter, for ₺12 proc. money... part of a 400 A grant to JAMES JOWERS
7 Apr 1749, conveyed to JOHN ASHLEY JUR, then to THOMAS WARD 2 Dec 1751, N side
Great PEe Dee, on a branch of Little River, Buflow Run, 200 A...THOMAS WARD (T)
(SEAL), Wit: RICHD. DOWNS, GEORGE CLEMOND (X).

Pp. 289-290: 20 Dec 1752, ELIZABETH KEMP of Anson Co., widow of WM KEMP, to
              THOMAS TOMKINS of same, planter, 100 A on S side Greate Pee
Dee, part of a 400 A tract laid out to WM KEMP SENR...ELIZABETH KEMP (E) (SEAL),
Witt AMBROSE STEELE, ANDREW COX (A).

Pp. 290-291: 18 Dec 1752, JOHN McDANIEL of Anson Co., planter, to ANDREW FALKIN-
              BROUGH of same, planter, for ₺35 Va. money, 150 A on S side Pee
Dee, N side Jones Creek, granted to BENJAMIN HORN 3 Dec 1746, conveyed to
McDANIEL 19 July 1751...JOHN McDANIEL (X) (SEAL), Wit: JAMES PICKETT, HENRY
FALBENRY (H).

Page 291: 15 Jan 1753, BENJAMIN DUMAS of Anson Co., to DAVID DUMAS, for s5 and
           fatherly love to his child...353 A on N side Great Pee Dee, adj. Widow
HARRINGTON's line...BENJAMIN DUMAS(SEAL), Wit: EDMOND LILLY, JEREMIAH DUMAS,
THOMAS GEORGE, BENJ. DUMAS.

Page 292: 15 Jan 1753, BENJAMIN DUMAS of Anson Co., to EDMOND LILLY and SARAH
           for s5 and fatherly love to his child...350 A on N side Great Pee
Dee, beg. at corner in Buffelow Island, S side of Ye Throwfare in Buffelow
Island...BENJ. DUMAS (SEAL), Wit: THOMAS GEORGE, JEREMIAH DUMAS, DAVID DUMAS,
BENJ. DUMAS.

Pp. 292-293: 1 Jan 1753, JOSEPH HALL of Anson Co., planter to ANDREW MOOREMAN JUR.
              of same, planter, for ₺20 Va. money...land on E side Pee Dee adj.
THOS MOOREMANs corner, 50 A part of 300 A granted to JOHN HITCHCOCK 22 May 1741...
JOSEPH HALL (SEAL), Wit: THOS MOOREMAN, BENJAMIN MIMS (✔).

Page 294: 15 July 1753, ISAAC NORMAN of Anson Co., planter, to JAMES PICKETT
           of same, land on S side Greate Pee Dee, on which sd. NORMAN lived
about 3 years...conveyed to NORMAN by JOSEPH WHITE, "deed yet lodge in Bladen
Office"...ISAAC NORMAN (SEAL), Wit: ANTHO. HUTCHINS, M. BROWN.

Page 295a:20 July 1753, JNO. CLARK of Anson Co., Esqr., to CHARLES ROBERTSON ,
           CALEP HOWELL, and ANDREW PICKENS ESQRS., 3 of HIs Majesties Justices of
the Peace, for s5 sterling money of Great Britain...5 acres, excepting 1 acre,
including the Court HOuse, prison Stocks, etc....JOHN CLARK (SEAL), Wit. A. F. SMITH,
JOSEPH WHITE.

Page 295a-295b : 23 Oct 1752, THOMAS RED of Augusta, GA., appoint trusty friend
              JOSEPH WHITE of Anson Co., lawful attorney...to receive payments...
tract at Mount Pleasant whereon CALEB HOWELL now resides unlawfully...THOMAS RED
(SEAL), Wit: SAML DAVIS, HENRY EENDRY, ANTHY. HUTCHINS.

Pp. 295b-296: 16 Jan 1753, JEREMIAH SWAN of Anson Co., for ₤10 to JAMES LEE of
"Hedgecomb County"...land on S side Lains Creek, to southward of
McCULLOCKs line...granted 7 Oct 1747, 200 A....JEREMIAH SWAN (SEAL), Wit: JAMES
ADAMS, RICH. YARBRUIGH, HENERY STOKES.

Pp. 296-297: 16 Jan 1753, EDMUND CARTILEDGE of Anson Co., to WM. TERRY, for
₤10...land on N side Greate Pee Dee...THOMAS JONES lower corner....
Lick Branch...12 1/2 A, part of 200 A granted to THOS JONES 10 Apr 1745 &
conveyed to EDMUND CARTILEDGE 12 Apr 1749...EDMD CARTILEDGE (SEAL), Wit: ALEX.
OSBURN, JAMES CARTER.

Pp. 297-298: 14 Nov 1752, JOHN HORNBACK of Anson Co., to JACOB JEANKINS of same, for
₤108 S. C. money...150 A on W side Pee Dee, adj. JOHN GRADYs line,
WM LETTILE line, JOHN JEANKINS line, E side Long Island...JOHN HORNBACK (SEAL),
Wit: JAMES BYLSS (X), JOHN JENKINS.

Page 298: 25 Aug 1752, THOMAS JONES of Bladen Co., **planter**, to WILLIAM LITTLE
of Anson Co., for ₤40 Va. money...400 A on S side Pee Dee, adj. lands
of HEZEKIAH RUSS...THOMAS JONES (SEAL), Wit: <u>CLEB</u> HOWELL, JAS. GILLESPIE, JNO
LANE.

Page 299: 23 Apr 1753, NATHAN MILLS of Anson Co., to HENERY DOWNS of same, for ₤60
Va.. money , part of a tract granted to his father ROBERT MILLS 22 Nov
1746, conveyed to him by deed 15 Jan 1751, for 500 A...but afterward proved not
to be so much, MATHEW MILLS having an older deed for 100 A and ROBERT PARK has an
older patten that took away 97A...therefore 300 A...NATHAN MILLS (M) (SEAL), Wit:
JOHN SMITH, TOWNSEND ROBINSON.

Pp. 299-300: 15 Jan 1753, WILLIAM PHILLIPS Esqr. of Anson Co., to CALEB TOUCHSTONE
of same, Blacksmith, for ₤20 proc. money...land on N side Great
Pee Dee...3/4 mile above JAMES DENSON's...conveyed to PHILLIPS by deed from
NICHLDS SMITH 5 Oct 1748... WM. PHILLIPS (SEAL), Wit: JNO DUNN, JAS CARTER.

Pp. 301-302: 23 Aug 1752, JOHN HORNBACK of Anson Co., to WILLIAM LITTLE of same,
for ₤60,S. C. money...part of a tract where HORNBACK formerly lived...
50 A on S side Great Pee Dee, adj. JOHN JENKINS line...JOHN HORNBACK (SEAL), Wit:
JOHN HALL (H), HENERY WALKER.

Pp. 302-303: 16 & 17 Jan 1753, JOHN CLARK of Anson Co., planter, to RICHD HUGHES
of same, (lease s5, release ₤50, lease says"RICHD. HUGHES of Eas
Collen, Chester Co., Pa."), land on S side Broad River, where sd. CLARK lately
lived, 600 A...JOHN CLARK (SEAL), Wit: SAML. BRYON, JOHN DUNN.

Pp. 304-306: 13 & 14 July 1753, LENORD KILLION & MARGETT his wife of Anson Co.,
to PETTER CLUBB of same, (lease s5, release ₤30 Va. money)...315 A
granted to KILLION 11 Apr 1752...LENORD KILLION (L) (SEAL), MARGETT KILLION (M)
(SEAL), Wit: JAMES ARMOUR, JOHN THOMAS.

Pp. 306-308: 22 & 23 June 1753, GEORGE RENICK & MARY his wife of Anson Co., to
JOHN WILLSON (lease s5, release ₤34 Va. money)...land on S side S
fork Catawba on a Little Creek, 300 A on a branch that runs into Alison's Creek,
adj. JAMES CAMPBELLs, granted to RENICK 2 Apr 1753...GEORGE RENICK (SEAL), MARY
RENICK (SEAL), Wit: JNO THOMAS, WILLIAM WATSON.

Pp. 308-309: 22 & 23 June 1753, GEORGE RENICK & MARY his wife to JOHN WILLSON
(lease s5, release ₤34 Va. money)...350 A on S side Cataba, below place
GEORGE CATHEY claims, adj. JOSEPH CLARKs, JOHN DAVIS...granted to RENICK 21
March 1753...GEORGE RENICK (SEAL), MARY RENICK (SEAL), Wit: JOHN THOMAS, WILLIAM
WATSON.

Pp. 309-311: 29 Mar 1753, JOHN LARGE & ESTER his wife of Anson Co., to HENERY
KNEELY of same, (lease s5, release ₺30 Va. money)...250 A on S
side Cataba, granted 27 Sept 1751 to sd. LARGE...JOHN LARGE (SEAL), ESTER LARGE
(0) (SEAL), Wit: ALEX. OSBURN, HENERY ONEILL.

Pp. 312-314: 25 Dec. 1752, GEORGE CATHEY JUNIOR of Anson Co., planter, to WILLIAM
MACKEY of same, planter, (lease s5, release ₺40 sterling)...613 A
adj. JAMES ALEXANDER....GEORGE CATHEY (SEAL), Wit: JAMES CARTER, JNO DUNN.

Pp. 314-315: 12 Jan 1753, JAMES ALEXANDER of Parish of St. George, Anson Co.,
planter, to son JAMES ALEXANDER JUNIOR of same, planter, half of
640 A on Cadle Creek...for love & good will...JAMES ALEXANDER (SEAL), ANN
ALEXANDER (a), Test: WM MACKEY, HENRY HENDRY.

Pp. 315-315b: 12 Jan 1753, JAMES ALEXANDER to son DAVID of Anson Co., planter,
for love and good will...half of 640 A...so as not to hurt improvements
made by my son ROBERT...JAMES ALEXANDER (SEAL), ANN ALEXANDER (a) (SEAL), Wit:
WM. MACKEY, HEN. HENDRY.

Page 315b: 12 Jan 1753, JAMES ALEXANDER to daughter ELENER ALEXANDER for love &
good will...gray mair & three cow yearlings...JAMES ALEXANDER (SEAL),
Test: WM MACKEY, HEN. HENDRY.

Pp. 315b-316: 12 Jan 1753, JAMES ALEXANDER to son ROBERT for love & good will...
half of 640 A & dwelling house where I now live...JAMES ALEXANDER (SEAL), ANN
ALEXANDER (a) (SEAL), Wit: WM. MACKEY, HENRY HENDRY.

Page 316: 20 June 1753, JOHN WILKINS to JOHN ANDERSON of Rowan Co., planter, for
₺20 proc. money...mare & colt...JOHN WILKINS (Ŧ) (SEAL), Wit: WM.
HARRISON, JASPER CHARLTON.

Pp. 317-318: 2 & 3 Dec 1751, JAMES McMANUS of Northampton Co., N. C. Gentleman,
to THOMAS CHILD of Wilmington, Esqr., and FRANCES CORBIN of Edenton
Esqr.,(Lease s5, release ₺20)...4000 A in Anson or Bladen, between Grant's Creek
and Marlin Creek, beg. at GEORGE CATHEYs corner...JAS McMANUS (SEAL), Wit: JAS.
WALLACE, JAMES CAMPBELL.

Pp. 319-321: 5 & 6 Jan 1753, EDWARD HUGHES of Anson Co., to NICHOLAS HARFORD (lease
s5,release ₺30)...331 A, adj. S bank of Yadkin, land on RICHARD
WYNSECT...EDWARD HUGHES (SEAL), Wit: FRANCES JAMES, WILLIAM BROOKSHIRE (W).

Pp. 321-322: 20 & 21 Apr 1753, SAMUEL WILKINS of Anson Co., to JONATHAN WILKINS,
his son, of same, (lease s5, release ₺50), land on S side Cattaba,
adj. NATHANIEL HARRIs's line...SAML WILKINS (SEAL), Wit: JAMES ROBERTS, SAMUEL
BEESON.

Pp. 323-324: 13 & 14 Apr 1753, ALEXANDER OSBORNE, Gent., & AGNES his wife of
Anson Co., to JAMES HARRES (lease s5, release ₺45 Va. money)...
plantation where sd. HARRES now lives...600 A on fork of Rockey River...McCULLOHs
line...granted to sd. OSBORNE 7 Apr 1752...ALEX. OSBORNE (SEAL), AGNES OSBORNE (SEAL),
Wit: JOHN BRAVARD, ROGER LAWSON.

Pp. 324 326: 12 & 13 June 1752, THOMAS RIDGE of Anson Co., planter, to MORDECAI
MENDENHALL of same, planter, (lease s5, release L1-- Va. money)...
land on N side Richland Creek, below BENJAMIN WELL...1134 A, 2 tracts granted to
RIDGE by EARL OF GRANVILLE, 25 March 1752...THOMAS RIDGE(SEAL), Wit: JAS CARTER,
ELIJAH MacCOY.

Pp. 327-329: 5 & 6 Jan 1753, MORGAN BRYAN of Anson Co., to MORGAN BRYAN JUR. (lease s5, release ₺20)...land on N side Yadkin, 4 or 5 miles above mouth of Elk River, 150 1/2 acres...MORGAN BRYAN (SEAL), Wit: SAML BRYAN, EDWD HUGHES.

Pp. 329-330: 5 & 6 Jan 1753, MORGAN BRYAN to WILLIAM BRYAN (lease s5, release ₺20) ...land on N side Yadkin, a little below Springfield, 310 A... MORGAN BRYAN (SEAL), Wit: SAML. BRYAN, EDWD. HUGHES.

Pp. 330-331: 5 & 6 Jan 1753, MORGAN BRYAN to JAMES BRYAN (lease s5, release ₺20)... land on N side Yadkin, adj. CAPT SAMUEJ DAVIS's line...319 A... MORGAN BRYAN (SEAL), Wit: SAML BRYAN, EDWD. HUGHES.

Pp. 332-333: 5 & 6 Jan 1753, MORGAN BRYAN To SAMUEL BRYAN (lease s5, release ₺20)...land on S side Deep Creek that runs into Yadkin, 300 A... MORGAN BRYAN (SEAL), Wit: FRANICS JAMES, EDWD. HUGHES.

Pp. 334: 19 Sept 1753, WILLIAM WATSON to WILLIAM McNIGHT SENR., for 20 Pistoles, 400 A S side Cataba, head of Allison's Creek. above JAS. WILSONs survey...granted to WATSON 13 Aug 1753...WILLIAM WATSON (SEAL), Wit: WALTER CARRUTH, JAMES CARRUTH.

Pp. 334-335: 5 & 6 Jan 1753, MORGAN BRYAN to JOHN BRYAN (lease s5, release ₺20) ...land on N side Yadkin, below Mill Creek, Mulberry field...313 A ...MORGAN BRYAN, (SEAL), Wit: EDWD. HUGHES, SAML. BRYAN.

Pp. 336-337: 15 & 16 July 1753, WILLIAM PHILLIPS , Esqr. of Anson Co., to JOHN CLARK of same, Esqr., (lease s5, release ₺150)...land on S side Great Pee Dee by mouth of Harmer's Gut...300 A...WILLIAM PHILLIPS (SEAL), Wit: JNO DUNN, JAMES ARMOR, JNO THOMAS.

Pp. 338-339: 27 & 28 Sept 1753, PETER ELLIOT (ELLET) of Anson Co., to JAMES DAVIS of ROWAN Co., (lease s5, release ₺9 Va. money)...150 A about 3 miles below JOHN PRICE's...granted to ELLET 7 Oct 1749... PETER ELLET (P) Wit: EVAN JONES, ALEX. LEWIS.

Pp. 340-341: 16 & 17 Jan 1754, DANIEL TOUCHSTONE of Anson Co., planter, to BENJAMIN SMITH, of same, (lease s5, release ₺20 sterling)...land on S side Great Pee Dee, 100 A...DANIEL TOUCHSTONE (SEAL), Wit: CHAS. BETTY, JNO DUNN.

Pp. 324-344: 17 & 18 Jan 1754, BENJAMIN SMITH of Anson Co., Planter, to WILLIAM & ZACHARIAH PHILLIPS of same, (lease s5, release ₺20 sterling)... land on S side Great Pee Dee, below Brown Creek, adj. THOS GEORGE's land, 260 A ... BENJN. SMITH (B) (SEAL), Wit: JOHN DUNN, JAMES McDUGEL.

Pp. 344-345: 20 June 1752, WILLIAM ROBINSON of Augusta Co., VA., to WILLIAM BEARD of same, for ₺4 Va. money...land on N side of Carttapa River, on S side Cane Creek, called Rum Creek, granted to ROBINSON 3 Apr 1752, 400 A....WILLIAM ROBINSON (SEAL), Wit: WM. NUTT (W), ROBERT RAMSEY, SAMUEL DUNLAP.
    ROBERT CONINGHAM and BENJAMIN BURDING two of His Majesties Justices for Augusta Co., appeared and acknowledge above to be his hand and seal.

Pp. 345-346: 1 & 2 Jan 1754, LENORD KILLION & <u>MARYGREAT</u> his wife of Anson Co., to
          GEORGE BROWN of same, (lease s5, release Ⱡ32s10 Va. money)...land
on S side Cataba River, Killions Krick, 59 A, granted 30 Sept 1749 to KILLION...
LENORD KILLION (L) (SEAL), MARYGREAT KILLION (M) (SEAL), Wit: German Signature
[-----KELIEN?], HENERY JOHNSTON, JNO THOMAS.

Pp. 346=347: 19 & 20 Oct 1753, WILLIAM PHILLIPS of Anson Co., Esqr., to CALEB
          TOUCHSTONE of same, (lease s5, release Ⱡ20 Va. money)...200 A
adj. Great Pee Dee conveyed to PHILLIPS by NICHOLAS SMITH...WM. PHILLIPS (SEAL)
Wit: TOWNSEND ROBINSON, HENERY WALKER.

Page 348: 19 Oct 1753, JONATHAN WILKINS of Anson Co., planter, to JOHN CLARK of
same, Esqr., for Ⱡ50 ...500 A, half of 1000 A patented to SAMUEL WILKINS &
conveyed to his son JONATHAN being opposite the place where JAMES ROBINSON now
lives...JONATHAN WILKINS, Wit: SCOTT. DAVID, HUMPHRY SMART.

Pp. 348-349: 17 July 1753, PETER PRESLEY of Anson Co., planter, to WALTER GIBSON,
          of same, for Ⱡ25...land on N side Rockey River, southward of
McCOLLOCK's land...200 A, conveyed to PRESLEY by deed 8 Oct 1747...PETER PRESLEY
(P) Wit: AMBROSE STEELE, ANTH. HUTCHINS.

Pp. 349-350: 15 Sept 1753, JOHN STONE of Anson Co., to JACOB RICHARD of same, for
          Ⱡ12 Va. money...land on N side Great Pee Dee, lower south of
mouth of Huwarry River, 300 A granted to JOHN STONE...JOHN STONE (HHꞱ) (SEAL),
Wit: EDMOND LILLY, DAVID DUMAS, WILLIAM CRITTEND.

Pp. 350-351: 19 Oct 1753, JOSEPH WHITE of Anson Co., Edqr., to JOHN CLARK of same,
          Esqr., forⱠ 50 VA. money, 300 A on Mount Pleasant, granted to THOMAS READ
22 Nov 1746, and now sold by power of attorney dated 23 Oct 1752...JOSEPH WHITE,
Wit: HEN. HENDRY, HUMPHRY SMAR.

Page 351: 27 July 1753, WILLIAM NEWBERRY of Anson Co., carpenter, to STEPHEN BROWN,
          of same, planter, for Ⱡ25 Va. money...170 A on N side Pee Dee below
mouth of Mountain Creek...granted to JOHN HAMER 29 SEpt 1750...WM. NEWBERRY (W)
(SEAL), Wit: M. BROWN, M. BROWN JUR.

Page 352: 12 Apr 1753, JOHN FRANCIS of Anson Co., planter, to RICHARD TOUCHSTONE
          for Ⱡ52, Va. money ...land granted to sd. FRANCIS 21 June 1746, 300 A
on N side Great Pee Dee, adj. Littel River...JOHN FRANCIS (SEAL), MARYAN FRANCIS (X)
(SEAL), Wit: M. BROWN, WM. DOWNS.

Pp. 352-353: 5 Sept 1759, FRANCIS MACKILWAIN of Anson Co., surveyor, to JOHN LEETH,
          of same, planter, for Ⱡ30 Va. money...200 A granted to MACKILWAIN 11
Apr 1749 sold to SAMUEL FRENCH and then to MACKELWANE, 17 Jan 1750/1, on S
side P. D. , both sides Cedar Creek...FRANCIS MACKILWEAN (SEAL), Wit: ANTHONY HUTCHINS
M. BROWN.

Page353: 8 Aug 1753, HENRY DOWNS of Anson Co., planter, to RICHARD DOWNS for Ⱡ20
Va. money, part of a 500 A grant to ROBERT MILLS 22 Nov 1746, conveyed to his
son NATHAN MILLS then to HENERY DOWNS..PATTON line...PARKE's line...100 A...
HEN. DOWNS (SEAL), Wit: JOHN STONE (HHꞱ), BENJ. VINES (X).

Pp. 354-355 : 12 Jan 1754, ROWLAND WILLIAMS of Anson Co., planter, to EMANUEL COCKER
          formerly of New Jersey, for Ⱡ24 Va. money...150 A, part of a 300 A
grant to SAMUEL HOUGH 16 Apr 1750 on S side Great Pee Dee on Brown Creek, conveyed
by HOUGH to ROWLAND WILLIAMS...ROWLAND WILLIAMS (W), Wit: FRANCES HOUGH (X), SAMUEL
HOUGH.

Pp. 355-356: 6 Jan 1754, JACOB SUMARAL of Anson Co., planter, to DANIEL TOUCHSTONE
            of same, planter, for ₤22 Va. money...part of a grant of 500 A
to JOHN ASHLEY 22 Nov 1746, sold to SAMUEL ARNOLD 28 March 1748, to JOHN McDANIEL
22 July 1750, to SUMARAL 19 Apr 1751...on upper side of mouth of Little River...
JACOB SUMARAL (SEAL), Wit: M. BROWN, EMANUEL COCKER, GARROT ONEAL (J).

Page 356: 2 Oct 1753, SAMUEL YOUNG to JOSEPH KERRAL, for ₤20 Va. money and bonds
            for the rest, 354 A on S side Cataba, N side Crowder's Creek, below
JOHN LITTLE's survey, patent to SAMUEL 1753...SAML YOUNG (SEAL), Wit: HENERY
HENDRY, THOMS McQUOWN.

Pp. 356-357: 2 Oct 1753, SAMUEL YOUNG to JOSEPH KERRAL, for ₤35 Va. money, 520
            A on S side Cataba, N fork Fishing Creek...THOMAS WALKER's corner
...granted to YOUNG 31 Aug 1753...SAML. YOUNG (SEAL), Wit: HENERY HENDRY, THOS
McQUOWN.

Page 357: 6 Dec 1753, ANDREW MOREMAN JUR. of Anson Co., planter, to TOWNSEND
            ROBINSON of same, Gent., for ₤ 10 money of Great Britain...246 A
on both sides Little River of Pee Dee...JOHN McKOY's corner...HENERY DOWNS
line...ABRAHAM BOYD's land...granted to MOREMAN 31 Aug 1753...ANDREW MOREMAN
JUR. (SEAL), Wit: CHARLES ROBINSON, WM. DOWNS.

Pp. 358-359: 15 Jan 1754, JOSEPH HALL of Anson Co., planter, to BENJAMIN MIMS
            of same, planter, for ₤25 Va. money...land on SE side Hitchcock's
Creek, 250 A, adj. ANDREW MOREMANs line...granted to HALL 31 Aug 1753...JOSEPH
HALL ( ) (SEAL), Wit: JNO. DUNN, JON. GRIG (I).

Pp. 359-360: 16 Jan 1754, JOHN McKOY of Anson Co., planter, to TILMAN HOLMES of
            same, planter, for ₤10 sterling...150 A on N side Great Pee Dee
upper side of Little River, opposite Chicks Island...granted to McKOY 11 Oct
1749...JOHN MACKAY (I) (SEAL), Wit: CHARLES ROBINSON, HENERY HENDRY.

Pp. 360-361: 13 Jan 1754, HENERY FALKENBURGH of Anson Co., planter, of TARRANCE
            CARREL of same, planter, for ₤22s10 Va. money...land on Nside Great
Pee Dee, near mouth of Naked Creek...granted to FALKENBURGH 13 Jan 1754...
HENDRICK WALKINBARG (SEAL), Wit: ISAAC FALKENBURGH (I), WILLIAM HOWELL, CALEB
HOWELL.

Pp. 361-362: 14 & 15 July 1753, GEORGE CATHEY JUR & SARAH his wife of Anson
            Co., to CHARLES McPETTERS , (lease s5, release ₤32 Va. money)...
land on S side Cataba, opposite ROBERT RENNIXs land... 325 A, granted to sd.
CATHEY 7 Oct 1749 ...GEORGE CATHEY (+) (SEAL), SARAH CATHEY (C) (SEAL), Wit:
ALEX. McCONNELL, GEORGE RENICK.

Pp. 362-364: 1 & 2 Jan 1754, JOHN KILLION of Anson Co. to JACOB BROWN of same
            (lease s5, release ₤32 Va. money)...land on S side Cataba ...
on Leapers Krick, 1000 A, granted to KILLION 30 Sept 1749...JOHN KILLION (I)
(SEAL), Wit: DANIEL O'CAIN, GEORGE BROWN, JNO. THOMAS.

Pp. 364-365: 11 & 13 Jan 1753, SAMUEL COBORN & MARGRET his wife of Anson Co.,
            to HENERY JOHNSTON of same, (lease s5, release ₤20 Va. money)...
land on S side Cataba, 260 A...granted to COBORN 29 Sept 1750...SAMUEL COBORN
(X) (SEAL), MARGT. COBORN (X) (SEAL), Wit: JON. BETTY, ALEX. OSBURN, HENRY HENDRY.

Page 365: 29 July 1753, THOMAS LEE to THOS WRIGHT, for ₤20 Va. money...100 A
on Bear Creek, THOMAS LEE's old place...THOMAS LEE (SEAL), MARGERY
LEE (SEAL), Wit: ANDREW PICKENS, MATT. PATTON.

Pp. 366-367: 26 July 1753, THOS. LEE and MARGERY his wife to THOS. WRIGHT, for
₤20 VA. money...134 A on Bear Creek, a fork of Cane Creek...THOMAS
LEE (SEAL), MARGERY LEE (SEAL), Wit: ANDRW. PICKENS, MATT. PATTON.

Pp. 368-370: 13 March 1754, THOMAS GILL & HANNA his wife to JOHN ARNOL PENDER
for ₤20 sterling...130 A in Waxaw on Gills Creek...THOMAS GILL
(SEAL), HANNA GILL (H) (SEAL), Wit: THOMAS WRIGHT (T), BEEN [BOON] MADDOX (X),
ANDREW MACKOWN (ᛗ).

Pp. 370-371: 19 Oct 1753, SAMUEL MOORE & SARAH his wife of Anson Co., to PETER
CLUBB of same, for ₤35 Va. money...250 A on S side Cataba, both
sides Killion's Creek, between KILLION's and ROBERT LEEPER's lines...[incomplete].

"Begun to Register Henry Hendry Public Register As Followeth"

Pp. 372-374: 16 Apr 1755, HUGH PARKE (PARKS) and MARGRET his wife of Rowan
Co., to JOHN SNODY of Anson Co (lease s5, release ₤20 proc.
money)... land on E side CAudle Creek, adj. DAVID TEMPLETON land, line of
DAVID HOUSTON, EARL GRANVILLE's line, THOMAS McQUOWNs land, HENRY HENDRYs
line...205 A granted to PARKS 24 Sept 1754...HUGH PARKS (SEAL), MARGRET PARKS
(ᛗ) (SEAL), Wit: THOS McQUOWN, HENRY HENDRY.

Pp. 375-376: 6 & 7 Dec 1754, JONATHAN HOWMAN & REBECCA his wife of Anson Co.,
to JACOB FORNEY of same, Millright (lease s5, release ₤11 Va. money)
...320 A on S side Cataba, on middle fork of Killion's Creek above KILLION's
land, the place formerly surveyed for CONRAD POVE, granted to HOWMAN 17 May
1754...JONATHAN HOWMAN (SEAL), REBECCA HOWMAN (/) (SEAL), Wit: CHAS. BETTY,
ADAM MEEK, JON. THOMAS.

Pp. 378-380: 9 & 10 Dec 1754, JOHN ARNOL PENDER, Mill carpenter, and WILLIAM
ARDREY, both of Anson Co., to JAMES ARMOUR of same, miller (lease
s5, release ₤41s5d6 Va. money)...land on both sides of Camp Creek, E side
Catawba, 400 A...granted to PENDER & ARDREY 6 Mar 1754...JOHN ARNOL PENDER (SEAL),
WILLIAM ARDREY (SEAL) ,Wit: ANDREW PICKINS, JAMES PATTON.

Pp. 381-383: 29 & 30 Dec 1754, MICHAEL FALINGER of Anson Co., to MICHAL RUDISALY
(lease s5, release ₤10 Va. money)...part of 400 A, on S side Catawba
on Leeper's Creek, above where MARTIN FALINGER now lives...granted 24 Sept 1754
...200 A....MARTIN FALINGER (SEAL), Wit: HENRY JOHNSTON, SAML. COBRON, LENORD
KILLION.

Pp. 384-386: 16 & 17 Feb 1755, JOHN WHITE of Anson Co., to ROBERT McCORKELL of
same, (lease s5, release ₤15 Va. money)...300 A on N side Cataba,
adj. WM. WHITE's corner, JOSEPH WHITE"s line...JOHN WHITE (SEAL), Wit: DAVID
WHITE, STEPHEN WHITE, BENJ. JOLLEY.

Pp. 386-389: 3 & 4 Jan 1755, JONATHAN WILLKOY (WILLKEY) to NATHANIEL MILLER
                (lease s5, release ₤60 Va. money)...place which JAMES BULLOCKlives
on HIckory Creek, 400 A...JONATHAN WILLKINS (SEAL), Wit: ALEX. LOCKHART, JAMES
HOWARD.

Pp. 390-392: 17 Jan 1755, CAPT. ROBERT McCLANACHAN of Anson Co., to JOHN PICKINS
                of same, Gent., (lease ₤50, release ₤55), 500 A on W side Catawba
opposite mouth of 12 miles creek...ROBERT McCLENACHAN (SEAL), Wit: DAVID WHITE,
SAML. BURNET, MATHEW GILLISPIE.

Pp. 392-394: 16 Jan 1755, JOHN WHITE of Anson Co., to JOHN LYNN of same (lease
                s5, release ₤16 Va. money)...250 A N side Cataba, S side Waxaw
Creek, adj. JOSEPH WHITE, WILLIAM McKEE, JOHN KELLEY...JOHN WHITE (SEAL), Wit:
DAVID WHITE, STEPHEN WHITE, BENJ. JOLLEY.

Pp. 394-399: 10 Dec 1754, DANIEL RODGERS & JANE his wife of Anson Co., to
                ARCHIBALD McDOWEL of same, for ₤42 proc. money...300 A on Fishing
Creek...DANL. RODGERS (X) (SEAL), JANE RODGERS (𝄐) (SEAL), Wit: WM TAYLOR, JAMES
HOWARD (X), ANDREW PICKINS, JOHN PICKINS.

Pp. 400-401: 19 Apr 1754, JAMES HANSURE of Anson Co., planter, to CHARLES WHITEACRE
                of same, for ₤40 Va. money...333 A on Buffulow Creek...granted to
HANSURE 3 Sept 1753...JAMES HANSURE (𝄐) Wit: JOHN CLARK, RICHARD BOOKER, FRANCES
AWBERRY.

Pp. 402-405: 9 & 10 Dec 1754, SAMUEL GILKEY of Anson Co., to JOHN HAMELTON of
                same (lease s5, release-₤45 Va. money)...land on S side Broad River,
abt. 3 miles below GABRIEL BROWN's land...600 A...SAML. GILKEY (SEAL), Wit: JOHN
CLARK, SAML. YOUNG, WILLIAM WILLSON.

Pp. 406-409: 18 Dec 1754, THOMAS HUES of Anson Co. to ADAM DICKINSON of same,
                (lease s5, release ₤12 Va. money)...land on N side Broad River
on Clark's Creek just below the great Lick, 600 A...THOMAS HUGHES (SEAL), Wit:
JOHN CLARK, JOHN McCLENACHAN, WILLIAM WILLKINS.

Pp. 409-410: 17 Dec 1754, THOMAS HARRINGTON of Anson Co., planter, to BENJ.
                DUMAS of same, for ₤150 Va. money...270 A, N side Great Pee Dee...
line of JOHN CHEEK...100 taken up by JOHN GILES and the other by THOMAS HARRINGTON
by patent 1754...THOMAS HARRENTON (T) (SEAL), Wit: EDMOND LILLEY, JOHN CULPEPPER,
SARAH LILLEY.

Pp. 411-412: 18 Jan 1755, JOHN HORNBACK of Anson Co., to NATHANIEL CHAMBERS,
                planter, for ₤23 Va. money...100 A on S side Great Pee Dee, beg.
at lower end Stone's Island against mouth of Island Creek, part of a tract laid
out for JOHN NUBERRY, granted to JOHN NUBURY 7 Oct 1747...JOHN HORNBACK (SEAL),
Wit: AMBROSE STEELE, THOS MOORMAN.

Pp. 413-414: 4 Dec 1754, SAMUEL HOUGH of Anson Co., planter, to ANTHONY HUTCHINS
                of same, for ___ proc. money...60 A, part of a grant to JAMES BENTLEY
26 Nov 1746...conveyed to THOMAS HARRINGTON 26 Apr 1748, then to SAMUEL HOUGH
16 July 1751...land on N side Great PEe Dee on upper side of mouth of Dry
Creek...SAMUEL HOUGH (SEAL), Wit: JAMES MACKELWEAN, JAS. NICHOLSON, ROWLAND
WILLIAMS.

Pp. 414-416; 27 & 28 Oct 1754, GEORGE RENICK of Anson Co., to JOHN BLACK of same,
(lease s5, release Ł43 Va. money)...land on N side Cuttawba, abt.
2 miles up Ellet's Creek, 300 A which RENICK now lives on....granted to RENICK
15 Apr 1752...GEORGE RENICK (SEAL), Wit: THOMAS BLACK, WILLIAM BLACK , JOSIAS
BLACK.

Page 417: 22 Aug 1750, HENRY SUMMERLIN of Anson Co., planter, to THOS UNDERWOOD,
Carpenter, for Ł15 Va. money...100 A on S side of N fork of Little
P. D....granted to HENRY SUMMERLIN SENR 9 Sept 1754...HENRY SUMMERLIN SENR
(SEAL), Wit: WILLIAM SMITH, HEZ. RUSS.

Pp. 418-419: 30 March 1753, WILLIAM GAMBRELL for s4 proc. money to MARY GAMBRELL...
150 A on S side Great Pee Dee, on SE side Brown Creek, 6 or 7
miles about the mouth, granted to GAMBRELL by deed 18 ___ 1751...[dated at end
16 Apr 1753]...WILLIAM GAMBRELL (G) Wit: DAVID JONES, WILLIAM CURRIE, JOHN
HUTCHINS.

Page 420: 30 Aug 1754, WILLIAM NEWBERRY of Anson Co., Carpenter, to STEPHEN
BROWN of same, planter, for Ł10 Va. money...100 A granted to NEWBERRY
17 Nov 1753, on a branch of Cartledges Creek...WILLIAM NEWBERRY (X) (SEAL), Wit:
MORGAN BROWN, WM. FERRAL.

Pp. 421-422: 30 Sep 1754, GABRIEL BROWN of Anson Co., planter, to CHARLES
WHITEACRE, for Ł50 Va. money...200 A on S side Broad River at
mouth of a large creek, land known as Ranggers Lady...granted to sd. BROWN
5 Apr 1752...GABRIEL BROWN (SEAL), Wit: JAMES LORE, WILLIAM HUGHES.

Pp. 423-424: 23 Jan 1755, COL. JOHN CLARK of Anson Co. to BENJ. DUMAS of same, for
Ł30 proc. money of N. C....land on N side Great Pee Dee adj. PHILIP
HENSON's line, McANTHONY WHITE's line, 50 A granted 1751...JOHN CLARK (SEAL),
No wit.

Pp. 424-425: 27 Sep 1754, JOHN CONYERS of Anson Co., Hunter, to JANE CRUNK
of Rowan Co., for Ł51 Va. money...200 A on N side Broad River
above FANNINs land...granted to CONYERS 3 Sept 1754...JOHN CONYERS (SEAL), Wit:
JOHN CLARK, JNO. _____.

Pp. 426-427: 5 Aug 1754, RICH'd MILLER of Anson Co., planter, to JONATHAN
WILKEE of Rowan Co., for Ł80 Va. money...land on Thicketty
Creek bought of JAMES BULLOCK on S side of Creek below WILLIAM GREEN's land...
400 A, granted to RICH'D MILLER , 16 May 1752...RICH'D. MILLER (SEAL), Wit:
JOHN CLARK, NATHAN MILLER, MARY CLARK.

Pp. 427-428: 3 Mar 1753, ABRAHAM ODAM of Anson Co., to WILLIAM LITTLE of same, for
Ł250 Va. money...700 A on Great Pee Dee, 300 pattented to SOLOMON
HUGHES 20 Apr 1745, & 400 pattented by WILLIAM TURNER adj. to GEORGE SENIOR's upper
corner...ABRAHAM ODAM (SEAL), Wit: HENRY GAINIE, PHILLIP LYNCH, WM. PLUNKET.

Pp. 429-430: 1 Dec 1753, SAMUEL GILKEY of Anson Co., to ALLEXANDER LORRACT for
Ł5s10 Va. money...510 A on S side Broad River on McDowel's Creek
near McDOWEL's line...granted to GILKEY, 11 May 1753...SAML. GILKEY (SEAL), Wit:
JOHN CLARK, SAML. YOUNG.

Pp. 431-432: 4 July 1754, ROBT. McCLENACHAN of Anson Co., Gent. to THOMAS LAND
of same, weaver, for ₤10 money of Great Britain...213 A on W side
Cataba at CASPER CULPE corner, granted to McCLENACHAN 25 Feb 1754...ROBT.
McCLENACHAN (SEAL), Wit: CHARLES ROBINSON, JAMES PATTON, WILLIAM FLEMING.

Pp. 432-433: 1 Dec 1753, THOMAS POTTS & SAMUEL BEASON of Anson Co. to JOSEPH
MELIGAN of same, for ₤32 Va. money...land on S side Catawba on both
sides Pott's Creek...granted to POTTS & BEASON 3 Sept 1753...THOMAS POTTS (SEAL),
SAML. BEASON (SEAL), Wit: JNO. CLARK, JNO. WILKINS.

Pp. 434-435: 21 Dec 1754, WILLIAM GAMBRIEL of Anson Co. planter, to ANTHONY
HUTCHINS of ₤20 proc. money...100 A, part of a tract granted to
JAMES BENTLEY 26 Nov 1746, conveyed to THOMAS HARRINGTON 26 Apr 1748, to SAMUEL
HOUGH 16 July 1752, part of a tract conveyed by HOUGH to JOHN GAMBRIEL, who died
intestate, therefore fell to WILLIAM being the eldest son...on N side Pee Dee,
adj. grant to JACOB COLLSON...WILLIAM GAMBREL (SEAL), Wit: JAMES NICHOLSON, FRANCES
HOUGH, SAML. HOUGH.

Pp. 436-437: 2 Oct 1754, JOHN HAMER of Anson Co., to EPHRIAM TYLER, planter, of
same, for ₤8 Va. money...land on S side Great Pee Dee, adj. to sd.
river, adj. JOHN NEWBERRY's above Island Creek, JOHN MACKEY's corner...granted to
HAMER 5 Feb 1754, 100 A...JOHN HAMER (SEAL), Wit: TELISON KIBLE, JAMES LILES.

Pp. 437-439: 23 & 24 Jan 1755, JOHN HALL & ELIZABETH his wife of Anson Co., to
JOHN VANHOUSER, of same (lease s5, release ₤40 Va. money)...100 A
(200 A ?) on S side Pee Dee, adj. to sd. river, below the Alligator Pond...
JOHN HALL (SEAL), Wit: HENRY STOKES, BENJ. GRIFFETH.

Pp. 440-442: 23 & 24 Jan 1755, JOHN CLARK of Anson Co., to SAML. WILKINS
(lease s5, release _____), land that JOHN CLARK, ESQR. bought of
WILLIAM PHILLIPS, ESQ. that the Court House now stands on, 300 A...JOHN
CLARK (SEAL), Wit: WILLIAM PHILLIPS, JAMES HUTCHINS.

Pp. 443-445: 23 & 24 Jan 1755, SAMUEL WILKINS of Anson Co., to JOHN CLARK, ESQR.
(lease s5, release _____), 600 A on S fork Cuttawba, bought of
JOHN CLARK, part of 1000 A on S side of river opposite sd. land...SAMUEL
WILKINS (SEAL), Wit: WM. PHILLIPS, JAMES HUTCHINS.

Pp. 446-449: 9 & 10 Dec 1754, GEORGE GILLESSPEY of Lancaster Co., Pa., to
ROBT. DUGGAN of Anson Co., (lease s8, release ₤8 Pa. Money)...
497 A on south side Fair Forest including the Little River path...GEORGE
GILESSPEY (SEAL), by SAML. YOUNG, Wit: JOHN CLARK, JAMES MACKELWEAN, ADAM
DICKINSON.
Power of attorney granted to SAML. YOUNG from GILESSPEY 15 Aug 1754.
[This land now in S. C.]

Page 450: Blank.

Pp. 451-454: 18 & 19 Dec 1754, SAMUEL GILKEY to ADAM DICKINSON (lease s5, release
₤30 Va. money)...land on S side Broad River, on Gilkey's Creek,
600 A...SAML. GILKEY (SEAL), Wit: JOHN CLARK, ALLEX. LOCKHART, WM. WILKINS.
[This land now in S. C.]

Pp. 454-455: 15 July 1755, BENJAMIN DUMAS of Anson Co., to JOHN FANHOOSO, for
₤20 Va. money...land on S side Pee Dee opp. to Long Island...
granted 23 Feb 1755...BENJ. DUMAS, MARTHA DUMAS, Wit: JEREMIAH DUMAS, JOHN
McQUEEN, JOHN FANHOOSO (X).

Pp. 456-459: 9 & 10 Dec 1754, JOHN CLARK & MARY his wife of Anson Co., to
JOHN FENISTER (lease s5, release Ŀ40 Va. money)...land on S
side Broad River, adj. LOVE's line, 400 A...JOHN CLARK (SEAL), MARY CLARK (SEAL),
Wit: SAML. YOUNG, ALLEX. LOCKHART, SAML. GILKEY.
[This land in present Union Co., S. C.]

Pp. 460-463: 8 & 9 Jan 1755, SAMUEL GILKEY to ADAM DICKINSON (lease s5, release
Ŀ30), 600 A S side Broad River, both sides King's River...SAMUEL
GILKEY (SEAL), Wit: ALLEX. LOCKHART, WM. WILKINS, JOHN CLARK.
[This land in present S. C., King's River now Enoree River]

Pp. 464-467: 25 & 26 1754, JAMES MITCHEL & MARGARET his wife of Anson Co.,
to HENRY FOSTER of same (lease s5, release Ŀ13 Va. money)...380
A on S side Broad River, on Great Creek of Little River, adj. GEORGE STOREY's
line...JAMES MITCHOL (S), MARG'T MITCHEL (SEAL), Wit: JOHN CLARK, JAMES MITCHEL,
THOMAS MITCHEL.
[This land in present S. C., Great Creek of Little River, now
Fairforest Creek.]

Pp. 467-470: 11 & 12 Dec 1754, JOHN CLARK to WILLIAM MOORE (lease s5, release
Ŀ50 Va. money)...700 A on Broad River, bought of JOSEPH HOLLINGS-
WORTH & JOHN STUART, opposite to mouth of Sandy River [not signed]...Wit:
SAML. YOUNG, JOHN OATES.

Pp. 471-474: 18 & 19 Dec 1754, JOHN CLARK to JOSEPH FENISTER (lease s5, release
Ŀ30 Va. money)...land on Thickety Creek, 800 A granted to
CORNELIUS O'NEAL 3 Sept 1753, then sold to CLARK...JOHN CLARK (SEAL), Wit:
SAML. YOUNG, ALLEX. LOCKHART, JOHN WILLSON.
[This land in present Cherokee Co., S. C.]

Pp. 477-479: 16 & 17 Dec 1754, ANDREW ALISON & MARG't his wife of Rowan Co.,
to ALLEX. McCALLISTER, late of Anson Co. (lease s5, release Ŀ55 Va.
money)...640 A on S side Cuttawba River on Indian Camp Creek, taking in Ye
Indian Old Fields on S side of sd. Creek, granted to sd. ALISON 3 Apr 1752...
ANDREW ALISON (SEAL), MARGARET ALISON (SEAL), Wit: GEORGE DAVISON, HENRY HENDRY.

Page 480: 21 Apr 1754, JOHN PRESLY of Anson Co. , to WALTER GIBSON of same, for
Ŀ25 proc. money of N. C., land on N side Rockey River, 200 A, granted
to PRESLY 11 Apr 1750...JOHN PRESLY (ƛ), Wit: WILLIAM TERRY, WILLIAM DOWNS.

Pp. 481-482: 11 Mar 1755, CHARLES & BENJAMIN MOOREMAN, planter, of Anson Co.,
to ANDREW MOREMAN JUR. of same, for Ŀ40 Va. money...land on S
side Great P. D. at mouth of Walker's gut...200 A conveyed to them by JOHN
HORNBACK...CHARLES MOOREMAN (X) (SEAL), BENJAMIN MOOREMAN (SEAL), Wit: JOHN
COLLSON, MARSHALL DIGGS.

Pp. 482-484: 15 & 16 Mar 1755, THOMAS PATTON (PATEN) of Anson Co., to ANDREW
LYNN of same (lease s5, release Ŀ5 Va. money)...land on S side
Cuttawba on Suggar Creek, below his other survey...THOMAS PATTON (SEAL), Wit:
ANDREW PERKINS, PATT KER, ROBT. RAMSEY.

Page 485: 21 Apr 1755, WALTER GIBSON of Anson Co., planter, to JOHN PRESLY, for
Ŀ50 proc. money of N. C., land on S side Pee Dee, adj. ROBT. PARKE's
land, 200 A...WALTER GIBSON (W), Wit: WM. TERRY, WM. DOWNS.

Pp. 486-487: 21 Apr 1755, JOHN HORNBACK of Anson Co., planter, to NATHANIEL
                CHAMBERS, planter, for ₤35 Va. money...land on S side Great Pee
Dee to ye mouth of Island Creek...part of a tract laid out for JOHN NEWBERRY,
200 A, 7 Oct 1747...JOHN HORNBACK (SEAL), Wit: STEPHEN TOUCHSTONE, LEONARD HODGEN.

Page 487: 17 Jan 1755, BENJ. GRIFFETH of Anson Co., planter, to THOMAS DAVIS
                of same, for ₤5 Va. money...land on S side Great Pee Dee, abt. 6 miles
above the fork at the mouth of the Cabin Branch...granted to GRIFFETH 31 Aug
1753...BENJN. GRIFFETH (B) (SEAL), Wit: JOHN COLLSON, WM. DOWNS, WM. DOWNS, JUR.

Pp. 488-490: 12 & 13 Feb 1755, SAML. McELVENEY, miller of Anson Co., to JOHN
                & ARCHIBALD CROCKETT, Yeoman, of same, (lease s5, release ₤44 Va.
money)...528 A at ANDREW PICKINs line on N side Waxhaw Creek...SAMUEL McELVENEY
(SEAL), Wit: WM. KING, JAMES McCORKALL, WILLIAM DAVIS.

Pp. 491=493: 2 & 3 Feb 1755, THOMAS MACKELHENNY to CHARLES BURNET, both of
                Anson Co., (lease s5, release ₤40 Va. money)...land on N side
Cuttawba, including an improvement bought of THOMAS GILES, on Reedy Creek,
600 A...THOMAS McELHENNY (SEAL), JEAN McELHENNY (X) (SEAL), Wit: ANDREW PICKINS,
MEAL McGLAUGHLIN, SAMUEL BURNET.

Pp. 493-495: 3 Feb & 2 May 1755, ROBERT McPHERSON of Rowan Co., to JAMES HUEY
                of Rowan Co., (lease s5, release ₤20)...land on N fork of S fork
of Sandy River, adj. JOHN CLARK's line...400 A...ROBERT McPHERSON (SEAL), Wit:
HENRY HENDRY, JAMES PICKETT.

Pp. 496-498: 28 & 29 Jan 1754, WILLIAM ALLEXANDER, Merchant, to JOHN PATERSON,
                planter, both of Rowan Co., (lease s5, release ₤10)...land on N
side Cuttawba, S side of Twelve Mile Creek...496 A...WILLIAM ALLEXANDER (SEAL),
Wit: JOHN McCALPIN, HENRY HENDRY.

Pp. 498-499: 16 Oct 1755, CALEB TOUCHSTONE, Blacksmith, to STEPHEN TOUCHSTONE,
                planter, to ₤10 proc. money...land on W side of a branch running
into Mountain Creek, 200 A...CALEB TOUCHSTONE (SEAL), Wit: HENRY TOUCHSTONE, JOHN
MACKLANE.

Pp. 499-500: 16 Oct 1754, EDMOND LILLY of Anson Co. to JOHN LILLEY of Albemarle Co.,
                Va., for s5 Va. money...land on N side Pee Dee, upper end of
Buffelow Island, 197 A, granted to EDMOND LILLEY 1753...EDMOND LILLY (SEAL), Wit:
WM. LILLY, WILLIAM QUEEN.

Pp. 500-501: 16 Oct 1754, ANDREW MOORMAN to CHARLES & BENAJMIN MOORMAN, for
                ₤60 Va. money..land laid out for WILLIAM STONE, conveyed to ANDREW
MOORMAN by deed Jan. 1752, and 50 A adj. to it laid out for JOHN HITCHCOCK,
conveyed to JOSEPH HALL 27 Jan 1750, & then to ANDREW MOORMAN...on E side Great
Pee Dee, adj. SOLOMON HUGHES & THOS MOORMAN's land, 250 A granted to STONE
20 Apr 1745...granted to HITCHCOCK 25 May 1741...ANDREW MOORMAN (SEAL), Wit:
CHARLES ROBINSON, TOWNSEND ROBINSON.

Page 502: 1 May 1754, RICH'D TOUCHSTONE of Anson Co., planter, to STEPHEN
                TOUCHSTONE of same, for ₤20 proc. money,...part of 300 A granted
to JOHN FRANCIS 21 June 1746, conveyed to RICHARD TOUCHSTONE...on Lake Island,
50 A...RICHARD TOUCHSTONE (X)(SEAL), Wit: MORGAN BROWN, DANIEL TOUCHSTONE.

Pp. 503-506: 14 & 15 Feb 1754, JOHN PATERSON & ELIZABETH his wife of Rowan Co.,
        to WILLIAM NUTT, JUR. of Anson Co., (lease s5, release Ƚ23)...
496 A on N side Cuttawba, S side Twelve Mile Creek...JOHN PATERSON (SEAL),
ELIZABETH PATERSON (Ϛ) (SEAL), Wit: HENRY HENDRY, JAMES McCORKALL.

Pp. 506-507: 12 Oct 1754, JAMES WAUGHNY of Anson Co., to JOHN BIRD of Cumberland
        Co., Pa., (lease s5d9, release L32s10 Va. money)...land on S side
Cuttawba, S fork of Crodas Creek, 550 A, granted to WAUGHNY 18 Nov 1752...JAMES
WAUGHNY (SEAL), Wit: JOHN CLARK, NATH'L ALLECANDER.

Pp. 508-509: 12 Oct 1754, JAMES WAUGHNY of Anson Co. to HENRY VERNOR of same,
        for Ƚ15 Va. money...land on S side S fork Cuttawba, on a branch of
Crodas Creek, 650 A granted to WAUGHNY 29 Mar 1753...JAMES WAUGHNY (SEAL), Wit:
JOHN CLARK, ALLEXANDER WALLAGE, MOSES FERGUSON.

Page 510: 15 Oct 1754, TORRANCE CARREL of Anson Co., planter, to JOHN LEATH of
        same, Yeoman, forƚ _____, Va. money..._____ A granted to HENRY FALKEN-
BURG, 6 Apr 1750, conveyed by FALKENBURG, ___Jan.1754...land on N side Pee Dee,
near mouth of Naked Creek, 80 A...TORRANCE CARREL (ÐÐ) (SEAL), Wit: MORGAN
BROWN, WILLIAM DOWNS.

Page 511: 22 Feb 1754, JAMES LARRIMORE of Anson Co., Taylor appoints ANDREW
        PICKINS, ESQR. his lawfull attorney...JAMES LARRIMORE (SEAL), Wit:
WILLIAM PICKINS, ARCHIBALD CROCKETT.

Pp. 512-513: 10 Jan 1754, JOHN KIMBROUGH of Anson Co., to WILLIAM LITTLE of same,
        for Ƚ250 Va. money..640 A on Great Pee Dee, bought of JOHN WESTFIELD...
JOHN KIMBORUGH (SEAL), Wit: NATHANIEL KIMBROUGH, EDMOND IRBY, JEREMIAH ATWOOD.

Pp. 513-514: 8 Mar 1754, WILLIAM BEDINGFIELD of Anson Co., planter, to WILLIAM
        LITTLE of same, for Ƚ25 Va. money...130 A granted to sd. BEDINGFIELD
25 Feb.¹ 1754...WILLIAM BEDINGFIELD (SEAL), Wit: JAMES FILLESPIE, EDMOND IRBY.

Pp. 514-515: 8 Mar 1754, HENRY BEDINGFIELD of Anson Co., to WILLIAM LITTLE of
        same, for Ƚ10 Va. money...200 A granted to HENRY BEDINGFIELD
25 Feb 1754...HENRY BEDINGFIELD (SEAL), Wit: EDMOND E. IRB Y, GOLDMAN
KIMBROUGH, WILLIAM BEDINGFIELD.

Pp. 516-517: 1 March 1754, WILLIAM LITTLE of Anson Co., to JOHN STAFFORD of same,
        for Ƚ20 Va. money...land on S side Pee Dee, adj. JCHN JENKINS' line
50 A...WILLIAM LITTLE (SEAL), Wit: ROBERT AMMONS (X), WILLIAM MORRISE.

Page 517: 16 July 1754, HENRY WALKER of Anson Co., to JAMES ADAMS for ten pistoles
        ...land on S side Pee Dee, below the mouth of Rockey River, 135 A...
HENRY WALKER (SEAL), Wit EDMOND LILLY, JEREMIAH DUMAS, JOSEPH CULPEPPER.

Page 518: 5 Feb 1754, GEORGE DOBBS of Craven Co., S. C., to JAMES MATHEWS of
        same, for Ƚ 30 Va. money...land on S side Great Pee Dee, both sides
of Thompson's Creek, 150 A...granted to sd. DOBBS 13 Apr 1749...GEORGE DOBBS
(S) (SEAL), Wit: JOHN JURVIS, DURHAM HILLS.

Pp. 519-520: 24 Dec 1753, CURTIS WOODS of Anson Co., Hunter, to JOHN GORDEN
        of Berkley Co., S. C., for Ƚ5 proc. money...300 A on S side Teager
River, including an improvement where old Mr. JENNINGS formerly lived, claimed
by STEPHEN HOLSTON, at mouth of a branch below THOS JENNINGS...granted to sd.
WOODS 31 Aug 1753, 300 A...CURTIS WOODS (+) (SEAL), Wit: JOHN CLARK, GABRIEL
BROWN, SAMUEL YOUNG.
        [This land now in S. C., Teager River is Tyger River]

Pp. 520-521: 4 July 1754, SAML MARTEN of Craven Co., S. C. to TOWNSEND ROBINSON
of Anson Co., N. C. for ₤50 proc. money...land on S side Pee Dee,
above the mouth of Little River...opposite to a bluff in DENSON's land, 300 A...
SAMUEL MARTEN (SEAL), Wit: PATTR. KER, LAURANCE BRYAN, JAMES PICKETT.

Pp. 522-524: 28 Jan & 1 Mar 1755, THOMAS UNDERWOOD of Anson Co., to PATRICK KER
of same, (lease s5, release ₤16 proc. money)...400 A on upper side
of Brown Creek...THOMAS UNDERWOOD (SEAL), SARAH UNDERWOOD (3) (SEAL), Wit:
HENRY HENDRY, SAML. YOUNG.

Pp. 525-527: 13 & 14 June 1754, SAMUEL BEASON of Anson Co., planter to JOHN
RAMSOUR of same (lease s5, release ₤50 Va. money)...land on N side of South
fork & E side of Clark's Creek...320 A...SAML. BEASON (SEAL), Wit: HENRY JOHNSTON,
JAMES ARMOUR, JOHN THOMAS.

Page 527: 30 Oct 1753,BENJAMIN VINES of Anson Co., to TOWNSEND ROBINSON, for
₤10 proc money...Bay mear and other stock known as Eliby's gang...
BENJAMIN VINES (8) (SEAL), Wit: CHARLES ROBINSON, WILLIAM DOWNS.

Pp. 528-529: 25 & 26 Feb 1754, ROBERT LEEPER & CATHERINE his wife of Anson Co.
to ADAM SNIDER (lease s5, release ₤60 Va. money)...land on S side
Catawba, Leeper's Creek, 300 A granted to LEEPER 8 Oct 1751...ROBERT LEEPER
(SEAL), CATHERIN LEEPER (K) (SEAL), Wit: ROBERT PATRICK, ABRAHAM KURKENDAL, JOHN
THOMAS.

Pp. 530-531: 23 & 25 Mar 1754, CHARLES BETTY of Anson Co., to SAMUEL COBRON of
same, (lease s5, release ₤5 Va. money)...land on S side Cutawba
on Bever Dam branch, adj. SAMUEL COBRON's corner...granted to BETTY 23 Feb 1754
[acreage not given]...CHARLES BETTY (SEAL), Wit: SAMUEL WILSON, JAMES ARMOR.

Pp. 532-533: 11 Oct 1754, ANDREW COX of Anson Co., to STOKES EMMONS of same,
"for other good causes & Consideration" 50 A, part of a 400 A
grant to WILLIAM KEMP on S side Pee Dee, Mill Creek, including plantation
where ANDREW COX formerly did dwell...ANDREW COX (A) (SEAL), Wit: TOWNSEND
ROBINSON, BURLINGHAM RUDD.

END OF VOLUME B

ANSON COUNTY DEEDS VOLUME C-1

Pp. 1-2: 17 & 18 Apr 1755, JOSEPH WHITE & ELIZABETH his wife of Anson Co.,
          to JOHN LYNN of same, (lease s5, release ₤45 s3 Va. money)...
643 A on S side Waxhaw Creek, adj. JOSEPH WHITE's line...JOSEPH WHITE (SEAL),
ELIZABETH WHITE (O) (SEAL), Wit: ANDREW PERKINS, JAMES McCORKALL, SAML. BARNET.

Pp. 3-4: Blank.

Page 5: __ Dec 1754, JACOB PAUL of Anson Co., planter, to ANTHONY HUTCHINS of
         same, planter, for ₤30 proc. money...200 A on E side Brown Creek, granted
to JACOB PAUL 28 Sept 1754...JACOB PAUL (SEAL), Wit: THOMAS HERRINGTON (T), THOS.
PIPER (X), JOHN JACKSON.

Page 6: Blank.

Pp. 7-8: 9 & 10 Apr 1754, GEORGE HEAKER & MARGARET his wife of Anson Co. to
         WILLIAM HEAKER (lease s5, release ₤10 Va. money)...land on S side
Catawba, part of plantation where sd. GEORGE now liveth, 200 A granted to
GEORGE HEAKER 30 Aug 1753...GEORGE HEAKER (SEAL), MARGRET HEAKER (X) (SEAL),
Wit: DANIEL O CAIN, JEAN THOMAS, JOHN THOMAS.

Pp. 9-10: Blank.

Pp. 11-13: 20 & 21 Aug 1754, JOHN SIGLE & wife ELIZABETH & MATHIAS CLAUS of
           Anson Co., to BOSTIAN BEST of same, (lease s5, release ₤20 proc.
money)...land on S side Catawba, on Andrew Rilloan's Creek, abt. a mile above
ANDREW RILLOAN, JUNR., granted to SIGLE & CLAUS 23 Feb 1754, 200 A...JOHN SIGLE
(SEAL), ELIZ. SIGLE (X) (SEAL), MATHIAS CLAUS (|||) (SEAL), Wit: PETER HAYLE,
ANN BLACK, JOHN THOMAS.

Page 14: Blank.

Pp. 15-16: 16 Oct 1754, TOWNSEND ROBINSON of Anson Co., to JOHN WOODS of same,
           for ₤11 proc. money...land on W side of Little River of Pee Dee,
between land on HENRY DOWNER & TILLMAN HOLMS, part of a 246 A tract granted to
ANDW. MOORMAN JUNR., 21 Aug 1753 & sold to sd. ROBINSON...TOWNSEND ROBINSON
(SEAL), Wit: JAMES JOWERS, CHARLES ROBINSON JUNR.

Pp. 17-18: 1 & 2 Mar 1754, MATHEW KEYEKENDALL & MARY his wife of Anson Co., to
           PETER KEYEKENDALL of same, for ₤15...land on S side Catawba on Lepers
Creek, half of sd. MATHEW's place where he did live, 150 A granted to sd. MATHEW
1 Apr 1750...MATHEW KEYEKENDALL (O) (SEAL), MARY KEYEKENDALL (X) (SEAL), Wit:
JOHN KEYEKENDALL, ANDREW HAMPTON, CHARLES DUNLAP.

Page 19: Blank.

Pp. 20-23: 4 & 5 Mar 1754, MATHEW KEYEKENDALL & MARY his wife to ANDREW HAMPTON
           all of Anson Co., for ₤28 Va. money...land on S side Catawba, S side
Leapers Creek, 150 A granted to sd. KEYEKENDALL 1 Apr 1750...MATHEW KEYEKENDALL
(O) (SEAL), MARY KEYEKENDALL (X) (SEAL), Wit: JOHN KUYKENDAL, PETER KUYKENDAL,
CHARLES DUNLAP.

41

Pp. 24-26: 25 & 26 Feb 1754, ROBERT LEOPARD & KATHERN his wife of ANSON Co.,
     to PETER ANSTER (lease s5, release ₺20 Va. money)...land on S side
Cattawba, above the great shoal on both sides Leepers Creek, including COBRON
& CATHEYs Camp, 200 A granted to sd. ROBERT LEEPER 31 Mar 1753...ROBERT
LEEPER (SEAL), CATHERIN LEEPER (SEAL), Wit: ROBT. PATRICK, ABRAHAM KUYKENDAL,
JOHN THOMAS.

Page 27: Blank.

Pp. 28-30: 16 & 17 May 1754, ABRAHAM KUYKENDALL & ELIZABETH his wife to WILLIAM
     ADEAR of same, for ₺36 Va. money, land on S side Cuttawba, on fork
of Fishing Creek, below GEORGE RONDERK's entry, 570 A, granted to sd. KUYKENDALL
29 Mar 1753...ABRAHAM KUYKENDALL (SEAL), ELIZABETH KUYKENDALL (SEAL), Wit:
JOHN KUYKENDALL, JOSEPH HARDEN, CHARLES DUNLAP.

Pp. 31-34: 10 & 11 Dec 1753, JOHN KUYKENDALL & REBECCA his wife of Anson Co.,
     to PETER KUYKENDALL of same, for ₺20 Va. money, land on S side Cuttaw-
ba, a N branch of Fishing Creek, granted to JOHN KUYKENDALL 30 Aug 1753 [acreage
not given]...JOHN KUYKENDALL (SEAL), REBECCA KUYKENDALL (SEAL), Wit: ANDREW
HAMPTON, ABRAHAM KUYKENDALL, CHARLES DUNLAP.

Pp. 35-37: 10 & 11 July 1754, WILLIAM WATSON of Anson Co., to BENJAMIN HARDEN
     of same, (lease s5, release ₺30 Va. money)...land on N side Cuttawba
above GEORGE RENICKs line...granted to WM. WATSON 28 Feb 1754...[acreage not
given]...WILLIAM WATSON (SEAL), Wit: ANDREW BERRY, WILLIAM PRICE, JOHN THOMAS.

Page 38: Blank.

Pp. 39-41: 9 & 30 July 1754, MICHEL MILLER of Anson Co., to DEVALT PAFF, planter,
     of same, (lease s5, release ₺30 Va. money)...300 A on S side Cuttawba,
both sildes Rilloans Creek, adj. RILLOANS corner...granted to MICHEL MILLER
23 Feb 1754...MICHEL MILLER (SEAL), Wit: DANIEL O CAIN, JEAN THOMAS, JOHN THOMAS.

Pp. 42-45: 26 & 27 Dec 1753, WILLIAM HENRY & IZABELLA his wife of Anson Co., to
     ALLEXANDER ROBINSON of same, (lease s5, release ₺10 Va. money)...
land on S side Cuttawba on sd. HENRYs line...along Scholars head line...200 A
granted to WM. HENRY 3 Sept 1753...WILLIAM HENRY (SEAL), ISABELLA HENRY (SEAL),
Wit: ABRAHAM KUYKENDALL, ADAM SNIDER, JOHN THOMAS.

Page 46; Blank:

Pp. 47-49: 22 & 23 May 1754, ISAAC TAYLOR of Anson Co., to JOHN MATHEWS of same,
     (lease s5, release ₺20 sterling)...land on both sides Fishing Creek,
200 A...ISAAC TAYLOR (SEAL), Wit: ANDREW PICKENS, JAMES PATTON, HENRY WHITE.

Pp. 50-51: Blank.

Pp. 52-54: 21 & 22 June 1754, WILLIAM JONES, Showmaker, of Anson Co. to JAMES
     JOHNSTON, planter of Rowan Co., (lease s5, release ₺20 Va. money)...
500 A on N side of S branch of Fishing Creek, below SAMUEL MOORE's corner...
WILLIAM JONES (SEAL), Wit: WILLIAM COURTNEY, HENRY HENDRY.

Page 55: Blank.

Pp. 56-59: 5 & 6 Feb 1754, THOMAS LEE & MARGERY his wife of Anson Co., to
          DAVID KARE of Rowan Co. (lease s5, release ₤30 proc. money...
160 A on Cain Creek...THOMAS LEE (SEAL), MARGERY LEE (SEAL), Wit: JAMES
JOHNSTON.

Page 60: Blank.

Page 61: 16 Feb 1754, WILLIAM BROWN of S. C. Labourer, to BENJAMIN CLARK of
          Colleny of Va., Labourer, for ₤15 proc. money...land on N side Pee
Dee, near the great falls of the Pee Dee, near Beaver Dam Creek, 300 A granted
to WILLIAM BROWN, 7 Nov 1753...WILLIAM BROWN (SEAL), Wit: ANDREW MOORMAN
JUNR., BENJAMINE NIMS, JOHN WEBB.

Page 62: Blank.

Page 63: 16 Feb 1754, WILLIAM BROWN of S. C., Labourer, to CHRISTOPHER
          CLARK of Colleny of Va., Labourer, for ₤10 proc. money...200 A
on N side Pee Dee, abt. half a mile below the mouth of Wood Run, granted
to WILLIAM BROWN 17 Nov 1753...WILLIAM BROWN (SEAL), Wit: ANDREW MOORMAN
JUNR., BENJAMIN NIMS, JOHN WEBB.

Page 64: Blank.

Pp. 65-66: 19 July 1754, JAMES LARIMORE, Late of Anson Co., Taylor, to WILLIAM
          DAVIS, carpenter, of same, for ₤20 sterling...418 A granted to
JAMES LAREMORE 17 May 1754...By virtue of a power of attorney to ANDREW
PICKINS, Esqr...ANDREW PICKINS (SEAL), JAMES LAREMORE (SEAL), Wit: GELEN
O HELY, HENRY HENDRY.

Pp. 67-68: 19 Dec 1753, FELEX KENNEDY of Anson Co., to JOHN KENNEDY of same,
          for ₤50...land in the Waxhaw, on N side Wateree River in Anson
Co., adj. WILLIAM TAYLORs line...300 A granted 5 Apr 1753...FELEX KENEDY
(SEAL), ANN KENEDY (SEAL), Wit: ANDREW PICKINS (SEAL), JACOB TAYLOR.

Pp. 69-70: Blank.

Page 71: 16 Mar 1754, PETER SMITH of Anson Co., to JAMES LAND, Cordwinder,
          for ₤20 sterling...land on both side Rockey Creek, 340 A granted
to PETER SMITH 6 Apr 1753...PETER SMITH (SEAL), Wit: WILLIAM PICKINS, JOHN
KENEDY, PATRICK KER.

Page 72: Blank.

Pp. 73-74: 6 Apr 1754, JOHN HAMER of Anson Co., Gent., to WILLIAM FERRAL of
          same, for ₤70 sterling...land granted to JOHN NEWBERRY 8 Oct
1747, 545 A ...S side Mountain Creek...200 A, conveyed by JOHN NEWBERRY to
JOHN HAMER 19 June 1752...JOHN HAMER (SEAL), Wit: MORGAN BROWN, ELIZ. BROWN.

Pp. 75-76: 19 Apr 1754, JOHN HAMER to WILLIAM FERRALL, for ₤10...100 A
          granted to HAMER 31 Aug 1753 on upper part of Mountain Creek...
JOHN HAMER (SEAL), Wit: MORGAN BROWN, STEPHEN BROWN.

Page 77: Blank.

Pp. 78-79: 29 Nov 1753, CORNEALOS O NEAL of Anson Co., Shoe Maker, to JOHN
            CLARK, for £25 Va. money...800 A on Hickly Creek...CORNEALOS
O NEAL (SEAL), Wit: JOHN O NEAL, BABRIEL BROWN.

Pp. 80-83: 4 Dec 1754, JOHN McDOWELL of Anson Co., to JAMES HARRISS of same,
            (lease s5, release £16 s5)...land on S side Broad River, on
a branch of Little River, 640 A ...granted to sd. McDOWELL 18 Nov 1752...
JOHN McDOWELL (SEAL), Wit: NATHANIEL ALEXANDER, SAMUEL McCLEREY.

Pp. 84-85: Blank.

Page 86: 3 Feb 1755, JOSEPH THEIMS of Cumberland Co., N. C., planter to
            WILLIAM NEWBERRY of Anson Co., carpenter, for £25 Va. money...300
A on N side Pee Dee on S side Mountain Creek, on both sides of Dry fork...
granted to sd. THEIMS 28 Sept 1754...JOS. THEIMS (X) (SEAL), Wit: MORGAN
BROWN, JOHN NEWBERRY, STEPHEN BROWN.

Page 87: Blank.

Page 88: 21 July 1755, WILLIAM STONE of Anson Co., to WILLIAM QUEEN of same,
            for £6 Va. money...100 A granted to sd. STONE 23 Dec 1754...on
Little River of Pee Dee, below mouth of Ridge Creek...land where WILLIAM
QUEEN now lives...WILLIAM STONE (M) (SEAL), Wit: WILLIAM DOWNS, CHARLES
ROBINSON.

Pp. 89-90: Blank.

Pp. 91-92: 5 Nov 1754, JOSEPH KEMP of Anson Co., to WILLIAM HALEY of Colleny
            of Va., for £75 Va. money...land on E side great Pee Dee. 213 A,
part of a tract laid out for SOLOMON HUGHES...600 A granted 22 May 1741...
JOSEPH KEMP (K) (SEAL), Wit: JOSEPH HALL, JOHN WEBB, THOMAS MOORMAN.

Page 93: Blank.

Pp. 94-97: 11 & 12 Apr 1755, NATHENIEL ALLEXANDER of Anson Co., to DANIEL
            ALLEXANDER of same, (lease s5, release £30 s5)...land on N
side Cutawba on Buffelow Creek on ye upper side of DAVID HUSTONs survey,
387 A granted to sd. NATHENIEL 23 Feb 1754...NATHL. ALLEXANDER (SEAL), Wit:
ANDREW BARRY, EDWARD GYLLES.

Page 98: Blank.

Pp. 99-101: 5 & 6 Mar 1755, GEORGE RENICK & MARY his wife of Anson Co., to
            WILLIAM PEDERICK of same, (lease s5, release £7 s10)...land
on N side Cuttawba, both sides of quir Creek, 200 A granted to GEORGE
RENICK 31 Mar 1753...GEORGE RENICK (SEAL), MARY RENICK (SEAL), Wit: ANDREW
BARRY, WILLIAM B. WATSON, RICHARD BARRY.

Page 102: Blank.

Pp. 103-105: 7 & 8 May 1754, ROBERT McPHERSON of Rowan Co., to JOHN McCAPIN
of Rowan Co., (lease s5, release Ƚ3)...land on S side Broad
River, on Bush River, 360 A adj. GEORGE DERUMPLES corner & line...ROBT.
McPHERSON (SEAL), Wit: HENRY HENDRY, JAMES PICKETT.
[This land is now in present Laurens and Newberry Counties, S. C.
This land was granted to ROBERT McFARSON, Land Grant Office, Bk.
13, p. 10. DERUMPLE is a mis-pronunciation of DALRYMPLE.]

Pp. 106-107: Blank.

Pp. 108-110: 15 Jan 1755, ANDREW LYNN & SARAH his wife of Rowan Co., to
RICHARD COUSHER of Anson Co., (lease s5, release Ƚ5)...91 A
on both sides Giles Creek..waters of Cuttawba on E side...adj. JOHN PHILLIPS
line...ANDREW LYNN (SEAL), SARAH LYNN (SEAL), Wit: ANDREW PICKENS, ROBT.
RAMSEY, JOSEPH WHITE.

Pp. 111-112: Blank.

Pp. 113-116: 12 & 13 July 1755, JAMES KUYKENDAL & SARAH his wife of Anson Co.,
to JOHN KUYKENDAL of same, for Ƚ40 Va. money, 300 A on Kuykendal's
Creek, part of a large survey of JAMES KUYKENDAL granted 1 Apr 1751...
JAMES KUYKENDAL (SEAL), SARAH KUYKENDAL (SEAL), Wit: ETON MOOLEY, WILLIAM
HENRY, FREDERICK HAMBRIGHT.

Page 117: Blank.

Pp. 118-119: 6 Mar 1755, JOHN GRIGGS of Anson Co., to JOSEPH WHITE of same,
for Ƚ12 Va. money...on S side Pee Dee, below the Wagon ford...
granted to JOHN GRIGGS 30 Sept 1748...JOHN GRIGGS (Ⅰ) (SEAL), Wit: ANTHO.
HUTCHINS, FRANCES HOUGH.

Page 120: Blank.

Page 121: Grant from GEORGE II (GABRIEL JOHNSTON) to DAVID TEMPLETON, 600
A on Caudle Creek, N side Cuttawba...3 Apr 1752...GABRIEL JOHNSTON...
Enrold in Audr. Generls. Office 6 Apr 1752 P ALLEXR McCULLOCH Dep. Audr.
JOHN RICE, Dep. Sec:

Page 122: Blank.

Page 123: Grant from GEORGE II (NATHANIEL RICE) to DAVID TEMPLETON...300 A
on Coddle Creek, adj. his own land & McCULLOCK's line...18 Nov
1752 ...NATHANIEL RICE...JOHN RICE Dep Secr. Enrolled in Auditor Genls.
Office 1 March 1753 P ALLEXR. McCULLOCH Dep Audr.

Page 124: Blank.

Page 125: Grant from GEORGE II (MATHEW ROWAN) to DAVID TEMPLETON...125 A
on N side Caudle Creek, adj. his own line & DAVID HUSTONs...MATHEW
ROWAN...JAMES MURRAY SENR, Secr. Enrolled in Audr. Genls. Office 10 Sept
1753 RICHD. LYON Pro. Audr.

Pp. 126-127: Blank.

Pp. 128-131: 1 & 2 July 1755, JAMES ARMOR & JANNET his wife of Anson Co., to
WILLIAM ALLEXANDER of Rowan Co., (lease s5, release Ł15)...
300 A on S side Cuttawba, granted to ARMOR 29 Sept 1750...JAMES ARMOR (SEAL),
JANNET ARMOR (SEAL), Wit: ANDREW BARRY, WILLIAM MOORE.

Pp. 132-133; Blank.

Pp. 134-137: 1 & 2 Dec 1754, CHARLES BETTY & THOMAS BETTY of Anson Co., to
JOHN THOMAS of same, Milright (lease s5, release Ł40 Va. money)
...land on S side Cuttawba, on Stoney branch, near JOHN BETTY land & above
where JOHN LITTLE now liveth, 400 A granted to CHARLES & THOMAS BETTY 31
Mar 1753...CHARLES BETTY (SEAL), THOMAS BETTY (SEAL), Wit: PATRICK KER,
HENRY JOHNSTON, WILLIAM LITLE.

Pp. 138-139: Blank.

Pp. 140-143: 13 & 14 Feb 1754, JOHN THOMAS & JEAN his wife of Anson Co., to
ELIJAH MASSEY of Kent Co., Maryland, (lease s5, release Ł24
Va. money)...448 A on S side Cuttawba, adj. JOHN LARGES corner, ANDREW
RELLIANS line...the plantation sd. JOHN formerly lived on, granted 17 May
1754,...JOHN THOMAS (SEAL), JEAN THOMAS (SEAL), Wit: JAMES ORMOND, CHARLES
McPECTORS, GEORGE RENICK.

Page 144; Blank.

Pp. 145-147: 27 & 28 Feb 1755, HUGH RODGERS of Anson Co., & ELIZABETH his wife
to HUGH KELLY of same (lease s5, release Ł 10 Va. money)...
land on both sides Lantees Creek, adj. JOHN LARGES seoond corner...S side
Cuttawba, adj. THOMAS BETTYs line...300 A...HUGH RODGERS (SEAL), ELIZABETH
RODGERS (SEAL), Wit: JAMES ARMOR, DAVID AMANUEL.

Page 148: Blank.

Pp. 149-153: 6 & 7 July 1755, JAMES ARMOR & JANNET his wife to GEORGE DENNEY
(lease s5, release Ł12 money of Va.)...land on S side Cuttawba,
on fork of Allison's Creek, adj. WILLIAM DICKEYs line, JAMES WILLSONS line,
300 A granted to JAMES ARMOR 27 Mar 1755...JAMES ARMOR (SEAL), JANNET ARMOR
(SEAL), Wit: SAML YOUNG, ROBT. McPHERSON, JOHN WITHROW.

Pp. 154-155; Blank.

Pp. 156-160: 28 Feb 1755, ROBT & ELIZABETH McCLANACHAN of Anson Co., to
THOMAS WILLIAMS of Chester Co., Pa., for Ł45 proc. money, 408
A, part of the plantation sd. MCCLANACHAN lives on...Adj. THOMAS FERRELS
line...W side Cuttawba...ROBT. McCLANACHAN (SEAL), ELIZ. McCLANACHAN (SEAL),
Wit: ANDREW PICKINS, JAMES PATTON.

Page 161: Blank.

Pp. 162-166: 22 & 23 Sept 1755, JOHN CLARK of Anson Co., to DERRICK RAMSEUR
of same, for (lease s5, release Ł42 Va. money)...land on S fork
Cuttawba, adj. JOHN ARMSTRONGs, 400 A...JOHN CLARK (SEAL), Wit: JOHN WILLKINS,
SAMUEL HAYWARD, JAMES ROBINSON.

Pp. 167-168: Blank.

Pp. 169-173: 13 & 14 Aug 1755, RICHARD RENELDS to MOSSES MOORE (lease s5,
                release £40 Va. money)...land on S side S fork Cuttawba, on
Renols Creek, including where he lately lived, 600 A granted to RENELDS
28 Mar 1755...RICHARD RANDLES (SEAL), Wit: DAVID HUDDELSTON, WILLIAM
HUDDELSTON, PATTR. KER.

Pp. 174-175: Blank.

Pp. 176-180: 22 & 23 1753, JOHN CLARK of Anson Co., to MARTIN COULTER of
              samer, (lease s5, release £80 Va. money)...400 A on N side
S fork Cuttawba, adj. JAMES ROBINSONs line...part of 1000 A granted to CLARK
...JOHN CLARK (SEAL), Wit: JOHN WILLKINS, W. SMITH, JAMES ROBINSON.

Pp. 181-182: Blank.

Pp. 183-187: 19 & 20 Sept 1755, JOHN CLARK of Anson Co., to GEORGE SHOEFOOT
              of same, (lease s5, release £55 Va. money)... land on S side S
fork Cuttawba, at ye Rockey ford...500 A granted to SAMUEL WILKINS, upper
end of sd. tract, opposite to ye mill, which CLARK bought of Sd. WILKINS...
JOHN CLARK (SEAL), Wit: ISAAC WEIDNEY, JOHN WILLKINS, JAMES ROBINSON.

Pp. 188-189; Blank.

Pp. 190-193: 24 & 30 Aug 1755, JAMES ARMOR & JANET his wife of Anson Co to
              DINNIS DYER of Rowan Co., (lease s5, release £12 Va. money)...
land on S side Cuttawba, adj. JOHN LARGES former line, 290 A granted to
JOHN LARGE 25 Sept 1754...JAMES ARMOR (SEAL), JANET ARMOR (SEAL), Wit:
JOHN CATHEY, WILLIAM LITTLE, JOHN THOMAS.

Page 194: Blank.

Pp. 195-198: 16 & 17 Sept 1755, HUGH KALLY of Anson Co., to WILLIAM LITLE
              of same, (lease s5, release £7 s10 proc. money)...land on both
sides Lantees Creek, S side Cuttawba, adj. JOHN LARGES second corner, JOHN
McCONELs line, THOMAS BETTYs line...granted to HUGH RODGERS, 31 Aug 1753...
HUGH KALLY (SEAL), Wit: ANDREW BARRY, CHARLES MOORE, JOHN THOMAS.

Page 199: Blank.

Pp. 200-204: 19 & 20 March 1755, THOMAS IRWIN & REBECCA his wife of Anson
              Co., to JOHN McDOWELL of same(Lease s5, release £16 s3 Va.
money)...200 A on a branch of McDOWELL Creek, adj. JOHN KALLERS line, McCULLOCHs
line...granted to IRWIN 23 Feb 1754...THOMAS IRWIN (SEAL), REBECCA IRWIN
(SEAL), Wit: JOHN THOMAS, ALLEXANDER McCONEL, ROBT. DENNEY.

Page 205: Blank.

Page 206: 2 Oct 1755, HENRY TOUCHSTONE & SARAH his wife, of Anson Co., to
              THOMAS PRESTWOOD SENR of same, for £20...200 A on N side great
Pee Dee, adj. DENSONs line...granted to JOSEPH WHITE I752...HENRY TOUCHSTONE
(SEAL), SARAH TOUCHSTONE (SEAL), Wit: ANDREW TOUCHSTONE, GARRET O NEILL,
STEPHEN PIECOCK.

Pp. 207-208: Blank.

Page 209: 28 Oct 1755, HENRY FALKENBOURG, of Anson Co., to JAMES PICKETT Gent.,
for ₺27 Va. money...200 A granted to JOSEPH WHITE 26 Sept 1746,
on S side Great Pee Dee, adj. JOHN LEETHs land...conveyed by WHITE to sd.
FALKENBOURG 2 Apr 1748...HENRY FALKENBOURG (SEAL), Wit: MORGAN BROWN, ANTHO:
HUTCHINS.

Pp. 210-211: Blank.

Page 212: 24 Oct 1755, WALTER GIBSON of Anson Co., to WILLIAM CULPEPPER of
same, for ₺15 Va. money...100 A on N side Rockey River against land
of sd. GIBSON, at mouth of Spring Branch...WALTER GIBSON (SEAL), Wit: EDMOND
LILLY, JEREMIAH DUMAS, JOHN CULPEPPER.

Page 213: Blank.

Page 214: No. 830. Grant from GEORGE II (MATHEW ROWAN) to SAMUEL ZEIKLAG,
176 A on W side Caudle Creek...25 Feb 1754...MATHEW ROWAN. JAMES
MURRAY Sec: Enrolled in Audr. Genls. Office 20 Feb 1754. RICHD. LYON Pro:
Audr.

Pp. 215-216: Blank.

Page 217: Grant from GEORGE II (MATHEW ROWAN) to ALLEXANDER DOBBIN, 250 A
on N side Cataba, a mile or two above the fork...6 Mar 1754...
MATHEW ROWAN, JOS VAIL Dep. Sec: Enrolled in Audr. Genls. Office 9 Mar
1754, RICHD. LYON Pro: Audr.

Pp. 218-219: Blank.

Page: 220: 4 March 1756, MATHEW IRWIN of Rockey River, Anson Co., taylor, to
JOHN GILMOR of Anson Co., Yeomen, for ₺4 money of Carolina...
sale of cattle...MATHEW IRWIN (SEAL), Wit: JOHN McCLEAN, McN. IRWIN, Proved
by JOHN McCLEAN 3 Apr 1756...NATHL. ALLEXANDER.

Page 221: 4 Mar 1756, MATHEW IRWIN to JAMES IRWIN, Black smith, for ₺4
money of Carolina...sale of cattle...MATHEW IRWIN (SEAL), Wit:
JOHN McCLEAN, JOHN GILMOR, Proved by McCLAN and GILMOR 3 Apr 1756.
3 Apr 1756, I, MATHEW IRWIN, do make over all my wheat and rye to JOHN McLEAN.
Wit JAMES IRWIN, JOHN GILMOR.

Page 222; Blank.

Pp. 223-227: 3 & 4 Sept 1753, JOHN BREVARD & JEAN His wife of Rowan Co., to
JOHN POTTS of Anson Co., (lease s5, release ₺40 Va. money)...
630 A granted to BREVARD 11 Apr 1752...JOHN BREVARD (SEAL), JEAN BREVARD (SEAL),
Wit: ALLEX. OSBURN, PAUL CUNNINGHAM, HENRY HENDRY.

Pp. 228-229: Blank.

Page 230: 19 Jan 1756, STOKES EMMONS of Anson Co., to THOS COYAL of same, for
₺ 30 proc. money...150 A surveyed for WILLIAM KEMP SENR, on Mill
Creek, the lower side of the Patent...STOKES EMMONS (SEAL), Wit: BENTLY
FRANKLIN, HENRY FULKENBOURG, JOSEPH SLOAN.

Page 231: Blank.

Page 232: 6 Dec 1755, THOMAS GEORGE of Anson Co. to PETER PRESLEY, for Ł50
proc. money...200 A on S side great Pee Dee at the mouth of Brown
Creek, granted to sd. GEORGE 4 Apr 1750...THOMAS GEORGE (SEAL), Wit: WILLIAM
PHILLIPS, BENJN. SMITH, ANN PHILLIPS.

Page 233; Blank.

Page 234: 8 Dec 1755, THOMAS UNDERWOOD of Anson Co., to PETER PRESLEY of same,
for Ł50 proc. money...100 A on S side of N fork of Litle P.D., conveyed from HENRY SUMERALL 24 Sept 1754...THOMAS UNDERWOOD (SEAL), Wit: WILLIAM
PHILIPS, "One Dutch Name," ZACH. PHILLIPS.

Page 235: Blank.

Page 236: 14 Apr 1755, THOMAS WILLIAMS of Anson Co., to JOHN THOMPSON of same,
for Ł30 Va. money...200 A on N side Pee Dee above mouth of Clarks
Creek...granted to sd. WILLIAMS 23 Feb 1754...THOMAS WILLIAMS (SEAL), Wit:
EDMOND LILLY, BENJN. VINES, SARAH LILLY.

Pp. 237-238: Blank.

Pp. 239-240: 8 Sept 1755, WILLIAM TERRY of Anson Co., to LAURENCE O BRIAN
for Ł6 proc. money...100 A on upper branch of S fork of
Cartlidges Creek, adj. EDMOND CARTLIDGEs upper corner, granted to WM. TERRY
9 March 1754...WM. TERRY (SEAL), Wit: TILLOSON KIBLE, EDMOND CARTLIDGE.

Page 241; Blank.

Page 242: __ Oct 1755, THOMAS BERRY of Anson Co., to CHARLES BERRY of same,
for Ł10 proc. money...175 A, part of a tract sd. THOMAS lives on,
on S side Pee Dee, both sides Smiths Creek...granted to JOSEPH WHITE &
FRANCIS MACKILWEAN 13 Apr 1749, conveyed by them to sd. THOMAS BERRY, 18
July 1752...THOMAS BERRY (S) (SEAL), Wit: MORGAN BROWN, SAM. DAVISON,
JONATHAN HELMS.

Pp. 243-244: Blank.

Pp. 245-246: 20 July 1755, TILMAN HELMS, of Anson Co., Labourer, to WM TERRY
Esqr., for Ł25 proc. money...150 A on N side Pee Dee and upper
side of Little River, opp. an Island formerly called Checks Island, granted to
JOHN McCOY 11 Oct 1749, and sold to TILMAN HELMS 16 Jan 1754...TILMAN HELMS
(SEAL), Wit: MORGAN BROWN, ELIZ. BROWN.

Page 247: Blank.

Pp. 248-249: 29 Jan 1756, GEORGE CLAMONS of Anson Co., to JOHN AVERET, for
Ł30 proc. money...100 A on W side Little River of Pee Dee, adj.
CHARLES ROBINSONs line, granted to CLAMONS 4 Apr 1750...GEORGE CLAMONS (SEAL),
Wit: JOHN FROHOCK, MORGAN BROWN, ADAM McCOOLL.

Page 250: Blank.

Pp. 251-252: 30 July 1755, TOWNSEND ROBINSON of Anson Co., to JAMES PICKETT
            of same, for Ł34 Va. money...200 A an S side great Pee Dee above
ye mouth of Little River, about half a mile above the wagon ford, granted to
NICHOLAS SMITH 13 Oct 1749 and conveyed by him to TOWNSEND ROBINSON...
TOWNSEND ROBINSON (SEAL), Wit: WM. HARRISON, JOHN DUNN.

Pp. 253-254: Blank.

Pp. 255-256: 28 Jan 1756, JAMES COWARD of Anson Co., to ARCHIBALD GRAHAM of
            same, planter, for Ł80 Va. money...190 A on E side Great P.D.,
on both sides of ye Mean Road about one mile from the river...granted to
JAMES COWARD 27 May 1754...JAMES COWARD (SEAL), Wit: HENRY DOWNS, AMBROSE STEELE,
JAMES McMANUS.

Page 257: Blank.

Pp. 258-259: 4 Sept 1755, HOPKIN HOWEL of Anson Co., planter, to DAVID HILDRETH
            of same, cooper, for Ł27 s16 proc. money...600 A on S side Pee
Dee on Watery Branch of Jones Creek...granted to HOPKIN HOWELE 11 Oct 1749
...HOPKINS HOWEL (SEAL), Wit: AMBROSE STELLE, THOMAS UNDERWOOD, DAVID LILES.

Page 260: Blank.

Page 261: 28 Oct 1755, THOMAS BARRY of Anson Co., to ELIZABETH BROADAWAY,
            husband of NICHOLAS BROADAWAY, and daughter of sd. THOMAS, for
Ł10...150 A on W side Pee Dee on Smith Creek, granted to JOSEPH WHITE &
FRANCIS MACKELWEAN 13 Apr 1749 and conveyed by them to sd. THOMAS BERRY
18 July 1852...THOS. BERRY (SEAL), Wit: MORGAN BROWN, SAML. DAVISON, JONATHAN
HELMS.

Pp. 262-263: Blank.

Pp. 264-265: 29 Oct 1755, PATRICK KER of Anson Co., to WILLIAM MONET, attorney
            at law, for Ł40 Va. money...400 A on S side Pee Dee on ye upper
side of Brown Creek, conveyed by THOMAS UNDERWOOD to PATRICK KERR, granted to
sd. UNDERWOOD _____ 175_...PATTR. KER (SEAL), Wit: HENRY DOWNS, JOHN DUNN.

Page 266: Blank.

Page 267: Grant from GEORGE II (MATHEW ROWAN) to JOHN BREVARD, 274 A on
            branches of Rockey River, adj. his former line...28 Sept 1754
MATHEW ROWAN.

Pp. 268-269: Blank.

Page 270: Grant from GEORGE II (MATHEW ROWAN) to JANE McWHORTER, 430 A adj.
            ALLEXE. OSBRUns corner...9 Apr 1753....MATHEW ROWAN.

Page 271: Blank.

Page 272: Grant from GEORGE II (MATHEW ROWAN) to MARY McDOWLE, 320 A on
            N side Catawba, both sides of the Midle Path...28 Feb 1754...
MATHEW ROWAN.

Page 273: Blank.

Page 274: Repeat of grant to JANE McWHORTER on p. 270. JAS MURRY, Sec.

Pp. 274-278: 9 & 10 Dec 1755, JOHN LITTLE & JANET his wife of Anson Co., to
JAMES LITTLE & ALLEXANDER LITTLE of same, (lease s5, release
Ł50)...300 A on S side Cattawba, where JOHN LITTLE now liveth...granted and
bought of JOHN McCONNELL...and the plantation left in the above JOHN LITTLEs
L. W. & T.....JOHN LITTLE (SEAL), JANET LITTLE (SEAL), Wit: GEORGE WEKER,
MARY DEWART, GEORGE RENICK.

Pp. 279-281: Blank.

Pp. 282-286: 9 & 10 Dec 1755, JOHN LITTLE and JANET his wife to ARCHIBALD
LITTLE (lease s5, release Ł30)...440 A on S side Cattawba on
Crowders Creek, SAML. COBRON camp...granted to sd. JOHN LITTLE 3 Apr 1753...
JOHN LITTLE,(SEAL), JANET LITTLE (SEAL), Wit: GEORGE HEKER, MARY DEWART,
GEORGE RENICK.

Pp. 287-288: Blank.

Pp. 289-294: 9 & 10 Aug 1755, SAML. YOUNG of Rowan Co., to JACOB SIMERMAN of
Anson Co., (lease s5, release Ł15 Va. money)...275 A on S side
S fork Cattawba betwixt Indean Creek and Bever Dam Creek, land formerly sur-
veyed for JOHN WELSH...SAML. YOUNG (SEAL), Wit: THOMAS POTTS, LAURANCE KUYSER.

Pp. 295-297: Blank.

Pp. 298-203: 16 & 17 July 1755, GEORGE CATHEY & SARAH his wife Anson Co., to
WILLIAM ALEXANDER of Rowan Co. (lease s5, release Ł7 s10)...
150 A on S side Cattawba, adj. JAMES ARMOR...granted to GEORGE CATHEY 29 Mar
1753...GEORGE CATHEY (SEAL), SARAH CATHEY (SEAL), Wit: JAMES ARMER, MICHAEL
OUSTER.

Pp. 302-304: Blank.

Page 305: Grant from GEORGE II (MATHEW ROWAN) to ALLAN ALEXANDER, 450 A on S
side Catawba, about 3 miles below ye lower mount...4 Sept 1753...
MATHEW ROWAN, JAS. MURRAY, Sec.

Page 306: Blank.

Page 307: Grant from GEORGE II (MATHEW ROWAN) to WILLIAM HALL, 300 A on N side
THOMAS GILLS Creek, about a mile and a half above the black river path
...24 Sept 1754...MATHEW ROWAN, JAMES MURRAY Sec:

Pp. 308-309: Blank.

Page 310: Grant from GEORGE II (MATHEW ROWAN) to WILLIAM HALL, 240 A on N side
Cataba, on head drafts of Rockey River...24 Sept 1754...MATHEW
ROWAN, JAMES MURRAY, Sec:

Pp. 313-314: Blank.

Page 315: Grant from GEORGE II (MATHEW ROWAN) to HENRY HENDRY 300 A on both
sides Caudle Creek, adj. THOMAS McCOWANS line...27 Sept 1751...
JOHN RICE Dep: Sec:
"So Ends the Registering of HENRY HENDRY April the 29th 1756.
Recd. ye Books from the above June the first p me ROBT. HARRIS Pr. R.
WILL HARRIS Augst. 16 1756
Register's Office."

Pp. 316-317: Blank.

Pp. 318-20: 16 Oct 1756, M the Brand on the Mounting Shoulder a Crop with a
peice taken out of the NOse Ear and a halfpenny cut out of the
off in the Lower Sides Ear the Brand and Mark of ADAM MEEK.

23 July 1757, WILLIAM STONE of Anson Co., planter, to JAMES GOLSBY
of same, planter, for ₺2 proc. money...200 A on NE side fo Bumpusses fork,
a branch of Little River, granted to sd. STONE 26 May 1757...WILLIAM STONE (M)
(SEAL), Wit: RICHD. DOWNS, SAML. PARSONS, JAMES ALLEY.

23 July 1757, WILLIAM FERRALL of Bladen Co., to MORGAN BROWN of
Anson Co. saveyor, for ₺45 proc. money...200 A granted to JOHN NEWBERY 6 Oct
1747...on a branch of Mountain Creek...sold by NEWBERRY to JOHN HAMER 19
June 1752...from HAMER to above FERRALL 6 Apr 1754...WM. FERRALL (SEAL), Wit:
JOHN HAMER, ANDREW BIEGLAN.

Page 321: Blank.

Pp. 322-323: 24 Jan 1757, EDWARD ELERBEE of Anson Co., planter, to ALEXANDER
GORDON for ₺50 Va. money...50 A on NE side Great Pee Dee, adj. to
where sd. GORDON now lives, conveyed to EDWARD ELRBEE, by JOHN ELERBEE decd.
by will dated 22 Sept 1751...EDWARD ELERBEE(SEAL), Wit: JOHN ELERBEE, JOSEPH
KEMP (K).

Page 324: 24 Apr 1758, SAMUEL WILKINS of Anson Co., to WILLIAM PICKETT of same,
for ₺100 proc. money...300 A on S side great Pee Dee, wheron the
Court House for Anson Co. now stands, granted to WILLIAM PHILLIPS...SAMUEL
WILKINS (SEAL), Wit: THO. PRESTWOOD, WILL TERRY, CORNELUS ROBISON.

Pp. 325-326: 29 July 1758, ANTHONY HUTCHINS of Anson Co., to JAMES PICKETT
JUR. for ₺100...200 A, part of 500 A granted to JOSEPH WHITE 26 Sept 1746,
on S side great Pee Dee, adj. JOHN LEETHs corner..sold by WHITE to HENRY
FALCONBURY 2 Apr 1740, then to JAMES PICKETT 20 Oct 1755, then to sd. HUTCHINS
20 Jan 1757...and another tract of 100 A wheron Sd. JAMES PICKETT now lives,
conveyed by ISAAC NORMAN to JAMES PICKETT L5 July 1753, then to ANTHONY
HUTCHINS 20 Jan 1757, and also a tract granted 13 Oct 1749 to NICHOLAS SMITH
on S side Great Pee Dee, above mouth of LIttle River...conveyed to TOWNSEND
ROBINSON, then to JAMES PICKETT, then to ANTHONY HUTCHINS 20 Jan 1757...ANTHO.
HUTCHINS (SEAL), Wit: JNO. HAMER, VIOLET PRIMROSE, THOS. PRESTWOOD.

Page 327: Blank.

Pp. 328-329: 10 July 1758, EDMUND CARTLIDGE and WILLIAM BLEWET of Anson Co.,
Yeoman, to JOHN CRAFORD, Yeoman, of same, for ₺100 proc. money...
137 1/2 A granted to sd. CARTLIDGE & BLEWET 1 July 1750 on N side Cartlidges
Creek, adj. THOMAS JONES line, WILLIAM BLEWETS corner, 1/2 of sd. tract...
EDM. CARTLIDGE (SEAL), WILLIAM BLEWIT (SEAL), Wit: M. BROWN, JAMES DOWNING,
WILLIAM TERRY.

Pp. 330-331: 15 Oct 1757, BENJAMIN DUMAS of Anson Co., planter, to JEREMIAH
DUMAS, his son, of same, for s5...270 A on N side Pee Dee, adj.
JOHN CHICKS line...100 A taken up by JOHN GILES and the other by THOS. HARRING-
TON...BENJAMIN DUMAS (SEAL), Wit: JOHN LILLEY, JAMES LARGUOT, JOHN MACKEANE.

Pp. 332-333: 24 Apr 1758, SAMUEL WILKINS of Anson Co., planter, to WILLIAM TERRY
of same, for Ł20 Va. money...300 A on S side Great Pee Dee at
mouth of Savanah Creek, conveyed to sd. WILKINS by JOSEPH WHITE...SAMUEL
WILKINS (SEAL), Wit: RICHD. DOWNS, RICHD YARBROUGH, JOHN FREMAN.

Pp. 334-335: 25 Apr 1758, WILLIAM STONE of Anson Co., to RICHARD DOWNS of
same, planter, for Ł30 Prov.money...100 A, part of 200 A
granted to ROBT. MILLS 24 Mar 1747 & conveyed to WILLIAM STONE...WILLIAM
STONE (M) (SEAL), Wit: WILLIAM CRITTENDEN, PHILLIP SELTON, JOHN COCKERILL.

Pp. 336-337: 31 Dec 1757, EDMOND CARTLIDGE of Anson Co., to JOHN COLE, of
same, Cordwinder, for 25 pistoles...350 A on N side Pee Dee,
Cartlidges Creek, on upper side of S fork...part of 400 A granted to sd.
CARTLIDGE 29 Sept 1750....E. CARTLIDGE (SEAL), Wit: L. O BRYAN, FRANCIS
O BRYAN, JAMES DOWNING, M. BROWN.

Pp. 338-339: 20 July 1757, BENJAMIN JACKSON of Anson Co., to RICHARD STREET,
for Ł6 Prov. money... 137 A on S side Thompson Creek, adj. JOHN
KUSHINGS line...JAMES MATHEWS line...line of MATHIS...granted to Sd. JACKSON
29 Sept 1750...BENJ. JACKSON (SEAL), Wit: JAMES SUNDRY (X), JOHN JACKSON.

Page 340: 28 Oct 1757, JAMES GOLSBE of Anson Co., to JOSEPH HATAWAY of same,
for Ł20 sterling...100 A on NE side Buposes Creek, on a branch
of Little River, granted to WILLIAM STONE 26 May 1757...JAMES GOLSBE (X)
(SEAL), Wit: HEN. DOWNS, R. DOWNS, JOHN DOWNS.

Pp. 341-344: 2 & 3 Sep 1757, MARTIN FALLINGER & BARBARA his wife of Anson Co.,
planter, to JACOB HOIL of same, weaver (lease s5, release Ł5
proc. money)..185 A on S side Cataba, S side Leepers Creek, adj. PHILIP
FALLINGERS line near LAWRANCE SNAPPs survey, part of 370 A granted to MARTIN
FALLINGER 30 Aug 1753...MARTIN FALLINGER (SEAL), BARBARA FALLINGER (A)
(SEAL), Wit: ADAM FRITZ, JOHN THOMAS, BASTIAN BEST, signed in German.

Page 345; Blank.

Pp. 346-348: 2 & 3 Sept 1757, MARTIN FALLINGER & BARBARA his wife to PHILIP
FALLINGER, taylor, (lease s5, release   proc. money)...185 A
on S side Catabo on S fork Leepers Creek, adj. JACOB HOILs land, near LAWRANCE
SNAPPs survey, half of tract granted to sd. MARTIN FALLINGER 30 Aug 1753...
MARTIN FALLINGER (SEAL), BARBARA FALLINGER (A) (SEAL), Wit: ADAM FRITZ, JOHN
THOMAS, BASTIAN BEST, signed in German.

Page 349: Blank.

Pp. 350-352: 2 & 3 Sept 1757, MARTIN FALLINGER & BARBARA his wife to ADAM
SIGHTS, Taylor (lease s5, release Ł5 s15)...200 A on N side of
S fork of Catabo, adj. LAWRANCE SNAPPs line on a N branch of Leepers Creek,
patented to sd. FALLINGER 28 Mar 1755...MARTIN FALLINGER (SEAL), BARBARA
FALLINGER X() (SEAL), Wit: JACOB HOIL (H), JNO. THOMAS, BASTIAN BEST, signed
in German.

Page 353: Blank.

Pp. 354-356: 19 & 20 Nov 1756, ALLEXANDER OSBORN & AGNES his wife of Rowan
        Co., to the Rev. JOSEPH TATE of Lancaster Co., Pa. (lease s5,
release Ⱡ53 Va. money)...600 A below DEVISONs Loggs on both sides Sfork
Rockie River...ALEXANDER OSBORNE (SEAL), AGNES OSBORN (SEAL), Wit: HANCE
McWHORTER, WALTER CARRUTH.

Page 357: Blank.

Pp. 358-361: 19 & 20 Jan 1758, JOHN ANDERSON of Rowan Co., planter, to JOHN
        DUNN and WILLIAM CUMMING of Rowan Co., attornies (lease s5,
release Ⱡ50 proc. money)...300 A on NE side of S fork of Catawba, adj. sd.
ANDERSON old line, Clarks Creek, deeded from Estate of Granville 26 Nov
1757...JOHN ANDERSON (SEAL), Wit: JNO FERRELL, JNO WILLIAMS (Ⱡ).

Page 362: Blank.

Pp. 363-364: 23 July 1757, JOHN HAMER Of Anson Co., yeoman, to THOMAS
        DOWNER of same, carpenter, for Ⱡ5 proc. money...land granted to
sd. HAMER 25 May 1757, on S side of Island Creek in the line of a tract
surveyed for NEWBORG , 150 A...JNO HAMER (SEAL), Wit: WILL HARRISON, JOHN
FROHOCK.

Pp. 365-367: 1 & 2 Apr 1757, SAMUEL COBRON & MARGREAT his wife to JAMES KUY-
        KENDAL (lease s5, release Ⱡ36 proc. money)...319 A on Leepers
Creek, on the Indian path about two miles from JACOB KUYKENDALLs, granted to
COBRON 1 Mar 1753...SAMUEL COBRON (+) (SEAL), MARGREAT COBRON (M) (SEAL),
Wit CHRS. BETTY, JOHN KUYKENDALL, JNO. THOMAS

Pp. 368-371: 1 & 2 Apr 1757, SAMUEL COBORN & MARGREAT his wife to JAMES Kuy-
        KENDALL (lease s5, release Ⱡ10 proc. money)...132 A on Beaver
Dam Branch, S side Catabo, adj. SAMUEL COBORNs line...granted 23 Feb 1754 to
CHARLES BEATY, then conveyed to COBRON 25 Mar 1754...SAMUEL COBRON (X) (SEAL),
MARGREAT COBORN (M) (SEAL), Wit: CHRS. BEATTY, JOHN KUYKENDALL, JNO. THOMAS.

Pp. 372-374: 15 & 16 May 1758, JOHN MOORE of Anson Co., planter, to JARAMIAH
        POTTS, planter, (lease s5, release Ⱡ11 s4)...part of 600 A
conveyed to JOHN MOORE by EVAN LEWIS, 170 A on N side Indian Creek, a south
branch of the S fork of Catabo...adj. JOSEPH CLOUD, JARAMIAH POTTS...JOHN MOORE
(Ⱡ)(SEAL), Wit: SAMUEL BEASON, JOSEPH CLOUD, FRANCES BEATY.

Page 375: Blank.

Page 376: 13 Aug 1757, WILLIAM LITTLE of Anson Co., to JOHN PICKETT of King
        George Co., Va., for Ⱡ100 proc. money...400 A on S side great Pee
Dee, adj. lands of THOS. THOMPKINS, formerly HIZIKIAH RUSS...WM. LITTLE (SEAL),
Wit: JAS. PICKETT, MAR: KIMBROUGH.

Page 377: Blank.

Pp. 378-381: 9 & 10 Aug 1755, JAMES ARMOR & JANET his wife of Anson Co., to
JOHN MILLER of same, planter, (lease s5, release Ḽ60 Va. money·)
...315 A, adj. JOHN PRICE's corner...granted to JAMES ARMOUR by L. &. R. 16 &
17 July 1753...(Book B, N. 2, pp. 283-284)...JAMES ARMOR (SEAL), JANET ARMOR
(SEAL), Wit: JNO. DAVIES, SAML. WILSON, BENJAMIN HARDIN.

Page 382: Blank.

Pp. 383-384: 3 June 1758, PETER BRIEL of Oley Township, Berks Co., Pa.,
yeoman, to DERICK RAMSOEUR of Anson Co., yeoman, weaver, for
Ḽ8 Pa. money...land granted to BRIEL 3 Dec 1753, on S fork Catabo River...
adj. LAMBERT's line...PETER BRIER, signed in German, Wit: JACOB FARNNING,
JOHN RAMSOUER, MATHW. HENDERSON. Proved by JACOB FARNNING 29 Nov 1758.

Pp. 385-388: 10 & 11 Feb 1758, GEORGE RENICKS & MARY his wife of Anson Co.,
to ADAM MEEK of same, (lease s10, release Ḽ30)...300 A on
N side Catabo, about a mile and a half from the river, including the forks
of Renicks run...granted to RENICKS 31 Mar 1753...also 100 A adj. sd. tract
granted 30 Aug 1753...GEORGE RENICKS (SEAL), MARY RENICKS (SEAL), Wit: SAML.
WILLSON, JOHN PRICE, ALEXR. LEWIS.

Page 389: Blank.

Pp. 390-391: 18 Jan 1759, THOS. RENOLDS & MARY his wife of Anson Co., to
ALLEXANDER RENOLDS, son of sd. THOMAS REYNOLDS, for paternal
love and affection...on Bufelow creek that runs into Broad River, 250 A
granted 30 Aug 1753...THOMAS REYNODLS (X) (SEAL), MARY REYNOLDS (X) (SEAL),
Wit: RICHARD RYNOLBE (+), JNO. THOMAS.

Pp. 392-395: 14 & 15 Feb 1757, PETER OYSTER & MARY his wife of Anson Co., to
SAMUEL BICKERSTAF of same, (lease s5, release Ḽ8 NC money)...
land on N side of S fork of Catabo, 320 A granted to PETER OYSTER 23 Feb 1754
...PETER OSTER, signed in German, MARY OYSTER (O) (SEAL), Wit: PETER BAUM-
GARNERE JUR., JNO. THOMAS.

Page 396; Blank.

Pp. 397-399: 16 & 17 May 1758, GEORGE CATHEY of Anson Co., planter to MARTIN
PIFER of same, Inholder, (lease s5, release Ḽ50 NC money)...
300 A on S side Catabo, adj. SAMUEL CORBON and the Dutchmans Island, including
the place where ANDREW CATHEY formerly lived...GEORGE CATHEY (+) (SEAL), Wit:
JOHN CATHEY, JOHN DUNN.

Page 400: Blank.

Page 401: 30 Sept 1758, JOHN BRAVARD & JEAN his wife of Rowan Co., to JOHN
ANDERSON of Anson Co., for Ḽ15, 600 A on N side Catabo River, below
Gass Creek, near EDWARD CHUSICKS corner & on E side Indian path that leads from
CHARLES McDOWELs to the Catabo Nation, granted 31 Aug 1753...JOHN BRAVARD
(SEAL), JEANE BRAVARD (SEAL), Wit: ANDW. BAR RY, EPHRAIM BRAVARD.

Pp. 402-403: 20 Mar 1758, JAMES PICKET, of Anson Co., to JAMES ROBINSON, planter,
...in 1757 suit was rendered in Supream Court of Salisbury against
JAMES ARMOR at suit of THOMAS ARMOR of Kingdom of Ireland for Ḽ39 s19 d8 proc.
money...land on both sides of Camp Creek, waters of Catabo, 400 A...JAS
PICKET (SEAL), Wit: WILL CUMMING, ROBT. McCLENACHAN.

Page 404: 12 Nov 1757, JOSEPH HARDIN & JEAN his wife of Anson Co., to JOHN
SMITH, for ₤16 s10...150 A on N side Catabo River, including
Island below Tuckaley's foard, granted to JOSEPH HARDIN, 26 March 1755...
JOSEPH HARDIN (SEAL), JEAN HARDIN (‡) (SEAL), Wit: JNO THOMAS, JAS. MOORE,
BENJAMIN HARDIN.

Pps.405-406: Blank.

Pp. 407-409: 18 Jan 1757, JACOB FALKENBURY of Anson Co., to HENRY FALKENBURG
of same, (lease s5, release ₤100 proc. money)... 125 A on
S side great Pee Dee...JACOB FALKENBURG (‡) (SEAL), Wit: SAMUEL BERRY, THOMAS
BERRY, NICOLAS BROADY, WILLIAM HOWELL.

Pp. 410-411; Blank.

Pp. 412-413: 25 Apr 1758, ISAAC FALKEBURGH of Anson Co., planter to HENRY
FALKENBURGH, for ₤50 proc. money...on S side great Pee Dee,
Pleasant Hill, 200 A granted to JOHN FUTZJARRALL 30 Setp 1746, then to sd.
ISAAC 17 Apr 1754...ISAAC FALKINBOROUGH (ʂ) (SEAL), Wit: JAS. HUTCHINS,
SAMUEL BERRY, DAVN. HILDREATH.

Pp. 414-416: 26 & 27 Aug 1757, MARTIN SCHUCHMAN of Anson Co., to ABRAHAM
KUYKENDALL of same, for ₤10 proc. money..315 A on S side Catabo
opp. to Great Sholes, granted to SCHUCHMAN 23 Feb 1754...MARTIN SCHUCHMAN
(SEAL), Wit: FREDERICK HAMBRIGHT, ANDREW McNABB, BENJA. BROWN.

Pp. 417-418: 10 Aug 1758, JOHN HOOD of Anson Co., to BARTLEY WHITE of same,
for ₤6 ...100 A on Camp Creek, granted to HOOD 25 Feb 1754...
JOHN HOOD (‡) (SEAL), CATHERINE HOOD (ᴄ∩) (SEAL), Wit: ROBT. McCLENACHAN,
ROBT. WILSON.

Pp. 419-420: 26 Apr 1758, JAMES PICKETT of Anson Co., Esquire, to WILLIAM
WILLIAMS of same, Hatter, ...whereas RICHARD did recover against
GEORGE MOORE planter on 4th Tuesday in Oct 1757...good etc. of sd. MOORE be
sold...and case against MOORE by JOHN DUNN, Gentleman, one of the attornies...
for ₤5 s 18 proc. money...270 A on E side Catawba...JAMES PICKETT (Sheriff)
(SEAL), Wit: ANTHO. HUTCHINS, JOHN DUNN

Page 421: Blank.

Pp. 422-426: 7 Dec 1758, JOHN HAMER of Anson Co., planter, to THOMAS LIDE of
Cravin Co , S.C. (lease s5, release ₤60)...640 A sold by
ARTHUR DOBBS to EDMD CARTLEDGE 26 Nov 1757 on NE side Pee Dee on N side
Cartlidges Creek, sold by CARTHLEDGE to TELLOTIN KIBBLE 18 Oct 1758, then to
JOHN HAMER 26 Oct 1758...JNO. HAMER (SEAL), Wit: JOHN CRAWFORD JR., ALLEXR.
GORDON.

Page 427: Blank.

Page 428: 15 Jan 1759, ISAAC ODOM of Anson Co., to JOHN OVERSTREET, for ₤20
proc. money...100 A on shoeheel...ISAAC ODOM (SEAL), Wit: HENRY
OVERSTREET, ARCHD. McKISSAK.

Page 429: Blank.

Pp. 430-433: 10 & 11 Jan 1757, JOHN WITHROW & MARY his wife to ROBERT PRITCHET
(lease s5, release ₤10)...300 A on N side Broad River, mouth of
Bufelow Creek, granted to JOHN WITHROW 4 Sept 1753...JOHN WITHROW (6) (SEAL),
MARY WITHROW (R) (SEAL), Wit: SAML. YOUNG, LUKE DEAN.

Pp. 434-435: Blank.

Pp. 436-437: 13 Nov 1758, WILLIAM TERRY Of Anson Co., to MATHEW REFORD of
same, for ₤60 Proc. money... on N side Pee Dee, upper side of
Little River, opposite to island formerly called Checks Island, 150 A
granted to JOHN McCOY 11 Oct 1749...WM. TERRY (SEAL), MARY TERRY (SEAL),
Wit: RICHD. YARBROUGH, CHARLES COX (X).

Page 437: 24 Nov 1758, JOHN LYLY of Anson Co., to BENJAM. DUMAS of same, for
₤100 proc. money...land on N side Great Pee Dee, upper end of
Buffelow Island, 97 A...conveyed from EDMOND LILLY to JOHN LILLY 16 Oct
1753...JOHN LILLY (SEAL), Wit: JERH. DUMAS, DAVID SNEED, HILLER WILEDER (I).

Page 438: Blank.

Pp. 439-441: 13 Feb 1756, JAMES MEANS and RACHEL his wife of Anson Co.,
shoe maker, to JOHN LATTA, farmer, of same, (lease s5, release
₤40 Carolina money)...278 A, on both sides of a branch of Fair Forest Creek,
granted 18 Nov 1752 to JAMES MEANS...JAMES MEANS (SEAL), RACHEL MEANS (C)
(SEAL), Wit: HENRY FOSTER JOSEPH KELSO.
                [This land now in S.C.]

Pp. 442-445: 6 & 7 Sept 1756, ROBERT RENICK of Augusta Co., Va., to GEORGE
DENNIS of Anson Co., (lease s5, release ₤35 Va. money)...175 A
on N side Cataba, a mile or two above Leepers Creek...ROBERT RENICK (SEAL),
Wit: GEORGE RENICK, ANN RENICK (T).

Page 446: 28 Jun 1758, JAMES PICKET, high sherif of Anson Co., to THOMAS
PRESTWOOD, planter,...suit brought by POTTS, late of sd. county,
against JOSEPH SHITE, Esqr...sherif sells "at publick vendue" 100 A on S
side great Pee Dee, granted to JOHN GRIG, for s 21 proc. money...JAS.
PICKET (SEAL), Wit: GEORGE THUSTON, HUM: YARBROUGH.

Page 447: Blank.

Page 448: 20 Jan 1759, HENRY TIPPIN of Anson Co., to daughter SA RAH TIPPIN...
gift of entire estate...HENRY TIPPIN (H), Wit: JOHN WOOD, THOS. PRESTWOOD.

Pp. 449-451: 20 Apr 1759, EDWARD GIVINS & AGNAS his wife of Anson Co., to
JAMES HUGGINS of same, (lease s5, release ₤20 Va. money)...
160 A opposite mouth of Stoney Creek, S side Catawba, granted to THOMAS
ROBINSON 4 Apr 1750...sold to GIVINS 22 Oct 1752...EDWARD GIVINS (O) (SEAL),
AGNESS GIVINS (g) (SEAL), Wit: ROBT. McCLENACHAN, DAVID TEMPELTON.

                    So Ends Book C, N: 3
                    B Me ROBERT HARRIS JUNR
                        October the 10th 1759

VOLUME 7

Note: These are some early deeds at the beginning of Volume 7 which fall into the period concerning these abstracts. Page 17 of this volume begins with a deed in 1776 and pages following date from there.

Pp. 1-3: 1 & 2 Apr 1757, SAMUEL COBURN & wf MARGARET of Anson, to PATRICK McKINDRICK, (lease s5, release ₤12), 302 A on S side Catawba, including an Indian path below the mouth of Dutchman's Cr., granted to sd. COBURN 24 Sept 1754... SAMUEL COBURN (X) (SEAL), MARGARET COBURN (X) (SEAL), Wit: CHARLES BEATY, JOHN KUYKENDALL.

Pp. 4-6: 29 & 30 Aug 1757, BENJAMIN THOMASON & wf MARGARET of Anson, to ALEXANDER THOMASON (lease s2, release ₤20 sterling)...land on the Waxhaw and Runs Cr., N side Catawba, adj. BAIRDs line, THOS SIMSONS line, 200 A...BENJAMIN THOMASON (SEAL), MARGARET THOMASON (X) (SEAL), Wit: Thos. M'ELHENY, CHARLES BURNETT, SAMUEL BURNETT.

Page 7: Blank.

Page 8: 16 Aug 1754, WILLIAM HENRY & IZABELLA his wife of Anson, to ANDREW McNABB, for ₤10...300 A on S side Catawba where sd. HENRY now lives, granted to HENRY 28 Feb 1754...WILLIAM HENRY (SEAL), IZABELLA HENRY (SEAL), Wit: SAMUEL YOUNG, JAMES McCORD.

Pp. 9-11: 5 & 6 Feb 1760, JAMES ARMSTRONG of Anson Co., Maltster, to GEORGE RUT-LEDGE, of same, planter, (lease s5, release s14)...land on Dutchmans Cr., part of a tract granted to ROBERT LEEPER 31 Mar 1750, & sold by L. &. R. to sd. ARMSTRONG and afterwards found to intersect into sd. GEORGE RUTLEDGES land granted to him 20 May 1754...JAMES ARMSTRONG (SEAL), Wit: JOHN ARMSTRONG, FRANCIS BEATY.

Page 12: Blank.

Pp. 13-15: 10 Nov 1756, THOS GORDON & wf ELIZABETH of "County of Berkley & province of South Carolina" to JOHN GORDON, brother of sd. THOMAS, of same (lease s5, release ₤20 proc. money), land in Anson Co., patented 23 Feb 1754 on N side Enoree, adj. place where RUTH GORDON widow now lives...sd. THOMAS, son of MR. JOHN GORDON decd....THOMAS GORDON (SEAL), ELIZABETH GORDON (X) (SEAL), Wit: JACOB BROWN, BENJ. GORDON, ADAM McCOOLL.

Page 16: Blank.

58

Page 1: 1 Jan 1761, BENJAMIN SMITH of Anson Co., to WILLIAM CRITTENDEN, for Ł25
proc. money...100 A on SW side Great Pee Dee...YOUNGS land...ROBERT PARK's
...THOMAS GEORGE's land...WILLIAM YEARLY's corner...BENJAMIN SMITH (SEAL), Wit:
ROBERT LEE, WILLIAM YEARLY (W), ZACHARIAH PHILLIPS (3).

Pp. 2-5: 1 & 2 May 1760, JAMES McCLELLAND & wf JENNET of Anson Co., to JOHN BURNET
of Rowan Co. (lease s5, release Ł 10)...300 A on N side Catawba, adj.
JOHN BRAVARDs & ROBERT TENNENs...JAMES McCLELLAND (I) (SEAL), JENNET McCLELLAND
(C) (SEAL), Wit: JOHN BRANDON, JOHN PATTERSON, JOHN NISBET.

Page 6: Blank.

Pp. 7-8: 30 Dec 1760, JOHN COLE of Anson Co., yeoman, to STEPHEN COLE of same, hatter, for Ł20 proc. money...lower part of 400 A granted to EDMUND CARTLIDGE
29 Sept 1756, and conveyed to JOHN COLE 31 Dec 1757...100 A...JOHN COLE (SEAL),
Wit: Wm COLE, Wm COLEMAN (X).

Page 9: 2 March 1761, WILLIAM HOLTON to CHARLES SMITH, for Ł11, 100 A in Anson Co.,
on the NE side of Pee Dee River...N side of big creek...WILLIAM HOLTON (SEAL),
Wit: THOS HARRINGTON (+), SAML. PERSONS.

Pp. 10-11: 4 May 1761, WILLIAM PELLAM of Anson Co., planter, to JOHN HELMS of same,
for Ł32...200 A granted to sd. HOLTON, 1 July 1758, on the NE side of
Great Buffalo Creek of Little River...JOHN STONEs land...WILLIAM PELLAM (P) (SEAL),
Wit: CHAS. ROBINSON, GEO. HELMS.

Pp. 12-13: 15 June 1760, JOHN HORNBACK & wf EVE of Anson Co., planter, to DANIEL
MURPHY, for Ł20...100 A granted to HORNBACK, 21 Oct 1758...S side Pee
Dee, N side Jones Creek, adj. JOHN WALTERS land, DANIEL SHORTS land...JOHN HORN-
BACK (SEAL), EVE HORNBACK (SEAL), Wit: M. BROWN, WM. FIELDING, JAMES SHORT (X).

Page 14: 18 Mar 1761, JESSE BOUNDS of Anson Co., planter, to RICHARD YARBROUGH,
for Ł10 proc. money...75 A on W side Falling Creek, adj. RICH'D DEAR-
MAN's line, granted to JESSE BOUNDS 15 Dec 1760...JESSE BOUNDS (+) (SEAL), Wit:
JOHN CRAFFORD, JAMES BOUNDS, ANNE CRAFFORD.

Pp. 15-16: ___ May 1761, JOHN SMITH of Anson Co., planter, to WILLIAM SMITH, for
Ł25, 100 A on S side of Little River, THOMAS HOLMES upper corner...
Thicketty Creek...granted to JOHN SMITH 5 Dec 1760...JOHN SMITH (SEAL), Wit: WM.
QUEEN (X), MARGARET QUEEN (X), RICHARD DOWNS.

Page 17: Blank.

Pp. 18-19: 17 Apr 1761, JOHN LONG & wf MARY of Anson Co., Black Smith, to JOHN
COLE of same, yeoman, for Ł7s10...120 A on N side of S fork of Cart-
lidges Creek, at JOHN COLE's upper line, land he bought of EDMD CARTLIDGE...
THOS MASONS land...GEO. MARTINs land...granted 5 Dec 1760...JOHN LONG (SEAL),
MARY LONG (X) (SEAL), Wit: BENJ. MARTIN, JOHN CUNDALL.

Page 20: 7 Dec 1759, HENRY FALKENBOROUGH SENR of Anson Co., for natural love and
affection to beloved grandson JACOB FALKENBOROUGH, son of ISAAC FALKEN-
BOROUGH...half of the tract on S side Pee Dee on both sides of mouth of Little
Creek and one bay mare and a cow...HENRY FALKENBOROUGH (HH) (SEAL), Wit: BENJ.
MARTIN, SAM'L BERRY.

Pp. 21-22: 20 Sept 1760, JAMES McMANUS & wf MARY, planter of Anson Co., to GEORGE
MILLER of same, for ₤15 Va. money...land on both sides of Linches Creek
part of 206 A, 100 A, granted 1750...between MILLER and CARTLIDGEs land...JAMES
McMANUS (SEAL), MARY McMANUS (SEAL), Wit ISAAC WIEDNER, FREDERICK HENDRY.

Pp. 23-24: 20 Sept 1760, JAMES McMANUS & wf MARY to MICHAEL MILLER SENR, for ₤21 Va.
money...part of 206 A on Linches Creek, 140 A...granted 1750...JAMES
McMANUS (SEAL), MARY McMANUS (SEAL), Wit: ISAAC WEIDNER, FREDERICK HENDRY.

Pp. 25-26: 20 Sept 1760, JAMES McMANUS & wf MARY to SAMUEL GAY (GEY), for ₤17s6d18
Va. money...land on both sides of Hills Creek, part of 1011 A granted___
...100 A...JAMES McMANUS (SEAL), MARY McMANUS (SEAL), Wit: FREDERICK HENDRY, FARQ'D
CAMPBELL.

Pp. 27-30: 8 & 9 June 1758, JOHN KENNEDY & wf ELIZABETH of Anson Co., to THOMAS
CLARK of same, planter, (lease s5, release ₤19 proc. money)...land on
E side Catawba, on both sides Long Creek, adj. JOHN ANDERSON, FRANCIS BEATY, BRA-
VARD...including JOHN KENNEDYs improvement...patent #15, 26 Nov 1757...300 A...
JOHN KENNEDY (SEAL), ELIZABETH KENNEDY (SEAL), Wit: ANDREW BARRY, RICHARD BARRY.

Page 31: Blank.

Page 32: 10 Nov 1758, BENJAMIN & JOHN HARDEN to DAVID STANLEY, for ₤60 proc. money
...320 A on E side Catawba above YOUNGS and CHARLES BEATYs land, including
the place wheron STANLY lives...BENJAMIN HARDIN (SEAL), JOHN HARDIN (SEAL), Wit:
JAMES ERWIN, JOHN _____, JOSEPH HARDIN.

Page 33: 1 Jan 1760, JAMES ALLEY of Anson Co., to JOHN CARPENTER of same, for ₤30
proc. money...100 A on S side Cedar Creek...JAMES ALLEY (SEAL), Wit:
SAMUEL PERSONS, WILLIAM QUEEN (X), JOHN LEWIS (⌐).

Pp. 34-35: 3 Oct 1758, WILLIAM BLEWET & EDMUND CARTLEDGE of Anson Co., to JOHN
HUSBANDS, for ₤10...land on E side Great Pee Dee...WM. BLEWETS old tract
...patent to BLEWET 30 Sept 1748 & a patent to BLEWET & CARTLEDGE...WILLIAM BLEWET
(SEAL), E. CARTLEDGE (SEAL), Wit: JOHN LONG, GEORGE MARTIN.

Page 36: 15 July 1760, WILLIAM TAYLOR to son JACOB TAYLOR of Waxaw Settlement...
for good will & affection...land I now live on and cattle...WILLIAM
TAYLOR (X) Wit: ROBERT McCLENACHAN, SAMUEL THOMPSON, ELIZABETH McCLENACHAN.

Pp. 37-38: 20 Nov 1759, JAMES DOWNING of Anson Co., planter, to MORGAN BROWN,
Gent., for ₤15...300 A (except 100 sold to JOHN CRAWFORD) on N side
Pee Dee on Cartledges Creek...granted to ENOS THOMAS 1 July 1758...JAMES DOWNING
(SEAL), Wit: VIOLET PRIMROSE, JOHN PARSONS (+).

Page 39: 25 July 1760, BENJAMIN SMITH of Anson Co., to WILLIAM YERLY for ₤18 proc.
money...land on S side Great Pee Dee...AARON SMITHs corner, Youngs Island
...75 A...BENJAMIN SMITH (B) (SEAL), Wit: DAVID DUMAS, WILLIAM SNUGGS (X), RICHARD
SNUGGS (R).

Page 40: Blank.

Pp. 41-42: 10 Jan 1761, WILLIAM TERRY of Anson Co., Yeoman, to SAMUEL WILKINS, for
₤6 proc. money...50 A adj. JAMES DENSON, near the Terry Landing, granted
5 Dec 1760...WM. TERRY (SEAL), Wit: JER. TERRY, JOHN GRINNEN, LAURENCE FRANKLIN.

Pp. 42-46: 25 Oct 1759, JOHN HAMER, ESQR. Sheriff, of Anson Co. to JOHN BRANDON of
Rowan Co....on the 4th Tuesday in Feb. 1758 at a Supreme Court held at
Wilmington, JOHN BRANDON recovered against JAS. CARTER, late of Rowan Co....land
on S fork Catawba at the Beaver Dam branch, 703 A...JOHN HAMER (SEAL), Wit: ROBERT
HARRIS, BENTLY FRANKLIN.

age 47: Blank.

Pp. 48-49: 18 July 1761, DAVID TEMPLETON SENR of Anson Co., to ARCHIBALD TEMPLETON,
for ₺5 proc. money...300 A granted to sd. DAVID 18 Nov 1752, on N side
Catawba, Coddle creek, adj. his own and McCULLOCKs land...DAVID TEMPLETON (   )(SEAL),
ANNE TEMPLETON (X) (SEAL), Wit: JOHN DAVISON, JOSEPH TENNER, HENRY HENDRY, NATHANIEL
ALEXANDER.

Pp. 50-51: 27 July 1761, DAVID TEMPLETON SENR., to "my son SAMUEL TEMPLETON" of same,
for s5 sterling, 210 A, part of 600 A granted to sd. DAVID 3 Apr 1752
on Coddle Creek, the plantation I now live on...L. W. & T. of DAVID TEMPLETON SENR
dated 26 July 1761...DAVID TEMPLETON (SEAL), ANN TEMPLETON (X) (SEAL), Wit: JOSEPH
TANNER, HENRY HENDRY, NATHANIEL ALEXANDER, ROBERT McDOWEL.

Page 52: 27 July 1761, DAVID TEMPLETON SENR to JAMES TEMPLETON my son...for s5
sterling...250 A, part of 600 A granted 3 Apr 1752, adj. DAVID HUSTON...
DAVID TEMPLETON (SEAL), ANN TEMPLETON (X) (SEAL), Wit: JOSEPH TANNER, HENRY HENDRY,
ROBERT McDOWEL, NATH'L ALEXANDER.

Pp. 53-54: 27 July 1761, DAVID TEMPLETON SENR to DAVID TEMPLETON JR., for s5...
two tracts granted 30 Aug 1753, 125 A on N side Coddle Creek adj. his
own & DAVID HUSTON...the other 140 A, part of 600 A granted 3 Apr 1752...DAVID
TEMPLETON (SEAL), ANN TEMPLETON (X) (SEAL), Wit: JOSEPH TANNER, ROBERT McDOWEL,
HENRY HENDRY, NATH'L ALEXANDER.

Pp. 55-56: 10 Nov 1758, THOMAS COCKERHAM, planter, to PATRICK SAUNDERS, for ₺20
...tract granted to WILLIAM TERRY on the NE side P. D. on S fork
Mountain Creek, granted 27 Sept 1756, 300 A...adj. JOSEPH COCKERHAM,...THOMAS
COCKERHAM (X) (SEAL), Wit: CHARLES ROBINSON, CORNELIUS ROBINSON.

Pp. 57-58: 17 Apr 1759, JOHN DUNN ESQR. of Rowan Co., to JOHN DAVIDSON of Anson Co.,
black smith, for ₺50 proc. money...land granted to HENRY HENDRY 27 Sept
1751...sold at publick vendue by an execution recovered in the Court of Anson at
the suit of SAMUEL WILSON, SAMUEL McCLEARY, &c...300 A, adj. THOMAS McQUAWNS giving
line on both sides Coddle Creek...JOHN DUNN (SEAL), Wit: JAMES GOUNT, HENRY HENDRY.

Pp. 59-60: 24 May 1759[?]..."in the 32nd year of the reign of George II"...ARTHUR
DOBBS to MARTIN FIFER, planter, for ₺43 s10, 455 A near Buffalo Creek...
ARTHUR DOBBS (SEAL), Sit: THOMAS McGUIRE, WM. POWELL.
24 March 1762, Received of MARTIN FIFER ₺37s10 with ₺6 proc. money....
THOMAS McGUIRE on behalf of the Governor.

Page 61: Blank.

Pp. 62-63: 22 July 1761, JAMES McMANUS of Anson Co., planter, & wf MARY to MICHAEL
WHITENER of same, for ₺3 s12 d 5 Va. money, part of 1011 A granted 1748,
adj. JAMES ROBINSON's line, 120 A...JAMES McMANUS (SEAL), Wit: ISAAC WEIDNER, JACOB
WEIDNER.

Pp. 64-65: 9 Apr 1761, JAMES McMANUS of Anson Co., Gent., to ANTHONY THUNDERBURK,
for ₤12 Va. money...on fork Wildcat adj. CAPT. WADDLES, PETER CENESTRE,
100 A...JAMES McMANUS (SEAL), MARY McMANUS (SEAL), Wit: JACOB _____, ____ _____,
ISAAC WEIDNER.

Pp. 66-67: 20 Sept 1760, JAMES McMANUS & wf MARY to PETER BELLER, for ₤18 Va. money
...land on Hills Creek, part of a grant of 1011 A in 1750...100 A...
JAMES McMANUS (SEAL), MARY McMANUS (SEAL), Wit: ISAAC WEIDNER, FREDERICK HENRY,
signed in German.

Pp. 68-69: 22 July 1761, JAMES McMANUS & wf MARY to JAMES ROBINSON for ₤35 Va. money
...part of a 1011 A granted in 1748 on head of Hill Creek between MICHAEL
WEIDNER and RICHARD SPITE, 304 A...JAMES McMANUS (SEAL), MARY McMANUS (SEAL), Wit:
ISAAC WEIDNER, THOMAS PAGE.

Pp. 70-71: 1 July 1761, ALEXANDER GORDON of Anson Co., to JOHN COLE of same, for
₤ 5 proc. money... 1/2 A in Prince George Town in Anson Co., adj. "Mr.
STEPHEN his lot," part of a 650 A grant 14 Mar 1745, granted to JOHN ELLERBY decd...
ALEXANDER GORDEN (SEAL), Wit: WM. TEMPLE COLE, JOHN CULEASTER.

Page 72: Blank.

Pp. 73-74: 1 July 1761, ALEXANDER GORDEN to STEPHEN COLE of Bladen Co., Merchant,
for ₤5...a lot 1/2 A in Prince George Town, adj. JOHN COLE, part of
a grant to JOHN ELLERBEY 14 Mar 1745... ALEXANDER GORDEN (SEAL), Wit: JOHN CULEASTER,
WM. TEMPLE COLE.

Page 75: 27 Jan 1762, BENJAMIN HARDIN SR. Of Anson Co., to BENJAMIN HARDIN JR. of
same, for natural love & affection... BENJAMIN HARDIN (B) (SEAL), Wit:
RICHARD BERRY, ABRAHAM SCOTT, JOHN THOMAS.

Pp. 76-77: 27 Feb 1758, SAMUEL BEASON to JAMES McAFEE, for ₤13s13...land on N side
of S fork of Catawba, on S side Clarks Creek, adj. PRESTON GOFORTH's.
230 A granted 17 May 1754 to sd. BEASON...SAMUEL BEASON (SEAL), Wit: JOHN PATTON,
ALEXR. LEWIS.

Pp. 78-80: 16 & 17 July 1760, JOHN WILSON of Anson Co., to ROBERT ADAMS, of Rowan
Co., (lease s5, release ₤26s10)...350 A on S side Catawba below the place
where GEORGE CATHEY claims...Allison's Creek, adj. JOSEPH CLARK, JOSEPH DAVIS...
granted to GEORGE RENICKS...JOHN WILSON (SEAL), Wit: JOHN THOMSON, ALEX'R LEWIS.

Page 81: Blank.

Pp. 82-84: 16 & 17 July 1760 , JOHN WILSON to ROBERT ADAMS, (lease s5, release ₤26s10
...300 A on S side S fork Catawba, adj. JAMES CAMPBELL's land...JOHN
WILSON (SEAL), Wit: JOHN THOMSON, ALEX'R LEWIS.

Page 85: Blank.

Pp. 86-87: 10 Jan 1760, JACOB LIPHAM of Anson Co., Taylor to "WILLIAM BLACK, JUNR.
son to WILLIAM & HELEN Daughter to GEORGE METLAND merchant in Aberdeen,"
for ₤30 proc. money...240 A granted to sd. LIPHAM 6 Mar 1759...JACOB LIPHAM (SEAL),
Wit: JOHN CRAWFORD, CHARLES THOMPSON, ANDREW PRESLAR (A).

Page 88: 4 Mar 1760, BARTLEY WHITE & wf LYDIA of Anson Co., to GEORGE KENNDY &
WILLIAM FERRELL both of same, for ₤15 s15...100 A on Camp Creek...
BARTLEY WHITE (SEAL), LYDIA WHITE (X) (SEAL), Wit: ROBERT RAMSEY, THOMAS DAVIS,
ROBERT GALT (X).

Pp. 89-90: 10 Apr 1761, JOHN COLEMAN, of Anson Co., planter, to JOHN CARTWRIGHT, of
same, planter, for ₤12 Va. money...100 A on P. D. adj. JOHN FRANCES.
granted to THOMAS HOLMES 7 Apr 1749, conveyed to THOMAS COLEMAN, father of sd. JOHN
COLEMAN, as pr. deed 25 Dec 1749...JOHN COLEMAN (₤) (SEAL), Wit: THOMAS DOWNER, JOHN
DOWNER (X), JAS. PICKETT.

Page 91: 4 May 1761, JAMES GOLDSBY to JAMES SHEPHERD of "County Allifax," for
₤20...200 A granted to sd. GOLDSBY 21 Oct 1758...JAMES GOLDSBY (J)
(SEAL), Wit: JACOB SHEPHERD, JAS. PICKETT, JR. WM. PICKETT.

Page 92: Blank.

Pp. 93-94: 25 Feb 1761, JOHN STONE SENR. of Anson Co., planter, to JOHN STONE, JR.
of same, planter, for ₤30 part of a granted of 400 A to JAMES SEWERS 7
Apr 1749, conveyed by SEWERS to JOHN ASHLEY, JR., then to THOMAS WARD, then to JOHN
STONE SENR...on N side Pee Dee, on a branch of Little River known as Buffalo...
200 A...JOHN STONE (₤) (SEAL), Wit: THOMAS HARRINGTON (+), CHARLES ROBINSON.

Page 95: 2 Feb 1761, THOMAS SUGG of Anson Co., planter, & wf MARY to GEORGE SUGG of
same, for ₤10 proc. money...100 A granted to THOMAS SUGG, 1 July 1758...
THOMAS SUGG (SEAL), MARY SUGG (SEAL), Wit: JNO JETFREY, THOMAS FRANKLIN, JAMES
ATTAWAY.

Page 96: Blank.

Page 97: 2 Feb 1761, THOMAS WARD of Anson Co., planter, & wf MARY to JOHN JEFFERY
for ₤19 proc. money...100 A granted to THOMAS WARD 5 Dec 1760 on each
side of Little River...THOMAS WARD (₤) (SEAL), MARY WARD (ω) (SEAL), Wit: THOMAS
FRANKLIN, JAS. ATTAWAY, THOS. SUGG.

Pp. 98-99: 31 Jan 1761, JOHN CROUCH of Anson Co., to NATHANIEL DENNIS, planter, of
same, for s5...land on W side Thicketty Creek, 100 A granted to sd.
CROUCH 5 Dec in the 34th year of our reign[1760]...JOHN CROUCH (X) (SEAL), Wit:
JOHN SMITH, ARCHIBALD BLACK, F. C. DOWNER.

Page 100: 3 Feb 1760, ROBERT RATFORD of Anson Co., laborer, to THOMAS JONES of same,
laborer, for ₤15 proc. money...land on NE side Pee Dee on the W side of
Rocky fork of Hitchcock Creek 1200 A granted to ROBERT RADFORD 27 Sept 1756...
ROBERT RATFORD (SEAL), JONATHAN LEWELLING, RICHARD LEWELLING (R).

Pp. 101-102: 22 Sept 1760, GEORGE KENNEDY & PHANEY his wife of Anson Co., to HUGH
NELSON, for ₤40 SC money...land on S side Brod River on Brown Creek,
300 A granted 3 Oct 1755...GEORGE KENNEDY (SEAL), PHANNY KENNEDY (3) (SEAL), Wit:
ROBERT McCLENACHAN, ROBERT RAMSEY, WM. ALEXANDER.

Page 103: Blank.

Page 104: 2 Feb 1761, THOMAS SUGG of Anson, planter, & wf MARY to THOMAS FRANKLIN
for ₤10 proc. money...100 A granted 1 July 1758 on W side Little River...
THOMAS SUGG (SEAL), MARY SUGG (SEAL), Wit: JOHN STEPHEN, JAS. ATTAWAY, JOHN
SIMMONS.

Page 105: Blank.

Pp. 106-107: 23 Jan 1761, FRANCIS ASHLEY & wf RACHEL of Anson, planter, to JAMES
LONG, house carpenter, for ₤20...part of a grant to JOHN ASHLEY &
conveyed to FRANCIS ASHLEY on the W branch of little River, adj. JORDAN ASHLEY...
100 A....FRANCIS ASHLEY (F) (SEAL), RACHEL ASHLEY (X) (SEAL), Wit: ANN HOVER,
CHARLES ROBINSON.

Page 108: 30 Jan 1761, THOMAS SUGG & wf MARY to THOMAS RANDOLPH, for ₤11s10 proc.
money...100 A granted to SUGG 1 July 1758 on each side of Little River
...THOS SUGG (SEAL), MARY SUGG (SEAL), Wit: THOS SUGG, JOSEPH ATTAWAY, THOS
FRANKLIN.

Page 109: Blank.

Page 110: 15 Aug 1761, JOHN BUTLER of Anson, to SHADRACK JACOBS of Orange Co.,
N. C., for ₤20...land on E side Little River on the fork of Clarks
Creek...Townsends fork...200 A...JOHN BUTLER (SEAL), Wit: RICHARD YARBOROUGH,
JAMES ADAMS, MARSHALL DAGGE.

Pp. 111-112: 4 May 1761, HENRY TOUCHSTONE of Anson Co., Turner, to JAMES SANDERS
of same, planter, for ₤16 proc. money...land on E side Mountain
Creek, Boons Branch...150 A granted to sd. TOUCHSTONE 10 Apr 1761...HENRY TOUCH-
STONE (SEAL), Wit: M. BROWN, ELIZABETH BROWN.

Page 113: 4 Nov 1761, ROBERT LEEPER & CATHERINE his wife of Anson, to NICHOLAS
LEEPER, for ₤35 proc. money...on N side of fork of Catawba, opp. to
ANDREW CATHEY's survey, 400 A granted to ROBT. LEEPER 31 Aug 1753...ROBERT
LEEPER (SEAL), CATHERINE LEEPER (X) (SEAL), Wit: WM. HENRY, WM. PATRICK, JNO.
THOMAS.

Page 114: Blank.

Pp. 115-118: 10 Sep 1760, JOHN ANDERSON & wf MARGARET to HENRY VERNOR, all of
Anson, for ₤17s12...480 A on Long Creek between THOMAS CLARK and
JOWRY's line...JOHN ANDERSON (SEAL), MARGARET ANDERSON (Ø) (SEAL), Wit: JOHN
THOMAS, RICHARD BARRY, WILLIAM DRUE.

Pp. 119-122: 20 & 21 Aug 1759, JOHN LINN of Anson, to JAMES LINN (lease s5,
release ₤17)...250 A on N side Catawba on S side Waxhaw Creek...
between JOSEPH WHITE, WILLIAM McKEEs, & SAMUEL THOMPSONs land...JOHN LINN (SEAL),
Wit: ROBT. McCLENACHAN, JAS. McCORKALL, MATTHEW FLOYD.

Pp. 123-125: 7 Dec 1758, GEORGE CATHEY JR., planter, & wf FRANCES of Rowan Co.,
to JOHN BRAVARD, ESQR. & ROBERT LUCKY, Wheelwright, Exrs. of L. W.
& T. of WILLIAM McKEE, decd...for s5...478 A on S side S fork Catawba...GEORGE
CATHEY (SEAL), FANNEY CATHEY (F) (SEAL), Wit: JOHN FROHOCK, NATHANIEL ALEXANDER,
JONATHAN DOWNS.

Page 126: Blank.

Pp. 127-128: 8 Aug 1760, RICHARD DOWNS of Anson, to BENJ. ROBERTS of same, both
planters, for ₤100 proc. money...land on Little River granted to
ROBERT MILLS 24 Mar 1747, then conveyed to WILLIAM STONE, then to RICHARD DOWNS
25 Apr 1758, 100 A...R. DOWNS (SEAL), Wit: WM. BROWN, JENKINS WILLIAMS (ʒ).

Pp. 129-130: 9 Jan 1760, WILLIAM BLEWET of Anson, Taylor & wf SARAH to GEORGE
CARTER of same, for ₤10 proc. money...125 A granted to sd. BLEWET
6 Mar 1759 on Cartledges Cr....WILLIAM BLEWETT (SEAL), SARAH BLEWETT (X) (SEAL),
Wit: RICHARD ROTTENBERRY, JAMES HALTMAN ( ).

Page 131: Blank.

Pp. 132-133: 1 May 1761, NATHANIEL HILLEN of Anson, to NATHANIEL HILLEN, JR. of
same, for ₤70 proc. money...400 A on NE side of great Pee Dee, above
mouth of Little River, adj. NICHOLAS SMITH, JACOB COLLSON...NATHANIEL HILLEN (SEAL),
Wit: ZACHARIAH SMITH, FRANCIS COOPER.

Pp. 134-135: 14 Nov 1760, HENRY FALKENBURY of Anson, planter, to JACOB FALKENBURY,
son of ISAAC FALKENBURY, for ₤60...200 A on S side Great Pee Dee,
granted to JOHN FITZJARRAL 30 Sept 1748...100 A conveyed from FITZJARRAL to HUGH
WILSON __ June 1750...& conveyed by FITZJARRAL & WILSON to ISAAC FALKENBURY 17
Apr 1751...conveyed from ISAAC to HENRY FALKENBURY 25 Apr 1758...HENRY FALKENBURY
(H) (SEAL), Wit: BENJAMIN MARTIN, NICOLAS PADWAY, THOMAS BENERRY.

Pp. 136-137: 16 Sept 1760, DANIEL SHORT of Anson, planter, to DANIEL MURPHY, of
same, for ₤20...100 A, part of 200 A, granted to sd. SHORT 4 Oct
1751 on N side Jones Creek...DANIEL SHORT (SEAL), Wit: W. BROWN, WM FIELDING,
JAMES SHORT (ℱ).

Page 138: Blank.

Pp. 139-142: 2 & 30 March 1761, JACOB COBURN & wf MARY of Anson to BOSTIN BEST of
same (lease s5, release ₤13),,,land on N side of S fork of Catawba
...opp to Kerkendall Mount...210 A granted to sd. COBURN 20 May 1754...JACOB
COBURN (SEAL), MARY COBURN (SEAL), Wit: JAMES MOORE, JEAN THOMAS, JOHN THOMAS.

Page 143: Blank.

Pp. 144-147: 24 & 25 Nov 1760, JEREMIAH POTTS, planter, to MOSES MOORE, both of
Anson, (lease s5, release ₤15)...170 A on Indian Creek, a S branch
of S fork of Catawba...being the land sold by JOHN MOORE decd who was killed by
the Indians, corner of JOSEPH CLOUD, decd...JEREMIAH POTTS (I) (SEAL), Wit:
ROBERT SLOAN, JAMES BEATY (X), FRANCIS BEATY.

Pp. 148-149: 10 July 1758, GEORGE CATHEY, SR & wf JEAN of Rowan Co., to JOHN TOOL
of Anson, grandson of sd. GEORGE & JEAN CATHEY, for natural love &
affection...land on S side of N br. Catawba, adj. SAM'L COR---, & LEEPER, being
the plantation that MATTHEW TOOL now lives on, 400 A, granted to GEORGE CATHEY 7
Oct 1749...GEORGE CATHEY (SEAL), JEAN CATHEY (I) (SEAL), Wit: ANDREW CATHEY, THOMAS
BRALY, ARCHIBALD CATHEY.

Page 150: 21 Apr 1761, THOMAS GILLESPIE of Rowan, planter, to JOHN REED of Anson,
planter, for ₤35...land on S side Catawba below the mouth of Davidson
Creek, 275 A...THOMAS GILLESPIE (SEAL), Wit: ROBERT HOLMES, JOHN HOLMES.

Page 151: Blank.

Pp. 152-153: 20 July 1759, ANDREW PRESLAR, SR of Anson, Blacksmith, to ANDREW PRES-
LAR, JR. for ₤10 proc....land on S side Rocky River, 100 A...granted
to PRESLAR 1751...ANDREW PRESLAR (SEAL), Wit: THOMAS BERRY, JOHN CULPEPPER, L.
CULCASTER.

Pp. 154-155: 3 Oct 1761,.JOEL PHILLIPS of Anson, planter, to NICHOLAS SMITH of
Cumberland Co., for ₤10 proc. money...land in Anson on SW side Pee
Dee, adj. WILLIAM POWELL's upper line, Gould's fork...200 A granted to sd. PHILLIPS
5 Dec 1760...JOEL PHILLIPS (𝒹) (SEAL), Wit: WILL REED, CHARLES ROBINSON.

Pp. 156-157: 28 June 1760, JOHN PARNALL of Anson, to WILLIAM PELLAM of same, planter,
for ₤20, proc. money...land on N side Pee Dee, E side Little River,
25 A adj. land granted to JOHN APLEY, part of 100 A granted to GEORGE HOLMES 11 Oct
1749...JOHN PARNALL (𝒶) (SEAL), Wit: SHADRACK DENSON, THOMAS HARRINGTON (T).

Page 158: Blank.

Pp. 159-160: 3 Oct 1761, THOMAS HARRINGTON of Anson, planter to JOHN ASHLEY of
same, for ₤10 proc. money...land on N side Pee Dee, on Cheeks Creek,
100 A granted to SAMUEL MACBEE __ March 1756, and conveyed to THOMAS HARRINGTON...
THOMAS HARRINGTON (T) (SEAL), Wit: CHARLES ROBINSON, THO. _____.

Pp. 161-162: 24 Dec 1760, JOHN HUSBANDS of Anson, to NICHOLAS BROADWAY of same,
planter, for ₤20 proc. money...land on SW side Pee Dee, adj. CALEB
HOWELL's upper corner called Mount Pleasant, JOHN GEORGE's lower corner on the
river bank near Grassy Island waggon ford, granted to HUSBANDS 5 Dec 1760, 200 A
...JOHN HUSBANDS (SEAL), Wit: M. BROWN, ELIZABETH BROWN.

Page 163: 14 Apr 1760, JOHN DAVIS of Anson, planter, to JOHN VANHOSE, Blacksmith,
of same, for ₤10 proc. money...land on SW side Great Pee Dee River, adj.
JOSHUA WEAVERS, JOHN HALLS, land he sold to VANHOSER...150 A granted 25 May 1757...
JOHN DAVIS(Ɨ D) (SEAL), Wit: EDMUND LILLY, THOMAS DAVIS,----- JACOB ------.

Pp. 164-165: 21 Dec 1761, JOHN McDANIEL of Anson, to PETER PRESLAR, for ₤20 proc.
money...land granted to THOMAS HOLESIS 7 Apr 1749...adj. JOHN FRANCIS
corner...conveyed to THOMAS COLEMAN 26 Dec 1749, after his death to his son
JOHN COLEMAN, 100 A...JOHN McDANIEL (SEAL), Wit: SAM'L PAGETT, WILLIAM PAGETT.

Page 166: 20 July 1761, JOHN LANTS & wf CATHERINE of Anson, to JACOB CULP, of same,
for ₤14 proc. money...land on Mill Cr., conveyed by ROBERT McCLENACHAN
ESQR. to THOMAS LANTS and also by him to sd. JOHN LANTS 15 Jan 1760...JOHN LANTS
((∴) (SEAL), CATHERINE LANTS (SEAL), Wit: WM. TEMPLE COLE, ROBERT McCLENACHAN,
JOHN SMITH. Recd from JACOB CULP ₤ 14 20 July 1761. JOHN LANTS (∴).
WM TEMPLE COLE.

Pp. 167-168: 20 Oct 1761, JOHN STONE, JR. planter, of Anson, to WILLIAM PELLAM, JR.,
planter, for ₤35...200 A on N side Pee Dee, on a branch of Little
River, called Buffalo Run, part of 400 A granted to JAMES JEWERS 1749, conveyed to
JOHN ASHLEY, JR. then to THOMAS WARD, then to JOHN STONE, JR....JOHN STONE (Ɨ)
(SEAL), Wit: GELER RERNALS, CHARLES ROBINSON.

Page 169: Blank.

Page 170: 24 Nov 1761, JOSEPH NOBBS, late of Anson, to WILLIAM COX, of Anson, for
£20 proc. money...part of a tract granted to sd. NOBBS & PETET GUSTAVES
31 March 1750, 250 A...150 A on Jones Cr...JOSEPH NOBBS (𝑋), (SEAL), Wit: THOMAS
KEMP, ISAAC BRUNSON.

Page 171: Blank.

Page 172: 8 Dec 1760, PHILIP MILLER, SR. Cooper, of Craven Co., N.C., to JOHN
SIPPERT of Anson, for £24 proc. money...land granted to sd. MILLER,
585 A, adj. JOHN BARNOT SHIOREWOLFS line...PHILIP MILLER (SEAL), Wit: FREDERICK
HARGET, JR.

Page 173: Blank.

Pp. 174-175: 26 Jan 1762, SHADRACK JACOBS of Anson, to ZACHARIAH SMITH, Black Smith,
of same, for £40 proc. money...land on E side Little River, on N side
Townsends fork of Cheek Creek...200 A granted to JOHN BUTLER 5 Dec 1760, conveyed to
JOHN LOW, then to RICHARD YARBROUGH, then to sd. JACOBS...SHADRACK JACOBS (SEAL),
Wit: SHADRACH DENSON, JR., JOSEPH JONES.

Page 176: 4 Jan 1762, WILLIAM CRITTENDEN of Anson, Carpenter, to BENJAMIN SMITH,
of same, planter, for £25 proc. money...100 A on W side Pee Dee in Youngs
Island, adj. ROBERT PARKS, THOMAS GEORGE...WILLIAM CRITTENDEN (SEAL), Wit: MARGRET
IRLEY (X), PETER PRESLAR (P), SHADRACH HOGAN.

Page 177: Blank.

Page 178: 19 Dec 1761, WILLIAM WILKINS of Anson, to WILLIAM THOMPSON of same, for
£20 proc. money...land on NW side Pee Dee on S side of a Branch of Goulds
fork of Linches Creek....WILLIAM WILKINS (SEAL), Wit: JOHN THOMPSON, JOHN WILKINS (𝑋).

Pp. 179-180: 16 Jan 1762, ROWLAND WILLIAMS of Anson, planter to JAMES HUTCHINSON, JR.
planter, of same, for £30 proc. money...land on N side Great Pee Dee,
100 A, part of a grant to JAMES BENTLEY 26 Nov 1746, conveyed to THOMAS HARRINGTON
26 Apr 1748, then to SAM'L HOUGH 16 July 1751, then to sd. WILLIAMS 20 May 1752...
ROWLAND WILLIAMS (R) (SEAL), Wit: HENRY STOKES, JOHN GIBSON, SAM'L RATLIFF.

Pp. 181-184:27 & 28 Jan 1760, MARTIN PHIFER & wf MARGARET, of Anson, Inn holder, to
JOHN HILL of same, planter, (lease s5, release £33s15)...land on S side
Catawba adj. SAMUEL COBURN & "the Dutchmans land" including the place where ANDREW
CATHEY formerly lived...granted to sd. PHIFER by L & R 26 & 27 May 1758...MARTIN
PHIFER (SEAL), MARGARET PHIFER (X) (SEAL), Wit: WM MOORE, JAMES DOCHERTY (𝑋).

Page 185: Blank.

Pp. 186-188: 3 & 4 Feb 1762, BENJAMIN ROBINSON of Rowan, weaver, to FRANCIS YOST,
of Anson, (lease s5, release £50)....land on Cat tail branch of
Buffalo Creek, near ANDREW PRESLARs line...granted to ROBINSON 20 May 1754...252 A
...BENJAMIN ROBINSON (SEAL), Wit: GEORGE HENC. BRINER [?] , HEINRICH _____,
[both German signatures].

Page 189: Blank.

Pp. 190-191: 8 Aug 1.761, JONATHAN LEWELLING of Anson, joiner, to THOMAS GIBSON,
        Laborer, for ₺11 proc. money...land on NE side Pee Dee, 100 A, part
of 200 A granted 5 Dec 1760 to sd. LEWELLING...JONATHAN LEWELLING (SEAL), Wit:
MARK COLE, JOHN BOUND.

Pp. 192-193: 5 Sept 1761, WILLIAM & ZACHARY PHILLIPS of Anson, to JOSEPH OATS of
        same, for ₺55...land on S side Pee Dee below mouth of Browns Creek,
adj. THOMAS GEORGE...260 A...tract run out for WILLIAM SMITH, conveyed to BENJAMIN
SMITH, then to sd. PHILLIPS 18 Jan 1754...WM PHILLIPS (SEAL), Z. PHILLIPS (SEAL),
Wit: JOEL PHILLIPS (X), ELIZABETH PHILLIPS (X).

Pp. 194-195: 5 Sep 1761, ZACHARY PHILLIPS to JOSEPH OATS, for ₺5...25 A on S side
        Pee Dee below mouth of Browns Creek, adj. land run for WM. SMITH,
conveyed from PETER PRESLAR to sd. PHILLIPS 25 Apr 1759...Z. PHILLIPS (SEAL), Wit:
WM PHILIPS, WILLIAM CRITTENDEN, JOEL PHILLIPS (X).

Page 196: 10 July 1761, JOHN BOLAND of Anson, to FRANCIS EATHERNTON of same, for
        ₺20 proc. money...land near mouth of Drowning Branch, granted to BOLAND
5 Dec 1761...JOHN BOLAND (B) (SEAL), Wit: JOHN KEARBY, COGER SNEAD (†††), WM BOLLIN.

Page 197: 28 May 1761, JOHN OVERSTREET of Anson, to MERIDAY ELLZEY, for ₺30 proc.
        money...100 A on Shoe Heel...JOHN OVERSTREET (₮) (SEAL), Wit: JOHN DUNBAR
(B), JAMES DULANY.

Page 198: Blank.

Pp. 199-200: 29 May 1761, WILLIAM BLEWETT, Taylor & wf SARAH of Anson, to THOMAS
        BLASSENGEN, for ₺__ , 102 A on S side Cartledges Creek, granted to
BLEWETT 6 Mar 1759...WILLIAM BLEWETT (SEAL), SARAH BLEWETT (X) (SEAL), Wit: XTOPHER
HUNT, JOHN LONG.

Pp. 201-202: 30 Oct 1761, GEORGE DOUGLASS & wf MARY of Anson to HENRY FOSTER of
        same, for ₺50...150 A granted to DOUGLAS 24 Sept 1754 on N side
Catawba on Cain Creek, tract sd. DOUGLASS now lives on, above WM MOORES land...
GEORGE DOUGLAS (SEAL), MARY DOUGLAS (SEAL), Wit: ROBT McCLENACHAN, JAMES BURNS,
JAS. JOHN.

Page 203: 5 Aug 1761, JONATHAN HELMS of Anson, planter, to AILEE YARBROUGH of same, for
        ₺5...land on W side Little River of Pee Dee, 50 A granted to HELMS 4 Apr
1750...JONATHAN HELMS (H) (SEAL), Wit: JOHN WILKINS(₮), WILL REED.

Page 204: Blank.

Page 205: 5 June 1761, RICHARD YARBROUGH of Anson, planter, to SHADRACK JACOBS of
        same, for ₺20...100 A adj. CHARLES ROBINSON...RICH'D YARBROUGH (SEAL),
EALEE YARBROUGH (X) (SEAL), Wit: JOHN CRAWFORD, WM WELCHEAR (X).

Pp. 206-207: 11 Feb 1761, BENJAMIN ROBERTS of Anson, planter to WILLIAM QUEEN of
        same, planter, for ₺30 proc. money...part of 200 A granted to ROBT.
MILLS 24 Mar 1747, conveyed to WM STONE, then to RICHD. DOWNS, then to BENJAMIN
ROBERTS...on bank of Little River, adj. STONE & WILLIAM CRITTENDEN, 100 A...
BENJAMIN ROBERTS (SEAL), Wit: SAM'L RATLIFF, WM. JONES (X).

Pp. 208-209: 20 Sep 1761, EDWARD SMITH OF Anson, planter, to HENLEY SNEAD, for ₺25
proc. money...land on NE side Pee Dee on S side Hitchcocks Creek, near
JOSEPH HALLs, 200 A, granted to sd. SMITH 5 Dec 1760...EDWARD SMITH (X) (SEAL), Wit:
WILLIAM WATKINS, ISREAL SNEAD (X).

Pp. 210-211: 4 Aug 1761, JOHN SMITH of Anson, planter, to JASPER SMITH of same,
planter, for ₺35 Va. money...land on E side of Little River of Pee
Dee, 200 A...JOHN SMITH (SEAL), Wit: SAM'L PARSONS, R. DOWNS.

Page 212: __ Aug 176_, CHARLES BERRY to THOMAS TALLANT, for ₺20 proc. money...land
on both sides Smiths Creek, adj. THOMAS BERRYs...175 A conveyed to THOMAS
BERRY 18 July 1852, & to CHARLES BERRY his son __ Oct 1755...granted to FRANCIS
McELWANE 13 Apr 1749...CHARLES BERRY (X) (SEAL), ELIZABETH BERRY (X) (SEAL), Wit:
BENJAMIN MARTIN, JAMES DENSON.

Page 213: Blank.

Page 214: 8 Aug 1761, JONATHAN LEWELLING of Anson, joiner, to THOMAS SMITH JR.
of same, laborer, for ₺11 proc. money...land on N side Hitchcock Creek...
JONATHAN LEWELLING (SEAL), Wit: MARK COLE, JOHN BOUNDS.

"Note the blanks in this & the preceding deed are occasioned by
the originals deeds being torn & C. Test Wm Hammon p Reg 20th Septr
1809"

Pp. 215-216: 25 Feb 1761, GEORGE KENEDY & WM FERREL & PHANY and ELIZABETH their
wives of Anson, to JOHN GREER Of same, for ₺20...110 A on both sides
Camp Creek...GEORGE KENEDY (SEAL), PHANY KENEDY (X) (SEAL), WM FERREL (SEAL),
ELIZABETH FERRAL (X) (SEAL), Wit: ROBERT McCLENACHAN, DAVID KERR.

Pp. 217-218: 2 Nov 1761, JACOB PAUL of Anson, brick layer to HUGH McBRIDE of same,
for ₺ __ land on SW side Pee Dee, on Jones Creek, 200 A granted to
sd. PAUL __ March 1761...JACOB PAUL (SEAL), Wit: JOHN DUNN, WM REED.

Pp. 218-220: 6 Aug 1761, SHADRACK JACOBS of Anson, planter, to ELIEE YARBROUGH of
same, for ₺20 proc. money...100 A on W side Little River of Pee
Dee...granted to GEO. CLEMONS 4 Apr 1750...SHACRACK JACOBS (SEAL), PATTY BRIAN
JACOBS (X) (SEAL), Wit: HENRY TOUCHSTONE, ZACHARIAH SMITH.

Pp. 220-221: 14 Dec 1761, NICHOLAS WHITE of Anson, planter, to JAMES SHORT, planter,
for ₺10 proc. money...100 A on S side Jones Creek...granted to sd.
WHITE 5 Dec 1760...NICHOLAS WHITE (X) (SEAL), Wit: JAS. PICKETT, JOHN PICKETT.

Pp. 221-222: 26 Sep 1761, JOHN CARTWRIGHT of Anson, planter, to JOHN McDANIEL of same,
for ₺12 Va. money...land on N side Pee Dee. adj. JOHN FRANCIS corner,
100 A...JOHN CARTWRIGHT (X) (SEAL), Wit: WM. TERRY, MARY TERRY.

Page 223: 10 Oct 1761, EDMUND NICHOLAS of Anson, to JOHN HALTON of same, for ₺7 ster-
ling...land on NE side Pee Dee on Denson fork, concluding the place called
Halton's cabbin, granted to sd. NICHOLAS 4 Oct 1758...EDMUND NICHOLAS (X) (SEAL),
Wit: JOSEPH ATTAWAY, JAMES GOLDSBE (J), WM QUEEN (X).

Pp. 224-225: 26 July 1759, PATRICK SAUNDERS of Anson, to LITTLE BIRD SHEPHERD, for ₺50
sterling...land granted to WM TERRY 27 Sep 1756, 300 A, sold by TERRY to
THOMAS COCKRAM, then to SAUNDERS, and now 100 A to SHEPHERD...(later JOHN LITTLEBIRD
SHEPHERD)...PATRICK SAUNDERS (X) (SEAL), Wit: M. BROWN, PAUL BARRINGER, GEORGE PENNING-
TON.

Pp. 226-227: 24 June 1760, GEORGE HELMS of Anson, planter, to ROWLAND WILLIAMS, JR. of same, planter, for ₺15 proc. money...100 A on N side Pee Dee...granted to sd. HELMS 21 Oct 1758...GEORGE HELMS (SEAL), Wit: JAMES WHITE, JOHN CROUCH.

Page 228: NORTH CAROLINA (SEAL), By virtue of His Magisties Commission as Receiver General, I appoint FRANCIS BEATIE, Esquire, as my deputy for Anson County... 22 Apr 1762. JOHN RUTHERFORD.

Pp. 229-231: 9 & 10 Aug 1758, THOS REYNOLDS & wf MARY of Anson to MAJOR ANDREW LEWIS of Augusta Co., Va. (lease s5, release ₺10)...land on Buffalow Creek, granted to sd. REYNOLDS 30 Aug ____ about 4 miles above the fork, 400 A...THOMAS REYNOLDS (X) (SEAL), MARY REYNODLS (X) (SEAL), Wit: GEORGE CATHEY, GEORGE RENICK.

Pp. 232-234: 15 Sept 1758, SAMUEL COBRON, planter, & wf MARGARET of Anson, to JOHN RICHMAN of same, planter, (lease s5, release ₺12)...200 A on S side Catawba joining where COBRUN now lives, granted to COBRUN 30 Aug 1753...SAMUEL COBRON (X) (SEAL), MARGARET COBRUN (M) (SEAL), Wit: ANDREW BARRY, RICHD BARRY, JENNETT BARRY.

Page 235: Blank.

Page 236: 20 July 1757, GEO. BROWN of Anson, planter, to JOHN WATKINS of same, for ₺12, part of 950 A on S side Catawba granted to LEONARD KILLIAN 30 Sept 1749, & conveyed by LEONARD & wf MARGARET 1 Jan 1754 to sd. BROWN...GEORGE BROWN (SEAL), EVE BROWN (E) (SEAL), Wit: JACOB ____, ANDREW CATHEY (C), JOHN THOMAS.

Pp. 237-240: 23 & 24 Oct 1761, WILLIAM MORRISON of Anson, planter, to HUGH McKNIGHT of Rowan, planter, (lease s5, release ₺2 s10 NC money)...640 A adj. E side Catawba, below mouth of Morrisons Creek...including Morrisons improvement... granted to MORRISON 13 Oct 1756...WILLIAM MORRISON (SEAL), Wit: WM. McKNIGHT, JAS. McKNIGHT, FRANCIS BEATY.

Pp. 241-243: 8 & 9 March 1762, JACOB SIMMERMAN of Anson, planter, to PETER SIMMERMAN, of same, planter, (lease s5, release ₺17 NC money)...230 A between Beaver Dam Creek and Indian Creek, on S side S fork Catawba R...part of 275 A granted by SAMUEL YOUNG to JACOB SIMMERMAN, by L & R, 9 & 10 Aug 1755...JACOB SIMMERMAN (SEAL), Wit: SAMUEL BIGGERSTAFF, FRANCIS BEATY.

Page 244: Blank.

Page 245: 5 Feb 1761, JOHN McGEE of Orange Co., NC, planter, & wf MARTHA, to THOMAS THOMSON, of Anson, planter, for ₺17 proc. money...land on N side Catawba, McGees branch, granted to McGEE in 1750...JOHN McGEE (SEAL), MARTHA McGEE (SEAL), Wit: ROBERT LICKIE, MARGARET JOHNSON (++).

Pp. 246-249: 29 & 30 Mar 1756, EDWARD GIVENS & wf AGNES of Anson, to MATHEW McCORCLE of same, shoe maker...(lease s5, release ₺100 Va. money)... land on N side Catawba, S side Beaver Dam Creek, 400 A in part of 2 surveys, S side Davidsons Creek... granted to sd. GIVENS 8 Oct 1751 & 3 Apr 1752...EDWARD GIVENS (SEAL), AGNES GIVENS (O) (SEAL), Wit: ANDREW BARRY, _____, _____ .

Pp. 250-252: 26 & 27 Oct 1761, JAMES HUGGINS & wf ISABELLA of Rowan, planter, to ANDREW HASLEP of Anson, planter, (lease s5, release ₺30 NC money)... 160 A on S side Catawba, granted to THOMAS ROBINSON 4 Apr 1750, then conveyed to EDWARD GIVENS 22 Oct 1752, then to sd. HUGGINS by L & R, 19 & 20 Apr 1759...JAMES

HUGGINS (SEAL), ISABELLA HUGGINS (I) (SEAL), Wit: JAMES TEMPLETON, SAMUEL CLEGG (∂).

Page 253: Blank.

Pp. 254-257: 16 & 17 Nov 1761, JOHN BEATY SENR of Anson, planter, to JOHN BEATY, JUNR, of same, planter, (lease s5, release Ⴆ10)...270 A on W side Catawba, part of 2 pattents whereon sd. BEATY SENR now lives...adj. THOMAS BEATYs line...JOHN BEATY (SEAL), Wit: THOMAS BEATY, FRANCIS BEATY.

Pp. 258-259: 24 June 1762, ARTHUR DOBBS, Gov. on NC, to MOSES SHELBY of Anson Co., for Ⴆ19 s13...180 A on branches of Clear Creek...ARTHUR DOBBS (SEAL), Wit: MARTIN PHIFER, WM POWELL.

Page 260: Blank.

Pp. 261-264: 1 & 2 Feb 1757, HANCE ADAM SNIDER & wf SARAH, of Anson, to JOHN WALKER of same, (lease s10, release Ⴆ10)...land adj. HANCE ADAM SNIDERs old plantation on Leepers Creek, on W side Catawba, at or near BOSTON BESTS line...200 A granted to SNIDER 13 Oct 1756...ADAM SNIDER (SEAL), signed in German; SARAH SNIDER (X) (SEAL), Wit: GEORGE BROWN, MARTIN _____, JOHN THOMAS J. P.

Pp. 265-266: 24 June 1762, ARTHUR DOBBS to JAMES HARRIS, of Anson, for Ⴆ30 s12 d8... 293 A near Clear Cr., adj. ADAM ALEXANDERs line, SAMUEL HARRIS' line... ARTHUR DOBBS (SEAL), Wit: MARTIN PHIFER, WM POWELL.

Page 267: Blank.

Page 268: 25 Sept 1758, FREDERICK HAMBRIGHT & wf SARAH, to WILLIAM ADEAR, all of Anson, for Ⴆ30 proc. money...300 A on S side Catawba, adj. JUDITH COBRUNS survey... including Tuckaseagee path, grant to HAMBRIGHT 30 Aug 1753...FREDERICK HAMBRIGHT (SEAL), SARAH HAMBRIGHT (SEAL), Wit: JAMES MOORE, JOHN DICKSON, JOHN THOMAS.

Page 269: Blank.

Pp. 270-271: 17 Aug 1762, ARTHUR DOBBS to ARTHUR MACKAY of New Hanover Co., N. C., for Ⴆ5 proc. money...255 A adj. JOHN PENNY's corner...ARTHUR DOBBS (SEAL), Wit: GEORGE ORMSBY, WM POWELL.

Oage 272: Blank.

Pp. 273-274: 18 May 1762, ARTHUR DOBBS to ELEANOR McDOWELL of New Hanover Co., Widow., for Ⴆ10 proc. money...640 A adj. MICHAEL PATTON's line on Buffaloe Creek, a branch of Rockey or Johnston River, adj. MOSES WHITEs line...ARTHUR DOBBS (SEAL), Wit: MARTIN PHIFER, WM POWELL.

Page 275: 22 Mar 1758, PETER OYSTER & wf MARY of Anson, to MICHAEL OYSTER of same, for Ⴆ10...land about a miles from ROBERT LEEPERs line, adj. to a 50 A tract sold by sd. OYSTERs to PETER CLUB, 260 A granted to PETER OYSTER 24 Sep 1754...PETER OYSTER (SEAL), MARY OYSTER (X) (SEAL), Wit: ABRAHAM SCOTT, PETER CLUBB (PC), JOHN THOMAS.

Page 276: Blank.

Page 277: ARTHUR DOBBS appoints WILLIAM POWELL of New Hanover Co., Gentleman, as attorney to collect in Anson Co....and to sell land in Anson Co....12 Oct 1762.... ARTHUR DOBBS (SEAL), Wit: JOHN ANCRUM, ARTHUR MACKAY.

Pp. 278-80: [no date], JOHN HARVEY & wf MARY to WILLIAM CLEGHORN, for Ł30 (lease & release)...land on N side Catawba, S side Cain Creek...JOHN HARVEY (SEAL), MARY HARVEY (X), Wit: JOHN ARNOLPENDER (Ŧ), WM BAIRD, ANDREW PICKENS.

Pp. 281-282: Blank.

Pp. 283-284: 24 June 1762, ARTHUR DOBBS to ADAM ALEXANDER of Anson, planter, for Ł28 s16 d10 proc. money...276 A on Clear Creek...ARTHUR DOBBS (SEAL), Wit: MARTIN PHIFER, WM POWELL.

Page 285: Blank.

Pp. 286-287: 24 June 1762, ARTHUR DOBBS to REES SHELBY of Anson, planter, for Ł12 s15 proc. money...122 A on Clear Creek...ARTHUR DOBBS (SEAL), Wit: MARTIN PHIFER, WM POWELL.

Page 288: Blank.

Pp. 289-291: 17 & 18 May 1762, CHARLES BEATY of Anson, planter, to JAMES YOUNG of August Co., Va., (Lease s5, release Ł20 Va. money)...795 A on N side Catawba, granted to CHARLES BEATY #304, 30 Aug 1753...CHARLES BEATY (SEAL), Wit: MATHEW YOUNG (X) FRANCIS BEATY, JAMES WATSON.

Page 292: Blank.

Pp. 293-294: 24 June 1762, ARTHUR DOBBS to JAMES McLANE of Anson, for Ł19 s17 proc. money...190 A adj. JOSEPH RODGERS line....ARTHUR DOBBS (SEAL), Wit: MARTIN PHIFER, WM POWELL.

Page 295: Blank.

Pp. 296-297: 24 June 1762, ARTHUR DOBBS to PHILIP WISER of Anson, planter, for Ł12 s4 d4 ...117 A on Great Cold Water Creek...ARTHUR DOBBS (SEAL), Wit: MARTIN PHIFER, WM POWELL.

Page 298: Blank.

Pp. 299-300: 24 June 1762, ARTHUR DOBBS to DAVID SPIKE of Anson, planter, for Ł25 s1 d8 ...240 A on Dutch Buffalo Creek...ARTHUR DOBBS (SEAL), Wit: MARTIN PHIFER, WM POWELL.

Page 301: Blank.

Page 302: 22 Nov 1758, SAMUEL COBREN & wf MARGARET to WILLIAM CLEGHORN, for Ł25 proc. money....378 A on S side Catawba, above sd. COBRENS line on Tuckasegee path, granted to JUDITH COBREN 30 Aug 1753, & conveyed by her & her husband JOHN CLEMMENS to sd. SAMUEL COBREN by L & R, 28 Dec 1755...SAMUEL COBREN (X) (SEAL), MARGARET COBREN (X) (SEAL), Wit: WILLIAM HAECKER, JOHN THOMAS.

Page 303: Blank.

Pp. 304-305: 24 June 1762, ARTHUR DOBBS to NICHOLAS WALTER, of Anson, planter, for Ł18 s12 proc. money...178 A on Little Cold Water Creek... ARTHUR DOBBS (SEAL), Wit: MARTIN PHIFER, WM POWELL.

VOLUME 6

Page 306: Blank.

Pp. 307-308: 24 June 1762, ARTHUR DOBBS to MARTIN BENNEGER of Anson, planter, for ₺38
            s13 d4 proc. money...378 A on Dutch Buffaloe Creek, adj. KINGs line...
ARTHUR DOBBS (SEAL), Wit: MARTIN PHIFER, WM POWELL.

Page 309: Blank.

Pp. 310-311: 24 June 1762, ARTHUR DOBBS to WILLIAM WHITE of Anson, planter, for ₺16 s10 d4
            ...158 A on S side Rockey River...ARTHUR DOBBS(SEAL), Wit: MARTIN PHIFER,
WM. POWELL.

Page 312: Blank.

Pp. 313-314: 24 June 1762, ARTHUR DOBBS to JOSEPH ROGERS of Anson, planter, for ₺24 s9
            proc. money...234 A formerly surveyed for WILLIAM CLARK between Buffaloe
Creek & three mile branch...ARTHUR DOBBS (SEAL), Wit: MARTIN PHIFER, WM POWELL.

Page 315: Blank.

Page 316: 30 Oct 1758, JOSHUA WEAVER Of Anson, planter, to TIMOTHY TAYLOR of same,
            for ₺20 Va. money...100 A on S side Pee Dee, 1/2 of tract gramted to WEAVER
3 Feb 1754...JOSHUA WEAVER (SEAL), Wit: JOHN DUNNE, JOHN COLLSON.

Pp. 317-318: 24 June 1762, ARTHUR DOBBS to PAUL BARRINGER, of Anson, planter, for ₺19
            s16 d8 proc. money...185 A on Dutch Buffaloe Cr.,..ARTHUR DOBBS(SEAL), Wit:
MARTIN PHIFER, WM POWELL.

Page 319: Blank.

Pp. 320-321: 24 June 1762, ARTHUR DOBBS to HENRY FURR of Anson, planter, for ₺32 s1 d4
            ...301 A on Dutch Buffaloe Cr....ARTHUR DOBBS (SEAL), Wit: MARTIN PHIFER,
WM POWELL.

Page 322: Blank.

Pp. 323-324: 24 June 1762, ARTHUR DOBBS to VALENTINE WEAVER, planter, of Anson, for ₺12
            s11 proc. money...120 A, adj. ANDREW RINCHART's line...ARTHUR DOBBS (SEAL),
Wit: MARTIN PHIFER, WM POWELL.

Page 325: Blank.

Pp. 326-327: 24 June 1762, ARTHUR DOBBS to JOHN ADAM BLACKWELDER, of Anson, planter, for
            ₺16 s16 d4 proc. money...156 A on Little Cold Water Creek...ARTHUR DOBBS
(SEAL), Wit: MARTIN PHIFER, WM POWELL.

Page 328: Blank.

Pp. 329-330: 24 June 1762, ARTHUR DOBBS to MATTHIAS BEAVER of Anson, planter, for ₺15 s5
            d4...146 A...ARTHUR DOBBS (SEAL), Wit: MARTIN PHIFER, WM POWELL.

Pp. 331-332: 24 June 1762, ARTHUR DOBBS to JOHN CORZINE, planter, for ₺24 s5 proc. money
            ...232 A on Buffaloe Cr....ARTHUR DOBBS (SEAL), Wit: MARTINPHIFER, WM
POWELL.

Page 333: Blank.

Pp. 334-335: 24 June 1762, ARTHUR DOBBS to NICHOLAS CORZINE, planter, for ₤30 s12 d8
...293 A on Great Cold Water Cr., first piece surveyed for MARTIN PHIFER
...ARTHUR DOBBS (SEAL), Wit: ROBERT HARRIS, WM POWELL.

Page 336: Blank.

Pp. 337-338: 24 June 1762, ARTHUR DOBBS to MICHAEL CLINE of Anson, planter, for ₤12 s13
d2 proc. money...121 A on Blackwelders branch of Little Cold Water Cr....
ARTHUR DOBBS (SEAL), Wit: MARTIN PHIFER, WM POWELL.

Page 339: Blank.

Pp. 340-341: 24 June 1762, ARTHUR DOBBS to WM LIPPER of Anson, for ₤19 s13 proc. money
...188 A on Dutch Buffaloe Creek....ARTHUR DOBBS (SEAL), Wit: MARTIN
PHIFER, WM POWELL.

Page 342: Blank.

Pp. 343-344: 24 June 1762, ARTHUR DOBBS to MOSES WHITE of Anson, planter, for ₤30 s2
proc. money...288 A, adj. KINGs line, where sd. MOSES WHITE now lives...
ARTHUR DOBBS (SEAL), Wit: MARTIN PHIFER, WM POWELL.

Page 345: Blank.

Pp. 346-347: 24 June 1762, ARTHUR DOBBS to SAMUEL HARRIS of Anson, planter, for ₤47 s6
d10...453 A on Clear Creek...ARTHUR DOBBS(SEAL), Wit: ROBERT HARRIS, WM.
POWELL

Page 348: Blank.

Pp. 349-350: 24 June 1762, ARTHUR DOBBS to SAMUEL HARRIS, son of JAMES HARRIS, of Anson
planter, for ₤11 s10 proc. money...110 A on Clear Cr., adj. REES SHELBY's
lower corner...ARTHUR DOBBS (SEAL), Wit: ROBERT HARRIS, WILLIAM POWELL.

Pp. 351-352: 24 June 1762, ARTHUR DOBBS to DANIEL ALEXANDER, planter, for ₤8 s5 proc.
money...79 A on Rocky River, where sd. ALEXANDER now lives...ARTHUR DOBBS
(SEAL), Wit: ROBERT HARRIS, WILLIAM POWELL.

Pp. 353-354: Blank.

Pp. 355-356: 24 June 1762, ARTHUR DOBBS to ANDREW REYNHART of Anson, planter,for ₤11 s14
proc. money...112 A on a branch of Adams Creek where he now lives...
ARTHUR DOBBS (SEAL), Wit: ROBERT HARRIS, WM POWELL.

Page 357: Blank.

Page 358: I, JOHN ARMOR, with consent of my mother JENNETE ARMOR, of Anson, do bind
myself to lear the mistery and art of the Taylor from JOHN BUCHANAN for 4
yrs. and 6 mo....1 July 1762...JOHN ARMOR (SEAL), JENNETT ARMOR (SEAL), JOHN BUGHANAN
(SEAL), Wit: JOHN WILSON, ROBERT HARRIS, JR. Proved 17 Aug 1762 before ROBERT HARRIS,
JR.,J. P.

Pp. 359-362: 20 & 21 Nov 1758, JOHN BARNS of Craven Co., S. C., planter, to JOHN BUCH-
ANAN of the Yadkin in N. C., dealer & chapman (Lease s5, release ₺50 &
one horse)...land on S side Catawba nigh to THOMAS LITTLEs survey...JOHN BARNS (SEAL),
Wit: HENRY ONEAL, WM DAVIDSON, JAMES SNOW. Proven by HENRY ONEAL before CHARLES WOOD-
MASON, JP for Craven Co.

Pp. 363-365: 24 & 25 Sep 1762, ROBERT SIMONSTON of Rowan Co.,planter, to REV. MR.
ALEXANDER CRAIGHEAD of Anson (Lease s5, release ₺10)...500 A on Indian
Camp Creek, adj. MATHEW TOOL's line, patent 25 Feb 1754...ROBERT SIMONSTON (SEAL),
MARGARET SIMONSTON (X) (SEAL), Wit: ANDREW ALLISON, MATT. LONG.

Pp. 366-369: 6 & 7 July 1762, HENRY VERNOR & wf BARBARA of Anson, to REV. MR ALEXANDER
CRAIGHEAD (lease s5, release ₺85 Va. money)...480 A on Long Cr., adj. THOS
CLARKS, & TOYs lines...HENRY VERNER (SEAL), BARBARA VERNER (X) (SEAL), Wit: ROBERT
HARRIS, JOHN BUCKANAN, ROBERT HARRIS, JR.

Pp. 370-372: 18 & 12 Dec 1759, JAMES HANNA of Anson, to THOMAS BLACK of same, (lease ₺5,
release ₺5)...204 A on Rocky Cr., above the plantation that CHARLES
KITCHENS lives on...JAMES HANNA (SEAL), Wit: ROB'T McCLENACHAN, JOHN KING.

Page 373: 20 Mar 1760, JOSEPH WHITE of Anson, planter, to WILLIAM PHILLIPS of same,
for ₺50...150 A on Lanes Creek, granted to JOSEPH WHITE, 1760, 300 A, known
as "Buty Spot"...JOSEPH WHITE (SEAL), Wit: JACOB PAUL, WM MITCHELL, ZAC. PHILLIPS.

Page 374: Blank.

Page 375: 23 Feb 1762, THOMAS DICKSON of Anson, to THOMAS MITCHELLE of same, for ₺30
proc. money...150 A on N side Jones Cr....THOMAS DICKSON (SEAL), Wit: JOHN
PARSONS, NICHOLAS WHITE (X).

Page 376: 10 Feb 1762, JOSEPH WHITE of Anson, to JACOB PAUL of same, for ₺70, 200 A
on Brown Creek, the place where sd. JOSEPH WHITE lately lived...JOSEPH WHITE
(SEAL), Wit: WM PHILLIPS, ZAC. PHILLIPS, WILLIAM MITCHELL.

Pp. 377-378: 20 Nov 1761, FRANCIS ASHLEY, planter, of Anson, to JAMES LONG, carpenter
of same, for ₺20 proc. money...land on W side Little River of Pee Dee...
adj. JORDAN ASHLEY...100 A part of a grant to JOHN ASHLEY & conveyed to sd. FRANCIS...
FRANCIS ASHLEY (X) (SEAL), Wit: HENRY TOUCHSTONE, CHRISTOPHER TOUCHSTONE.

Page 379:Blank.

Page 380: 5 Mar 1762, THOMAS DAVIS of Anson, to JOHN WILSON of same, for ₺21 proc.
money...200 A on Clark's Creek, N side Pee Dee, granted to sd. DAVID by deed
from WILLIAM HARRINGTON 27 Sept 1756, 200 A....THOMAS DAVIS (T) (SEAL), Wit: EDMUND
LILLY, DAVID SNEAD.

Page 381: Blank.

Page 382: 21 Mar 1759, JOHN BRIAN of Craven Co., SC., planter to PHILIP WALKER of same,
for ₺200 SC money..land on S side Broad, River on Thicketty Creek, formerly
belonging to WILLIAM GREEN, 350 A...JOHN BRIAN (SEAL), Wit: HUGH McDONALD, THOMAS POOLE.

Pp. 383-384: 1 Mar 1762, JAMES DUNN of Anson to WILLIAM SIMM of same, for ₺20 proc.
money...part of tract granted to JAMES ALEXANDER & conveyed to JAMES
DUNN 10 Feb 1759, adj. WILLIAM GIVINS line...245 A...JAMES DUNN (SEAL), ELIZABETH
DUNN (X) (SEAL), Wit: JOHN WILSON, ROBERT HARRIS, JR., ROBERT HARRIS SR.

Pp. 385-386: 10 May 1762, JOHN PARKER of Rowan, to SAMUEL WILSON of Anson, for ₺100 NC
money...land on S side Clarks R., at mouth of Fisher's Creek...400 A,
granted 9 Apr 1755 to SAMUEL WILSON & conveyed to PARKER...JOHN PARKER (SEAL), Wit:
STEPHEN JONES, ROBERT HARRIS, JR.

Pp. 387-389: 31 May & 1 June 1762, JAMES POTTS & wf SARAH of Anson, to JOHN LEECH of same
for (lease s5, release ₺15)...200 A adj. Governor's line, granted 21 Oct
1758 to sd. POTTS...JAMES POTTS (SEAL), SARAH POTTS (O) (SEAL), Wit: NATHANIEL ALEXANDER,
JOHN ROBINSON.

Page 390: Blank.

Page 391: 20 Mar 1762, JOSEPH WHITE of Anson, to ZACHARY PHILIPS of same, for ₺50...
land on SW side Lanes Creek, 300 A granted to JOSEPH WHITE, 1756, known
as Beauty Spot...JOSEPH WHITE (SEAL), Wit: WM PHILLIPS, JACOB PAUL, WILL MITCHELL.

Pp. 392-393: 17 June 1762, AARON SMITH of Anson Co., to WILLIAM CRITTENDEN of same,
for ₺51...land on S side Pee Dee, adj. ROBERT PARKES land, on Walker's
Island...300 A granted 26 Nov 1746 to JOHN GILES & conveyed to HENRY WALKER, 75 A
conveyed to AARON SMITH (SEAL), Wit: W. TERRY, ANDREW PRESLAR, FRANCIS SMITH.

Pp. 394-397: 7 & 8 May 1762, FRANCIS BEATY of Rowan, Surveyor to DAVID HAY of Anson,
planter, (lease s5, release ₺23 proc. money)...560 A on N side Catawba,
about a mile from path from JOHN FALL's, formerly WIDOW PICKENS, to the Catawba Nation,
formerly surveyed for HUGH HARRIS, granted to SAMUEL YOUNG 17 May 1754, conveyed by
YOUNG to BEATY...FRANCIS BEATY (SEAL), Wit: ALEX. LEWIS, SAMUEL BIGHAM.

Pp. 398-401: [deed incomplete] 1762, DAVID HAY, SENR of Anson, planter to DAVID HAY, JR.
of same, planter (lease s5, release ₺9 proc. money)...187 A, part of 560 A
granted to SAMUEL YOUNG 17 May 1754, then to FRANCIS BEATY, then to DAVID HAY...DAVID
HAY (SEAL), Wit: SAMUEL BIGHAM, FRANCIS BEATY.

Pp. 402-405: 15 & 16 Aug 1762, FRANCIS McELWAIN of Dobbs Co., NC, to FRANCIS BEATY of
Rowan Co., (lease s5, release ₺40)...600 A on S side S fork CAtawba on
both sides Fisher's Creek...granted to McELWAIN 17 May 1754...FRANCIS McELWAIN (SEAL),
Wit: THOMAS BEATY, HUGH BEATY.

Page 406: Blank.

Pp. 407-410: 20 & 21 Sept 1762, FRANCIS BEATY of Rowan Co., surveyor, to THOMAS BEATY of
Rowan, (lease s5, release ₺45)...200 A on E side Catawba, 1/2 or 3/4 mile
above JOHN BEATY's ford...granted to sd. FRANCIS 26 Nov 1757...FRANCIS BEATY (SEAL),
Wit: JOHN SLOAN, HUGH BEATY.

Page 411: Blank.

Page 412: 22 Feb 1762, MARY MOORE, widow of JOHN MOORE, decd of Anson, to MOSES MOORE,
for ₺___...land granted to EVAN LEWIS 10 Apr 1750...600 A conveyed to JOHN
MOORE by L & R 24 & 25 Oct 1755...& on 16 May did reconvey to JEREMIAH POTTS 170
and 300 A to JOSEPH CLOUD...MARY MOORE (SEAL), Wit: ABRAHAM SCOTT, RICHARD BARRY, JOHN
THOMAS.

Page 413: SAMUEL YOUNG to JOSEPH HARDEN & JOHN KUYKENDALL, 400 A 2 or 3 miles above
        FRANCIS McELWAIN's land and THOMAS ROBINSON's land [deed fragmentary, date
not given]...SAMUEL YOUNG (SEAL), Wit: _____ KUYKENDALL, SAMUEL COBRUN (X), JOHN HARDEN.

Pp.414-416: 22 & 23 Mar 1762, JACOB COOK & wf NANCY of Anson, to CHRISTOPHER PLES,
        of same, (lease s5, release ₺20)...land on S side Yadkin, both sides of
Buffaloe Creek, adj. JOHN BRANDON's land...195 A....JACOB COOK (SEAL), NANCY COOK (X)
(SEAL), Wit: DAVID DUNCAN, FRANCIS BEATY.

Page 417: Blank.

Pp. 418-421: [deed fragmentary], 1757, THOMAS HOLLINGSWORTH, son & heir at law to
        JOSEPH HOLLINGSWORTH of Anson & sd. THOMAS of Granville Co., S.C. to
ABRAHAM HOLLINGSWORTH his brother of Anson Co (Lease s5, release ₺___), 300 A
granted 4 Sept 1753 on S side Broad, including some Beaver dams on Cain Creek...THOMAS
HOLLINGSWORTH (SEAL), ISAAC COX Attorney, Wit: _____ McCOOL, EDWARD MUSGROVE, ISAAC
COOK.

Page 422; Blank.

Pp. 423-424: 3 May 1757, HUGH NELSON of Rowan Co., to WILLIAM HAGAN's(sic) of Anson, for
        ₺20 proc. money...land on N side Catawba, on twelve mile Creek including
the Creek on each side of the path that leads from the Catawba Nation to ANDREW PICKINS,
320 A...HUGH NELSON (X) (SEAL), Wit: JAMES LINN, SARAH LINN (X), WILLIAM LINN.

Pp. 425-426: 8 Jan 1760, JOHN ELKINS of Craven Co., SC, shoemaker, to WILLIAM WATKINS of
        Anson CO., N. C. , for ₺10 Va. money...land adj. JOSEPH HALL's line, N
side Hitchcock Creek, JOHN WEBB's corner, JAMES TERRY's...100 A granted to ELKINS 6
Mar 1759...JOHN ELKINS (X) (SEAL), Wit: BENJAMIN MIMS (X), MARSHALL DIGGS, ISREAL SNEAD
(X).

Pp. 427-428: 21 July 1759 , ARCHIBALD FISHER, Exr. of MECAIN FISHER & THOMAS STEEL,
        planters, to STEPHEN WHITE, Blacksmith, all of Anson, for ₺10 proc. money
...265 A...ARCHIBALD FISHER (SEAL), THOMAS STEEL (SEAL), Wit: ROBERT McCLENACHAN, JOHN
STEEL, THOMAS FERRAL.

Page 429: Blank.

Pp. 430-432: 20 Oct 1756, TOWNSEND ROBINSON of Anson, Gentleman, to THOMAS LAND of
        same, miller, for ₺5...546 A on S side Catawba, N side of S fork of
Rockey Creek...granted to sd. ROBINSON 3 Oct 1755...TOWNSEND ROBINSON(SEAL), Wit:
THOMAS PRESTWOOD, PATRICK KERR.

Page 433; Blank.

Pp. 434-435: 14 May 1762, SAMUEL PARSON of Anson, planter, to HENRY TIPPINS of same,
        planter, for ₺10 proc. money.. part of tract granted to WILLIAM STONE 3
Oct 1755 & conveyed by STONE to PARSONS on both sides N fork of Little River...100 A
...SAMUEL PARSON (SEAL), Wit: J. PICKETT, JR., NICHOLAS BOND.

Page 436: 25 Apr 1760, RICHARD SCRUGGS of Parish of St. George, District of Halifax,
        Georgia, sells to JACOB PAUL of same, one negro girl... RICHARD SCRUGS (SEAL),
Wit: MARTHA EMANUEL, DAVID EMANUEL.

END OF VOLUME 6

VOLUME 5

Page 1: 14 July 1766, WM SIMS of <u>Mecklingburg</u> Co., to Edmund Fanning of Town
of Childsburg, Orange County, N. C., for Ł10 proc. money...land on E
side Little River, Dry Creek...granted to sd. SIMS 13 Oct 1765...WILLIAM SIMS
(SEAL), Wit: J. EDWARDS, JOHN DUNN.
Proven Anson Co. Inferior Ct. July 1766, SAML. SPENCER, C.C.C.

Page 2: Blank.

Pp. 3-4: 22 July 1766, HENRY DOWNS, JR. of Mecklinburg, planter, to CORNELIUS
ROBINSON of Anson Co., for Ł110...300 A, part of a grant to ROBERT
MILLS 22 Nov 1746, conveyed to HENRY DOWNS, then to WILLIAM DOWNS, then to
HENRY DOWNS, JR....HENRY DOWNS (SEAL), No wit.
Proven July term 1766, SAML. SPENCER, C.C.C.

Page 5: 23 July 1766, JOHN HAMER of Craven Co., S. C. to CHRISTOPHER CLARK, of
Anson Co., for Ł20...land on lower side of Island Creek, 100 A, granted
31 Aug 1753 to sd. HAMER...JNO HAMER (SEAL), Wit: SAML. SPENCER, WM. <u>HAIMER</u>,
Proven July Ct. 1766, SAML. SPENCER, C.C.C.

Pp. 6-7: Blank.

Pp. 8-9: 10 Aug 1766, JOHN CARTWRIGHT of Anson, planter, to ROBT. POSTON of same,
for Ł25 proc. money...land adj. JONATHAN EVANS's line on Mountain Creek,
100 A, part of 200 A granted to JAS. POSTON 26 Apr 1763, & conveyed to JOHN
CARTWRIGHT...JOHN CARTWRIGHT (I C) (SEAL), Wit: JOHN CRAWFORD, JOSEPH DENHAM.
Proven July Ct. 1766, SAML. SPENCER, C.C.C.

Page 10: 25 Oct 1766, RICHARD ADAMS of Anson, planter, to WM. ADAMS, of same,
planter, for s5...part of a tract granted to ADAMS 5 Dec 1760, 300 A
...RICHARD ADAMS (R) (SEAL), Wit: JOHN BENNETT (I), JAMES ADAMS (I), JOHN
THOMAS.   Proven Oct. term 1766, SAML. SPENCER, C.C.C.

Page 11: Blank.

Page 12: 25 Oct 1766, RICHARD ADAMS to JOHN BENNETT,planter, for s5...part of
300 A granted 5 Dec 1760...RICHARD ADAMS (R) (SEAL), Wit: JAMES ADAMS
(I), WM ADAMS (A), JOHN THOMAS
Proven Oct. Ct. 1766, SAML. SPENCER, C.C.C.

Page 13: Blank.

Page 14: 25 Oct 1766, RICHARD ADAMS to JAMES ADAMS, planter, for s5...50 A,
part of 300 A granted to sd. ADAMS 5 Dec 1760...RICHARD ADAMS (R)
(SEAL), Wit: WILLIAMS ADAMS (A), JOHN BENNETT, JOHN THOMAS.
Proven Oct. term 1766, SAML. SPENCER, C.C.C.

Page 15: Blank.

Page 16: 29 Oct 1766, JOHN CRAWFORD of Anson Co., to EDWARD CHAMBERS, of same,
for Ł80...100 A granted 6 Apr 1765 to CRAWFORD...JOHN CRAWFORD (SEAL),
No Wit.   Proven Oct. term 1766, SAML. SPENCER, C.C.C.

Page 17: Blank.

Pp. 18-19: 25 Oct 1766, JOHN GIBSON, planter, & wf ANNA, to JOHN RYLE, planter,
for ₤40...land on S side Rocky River, S side Pee Dee, opp. EDMUND
LILLYs plantation, granted 2 Nov 1764, 140 A...JOHN GIBSON (SEAL), ANNA GIBSON
(X) (SEAL), Wit: JNO. PICKETT, SHADRACK HOGAN.
Proven Oct. Ct. 1766, SAML. SPENCER, C.C.C.

Pp. 20-21: 28 Oct 1766, THOMAS WILLIAMS of Anson, planter, to JOHN DAVIS, of
same, planter, for ₤26...140 A on SW side Pee Dee, at the mouth of
Davis Creek...McCULLOCKS line...sold to WILLIAMS by DAVID EVANS 20 Sept 1764,
granted 5 Dec 1760...THOMAS WILLIAMS (SEAL), Wit: CHARLES MEDLOCK, WILLIAM
COLEMAN (+), JOHN RYLE.
Proven Oct. term 1766, SAML. SPENCER, C.C.C.

Page 22: Blank.

Page 23: 15 May 1766, JOHN WOOD of Anson, to JOHN USSERY of same, for ₤110...
land on W side Pee Dee, on Cheeks Creek...adj. ROBERT KILLCREASES line
...150 A granted 27 Sept 1756...JOHN WOOD (-J) (SEAL), Wit: W. USSERY, LUKE
ROBINSON (H), CHRISTIAN ROBINSON (P).
Proven July Term 1767, SAML. SPENCER, C.C.C.

Page 24: Blank.

Page 25: 10 Feb 1759, BENJAMIN & CHRISTOPHER CLARK purchased land on JOHN KEMP 13
Nov 1751, 640 A granted to KEMP 21 Jan 1746...now divided...CHRISTOPHER
CLARK (SEAL), BENJAMIN CLARK (SEAL), Wit: ISAAC CLARK, MARSHALL DEGGS.

Page 26: Blank.

Page 27: 15 Nov 1758, SAMUEL FRENCH of Anson Co., planter, to ELIZABETH GRIGG...
land on SW side Pee Dee on E side Cedar Cr., upper side of Griggs spring
branch...100 A, part of 200 A granted 25 May 1757...SAMUEL FRENCH (SEAL), Wit:
GEORGE ONEIL (B), ANTHO. HUTCHINS.

Page 28: Blank.

Pp. 29-30: 8 Aug 1758, WILLIAM TERRY of Anson, Yeoman, to JAMES TERRY of same,
yeoman, for ₤40...land granted to THOMAS REDD 22 Nov 1746, 200 A on
N side P. D., ...THOS JONES corner, THS. REDDs line...sold by REDD to WM TERRY
25 Dec 1751...also part of tract granted to THOMAS JONES 10 Apr 1745, conveyed to
EDMUND CARTLIDGE 12 Apr 1749, then to TERRY 16 Jan 1753, 12 1/2 A...WM TERRY (SEAL)
Wit: HENRY DOWNS, BENJ. MARTIN, SAML O BRYAN.

Page 31: 5 Oct 1758, TILLOTON KEBLE of Anson to JOHN HAMER of same, for ₤10 proc.
money...land on Carthages Cr., being the land Keble bought of EDMUND
CARTHAGE [CARTLIDGE], 640 A granted to CARTLEDGE 26 Nov 1757...TILLOTSON KEBLE
(SEAL), Wit: BENJ. MARTIN, SAM. O BRYAN, ELIZ. PENNINGTON (X).

Page 32: Blank.

Page 33: 26 Oct 1756, WILLIAM TERRY, ESQ. of Anson, planter, for ₤30 to WILLIAM
BYRD of same...land on N side Pee Dee, Hitchcocks Cr., adj. THOMAS STAFFORD
WILLIAMS, granted to TERRY 15 Mar 1756, 300 A...WM TERRY (SEAL), Wit: TOW. ROBINSON,
MATTHEW RAIFORD.

Page 34: Blank.

Page 35: 24 Apr 1759, EDWARD ELLERBEE of Anson, to ALEANDER GORDON, of same, for ₤12
        proc. money...land in Prince George Town, near sd. GORDONs land, part of 650
A granted to JOHN ELLERBEE decd, 14 Mar 1745...3 A....EDWARD ELLERBEE (SEAL), Wit:
WM BLACK, WM HAMER.

Pp. 36-37: Blank.

Page 38: 5 May 1757, WM FERRALL of Bladen Co., farmer, to WILLIAM NEWBERRY of Anson,
        farmer, for ₤8 proc. money...1/2 of patent of 200 A granted 9 Sept 1756, on
N side Pee Dee, adj. Wm COLEMANS line...WM FERRALL (SEAL), Wit: THS. UNDERWOOD, ELIZ.
BROWN.

Page 39: Blank.

Pp. 40-41: 10 Aug 1758, DANIEL TOUCHSTONE of Anson, to JURDAN ASHLEY of same for "ten
        dollars"...100 A on N side Pee Dee, at mouth of Little River, patent unto
JOHN ASHLEY, sold by ARNOLD to JOHN McDANIEL, then to JACOB SUMMERLAIN, then to DANIEL
TOUCHSTONE...DANIEL TOUCHSTONE (SEAL), Wit: HENRY TOUCHSTONE, STEPHEN PADACK, RACHEL
TOUCHSTONE (R).

Page 42: 27 Nov 1757, MORGAN BROWN of Anson to JOHN PELLAM (PULLAN) of same, for s48
        ...land granted to sd. BROWN 26 Nov 1757, 100 A...M. BROWN (SEAL), Wit:
CHARLES ROBINSON, JOHN THOMAS.

Page 43: Blank.

Pp. 44-45: 26 July 1757, JAMES DENSON, JR. planter, to BENJAMIN VINES, both of Anson,
        for ₤10 sterling...100 A on W side Little River...granted to DENSON 15 Nov
1753...JAMES DENSON (J) (SEAL), Wit: SAMUEL _____, THOMAS HARRINGTON (T).

Page 46: Blank.

Page 47: 20 Feb 1759, JOHN ASHLEY of Anson Co., to FRANCIS ASHLEY of same, for ₤50
        ...300 A on N side Little River, adj. ROBINSONs line, JAMES DENSON, JURDEN
ASHLEYs...JOHN ASHLEY (E) (SEAL), Wit: ANDREW PRESLAR, RICHARD YARBROUGH, FREDERICK
TOUCHSTONE.   (E)

Page 48: Blank.

Page 49: 22 Jan 1759, JOEL YARBROUGH of Anson, planter, to SAMUEL DAVIS of same, plan-
        ter, for ₤20, land on E side P. D. River, adj. CHARLES ROBINSON, JOHN McCOY...
100 A, granted to JOHN AVERIDE 27 Sept 1756(?)...JOEL YARBROUGH (SEAL), Wit: RICHARD
YARBROUGH, HUN. YARBROUGH, THOS DAVIS.

Page 50: Blank.

Page 51: 26 Mar 1758, ZACHARIAH PHILLIPS of Anson to JOHN LEVERITT of same, for ₤20
        Va. money...200 A granted to sd. PHILLIPS 25 Nov 1757...ZACHERY PHILLIPS
(SEAL), Wit: W. BROWN, ROBERT McCLENCHAN, JAS. CUNNING.

Page 52: Blank.

Page 53: 8 July 1758, ZACHERY PHILLIPS to JOHN LEVERITT, for ₤40 Va. money...300 A on

S side Pee Dee, on E side of graindstone branch of Goulds fork granted 1 July 1758...
ZACHERY PHILLIPS (𝒵) (SEAL), Wit: M. BROWN, ROBERT McCLENACHAN, JAS. CUNNING.

Page 54: Blank.

Page 55: 3 Nov 1758, ARCHIBALD GRAHAM of Anson, to WILLIAM LITTLE of same, for ₤120
        proc. money...190 A on NE side Pee Dee & 112 A adj. other tract...dividing
line between GRAHAM & JAMES COWARD...ARCHIBALD GRAHAM (SEAL), Wit: HENRY CAINS,
ROBERT ABRAHAM.
                [This land later in Marlborough County, S. C.]

Page 56: Blank.

Page 57: 23 Jan 1758, EDMUND CARTLEDGE of Anson, to TILLOTSON KEBLE, for ₤5 proc.
        money...50 A granted to CARTLIDGE...E. CARTLEDGE (SEAL), Wit: LAURENCE O
BRYAN, THOMAS KEMP ( ).

Page 58: 25 July 1758, ANDREW PRESLAR, SR. of Anson, to THOMAS PRESLAR of same, plant-
        er, for ₤___, part of 264 A granted to ANDREW PRESLAR 4 Oct 1751, on N side
Rocky River, 64 A...ANDREW PRESLAR (SEAL), Wit: JESS. CUNNING, WILL CUNNING.

Pp. 59-60: Blank.

Page 61: 25 July 1758, ANDREW PRESLAR of Anson, to JOHN PRESLAR, JR.of same, for ₤10
        proc. money...part of tract of 264 A on S side Rocky River, granted 4 Oct
1751...Spring branch...Cabbin Branch...100 A...ANDREW PRESLAR (SEAL), Wit: JAS.
CUNNING, WILL CUNNING.

Page 62: Blank.

Page 63: 14 Sept 1756, EDWARD ELLERBE of Anson, planter, to THOMAS ELLERBE of same,
        for ₤85...150 A on N side Pee Dee...granted to sd. EDWARD ELLERBE from
JOHN ELLERBEE by will dated 22 Sept 1751...EDWARD ELLERBEE (SEAL), Wit: RUNNEL
BRIGHTWELL ( ), ALEX. GORDON.

Page 64: Blank.

Page 65: 20 Sept 1757, NICHOLAS BROADAWAY & wf ELIZABETH of Anson, to THOMAS TALLANT,
        for ₤15 Va. money... land on SW side Pee Dee, on Smith Cr., granted to
JOSEPH WHITE & FRANCIS McELWAIN, 13 Apr 1749, conveyed to TOMAS BERRY by deed 17 July
1752, then from sd. BERRY to his dau. ELIZABETH BROADAWAY by deed 28 Oct 1758, 150 A.
NICHOLAS BROADAWAY (N) (SEAL), ELIZABETH BROADAWAY (X) (SEAL), Wit: Wit: ISAAC (Ŧ)
FALCONBROUGH, SAMUEL BERRY, WILLIAM HOWELL.

Page 66: Blank.

Page 67:15 Oct 1757, JOHN COWIN & wf MARGARET of Anson, to JAMES BLACK, for ₤30...
        part of grant to COWIN 17 May 1754...200 A...JOHN COWIN (SEAL), MARGARET
COWIN (Q) (SEAL), Wit: JOHN BLACK,JR. THOS BLACK, JOHN THOMAS.

Page 68: Blank.

Page 69: 22 July 1757, JAMES MUCKLEROY of Anson, Blacksmith, for ₤5 proc. money, to
        ARCHIBALD BLACK... part of a grant to sd. MUCKLEROY 26 May 1757, part of 330
A...200 A....JAMES MUCKLEROY (SEAL), Wit: WILLIAM BLEWETT, JOHN LILLY, DARBY CAVES (X).
                (·ttt)

Page 70: Blank.

Page 71: 14 July 1757, JACOB BROWN of Anson, to WILLIAM CATHEY of same, for Ł8...
        land on S side Catawba, part of 1000A granted to JOHN KILLION, 30 Sept 1759
[1749?], sold to sd. BROWN 1 & 2 Jan 1754, 250 A...JACOB BROWN (SEAL), Wit:JEAN
THOMAS, JNO. THOMAS.

Page 72: Blank.

Pp. 73-74: 26 July 1756, JOHN HALL of Anson, to WILLIAM GAMBOL (GAMBLE) for s30...
        300 A on N side Rocky R., part of 400 A granted to sd. HALL 25 Feb 1754...
JOHN HALL (SEAL), Wit: HENRY STOKES, WILLIAM FILLSTEN.

Page 75: 4 Nov 1755, JOHN CLARK of Anson, to SAMUEL WELLS of same, for Ł___ Va. money
        ...land on S fork Sandy R..."concluding the place where CALEB DENDLE then
lived on"...300 A...JOHN CLARK (SEAL), Wit: THOMAS KITCHELL, ISAAC WELLS, JOHN WILSON.

Pp. 76-78: 30 Nov & 5 Dec 1758, JOHN CLARK of Anson, to JOHN DICKINSON of Augusta Co.,
        Va...(lease s5, release Ł100 Va. money)...land on S side Broad R., S fork
of Sandy R., including the improvements he bought of JOHN STEWART...(grantee later
referred to as ADAM DICKINS)...JOHN CLARK (SEAL), Wit: ADAM DICKINSON, JOHN LARSEY,
JOHN BUTLER.

Pp. 79-81: Blank.

Pp. 82-85: 24 & 25 Sept 1758, JOHN CLARK & wf MARTHA of Anson, to HUGH McLAIN of same,
        for Ł15...land on N side Cain Cr., a branch of Catawba R., 200 A part of
514 A granted to MARTHA PICKINS, now wf. of sd. JOHN CLARK, 20 May 1754...JOHN CLARK
(SEAL), .1ARTHA PICKINS (M) (SEAL), Wit: ROBERT McCLENACHAN, JNO SELLERS (S).

Pp. 86-88: Blank.

Pp. 89-92: 13 & 14 Jan 1759, ADAM MEEKS & wf ELIZABETH, weaver, to JAMES MILLER, cord-
        winder, (lease s5, release Ł600)...land on E side Catawba, adj. WILLIAM
PRINCES line, Subdivided from 2 tracts, 200 A & 300 A formerly granted to GEORGE
RENEX 31 Mar 1753 & 30 Aug 1753...ADAM MEEKS (SEAL), ELIZABETH MEEKS (Ł) (X) (SEAL),
Wit: ALEX. LEWIS, JAMES SHARP, ALLEN CAMPBELL.

Pp. 93-94: Blank.

Pp. 95-97: 22 & 23 Jan 1759, ROBERT RAMSEY & wf MARGARET of Anson, to ROBERT DUNLAP
        of same (lease s5, release Ł30 proc. money)...300 A on N side Catawba, on
both sides Cain Creek....ROBERT RAMSEY (SEAL), MARGARET RAMSEY (X) (SEAL), Wit: W.
DAVIS, SAMUEL DUNLAP, WM DRENEN (X).

Page 98: Blank.

Page 99: 24 Oct 1757, RICHARD DERMUND of Anson, laborer, to JOHN MESHO of same, planter
        for Ł50 proc. money...100 A, part of a grant to sd. DEMUND, 27 Sept 1756
on Mill Creek...RICHARD DERMUND (D) (SEAL), Wit: JOHN LONG, JOHN BROWN (Ł), JAMES
LEWIS.

Pp. 100-101: Blank.

Page 102: 21 Jan 1758, THOMAS LAND & wf ELEANOR, of Anson, to ALEXANDER RAMTERY of

Craven Co., SC, for ₺7 NC money...100 A on W side Catawba granted to LAND from
LINARD...THOMAS LAND (SEAL), ELEANOR LAND ( ) (SEAL), Wit: JAMES PATTON, ROBT.
McCLEANACHAN.

Page 103: 24 Oct 1757, WM RUSHING of Anson, planter, to JACOB CARTER, of same,
planter, 50 A in Anson Co....WM RUSHING (SEAL), Wit: JOHN PICKENS, STEPHEN JACKSON.

Page 104: Blank.

Page 105: 22 Apr 1758, SAMUEL NELLY of Anson, planter, to SAMUEL LUSK, for ₺10...
        300 A below the Saluda path on the E side of the branch that runs into
Fishing Creek...granted to SAMUEL NELLY, 24 Sept 1754...SAMUEL NELLY (SEAL), Wit:
SAMUEL THOMPSON, ROBERT McCLENACHAN.
        [This land now in S. C.]

Page 106: Blank.

Page 107: 8 Feb 1758, WILLIAM LANKFORD Of Anson, to CHAS. MEDLOCK, planter, of same,
        for ₺6...land on N side Pee Dee...2nd corner of a tract surveyed for JAMES
MUCKLEROY on S side Solomons Creek...WILLIAM LANKFORD (SEAL), Wit: THOMAS MOORMAN,
FRANCIS CLARK (FC), CHRISTOPHER CLARK.

Page 108: Blank.

Pp. 109-110: 27 Oct 1756, WM TERRY of Anson, planter, to THOMAS COCKROOM, planter,
        of same, for ₺30 sterling...land on N side Pee Dee, on S fork Mountain
Creek...300 A granted to sd. TERRY 27 Sept 1756...WILLIAM TERRY (SEAL), Wit:
MATHEW RUISFORD, TILLOTSON KEBLE.

Page 111: 3 June 1756, WILLIAM COCKTRUM of Anson, p tner, to ELISHA PARKER, of
        same, planter, for ₺15 Va. money...300 A on N side Pee Dee, in mouth of
Marquy Cr....granted to sd. WILLIAM CAHON 30 Mar 1756...WM COCKTRUM (SEAL), Wit:
CALEB TOUCHSTONE, DANIEL TOUCHSTONE.

Page 112: Blank.

Pp. 113-115: 15 & 16 May 1758, JOHN MOORE of Anson, planter, to JOSEPH CLOUD of same,
        weaver, for (lease s5, release ₺15 Va. money)...300 A on S side Indian
Cr., a branch of S fork Catawba, adj. JEREMIAH POTTS...JOHN MOORE (ɪ) (SEAL), Wit:
SAMUEL BEASON, JEREMIAH POTTS (I), FRANCIS BEATY.

Page 116: Blank.

Page 117: 29 Oct 1757, DARBY CAVE of Anson, planter, to DAVID GORDEN of Johnson Co.,
        gentleman, for ₺8 proc. money...100 A granted to ELIJAH HELLAN, 26 Mar
1757 & sold 6 June 1757 to CHS. DARBY CAVE...on Naked Cr., adj. STEPHEN BROWNS land...
DARBY CAVE (N) (SEAL), Wit: WM. CUMMING, JOHN VERILE.
        [This land now in S. C.]

Page 118: Blank.

Page 119: 16 Oct 1756, JOHN ALEXANDER of Anson, to ROBERT WELCH of same, for ₺50 proc.
        money...land on N side S fork Catawba below DEWK RAMSOEURS...granted to sd.
ALEXANDER 20 Mar 1756...JOHN ALEXANDER (SEAL), Wit: THOMAS POTTS, ALEXANDER LEWIS,
SAMUEL BEASON.

Page 120: Blank.

Pp. 121-124: 9 Mar 1758, ROBT MILLER & wf JEAN of Anson, to ROBERT DAVIS, ROBERT
RAMSEY, JOHN LINN, SAMUEL DUNLAP & HENRY WHITE, planter, of same
"for the good will & affection...& every of their greater advantages & conveniency
in attending upon divine worship at all stated or accasional times"...land on N
side Catawba within land joining WM McKEE near ALEXANDER NESBITT & on the south
end of said tract...sold unto JAMES BARNETT by sd. MILLER excepting this tract...
"beginning at a stake upon sd. So side of an house built for divine service including a spring"...to above as trustees for the use of the Presbyterian Congre-
gation of the Waxhaws...only for divine service conform to the practice of the
Church of Scotland...MR. ROBERT MILLER & JEAN his wife reserve for themselves one
seat within the North door of sd. house...ROBERT MILLER (SEAL), JEAN MILLER (SEAL),
Wit: ROBERT McCLENACHAN, JNO. CROCKETT, ANDREW PICKENS.

Pp. 125-27: 22 & 23 Feb 1758, ROBERT MILLER & wf JANE of Anson, to JAMES BARNETT,
planter, (lease s30, release ₤14)...land on N side Catawba, adj. WM
McKEE, ALEXANDER NISBET...except for 4 1/2 A on south end of sd. tract with a
house for divine worship & retiring house...ROBERT MILLER (SEAL), JEAN MILLER
(SEAL), Wit: ROBT. McCLENACHAN, JOHN KENNADA.

Pp. 128-30: Blank.

Pp. 131-133: 22 & 23 Dec 1757, JOHN ANDERSON of Rowan Co., to JOHN WILKINS of Rowan,
(lease s5, release ₤100)..."land in county of Rowan, formerly called
Anson"on S fork Clarks Cr. of S fork Catawba...400 A granted to WM SHERRILL 13
Sept 1749...JOHN ANDERSON (SEAL), Wit: JOHN DUNN, ROBERT GILLESPIE.

Pp. 134-135: Blank.

Pp. 136-138: 27 & 28 Mar 1757, JOHN BARNETT & wf ANN, to MR. ROBERT MILLER, Minr.
of the Waxhaws (lease s5, release ₤10 proc. money)....land on N side
Catawba, adj. WM McKEE, ALEX. NISBET including an old cabbin...JOHN BARNETT (SEAL),
ANN BARNETT (SEAL), Wit: ALEX. OSBORN, ROBERT McCLENACHAN, ANDW. PERKINS.

Pp. 139-141: Blank.

Pp. 142-144: 12 & 13 Jan 1757, HANCE ADAM SNIDER & wf SARAH of Anson, to JOHN WALKER
of same (lease s5, release ₤5)...land on NE side of his old plantation & Leopards Cr., W side Catawba, adj. PETER CLUB, BOSTON BEST, SNIDers old
line...granted to sd. SNIDER 13 Oct 1756...ADAM SNIDER (SEAL), [signed in German],
SARAH SNIDER (X) (SEAL), Wit: GEORGE BROWN, MOUTICE PEGUES, JNO. THOMAS JP.

Page 145: Blank.

Page 146: 21 July 1758, Anson Co.: BENJAMIN MIMS to son DAVID for natural love &
affection...all goods and chattles...one pewter dish, one feather bed,
one horse...BENJ. MIMS (X) (SEAL), Wit: THOS MOORMAN, JOSEPH HALL, BENJAMIN MOOR-
MAN (B).

Pp. 147-148: 21 July 1758, THOMAS LEONARD of Anson, to DAVIS LEONARD of same, for
₤10...220 A, the tract that sd. THOMAS LEONARD liveth on...on W side
Catawba, on upper corner of THOS LEONARDs survey...THOMAS LEONARD (T) (SEAL), Wit:
JAMES PATTON, ROBERT McCLENACHAN.

Page 149: 6 June 1758, CHRISTOPHER HUNT of Anson, planter, to JNO WEBB of same, planter, for ₺20 proc. money...land on N side Pee Dee, adj. BENJ. MIMS upper corner, on S side Hitchcock Cr., adj. JOSEPH HALL...part of 350 A granted to WEBB 25 May 1757, 150 A...CHRISTOPHER HUNT (SEAL), Wit: HENRY SNEAD, NATHANIEL CHAMBERS, THOMAS MOORMAN.

Pp. 150-151: Blank.

Page 152: 1 May 1758, JAMES DOWNING of Anson, yeoman to WM WATKINS of same, carpenter, for s 10 proc. money...tract granted to JAMES TERRY 26 Nov 1757 200 A, adj. JOHN WEBB, N side Hitchcock Cr....conveyed by sd. TERRY to sd. DOWNING 1757....JAMES DOWNING (SEAL), Wit: SAML DAVIS, WM HAILEY (H), GEO. CARTER.

Page 153: Blank.

Page 154: 24 Oct 1757, RICHARD DARMOND of Anson, labourer, to JAMES LEWIS of same, trader, for ₺50 proc. money...land granted to DARMOND 27 Sept 1757, 200 A on S side Mill Cr....RICHARD DARMOND (D) (SEAL), Wit: JNO BROWN (₮), JNO. MISHO, JNO. LONG.

Page 155: Blank.

Pp. 156-158: 9 & 10 Sept 1757, THOMAS HOLLINGSWORTH of Granville Co., SC, son & heir at law of JOSEPH HOLLINGSWORTH decd, to WM HOLLINGSWORTH, his brother, (lease s5, release ₺50)...land on S side Broad R., on lower Fish Dam Cr., called Clarks Mill Cr., granted 4 Sept 1753, 300 A...THOS HOLLINGSWORTH (SEAL), by ISAAC COX, atty. Wit: ADAM McCOOL, ISAAC COOK, EDWD. MUSGROVE.
          [This land now in Union County, S. C.]

Pp. 159-161: Blank.

Page 162: 6 June 1757, ELIJAH KELLAM of Anson, JR., to DARBY CAVE, for ₺12...100 A on upper side Naked Cr., granted to KELLAM 26 May 1757...ELIJAH KELLAM (SEAL), Wit: JNO. HAMER, M. BROWN.

Pp. 163-164: 27 July 1757, WILLIAM HICKS of Anson, for JOHN HICKS, JR. for ₺5... land on N side Pee Dee, 150 A part of a grant to GEORGE SINIOR, 400 A, 1743... WM HICKS (SEAL), Wit: ALEXANDER GORDON, JOHN BIDINGFIELD, JOSPH. KEMP (K).

Page 165: Blank.

Page 166: 23 Jan 1758, JOHN WEBB of Anson, planter, to CHRISTOPHER HUNT, planter, for ₺20 proc. money... land on N side Pee Dee, adj. BENJAMIN MIMS, JOSEPH HALL, S side Hitchcock Cr....1/2 of 300 A granted to sd. WEBB 25 May 1757...JOHN WEBB (SEAL), Wit: JAMES DOWNING, SAML. DAVIS.

Pp. 167-168: Blank.

Pp. 169-170: 4 Oct 1755, SAMUEL YOUNG of Rowan, to ALEXANDER McCLAIN of same, for ₺10 proc. money...270 A in Anson Co., adj. TYLA [TYREE?] HARRISES corner, S bank Catawba, above mouth of S fork Catawba...LEEPERs line...granted to sd. YOUNG 3 Oct xxix year of his majesties reign [1755?]...SAML YOUNG (SEAL), Wit: JOHN KERR, WM KERR.

Page 171: Blank.

Pp. 172-174: 5 & 6 Nov 1756, HANCE ADAM SNIDER & wf SARAH, Blacksmith, to JOHN
        WALKER, cooper, (lease s5, release ₺40 proc. money)...300 A on both
sides Leopards Cr., on W side Catawba, granted 8 Oct 1751 to ROBERT LEOPARD
[LEEPER?], sold to SNIDER 25 & 26 Feb 1754...ADAM SNIDER (SEAL)SARAH SNIDER (SEAL),
[both signed in German], Wit: Two German signatures, ANDREW BARRY, J.P.

Pp. 175-176: Blank.

Pp. 177-180: 19 & 20 Oct 1758, ROBERT BREVARD & wf SARAH of Rowan, to CHARLES HARRIS,
        farmer, of Anson (lease s5, release ₺65 Va. money)...600 A on br. of
Rocky River, granted to BREVARD 25 Feb 1754...ROBERT BREVARD (SEAL), SARAH BREVARD
(SEAL), Wit: ROBERT HARRIS, WILLIAM HARRIS.

Page 181: Blank.

Page 182: 25 July 1758, JOHN WEBB Of Anson, yoeman, to ISRAEL SNEAD, Planter, for
        ₺15 proc. money...part of 350 A on N sd. Pee Dee, adj. BENJAMIN MIMS,
S side Hitchcock Cr., JOSEPH HALL...100 A...granted to WEBB 25 May 1757...JOHN
WEBB (SEAL), Wit: THOS MOORMAN, WM WATKINS, CHRISTOPHER CLARK (C).

Pp. 184-184: Blank.

Page 185: 27 July 1758, WM NUTT Of Anson, planter, to WM BROWN, of same, planter,
        for ₺20...part of a grant to WM ALEXANDER, on E side Catawba, near bank
of 12 Mile Cr...WILLIAM NUTT (SEAL), Wit: HEN. DOWNS, JAMES LEAM.
        [This land now in S. C.]

Pp. 186-187: 22 July 1758, ANDREW NUTT & wf JANETT, of Anson, to WM BROWN of same,
        for ₺12...land on S side mouth of 12 Miles Cr., E side Catawba...adj.
ROBERT McCORKLES, SAML BURNETTS line, WM NUTTS line. .ANDW NUTT (SEAL), JENNETT
NUTT (SEAL), Wit: ROBERT McCLANACHAN, ADAM McCOOL.
        [This land now in S. C.]

Page 188: Blank.

Page 189: Anson County, St. George's Parish: BENJAMIN FOREMAN to wf MARY...all
        goods and chattels...20 Feb 1758...BENJ. FOREMAN (SEAL), Wit: SAMUEL
DAVIS, JOHN JAMES (‡), LAWRENCE O BRYAN.

Pp. 190-192: 29 & 30 Apr 1757, JOHN HANNA to MAGNES SIMONSON, both of Anson, (lease
        s5, release ₺6)...land on S side Broad R., on the lower Fish Dam
Crk., adj. THOS HOLLINGSWORTH, 150 A....JOHN HANNA (‡ H) (SEAL), Wit: ROBERT
McCLENACHAN, WILLIAM MOORE.

Pp. 193-194: Blank.

Pp. 195-196: 4 May 1754, JOHN OATS of Anson, planter, to JOHN HANNA of same, for
        ₺6 Va. money...land on S side Broad R., upper Fish Dam Cr., adj.
JNO. CLARKS survey...granted to sd. OATS 30 Aug 1753, 360 A...JOHN OATES (SEAL),
Wit: JOSEPH HOLLINGSWORTH, GEORGE STRODE.
        [This land now in S. C.]

Page 197: 10 Jan 1757, THOMAS LAND Of Anson, miller, to JOHN LEE of SC, for ₺16 NC
        money...546 A on S side Catawba, N side Rocky Cr....granted to TOWNSEND

ROBINSON 3 Oct 1755...sold to LAND 20 Oct 1756 [?]... THOMAS LAND (I) (SEAL), Wit
ELEANOR LAND (A) (SEAL), Wit: JNO. SALLIS, ROBERT McCLENACHAN.

Pp. 198-199: Blank.

Pp. 200-202: 10 & 11 Sept 1759, SAMUEL ZICKLEY & wf JEAN, of Anson, to JAMES POTTS,
            of same, for Ł20...175 A granted to ZICKLEG 25 Feb 1754...SAMUEL
ZICKLEG ( ) (SEAL), JEAN ZICKLEG ( ) (SEAL), Wit: NATHL. ALEXANDER, JOHN MOORE.

Page 203: Blank.

Pp. 204-207: 16 & 17 Feb 1758, PRESTON GOFORTH & wf RACHEL of Anson, to JOHN PATTON,
            of same, (lease s10, release Ł50)...250 A on E side S fork Catawba,
adj. JAS. WILSON...subdivided from tracts of 300 A & 400 A...PRESTON GOFORTH (X)
(SEAL), RACHEL GOFORTH (X) (SEAL), Wit: ALEXANDER DAVIS, JONATHAN LEWIS.

Page 208: Blank.

Page 209: 9 Apr 1755, SAMUEL WILSON of Anson, to JOHN PARKER of Rowan, for Ł100 NC
          money...land on S side Clarks River, at mouth of Fishers Cr...400 A
granted to sd. WILSON 28 Sept 1754...SAMUEL WILSON (SEAL), Wit: PIERCE COSVILLE,
PERSHANNA SHERRILL.

Page 210: Blank.

Pp. 211-212: 25 Sept 1758, THOS LAND of Anson, to THOMAS ADDISON of same, for Ł 20
            ...land conveyed from JOHN LEONARD to THOMAS LAND ____ 6 Apr 1753
___ A, on which SAMUEL WAGGONER hath made some improvements, on W side Catawba...
THOS LAND (I) (SEAL), ELEANOR LAND (A) (SEAL), Wit: ROBERT McCLENACHAN, R. DOWNS.

Page 213: Blank.

Page 214: 28 Aug 1758, NATHL CHAMBERS, late of Anson, planter, to WM COX, of same,
          planter, for Ł25 proc. money...land on S side Pee Dee, Island Cr., 500
A granted to JOHN NEWBERRY 7 Oct 1747,...NATHL. CHAMBERS (SEAL), Wit: DANIEL
MURFREE (D), WM FIELDING (X).

Page 215: Blank.

Page 216: 10 Apr 1758, HENRY WALKER of Anson, to AARON SMITH of same, for Ł30 proc.
          money...part of 300 A on S side Great Pee Dee, adj. ROBERT PARKS on
Walkers Island, adj. land WALKER sold to JAMES ADAMS, decd...75 A...granted to
JOHN GILES 26 Nov 1746...HENRY WALKER (SEAL), Wit: JOHN HALL, WM GAMBLE (m),
ROBERT LEE (R).

Page 217: 18 Oct 1758, EDMUND CARTLEDGE, planter, of Anson, to TILLOTSON KEBLE,
          for Ł100...land on N side Pee Dee, Cartledges Cr...640 A granted to sd.
CARTLEDGE 26 Nov 1757... E. CARTLEDGE (SEAL), Wit: SAML O BRYAN, THOS KEMP (T),
SARAH WALKER.

Page 218: Blank.

Page 219: 27 May 1758, WILLIAM PLUNKETT of Anson, planter, to AMBROSE STEELE, of same, yeoman, for Ⱡ20...225 A granted to PLUNKETT 25 May 1757 on N side Old Mill Cr., S side Pee Dee...WILLIAM PLUNKETT (W) (SEAL), Wit: JAMES HILDRETH, JOHN HORNBECK, JOHN HORNBECK, JR. (J).

Page 220: Blank.

Page 221: 25 Oct 1758, THOMAS HARRINGTON to GEORGE GIBSON, planter,of Anson, for Ⱡ20 Va. money...land on N side Pee Dee, on No fork Mountain Creek... 300 A...THOMAS HARRINGTON (X) (SEAL), Wit: JONATHAN DOWNS, WM UNDERWOOD, ANDW. BARRY.

Pp. 222-223: 20 Jan 1759, RICHARD COUSARD & wf MARTHA of Craven Co., SC, to GEORGE WHITE of Anson, for Ⱡ40...302 A on N side Catawba, Gills Cr. about one mile from sd. COUSARDs, granted 24 Sept 1754...RICHARD COUSARD (SEAL), MARTHA COUSARD (Λ) (SEAL), Wit: ROBERT McCLENACHAN, WILLIAM DAVIS.

Page 224: Blank.

Pp. 225-226: 27 Sept 1758, THOMAS LAND & wf ELEANOR of Anson, to REPENTANCE TOWNSEND of same, for Ⱡ5...part of 312 A on W side Catawba, conveyed from ROBT. McCLENACHAN to LAND by virute of a patent 23 Feb 1754, W side Mill Cr...THOS LAND (Ⱡ) (SEAL), ELEANOR LAND (A) (SEAL), Wit: ROBERT McCLENACHAN, R. DOWNS.

Pp. 227-228: 24 Jan 1759, JOHN WEBB of Anson, planter, to ISRAEL SNEAD, planter, for Ⱡ3s10...land on N side Hitchcocks Cr., below mouth of Long Branch, adj.WEBB...350 A granted to WEBB 25 May 1751, 35 A...JOHN WEBB (SEAL), Wit: JOHN ELKINS (Ⱡ), WILLIAM WATKINS, HEZEKIAH WATKINS.

Page 229: 16 Nov 1758, JACOB COCKERHAM of Anson, to RICHARD ADAMS, planter,of same, for Ⱡ10 proc. money...land on S side S fork Mountain Cr., GRAIMES fork...100 A granted 21 Oct 1758...JACOB COCKERHAM (X) (SEAL), Wit: CHS. ROBINSON, JAS. HUTCHINS.

Pp. 230-231: Blank.

Page 232: 17 Jan 1759, JOSEPH HALL of Anson, planter, to WM WATKINS of same, for Ⱡ10 Va. money...land on NE side Hitchcock Cr., at mouth of Marshy Branch ...100 A granted to sd. HALL 20 Feb 1754...JOSEPH HALL (SEAL), Wit: JOHN WEBB, JOHN ELKINS (Ⱡ).

Page 233: Blank.

Page 234: 30 Nov 1758, JOHN TABOR, JR. of Anson, planter, to THOMAS CONNERLY, planter, for Ⱡ10...land on S side Hitchcock Cr., 150 A adj. RICHARD BRADFORD... granted to TABOR 1 July 1758...JOHN TABOR (SEAL), Wit: THOS MOORMAN, JOHN BYARS (J), BENJA. MOORMAN (B).

Page 235: 2 Apr 1758, WM STONE of Anson, planter, to SAMUEL PARSONS of same, for Ⱡ20...100 A on both sides Little River of Pee Dee, granted to STONE 20 Mar 1757...WILLIAM STONE (ₘ) (SEAL), Wit: JOHN COCKERILL, WM CRITTENDEN, ELEANOR CRITTENDEN.

Page 236: Blank.

VOLUME 5

Page 237: 8 Mar 1759, DAVID HILDRETH of Anson, planter, to CHRISTOPHER CLARK of
same, planter, for b1 s8 proc. money...land granted to HOPKINS HOWELL
11 Oct 1749 on S side Pee Dee, Watery branch of Jones Cr....DAVID HILDRETH (SEAL),
Wit: MARSHALL DEEGGE, RICHARD GRIFFEN (X).

Page 238: Blank.

Pp. 239-241: 9 & 10 July 1755, JAMES WILLSON of Anson, to JOHN PATTON of Augusta Co.,
Va., (release b25 Va. money)...land on Allisons Cr., granted to sd.
WILLSON 1753, 424 A...JAMES WILLSON (SEAL), Wit: CHARLES COGDELL, SAMUEL YOUNG.
Acknowledged 25 May 1757, PETER HENLY, C. J.

Pp. 242-243: Blank.

Page 244: 8 June 1754, JAMES MACKELVEAN of Johnson Co., Esq., to RICHARD CASWELL, JR.
of same, Gentm., for b50 proc. money...land on N side Pee Dee, adj. ED-
WARD GRIFFETH, STAFFORD...granted to MACKELVEAN 23 Mar 1747...JAMES MACKELVEAN
(SEAL), Wit:FRANCIS MACKLEVEAN, ELIZABETH MACKELVEAN.
Proven by FRANCIS MACKELVEAN 12 Sept 1754. JAS. HASELL, C. T.

Page 245: 24 July 1757, JAMES MUCKLEROY of Anson, Blacksmith, to THOMAS LACY of same,
for b5 proc. money...land granted 26 May 1757, 350 A, adj. ARCHIBALD BLACKES
...JAMES MUCKLEROY (+++) (SEAL), Wit: WM BLEWITT, JOHN LILLY, DARBY CAVES (⟩⟨).

Page 246: Blank.

Page 247: 22 Nov 1757, WM BYRD of Anson, Labourer, to JOHNATHAN LEWELLEN, cooper,
for b30 proc. money...land on Et. branch of Hitchcocks Cr., NE side Pee
Dee, adj. THOMAS STAFFORD WILLIAMS...granted to RICHARD BRADFORD, 300 A, 15 Mar
1756...conveyed to WILLIAM TERRY, then to sd. BYRD...WILL BYRD Wit: WILL TERRY,
WILL BLEWETT, E. CARTLEDGE.

Pp. 248-249: 28 Oct 1758, ANTHONY HUTCHINS of Anson, Exr. of L. W. & T. of JOHN
LEETH, decd., to JAMES PICKETT, JR. for b20 s15 proc. money...land
on S side Pee Dee, both sides Cedar Cr., granted to FRANCIS MACKELWEAN 11 Apr 1749,
conveyed to SAML FRENCH 17 Jan 1753 & 5 Sept 1753 to LEETH...ANTHO. HUTCHINS
(SEAL), Wit: JOHN COLLSON, BENJ. RENNOLDS.

Page 250: 3 July 1758, THOMAS PRESTWOOD of Anson, to ANTHONY HUTCHINS, for b10...
100 A granted to GRIGG, conveyed to JOSEPH WHITE, then sold by JAS.
PICKETT, JR. Sheriff at public vendue...THOS PRESTWOOD (SEAL), Wit: GEO. THERSTON,
JAS. PICKETT, HUM. YARBROUGH.

Pp. 251-252: 24 Oct 1759, ARCHIBALD BLAKE, of Anson, planter, to CHARLES MEDLOCK
of same, planter, for b16 proc. money...land on NE side Pee Dee, both
sides Solomons Cr., adj. JAS. MUCKELROY, 200 A...granted to MUCKELROY, 26 May 1757,
330 A...ARCHIBALD BLACK (SEAL), Wit: JOHN FROHOCK, M. BROWN.

Page 253: 26 July 1756, JOHN MOORMAN of Anson, to FRANCIS CLARK, planter, for b5 Va.
money...250 A granted to MOORMAN 25 Feb 1754...JOHN MOORMAN (SEAL), Wit:
JAMES MUCKLEROY, JOHN HOUSE.

89

Page 254: Blank.

Page 255: 31 July 1759, GEORGE HILLIENS of Anson, planter, to JOHN PARNOLD, for
£10...25 A on E side Little River...granted to HILEN 11 Oct 1749...
GEORGE HELMS (SEAL), Wit: RICHARD YARBROUGH, DENNIS NOWLAND (2), MARY ANN FRANCIS (X).

Page 256: Blank.

Page 257: 14 Mar 1754, ISAIAH FILTON, son of ANN BONIDY, late of Craven Co., SC,
planter, do put myself apprentice to DANIEL REES to learn the art &
mystry of Plaining for 14 years...ASIAH HILTON (SEAL), DANIEL REES (SEAL), ANN
BONIDY (X) (SEAL), Wit: EVAN REES (rm), J. CURRY.

Page 258: I DANIEL REES Do Sign over my right and title to the within indenture to
JOHN HAGAN 27 ___ 1757. DANIEL REES, Wit: MARY REES (W).
I do sign over my right and title of the within indenture to JOHN LINN, JR. for value
Recd. 5 May 1757. JOHN HAGAN, Wit: JAS. LINN, WILLIAM HAGAN.

Pp. 258-259: 26 Apr 1758, THOMAS MOORMAN, of Anson, planter,to FRANCIS CLARK, planter, for£2s10(?) proc. money...part of land on NE side Pee Dee, granted
to sd. MOORMAN, 400 A...200 A...granted 26 May 1757...THOS MOORMAN (SEAL), Wit:
JOSEPH ATTAWAY, THOMAS WARD (X), BARNABA KEPPER.

Page 260: 25 Apr 1759, PETER PRESLAR of Anson, planter, to ZACHARY PHILIPS, planter,
for£5...land on S side Pee Dee, adj. WM SMITH, 25 A, the mouth of Brown
Cr....confirmed to PRESLAR by deed 6 Dec 1755...PETER PRESLER (P) (SEAL), Wit: M.
BROWN, AARON SMITH.

Page 261: Blank.

Pp. 262-263: 22 June 1756, JOHN SPAN of Johnson Co., to AMBROSE JOSHUA SMITH of
Rowan, for £150 Va. money...3 tracts: (1)400 A on Great Pee Dee, on
Walkers Island, about 2 miles below mouth of Rockey River (2) 100(?) A below mouth
of Browns Cr, Youngs Island...(3) 300 A below mouth of Dry Cr....granted to ROBERT
PARKS by 3 patents 28 Sept 1745 & 14 Mar 1745....Made over to JOHN SPAN 14 Oct
1747 & proven 14 Sept 1749...registered in Bladen Co. Book C., folio 126, June
26th 1750...JOHN SPAN (SEAL), Wit: STEPHEN CADE, JOHN CULPEPPER, ABRAHAM HAY (A).

Page 264: 27 July 1756, ALEC. McCOY of Anson, planter, to JAMES MUCKLEROY, Black-
smith, for £45 proc. money...land on S side Pee Dee, adj. land granted to
EDMUND CARTLIDGE, now McCOYs...granted to JOHN McCOY decd, 15 May 1756...ALCE
McCOY (+) (SEAL), Wit: JOHN BLASSINGAME, JACOB PER___.

Page 265: Blank.

Page 266: 9 Oct 1756, STEPHEN BROWN of Anson, to VIOLET PRIMROSE of same, for
£10 proc. money...100 A on a branch of Cartledges Cr., granted to WM.
NEWBERRY, 17 Nov 1753...BROWN (SEAL), Wit: JNO. HAMER, SARAH FIRTH.

Page 267: 8 Aug 1759, SAMUEL MACBY of ANSON, planter, to THOMAS HARRINGTON, for
£10 proc. money...100 A in Cheeks Cr., granted to MACBY 17 Mar 1756...
SAML MACBY (SEAL), Wit: JACOB COCKERHAM (X), CHARLES ROBINSON.

Page 268: Blank.

Page 269: 27 Jan 1757, ISAAC FALKENBURGH of Anson, planter, to JAMES MUCKLEROY,
          Blacksmith, of same, for Ł32 s10 proc. money...150 A granted to JACOB
FALKENBURGH 2 Mar 1754...ISAAC FALKENBURGH (Ɨ), (SEAL), Wit: WILLIAM HOWELL, JAMES
ADAMS, JAMES MUTHLK (??).

Page 270: Blank.

Page 271: 20 Dec 1756, JACOB FALKENBURGH, planter, to ISAAC FALKENBURGH for Ł20...
          150 A, granted to JACOB 2 Mar 1754...JACOB FALKENBURGH (Ɨ)(SEAL), Wit:
PHILIP HOWELL, NICHOLAS BROADAWAY (N), WILLIAM HOWELL.

Page 272: Blank.

Pp. 273-274: 12 & 13 Oct 1756, THOMAS COYLE & wf HELEN of Anson, to JOHN HAYES of
             same, for Ł10...150 A on both sides Mill Cr., S side Pee Dee, part of
400 A...THOMAS COYLE (0) (SEAL), HELEN COYLE (X) (SEAL), Wit: ELISHA PARKER (P),
ABNER ARENDALL, ARCHIB D GRAHAM.

Pp. 275-276: Blank.

Pp. 277-278: 18 Jan 1759, THOS REYNOLDS & wf MARY for natural love & affection to
             WILLIAM RYNOLDS...land on Kings Cr. of Broad River, 300 A granted to
sd. THOMAS 30 Aug 1753...THOMAS RYNOLDS (X) (SEAL), MARY RYNOLDS (X) (SEAL), Wit:
RICHARD RYNOLDS (X), JNO. THOMAS.

Pp. 279-280: 18 Jan 1759, THOS RYNOLDS & wf MARY to JOHN RYNOLDS, for natural love
             & affection...250 A on Buffalow Cr. of Broad River, adj. ALEX. RYNOLDS...
tranted to THOMAS RYNOLDS 30 Aug 1753...THOS RYNOLDS (X) (SEAL), MARY RYNOLDS (X)
(SEAL), Wit: RICHARD RYNOLDS (X), JNO. THOMAS.

Pp. 281-283: 17 & 18 Apr 1759, JOHN ALEXANDER of Anson, to JOHN BURNSIDE of Anson
             (lease s5, release Ł20 NC money)...land on S side Broad River, No
fork of Thicketty Cr., above WM. GREENS...400 A...JOHN ALEXANDER (SEAL), Wit: JOHN
THOMAS, JAMES ROBINSON, JOHN PATTON.

Page 284: Blank.

Page 285: 8 Aug 1760, WILLIAM PHILLIPS of Anson, to WM WILKINS of same, for Ł50...
          land on S side Pee Dee, Goulds fork, granted to PHILLIPS 1756...300 A...
WILLIAM PHILLIPS (SEAL), Wit: ANTHONY HUTCHINS, WILLIAM FIELDEN.

Pp. 286-289: 25 & 26 June 1754, HENRY O NEAL of Rowan Co., to JAS. JOHNSTON of
             same, (lease s5, release Ł20 proc. money)...land on S side Camp Cr.,
adj. THOS LEEs plantation, 270 A...HENRY O NEAL (SEAL), Wit: DAVID KERR, WALTER
LINDSAY.

Pp. 290-291: __ Oct 1759, JAMES JOHNSTON of Rowan, to STEPHEN GAMBLE, WILLIAM
             GAMBLE, & JOHN GAMBLE, all of Anson, for Ł30 proc. money...land granted
to HENRY ONEAL 17 May 1754, adj. plantation of DAVID KERR, 270 A...JAMES JOHNSTON
(SEAL), Wit: R. McCLENACHAN, HENRY WHITE, DAVID KERR.

Page 292: 1 Feb 1758, PETER OYSTER & wf MARY of Anson, to PETER CLUBB of same, for
Ł20...land on both sides Leepers Cr., including CATHEYs & COBURNs camp,
200 A granted to ROBERT LEEPER 31 Mar 1753, sold to OYSTER 25 Feb 1754...PETER
OYSTER (SEAL), MARY OYSTER (O) (SEAL), Wit: JEAN THOMAS, JOHN THOMAS,WILL PAUL (X).

Page 293: Blank.

Page 294: 1 Feb 1758, PETER OYSTER & wf MARY to PETER CLUBB, for s.5...part of 310
A granted to OYSTER 24 Sept 1754, adj. LEEPER...50 A...PETER OYSTER (SEAL),
MARY OYSTER (O) (SEAL), Wit: JOHN THOMAS, JEAN THOMAS, WILL PAUL (W).

Page 285: Blank.

Pp. 296-298: 5 & 6 Jan 1759, JAMES ARMSTRONG & wf JEAN of Anson, to WM SMITH of
same, for (lease s5, release Ł15 proc. money)...229 A on Beaverdam
Cr., that runs into S fork Catawba...granted to ARMSTRONG 30 Aug 1753...JAMES
ARMSTRONG (SEAL), JEAN ARMSTRONG (O) (SEAL), Wit: MARTIN ARMSTRONG, JOHN THOMAS.

Pp. 299-300: 31 Mar 1759, JOHN ANDERSON & wf MARGARET of Anson, planter, to ROBERT
BOYD of same, Weaver, for Ł27...393 A on Long Cr....granted to ANDERSON
17 May 1754...JOHN ANDERSON (SEAL), MARGT. ANDERSON (O) (SEAL), Wit: RICHD BERRY,
JENNETT BERRY.

Page 301: Blank.

Page 302: 6 Mar 1758, SAMUEL YOUNG of Rowan, to HUGH ROBINSON of same, for Ł9 proc.
money...land on N side Catawba, on N bank Waxhaw Cr., adj. JOHN LINNS,
formerly JOSEPH WHITES...granted to YOUNG 31 Mar 175_...SAMUEL YOUNG (SEAL), Wit:
JOHN WITHROW (✗), JAMES STORRY (J).

Page 303: 23 July 1759, PHILIP HERNDON of Anson, carpenter, to NICHOLAS WHITE,of
same, for Ł15 proc. money...320 A, 1/2 of 640 A granted to JAMES BABER
& conveyed to HERNDON, on SW side Pee Dee, granted 22 May 1741...PHILIP HERNDON
(SEAL), Wit: HEZA. RUSS, ROBT. ABRAHAM, WM DUKES.

Page 304: Blank.

Page 305: 5 Dec 1758, WILLIAM NUTT, SR. of Anson, to son ANDREW NUTT, all interest
in 162 A wheron AMBROSE MILLS now dwells...to son WM NUTT, JR. 272 A,
part of land I now live I now live on, surveyed by FRANCIS BEATY...to son JOHN NUTT
300 A where I now live...my wife ELEN...WM NUTT (W) (SEAL), Wit: NATHANIEL WALKER,
JAMES McCORKEL, HUGH McCAIN.

Page 306: Blank.

Page 307: 20 Sept 1760, JAMES McMANUS & wf MARY of Anson, planter, to FREDERICK
HENDRIC of same, for Ł30 Va. money..lower end of 999 A, granted 1750,
on both sides linches creek...150 A...JAMES McMANUS (SEAL), MARY McMANUS(SEAL),
Wit: ISAAC WEIDNER, GEORGE MILLER.

Page 308: Blank.

Page 309: 20 Sept 1760, JAMES & MARY MCMANUS to PETER GYST, for ₺20 Va. money...
part of 300 A granted 1756 on Wildcat Cr...JAMES McMANUS (SEAL), MARY
McMANUS (SEAL), Wit: ISAAC WEIDNER, FREDERICK HENDRIC.

Pp. 310-311: 15 Jan 1760, REPENTANCE TOWNSEND of Anson, yeoman, to JOHN LANTS,
Blacksmith, part of grant to ROBT. McCLENACHAN 25 Feb 1754, sold to
THOMAS LAND, then to TOWNSEND on W side Mill Creek...REPENTANCE TOWNSEND (SEAL),
MARY TOWNSEND (X) (SEAL), Wit: ROBERT McCLENACHAN, JOSEPH STEELL.

Page 312: Blank.

Page 313: 20 July 1757, JACOB BROWN of Anson, to JOHN HILL, for ₺15 proc. money...
land on S side Catawba, part of 1000 A granted to JOHN KELION 30 Sept
1749...conveyed to JACOB BROWN 1 Jan 1754, adj. PHILIP ERHART, 250 A...JACOB BROWN
(SEAL), Wit: GEORGE BROWN, JOHN THOMAS.

Pp. 314-315: 16 Nov 1759, THOMAS BINGHAM of SC, carpenter, to JOHN CRAWFORD of
Anson, for ₺100 proc. money...300 A on HItchcocks Creek, granted 4
Apr 1750 to "John Crawford South Carolina" & conveyed to BINGHAM 13 Dec 1755...
THOMAS BINGHAM (SEAL), Wit: THOS BLASSENGAM (B), JOHN HUSBANDS, Jurat, JOHN LONG.

Pp. 316-317: 27 Apr 1759, JAMES DOWNING of Anson, yeoman, to THOMAS CRAWFORD, for
₺8 s5 proc. money...part of 300 A granted to ENOS THOMAS 1 July 1758,
100 A...JAMES DOWNING (SEAL), Wit: RICHARD YARBROUGH, NICHOLAS WOLFORD (X), JOHN
CRAWFORD, JR.

Page 318: [no date], WM TERRY of Anson, for love & good will & affection to son
JAMES TERRY...300 A on S side Pee Dee, St. George's Parish at mouth
of Savannah Cr....WILL. TERRY (SEAL), Wit: NICHOLAS BOND, JOS. CULCASTER, JAMES
ALLEY.

Page 319: Blank.

Pp. 320-321: 26 Aug 1760, THOS McKELHENEY & wf JEAN of Anson Co., yeoman, to WM
RICHARDSON of same, for ₺30, 150 A...part of a grant 3 Apr 1752, 300
A on north side of Catawba River...THOMAS MCKELHENY (SEAL), JEAN McKELHENY (X)
(SEAL), Wit: ROBT. McCLENACHAN, SAMUEL DUNLAP, SAMUEL THOMPSON.

Pp. 322-323: 19 July 1760, JAMES ROBINSON & wf HANNAH of Anson, to ROBERT GANT
TYLER of same, for ₺20...400 A on both sides Camp Creek sold to sd.
ROBINSON by JAMES PICKETT, high sheriff of Anson Co., 20 Mar 1757...1/2 of 400 A,
200 A...JAMES ROBINSON (SEAL), HANNAH ROBINSON (O) (SEAL), Wit: ROBT. McCLENACHAN,
ELIZABETH SELLERS, RICHD. HUGHS.

Page 324: Blank.

Page 325: 5 Jan 1760, PHILIP WALKER, planter, of Craven Co., SC, to JOHN LATTA of
Anson, for ₺20...land on S side Catawba, S side Fishing Creek, near
JACOB TAYLORs line...300 A...PHILIP WALKER (SEAL), Wit: R. M. McCLENACHAN, JOS.
STEELE.

Page 326: Blank.

Page 327: 27 SEpt 1760, DAVID KERR & wf JEAN of Anson Co., to JAMES DUNN of same

for Ŀ40...160 A on Cain Creek...granted 6 Apr 1753...DAVID KERR (SEAL), JEAN
KERR (SEAL), Wit: ROBT. McCLENACHAN, A. (?) BATTREY.

Page 328: Blank.

Pp. 329-330: 28 Oct 1760, ROBERT McCLENACHAN & wf ELIZABETH to JOHN CASTOLO, Cord-
            winder, for Ŀ20 proc. money...land on W side Catawba, adj. THOS.
WILLIAMS plantation, part of 939 A granted to sd. MCCLENACHAN 24 Sept 1754...100
A...ROBERT McCLENACHAN (SEAL), ELIZABETH McCLENACHAN (SEAL), Wit: JACOB TAYLOR,
WM KENNEDY, SAMUEL THOMPSON.

Page 331: 19 Oct 1761, HENRY DOWNS of Anson Co., planter, to WM DOWNS of same,
           for Ŀ5 va. money...land on W side LIttle River, near DYSONs line...500
A, granted to ROBT. MILLS 22 Nov 1746...HENRY DOWNS (SEAL), Wit: WM CRITTENDON,
JAMES MADISON, JNOTH. DOWNS.

Page 332: Blank.

Page 333: 30 Oct 1760, WM PHILLIPS of Anson, to JOHN THOMPSON of same, for Ŀ21 s10
           ...land on S side Pee Dee on E side of grindstone fork of Goulds fork at
ZACHARY PHILLIPS...300 A granted to sd. WM 26 Nov 1757...WILLIAM PHILLIPS (SEAL),
Wit: DAVID DUMAS, JOEL PHILLIPS (X), THOMAS TALLANT.

Pp. 334-335: 20 Sept 1760, JAMES McMANUS of Anson, & wf MARY , planter, to ISAAC
            WIDNER, for Ŀ32 s10...land on Linches Creek, part of 999 A granted
1750...100 A...JAMES McMANUS (SEAL), MARY McMANUS (SEAL), Wit: JOHN DAY, FREDERICK
HENDRICK.

Page 336: 7 Sept 1759, HENRY FALKENBURG, SR. of Anson, to grandson HENRY FALKENBURG
           son of JACOB FALKENBURG, for natural love..., 134 A on Smith Creek, S side
Pee Dee also an iron gray horse...HENRY FALKENBURG (Ŧ B) (SEAL), Wit: BENJ. MARTIN,
SAML. BERRY.

Page 337: 24 July 1759, PETER PRESLAR of Anson Co., to JOHN HENRY of same, for Ŀ __
           ...land on S side of N fork of Little Pee Dee, 100 A granted to ____ & ‾
sold to THOMAS UNDERWOOD 24 Sept 1754, then to PETER PRESLAR 18 Dec 1755...PETER
PRESLAR (P) (SEAL), Wit: WM BLEWETT, M. BROWN.

Page 338: Blank.

Page 339: 6 Sept 1760, WALTER GIBSON of Anson, planter, to JOSEPH CULPEPER of same,
           planter, for good will & respect...100 A adj. Rockey River on spring Br...
WALTER GIBSON (W) (SEAL), Wit: JNO. CULPEPER, WILLIAM CULPEPER, JNOTH. DOWNS.

Page 340: Blank.

Page 341: 20 Sept 1759, JOHN BROWN of Anson, Cowkeeper, to JORDAN GIBSON of same,
           planter, for Ŀ50...land on N side Hitchcock Cr., granted to BROWN 6 Mar
1759, adj. JOHN CRAWFORD, JAMES HALLES, including ABRAHAM SELLERS improvement...
300 A...JOHN BROWN (Ŧ) (SEAL), Wit: M. BROWN, JAMES BROWN.

Page 342: Blank.

Page 343: 10 Dec 1760, THOMAS CONNALLY of Anson, to JOHN JAMES of same, for ₺30 ...300 A granted 5 Dec 1760 on N side Hitchcocks Cr...THOMAS CONNALLY (T) (SEAL), Wit: M. BROWN, ELIZABETH BROWN.

Pp. 344-345: 5 Feb 1761, MORGAN BROWN of Anson, yeoman, to GEORGE PENNINGTON of same, for ₺17 s 15 proc. money...land on N side Great Pee Dee, on S fork Mountain Creek, adj. GEORGE GOULDS land...600 A granted 15 Mar 1756... MORGAN BROWN (SEAL), Wit: CHARLES SPADEN (X), _____ R. POSTON ( ).

Page 346: Blank.

Pp. 347-349: 5 & 25 Feb 1761, ROBERT TINNEN & wf CATHERINE of Anson to ALLEN ALEX-ANDER of same (lease s5, release ₺35)... 164 A granted to sd. TINNEN 31 Mar 1753...ROBERT TINNEN (SEAL), CATHERINE TINNEN (T) (X) (SEAL), Wit: NATHL. ALEXANDER, EBENEZER ALEXANDER.

Page 350: 20 May 1760, GEORGE RENICK & wf MARY of Anson, to ABRAHAM SCOTT, for ₺15 ...land on S side Catawba, No fork of Fishing Creek, called Wild Cat Branch, 400 A granted to RENICK 28 Mar 1753...GEORGE RENICK (SEAL), MARY RENICK (SEAL), Wit: SAM MEEL, CHARLES McPETERS, JOHN THOMAS.

Page 351: Blank.

Pp. 352-353: 4 July 1759, JAMES PICKETT, JR. to JAMES PICKETT, SR. of Anson, for ₺90 ...200 A, part of 500 A granted 26 Sept 1746 to JOSEPH WHITE on S side Pee Dee, adj. JNO. LEETH... conveyed by JOSEPH WHITE to HENRY FALKENBURG 2 Apr 1748 and then to sd. JAMES PICKETT 28 Oct 1755, then to ANTHONY HUTCHINS 20 Jan 1757, then to sd. PICKETT, J.R 29 July 1757...also 100 A conveyed by ISAAC NORMAN to JAMES PICKETT 15 July 1753, then to ANTHONY HUTCHINS 20 Jan 1757, then to PICKETT, JR. 29 July 1758... J. PICKETT, JR. (SEAL), Wit: JESSE SUMMERALL (X), ANTHONY HUTCHINS.

Page 354: Blank.

Page 355: 10 June 1759, JAMES PICKETT JR. to JOEL PHILLIPS for 35 pistoles...200 A on both sides Cedar Cr., S side Great Pee Dee...granted to FRANCIS Mc-ELEVEAN 11 Apr 1749, conveyed by him to SAMUEL FRENCH & reconveyed by sd. SAML. FRENCH to sd. McELVEAN 17 Jan 1750, then conveyed to JOHN LEETH, decd & sold by ANTHONY HUTCHINS, Exr. to L. W. & T. of sd. JOHN LEETH to JAMES PICKETT, JR. 28 Oct 1758...J. PICKETT, JR. (SEAL), Wit: JOHN COLLSON, BENJ. RENNOLDS, ANTH. HUTCHINS.

Page 356: Blank.

Page 357: 14 Apr 1759, JOHN POSTON, SR. of Anson Co., Carpenter, to JOHN COLE, JR. of same, Cordwinder...land on N side Pee Dee adj. WM TERRY, JR. on S side Hitchcock Cr...100 A...JOHN POSTON (₮) (SEAL), Wit: BENJAMIN MARTIN, STEPHEN COLE.

Page 358: Blank.

Pp. 359-361: 6 & 7 Mar 1759, THOS McELHONY & wf JEAN of Anson (lease s5, release ₺20)...150 A on N side Catawba, commonly called Poplar Spring land... THOS McELHONY (SEAL), JEAN McELHONY (X) (SEAL), Wit: JOHN THOMAS, ROBT. McCLENACHAN.

Page 362: Blank.

Page 363: 20 Nov 1760, DAVID DOUTHETT of Anson, to GEORGE DOBBS of same, for Ł15
        Va. money...150 A on SW side Pee Dee in a branch of old Mill Cr., Babers
branch...granted to DOUTHETT 27 May 1760...DAVID DOUTHETT (SEAL), Wit: HEZ. RUSS,
GEORGE CARTER.

Page 364: Blank.

Page 365: 7 Nov 1759, JOSEPH WHITE, SR. of Anson, to JAMES DENSON, JR. of same,
        planter, for Ł20...land on S side Pee Dee, below the Waggon ford road...
100 A granted 1749, conveyed by GREGS [GRIGGS?], to JOSEPH WHITE...JOSEPH WHITE
(SEAL), Wit: SHA. DENSON, ZACH. PHILLIPS (X).

Page 366: Blank.

Page 367: 6 Feb 1761, HENRY DOWNS of Anson, to JAMES SHPPERD, late of Halifax Co.,
        Va., for Ł10 Va. money...land on SW side Pee Dee, adj. land surveyed
for WM PHILLIPS...100 A granted to DOWNS 26 May 1757...HENRY DOWNS (SEAL), Wit:
BENTLEY FRANKLYN, JAMES PARSONS, JAMES GOULDSBURY (X).
        Recd. Feb. 17, 1761, of MR. JAMES SHEPHERD Ł10 Va. money. HENRY _____.

END OF VOLUME 5.

Page 1: 9 Apr 1762, NICHOLAS SMITH of Cumberland Co., to BENJAMIN THOMPSON of Anson,
for ₤24 proc. money...land on S side Pee Dee, adj. WILLIAM POWELLS open line,
Goulds fork, 200 A granted to sd. SMITH 5 Dec 1760...NICHOLAS SMITH (SEAL), Wit:
JOHN THOMPSON, JOHN LEVERETT.

Page 2: 28 Sept 1761, WILLIAM CRAIG & SARAH THOMPSON, for natural love and affextion
to WILLIAM THOMPSON, ELISHA THOMPSON, JOHN THOMPSON, and MARY THOMPSON &
ELIZABETH THOMPSON, which are the three sons and two daughters of JOHN THOMPSON, decd...
five young breeding mares branded ɪ T...all above children are minors, mares shall
remain in our care until MARY becomes 18 which will be 15 Sept 1769...WILLIAM CRAIG
( ), SARAH THOMPSON (S), Wit: JOHN COLSON, SAML. RATLIFF.

Pp. 2-3: 31 July 1762, ALEXANDER GORDON of Anson, to JOHN ELLERBEE, for ₤10 proc.
money...100 A, part of 250 A granted to ALIX GORDON intrust for the orphans of JOHN ELLERBE, 23 Apr 1762...adj. JOHN ELLERBEs decd. line, THOS. ELLERBES
line...ALEX GORDON (SEAL), Wit: EDWARD ELLERBE, PHILLIP DILL.

Pp. 3-4: 22 Sept 1762, JOHN FROHOCK, ESQ. of Roan Co., to HUGH McLAIN, for ₤40 Va.
money...400 A granted to SAMUEL McCLEARY, 31 Mar 1753, then sold to FROHOCK
3 July 1758...JOHN FROHOCK (SEAL), Wit: THOMAS FROHOCK, JOHN PRICE.

Pp. 4-5: 26 Feb 1761, ANDREW FALKENBERRY of Anson, to THOMAS DIXON, of same, for ₤35
proc. money...land on N side Jones Cr., 150 A....ANDREW FALKENBERRY (SEAL),
Wit: JOHN HORNBACK, ISAAC FALKENBERRY (ɪ).

Page 6: 1 May 1758, BENJAMIN HARDIN & wf CATHRINE of Anson, to DAVID STANLEY, for
₤28 s10 proc. money...part of land on N side Catawba granted to WILLIAM
WATSON, 29 Feb 1754, 400 A...200 A sold to HARDIN 10 July 1754...BENJAMIN HARDIN
(SEAL), CATHERINE HARDIN (C) (SEAL), Wit: PETER KUYKENDALL, ANDREW HAMPTON, BENJM.
BROWN.

Pp. 7-8: 6 Dec 1762, TARRANCE CARRELL of Anson & wf ANN, to THOMAS TALLANT of same,
for ₤50 proc. money...land on Pee Dee at mouth of hacked Creek, into an
Island...80 A, granted 6 Apr 1750 to HENRY FALKENBERRY, conveyed to CARRELL, then
to JOHN LEATH 15 Oct 1754, then to CARRELL 2 Mar 1756...TARRANCE CARRELL (T) (SEAL),
ANN CARREL (N) (SEAL), Wit: W. BROWN, GEORGE PENNINGTON, ELIZ. BROWN.
[The chain of title in the above deed in unclear.]

Page 9: 24 Jan 1763, JOHN BROOKS of Anson, to JOHN CULPEPPER of same, for ₤10 NC
money...land on S side Rocky R., beginning at a branch, near the ford,
between JOHN BROOKES & JOHN LEE...Richardson Creek...JOHN BROOKS (B) (SEAL), Wit:
HENRY STOKES, AARON BURLISON, W. BROOKS.

Pp. 9-11: 25 Dec 1762, CALEB TOUCHSTONE of Anson, planter, to JOHN CARTRITE of same,
for ₤35 proc. money...part of 400 A granted to NICHOLAS SMITH, 5 Dec 1743,
conveyed to WILLIAM PHILLIPS, then to sd. TOUCHSTONE, 200 A on N side Great Pee Dee
...CALEB TOUCHSTONE (SEAL), Wit: NATH. HILLIN, JUR. JAMES SHEPPARD (J).

Page 11: 9 Feb 1763, WILLIAM THOMPSON of Anson, to JOHN LEVERETT of same, for ₤50
proc. money, on S side of a Branch of Goulds fork, linches Creek, 300 A...
granted to sd. THOMPSON 19 Nov 1762...WILLIAM THOMPSON (SEAL), Wit: BENJAMIN THOMPSON,
JOHN LEVERETT SEN. (ɪ).

Pp. 11-12: 20 Jan 1762, GEORGE CATHEY & wf MARGARET of Anson, to PETER KUYKENDALL
          of same, for ₤71 s10 proc. money...land on S side Catabo R., in the
fork of Fishing Creek, 800 A granted to sd. CATHEY 1753...GEORGE CATHEY (X) (SEAL),
MARGARET CATHEY (X) (SEAL), Wit: RICHARD BARRY, JOHN BLACK, JOHN THOMAS.
          [This land now in S. C.]

Pp. 12-14: 25 Oct 1763, JONATHAN HELMS of Anson, planter, to EDWARD SMITH, planter,
          for ₤22 proc. money...land in Anson Co., on S side Little Buffelow Creek
of Little River, 100 A granted to GEORGE HELMS 1758 "now in possession of JONATHAN
HELMS"...JONATHAN HELMS (H) (SEAL), Wit: CORNS. ROBINSON, JOHN POSTER (‡).

Page 14: 30 Mar 1762, FRANCIS ASHLY of Anson, to JOHN CARTRITE of same, for ₤30 proc.
          money...land on N side Pee Dee, adj. "LONGs intended line"...100 A, part of
a grant to JOHN ASHLEY...FRANCIS ASHLEY (SEAL), Wit: JAMES HUNTER, SHADRACH DENSON,
JAMES SHEPARD (J).

Page 15: 3 May 1762, AARON SMITH of Anson, to WILLIAM IRBY of same, for ₤40 proc.
          money...land on S side Pee Dee above the mouth of Brown Cr., 180 A...
AARON SMITH (SEAL), Wit: JOHN SMITH, ANTHONY HUTCHINS.

Page 15: 4 May 1762, JACOB CARTER of Anson, to JOB MEADOR of same, for ₤10...50 A
          on E side Thompson Cr., patented by WM RUSHING, 21 Feb 1757...JACOB
CARTER (‡ C) (SEAL), Wit: BENJAMIN JACKSON, WILLIAM RUSHING.
          [This land now in S. C.]

Page 16: 14 Dec 1762, ISAAC CLARK of Colony of Va., labourer, to SAMUEL SNEAD of Anson,
          labourer, for ₤60 Va. money...land on N side Pee Dee, adj. THOMAS MORMAN...
land laid out for ANDREW MORMAN, deeded to ISAAC CLARK 8 Oct 1752, adj. BENJAMIN
MOORMAN, & 500 A granted to sd. ISAAC CLARK 24 Apr 1762 & granted to ANDREW MOORMAN
21 Apr 1750...ISAAC CLARK (SEAL), Wit: WILLIAM WATKINS, JOHN FANE, PHILIP BURFORD.

Page 17: 9 Feb 1762, BENJAMIN JACKSON of Anson, planter, to JOHN MATHEWS of same,
          for ₤125 SC money...land on N side Thompson Cr., adj. WM RUSHING, adj.
JAMES MATHEWS, 190 A granted to sd. JACKSON...BENJAMIN JACKSON (SEAL), Wit: GEORGE
CARTER, JACOB CARTER (‡).

Page 18: Blank.

Page 19: 16 Jan 1763, BENJAMIN JACKSON of Anson, planter, to ABRAM PAUL of same,
          for ₤70 SC money...300 A on N side Thompson Cr., granted to JACKSON 25
May 1757...BENJAMIN JACKSON (SEAL), Wit: WILLIAM COLEMAN (W), JOB MEADORS (J).

Page 20: 8 Apr 1763, THOMAS WILLIAMS of Anson, to JOHN EDWARDS of same, for ₤26proc.
          money...land on SW side Pee Dee, E side Brown Creek, 100 A sold to WILLIAMS
25 July 1751...THOMAS WILLIAMS (SEAL), CHRISTIAN WILLIAMS (C--her mark) (SEAL),
Wit: WILLIAM LEVERETT, WILLIAM WIATT, JOHN COOK.

Pp. 20-21: ___ Jan 1763, THOMAS SMITH JUR. of Anson, "cord winer" to JONATHAN LEWEL-
          LING, SEN. Joyner, for ₤11 proc. money...100 A, part of 200 A on Hitch-
cock Cr., granted to sd. LEWALLING 5 Dec 1760, & sold to sd. SMITH...THOMAS SMITH
(T) (SEAL), Wit: JOHN CRAWFORD, THOMAS GIBSON, CHARLES MEDLOCK.

Page 22: 15 Jan 1763, HENRY TOUCHSTONE of Anson, to FREDERICK TOUCHSTONE of same, for ₤20 proc. money...250 A on E side Little River, except what RICHARD TOUCHSTONE conveyed to STEPHEN TOUCHSTONE...HENRY TOUCHSTONE (SEAL), Wit: MATHEW RAEFORD, CHARLES ROBINSON.

Page 23: 15 Jan 1763, HENRY TOUCHSTONE to FREDERICK TOUCHSTONE, for ₤10 proc. money ...140 A granted to sd. HENRY 10 ___ 1760, 70 A adj. to land RICHD. TOUCH-STONE bought of JOHN FRANCIS...HENRY TOUCHSTONE (SEAL), Wit: MATHEW RAIFORD, CHAS. ROBINSON.

Page 24: Blank.

Page 25: 29 Apr 1762, ROLAND WILLIAMS of Anson, to JONATHAN HELMS of same, planter, for ₤16 proc. money...100 A granted to GEORGE HELMS 21 Oct 1758...ROWLAND WILLIAMS (R) (SEAL), Wit: THOMAS BALDIN (T), CHARLES ROBINSON.

Page 26: 11 Oct 1762, ABRAM BAGGETT of Pitt Co., NC, to JOHN LONG of Anson, for ₤20 proc. money...land on **Beggetts** Branch, a drain of Cartledge Cr., 150 A granted to BAGGETT 5 Dec 1760...**ABRAHAM** BAGGETT (SEAL), Wit: JOHN CUNDALL, WILLIAM STUNKEY.

Page 27: 6 Feb ____, PETER KUYKENDALL & wf MARY of Anson, to JOSEPH HARDIN of same, for ₤34...land on S side Catabo, Fishing Creek, 400 A granted to JOHN KUYKENDALL 14 Aug 1753 & conveyed by him & wf REBECCA to sd. PETER 10 & 11 Dec 1753... PETER KUYKENDALL (SEAL), MARY KUYKENDALL (M) (SEAL), Wit: BENJAMIN HARDIN, BANAGE PENNETTON (+).

Page 28: 2 Feb 1762, WILLIAM STUTLEY SHERLY of Anson, to ISAAC DAVIS, son of HEZEKIAH DAVIS, for ₤5 proc. money...part of 200 A granted to SHERLY 26 Nov 1757, adj. JEREMIAH CLARK, 50 A...WILLIAM STUTLEY SHERLY (W) (SEAL), Wit: W. BROWN, JERE-MIAH CLARK (H),

Page 29: 6 Feb 1762, SAMUEL WILKINS of Anson, to JAMES SHEPARD of Halifax Co., Va., for 50 pistoles...part of 500 A granted to JAMES DENSON 22 Nov 1756, 100 A conveyed to WILLIAM DOWNS 22 June 1750, then to WM TERRY Oct 1757 & 100 A conveyed by JAS. DENSON to JAS. D. .SON JUR. 21 June 1750...conveyed by TERRY to SAMUEL WIL-KINS 24 Jan 1758...SAMUEL WILKINS (SEAL), Wit: W. BROWN, CHRISTN. GWUIN, WILLIAM WILKINS.

Page 30: Blank.

Page 31: 5 Feb 1762, SAMUEL WILKINS to JAMES SHEPARD, for 50 pistoles...50 A granted to WM TERRY 13 Dec 1760, adj. JAMES DENSON & the ferry...sold to sd. WIL-KINS...SAMUEL WILKINS (SEAL), Wit: W. BROWN, CHRISTO. GEWIN., WM WILKINS.

Page 32: 3 Oct 1761[?], WILLIAM PELLAM, JUR. of Anson, planter, to DENNIS NOLLAN of same, for ₤5 proc. money...land on NE side Little River, adj. JOHN ASHLEY...granted to GEOR. HELMS 11 Oct 1749, 25 A...WILLIAM PELLAM (W) (SEAL), Wit: CHARLES ROBINSON, WILLIAM McDANIEL (W).

Page 33: 2 Feb 1762, WILLIAM STUTLEY SHERLY of Anson, planter, to JEREMIAH CLARK, of same, planter, for ₤5 proc. money...part of 200 A gr. to SHERLY 26 Nov 1757, 150 A...WILLIAM SHERLY (WS), Wit: M. BROWN, JOHN CRAWFORD.

Page 34: Blank.

Page 35: 20 Sept 1762, ANTHONY HUTCHINS, Sheriff...suit the King against CALEB HOWELL
...400 A sold at public vendue to JOHN HAMER, for ₺12 s1...ANTHONY HUTCHINS
Shef. (SEAL), Wit: ALEXANDER GORDON, JAMES ATTAWAY.

Page 36: 15 Jan 1763, JOHN HAMER of Anson, Gent. to ANTHONY HUTCHINS, Sheriff, for
___...400 A bought at publick vendue...JNO HAMER (SEAL), Wit: JOHN DUNN,
M. BROWN.

Pp. 37-38: 9 Aug 1762, BENJAMIN MARTIN of Anson, to WILLIAM MOODY of same, for ₺50
proc. money...land on N side Pee Dee, granted to JACOB FALKENBERY 2 Mar
1754, then sold to JAMES McELROY 27 Apr 1757, then to BENJ. MARTIN 10 June 1758,
150 A...BENJM. MARTIN (SEAL), Wit: CHRISTOPHER HUNT, JOHN LONG, JOHN CUNDALL.

Page 38: 15 June 1763, JACOB PAUL of Anson, to HEZEKIAH WHITE of same, for ₺80...
land where sd. PAUL now lives on Brown Creek, granted to JOSEPH WHITE __
Sept 1754 & conveyed to sd. PAUL...JACOB PAUL (SEAL), Wit: JOSEPH WHITE, JOHN WHITE,
JACOB PAUL (J).

Pp. 39-40: 11 July 1763, JAMES POSTON of Anson, Labourer, to JOHN CUNDALL of same,
Blacksmith, for ₺5 proc. money...100 A on S side Mountain Cr., adj.
JONATHAN EVANS, part of a grant to sd. STON 20 Apr 1763 for 200 A...JAS POSTON
(SEAL), Wit: M. BROWN, ELIZ. BROWN.

Page 41: 11 July 1763, JAMES POSTON of Anson, to JOHN CARTRITE of same, for ₺5proc.
money...100 A adj. JONATHAN EVANS on Mountain Creek...JAMES POSTON (SEAL),
Wit: WM. NEWBERRY (W), M. BROWN, ELIZ. BROWN.

Page 42: 7 July 1763, JOHN CARTRITE of Anson, to JAMES SHEPPARD of same, for ₺20
proc. money...land on N side PD River., adj. JAMES LONG...JOHN CARTRITE
(★) (SEAL), Wit: SHADRACH DENSON, WILLIAM COLEMAN (W).

Page 43: 25 Jan 1763, JAMES SHORT of Anson, planter, to WILLIAM COX , planter, for
₺10 proc. money...land on SW side Pee Dee, S side Jones Creek, McDaniel
branch, 100 A granted to SHORT 2 Oct 1761...JAMES SHORT (I) (SEAL), Wit: HENRY
FALKENBURGH, JAMES FEE (+++), WM FIELDING.

Page 44: 8 July 1763, STEPHEN COLE to THOS CRAWFORD, for ₺18...one Lott or 1/2 A in
Town of Prince George on P D River, purchased of ALEX. GORDON, adj. JO
COLE, ALEX. GORDON...STEPHEN COLE (SEAL), Wit: WM LITTLE, WM CRITTENDEN, EDWARD
ELLERBEE.

Pp. 45-46: 4 May 1762, JOHN ASHLEY of Anson, planter, to TILMON HELMS of same, planter,
for ₺10...land on NE side Pee Dee, on a fork of Buffelow Cr., 100 A granted
to ASHLEY, 5 Dec 1760...JOHN ASHLY (I) (SEAL), Wit: CHAS. ROBINSON, ROBT. HARRIS, JUR.

Page 47: 17 Oct 1763, WILLIAM HICKS of Anson, to THOS WRIGHT, for ₺150 SC money...
150 A granted to ABRAHAM COLSON, 3 Oct 1748, adj. JOHN BERRYS, now JOHN
HAMERS...WILLIAM HICKS (SEAL), Wit: J. HULEASTER (CULCASTER?), JOHN WRIGHT.

Pp. 47-48: 29 June 1760, JOHN LONG of NC, Blacksmith, to THOMAS BLASSANGAM of same,
for ₺8 s5 proc. money...200 A granted to sd. LONG 24 Apr 1762, adj. WILL-
I. BLEWETTS home line, Baggetts branch, EDMUND CARTLEDGE, Cartledges Cr....JOHN
LONG (SEAL), Wit: JOHN CRAWFORD, THOMAS BLASAMGAM, WILLIAM MOODY.

Page 49: 22 Mar 1763, THOMAS FRANKLIN of Anson, Black smith, & wf ANN, to THOMAS
SUGGS, JUR. of same, for Ł9 proc. money...100 A granted to THOMAS SUGGS,
SENR. on W side Little River, 1 July 1758...BECK line...THOMAS FRANKLIN (SEAL), ANN
FRANKLIN (SEAL), Wit: JOSEPH MURPE, FRANCIS FEDWOCK (Ⴔ), THOS SUGGS SENR.

Pp. 50-51: 20 Sept 1763, JOSEPH OATS of Anson, to WILLIAM PICKETT of same, for Ł40
proc. money...25 A, part of 260 A on S side Pee Dee below Brown Creek, adj.
THOS GEORGE, adj. land run out for WM SMITH...JOSEPH OATS (SEAL), Wit: JAS PICKETT,
JAMES TERRY.

Pp. 51-52: 24 Nov 1762, JAMES ROBINSON of Anson, planter, & wf CATHERINE for Ł60
Va.,money to ENOCH RENFRO of same, ...304 A, part of 1011 A granted 1748
at head of hills creek adj. MICHAEL WEDNES...JAMES ROBINSON (SEAL), CATHARINE ROBIN-
SON (SEAL), Wit: GEORGE RENFRO (Ɍ), JOHN WELSH.

Page 53: 1 Oct 1763, THOMAS SUGG , JUR. of Anson, to WILLIAM SPENCER of same, for
Ł12 proc. money...100 A adj. THOS SUGGS SENR., tract granted to SUGGS
SENR. 1 July 1758...THOMAS SUGGS (Ƚ) (SEAL), Wit: JAMES ATTAWAY, JNO. JEFFERY, JAS.
JEFFERY.

Pp. 54-55: 11 Oct 1763, THOS. & ZACHARIAH MOORMAN, of Anson, planters, to ISHAM
HAILY of same, planter, for Ł25 Va. money...106 A, part of 213 A
once in possession of ANDREW MOORMAN, adj. WM HAILYS...640 A granted to SOLOMON HEWS,
22 May 1741...THOMAS MOORMAN (SEAL), ZACHARIAH MOORMAN (X) (SEAL), Wit: CHARLES
MEDLOCK, BENJAMIN MOORMAN (B), ARCHELOUS MOORMAN.

Page 56: 15 Sept 1763, PHILLIP HERNDON of Anson, planter, to WILLIAM RUSS, for Ł40
proc. money...land on SW side Pee Dee below Babers Cr., 220 A part of 640
A granted to JAMES BABER 22 May 1741, adj. NICHOLAS WHITE & land of sd. HERNDON "formally ROBINSONS"...PHILIP HERNDON (SEAL), Wit: GEORGE CARTER, JAMES BRUCE.

Page 57: 14 Feb 1758, HENRY SUMERALL of Craven Co., SC, planter, for Ł70 Va. money...
to DR. JOHN NEELLY of Anson, land on NE side Pee Dee adj. PHILIP HERNDON
...396 A, part of land JOHN HICKS conveyed to SUMERALL...HICKS plat bearing date
22 May 1741...HENRY SUMMERALL (H) (SEAL), Wit: ARCHIBD. GRAHAM, HEZ. RUSS, HUGH GIBSON.

Page 58: 24 Sept 1763, JOHN ASHLY of Anson, to JOHN EDWARDS of same, for Ł20 proc.
money...100 A on N side Chicks Cr., granted to SAML NIALBIC 17 Mar 1756 &
conveyed to ASHLY...JOHN ASHLY (Ŧ) (SEAL', Wit: THOS HELMS, JOHN DICKS, SARY
WHITEVILLE ASHLY (X).

Page 59: Blank.

Pp. 60-61: 8 Aug 1763, FEDRICK TOUCHSTONE & wf ROSE, CHRISTOPHER TOUCHSTONE & STEPHEN
TOUCHSTONE, all of Anson, planters, to JOHN USERY of NC, planter, for Ł125
proc. money...2 tracts: (1) granted to JOHN FRANCIS 20 June 1746 & conveyed to RICHD.
TOUCHSTONE, & bequeathed to sd. FEDR., CHRIT., & STEPHEN, 300 A on N side Pee Dee...
(2) 140 A adj. to above tract granted to HENRY TOUCHSTONE 10 May 1760 & conveyed to
FEDR. & CHRIST....FEDERICK TOUCHSTONE (SEAL), CHRISTOPHER TOUCHSTONE (SEAL), ROSE
TOUCHSTONE (R) (SEAL), STEPHEN TOUCHSTONE, Wit: JOHN WILLIAMS, CHAS. ROBINSON.

Pp. 62-63: 15 Oct 1763, JACOB UNDERWOOD of Edgecomb Co., NC, sole heir of THOMAS
            UNDERWOOD, late of Anson, carpenter, decd...to PHILIP HERNDON, for ₺25
proc. money...land granted 22 Apr 1762, surveyed by MORGAN BROWN on SW side Pee Dee,
Baubers Cr., adj. PHILIP HERNDON, THOS JONES, ROBINSON, BABERS, 300 A...JACOB
UNDERWOOD ( ) (SEAL), WiT: WM RUSHING, HEZ. RUSS.

Pp. 64-65: 22 Jan 1763, SAMUEL DAVIS of Anson, planter, to GEORGE TERRY, for ₺5 Va.
            money....200 A granted 24 Dec 1754 on N side P D, mouth of Lake Creek...
SAMUEL DAVIS (SEAL), Wit: JOHN TERRY, JAMES TERRY, ELIZABETH TERRY.

Pp. 65-66: 9 Aug 1763, WILLIAM LITTLE of Anson, to JOHN GILES, for ₺200 proc. money...
            200 A on S side Pee Dᵉ ₴, granted to SOLOMON HUGHS 25 Apr 1745, adj. GEORGE
SEAMOR, conveyed by HUGHS to MARMADUKE KIMBROUGH, then to sd. LITTLE...WILLIAM LITTLE
(SEAL), Wit: JOHN JENKINS, WM NORTON (X).

Pp. 67-68: 22 Jan 1763, PETER PRESLER, of Anson, to JOHN USERY of same, for ₺30 proc.
            money...land on N side Pee Dee, granted to THOMAS HOMES 7 Apr 1749...
adj. JOHN FRANCIS, conveyed to THOMAS ROBINSON by deed 26 Dec 1749, & property ascend-
ed to his son JOHN COLEMAN, who conveyed 100 A to JOHN MEADORS...PETER PRESLER (P)
(SEAL), Wit: J. DENSON, JAMES SHEPARD (J).

Pp. 68-69: 20 Oct 1763, DENNIS KNOWLAND of Anson, for ₺20 proc. money to JOHN HAMER
            JUR...200 A granted to sd. KNOWLAND 26 Nov 1757, adj. THOS. SKIPPER...
DENNIS KNOWLAND (2) (SEAL), Wit: M. BROWN, THOMAS FROHOCK.

Pp. 69-70: 23 Sept 1763, FRANCIS CLARK of Anson, planter, to JOHN HENN, Carpt., of
            same, for ₺40 proc. money...part of 400 A granted to THOS MOORMAN , 25 May
1757, 200 A conveyed to sd. CLARK 26 Apr 1758...FRANCIS CLARK (FC) (SEAL), Wit: WM.
TEMPLE COLES, BENTLEY FRANKLIN.

Pp. 71-72: 27 Oct 1763, NICHOLAS BROADAWAY of Anson, to CHARLES SPRADLIN of same,
            for ₺25 proc. money...land on SW side Pee Dee, adj. CALEB HOWELL, called
Mount Pleasant, adj. JOHN GRIGGS , near Grassy Island Waggon ford..granted to JOHN
HUSBAND, 5 Dec 1760, & so ld to BROADAWAY 24 Dec 1760...200 A...NICHOLAS BROADAWAY
(SEAL), Wit: JOHN COLE, WILLIAM COLE,M.BROWN.

Pp. 72-74: 15 & 16 May 1764, JAMES KEYKENDALL & wf SARY of Anson, to ADAM HAMPTON
            of same, for ₺50 va. money...land on S side Catabo R., on Keykendalls Cr.,
part of a survey of 300 A to sd. KEYKENDALL...granted 1 Apr 1751...JAMES KUYKENDALL
(SEAL), SARAH KUYKENDALL (I) (SEAL), Wit: JOHN KUYKENDALL, BENJAMIN HARDIN, CHARLES
DUNLAP.

Pp. 75-77: 29 Apr 1762, JOHN ANDERSON of Roan Co., to ALEXANDER WHITLOW of Roan Co.,
            for (lease s5, release ₺100 proc. money)...land on N side S forK Catabo,
S fork Clarks Cr., formally granted to WILLIAM SHERRILL 13 Sept 1749, 400 A...
JOHN ANDERSON (SEAL), Wit: ROBT. McMURREY, JOHN ADAMS (‡), ROBT. HARRIS, JUR.

Pp. 78-79: ____ 1754, JAS. COWARD of Anson, to FRANCIS MACKELWEAN of JOHNSTON CO.,
            NC, yeoman, for ₺50 proc. money...150 A in Craven Co., on N side New
[Neuse?] River, & s   side contenting [Cotentny?] Creek, between WM COWARDS &
HENRY SUMERALLS...granted to JAS. COWARD 21 May 1741...JAMES COWARD (SEAL), Wit:
THOS. TAYLOR, WM CANNELL, DAVIS JONES, ANTH. HUTCHINS.

Page 79: 17 Jan 1764, ABRAM PAUL of Anson, planter, for Ł32 NC money, to BENJ. JACK-
SON...300 A on N side Thompson Creek...ABRAHAM PAUL (SEAL), Wit: WILLIAM
PRESTWOOD, PETER PARTIN, SAML TOMKINS (S).
[This land now in SC.]

Page 80: 18 Nov 1763,   ROBERT RANEY of Johnson Co., NC, to the REVD. SAMUEL BRUCE
of Dublin, Kingdom of Ireland, for s5...land on S side Pee Dee, S fork
Jones Cr., adj. GEORGE RUD, 300 A, granted to sd. RANEY 22 Apr last...ROBT. RAINEY
(SEAL), Wit: ALEXANDER FORD, JOHN RAINEY.
Edenton pr. Proved by JOHN RAINY 23 Nov 1763, FRANS. CORGIN, ag.

Page 81: 21 Nov 1763, THOMAS HIGHTOWER of Anson, to WILLIAM MORRIS of same, for Ł30
...100 A on S side Pee Dee on Williams Creek including the pl tation where
the widow HIGHTOWER now lives...THOS HIGHTOWER (+) (SEAL), KIND NESS (X)(SEAL), Wit:
THOMAS WILLIAMSON, JOHN MORRIS (/).

Page 82: 15 Oct 1763, ELIZABETH GOULD of Bartee Co., NC, Extx of est. of her late
husband GEORGE GOULD, to JOHN CAMPBELL of same, Merchant, for Ł20 proc.
money pd. 29 Mar 1757...land on 3rd northern fork of Jones Cr., E side Pee Dee, 640
A granted to GEORGE GOULD 26 Mar 1748...ELIZABETH GOULD (SEAL), Wit: ROBT. RAINEY,
ALIX. FORD.

Page 83: 21 Nov 1763, WILLIAM IRBY of Anson, to RANDOLPH CHEEK of same, for Ł50
proc. money...land on S side Pee Dee, Brown Cr., 180 A...WILLIAM IRBY
(SEAL), Wit: DAVID DUMAS, BENJ. SMITH (B), MACAGAH PICKETT.

Pp. 84-85: 14 Oct .1763, JACOB UNDERWOOD of Edgecomb Co., NC, carpenter, to MORGAN
BROWN, JUR, son of MORGAN BROWN, for Ł65 proc. money...200 A on NE
Pee Dee, granted to MATHEW CREED 22 May 1741...JACOB UNDERWOOD (SEAL), Wit: JOHN
WEBB, NICHOLAS WHITE (N), GEO. TERRY.

Pp. 85-86: 17 Dec 1763, JOEL PHILLIPS of Anson, to JAMES HUTCHINS of same, for 25
pistoles...200 A on Cedar Cr., granted to FRANCIS McELWEAN 11 Apr 1749,
sold to SAMUEL FRENCH then to sd. McELWEAN 1y Jan 1750, then to JOHN LEATH 5 Sept
1753, then sold by ANTHO. HUTCHINS, Exr. of L. W. & T. of sd. LEATH, pursuant to the
will unto JAMES PICKETT, JUR. 28 Oct 1758, & then to PHILLIPS 10 June 1759...JOEL
PHILLIPS (SEAL), ELIZABETH PHILLIPS (SEAL), Wit: JOHN BODELY, WILLIAM PHILLIPS, LAC.
(ZAC.?) PHILLIPS.

Page 86: 16 June 1763, JACOB PAUL of Anson, to HEZ. WHITE of same, for Ł80...land
where sd. PAUL now lives on Browns Cr., granted to JOSEPH WHITE __ Sept
1754 & conveyed to sd. PAUL...JACOB PAUL (SEAL), Wit: JOSEPH WHITE, JOHN WHITE, JACOB
PAUL JUR. (J).

Pp. 87-88: 4 Nov 1762, LEONARD HIGDON to SAML. FLAKE for Ł30 proc. money...tract on
S side Pee Dee, Smiths Cr., granted to JOSEPH WHITE & FRANCIS McELWEAN,
13 Apr 1749, conveyed to THOMAS BERRY 8 July 1752, then to NICHOLAS BROADAWAY __
Oct 1755, then to THOMAS TALLANT, 20 Sept 1757, then to HIGDON 27 July 1762, 150 A...
LEONARD HIGDON (SEAL), Wit: BENJAMIN MARTIN, ISAAC FALKENBURGH (+).

Pp. 89-90: 26 Jan 1763, THOMAS HARRINGTON of Anson, planter, to GIBBEN JONES of same,
for Ł10...100 A on a branch of Mountain Cr., called Silver Rim, granted to
sd. HARRINGTON 24 Apr 1762...THOS HARRINGTON (SEAL), Wit: M. BROWN, THOS FROHOCK.

Pp. 90-91: 25 Feb 1763, GEORGE PENNINGTON of Anson, Sadaler, to JOSEPH DUNHAM of
same, for ₺115 proc. money...600 A on Mountain Cr., adj. GEORGE GOULDS,
granted to MORGAN BROWN 15 Mar 1756, conveyed to PENNINGTON 5 Feb 1761...GEORGE
PENNINGTON (SEAL), Wit: ROBT. POSTON (R), M. BROWN, ELIZ. BROWN.

Page 92: 28 Feb 1763, JOHN HORNBACK of Anson, to JAMES BRUCE of same, for ₺25 proc.
money...200 A on N side Jones Cr., adj. HOPKINS HOWELL & sd. HORNBACK...JOHN
HORNBACK (SEAL), Wit: ANDREW FALKENBURGH (A), ISAAC FALKENBURGH (Ɨ).
[From ORANGE COUNTY, VIRGINIA FAMILIES Vol. III, by W. E. Brockman,
p. 9, on a petition for a Gap Road, July 24, 1738 appear the names
of HENRY FALKENBOROUGH, ANDREW FALKENBOROUGH, JACOB FALKENBOROUGH,
and HENRY FALKENBOROUGH.]

Pp. 93-94: 10 Dec 1763, STEPHEN KEMP of Augusta, Georgia, Pack horse man, to JOSEPH
KEMP of Augusta, his brother...land in S side Pee Dee, adj. BENJAMIN
CLARK...STEPHEN KEMP (X) (SEAL), Wit: THOS. WATERS, THOS KEMP (T), ZAC. MOORMAN (X).

Page 95: 29 July 1763, CHARLES PATE of Anson, to THOMAS WILLIAMSON of same, for ₺40
...200 A on SW side Pee Dee, adj. WM POWELLS line in Goulds fork, where sd.
PATE now lives...CHARLES PATE (SEAL), SARAH PATE (X) (SEAL), Wit: AARON HART (A),
JOHN LARCERY (Ɨ).

Page 96: 3 Oct 1763, CHRISTOPHER GEWIN of Anson, for ₺30, to JOHN CARR of same, ...
100 A on SW side Pee Dee, where CARR now lives...adj. line run by JOHN
SHEPARD...CHRISTOPHER GEWIN (SEAL), Wit: THOMAS WILLIAMSON, THEFEHUS [THEOPHILUS?]
BAXTER, (TB).

Page 97: Blank.

Pp. 98-99: 1763, THOMAS ARRINGTON of Anson, planter, to JOHN JONES, planter, for ₺10
proc. money...100 A on Jones Cr., adj. JAMES JONES...THOMAS ARRINGTON, SR.
Wit: ISHAM HAILLY, WM HAILEY (X), GEO. MATHEWS.

Page 99: 2 Jan 1764, JOHN MATHEWS of Anson, planter, for ₺25 to JACOB JOHNSON of
same, planter, ...180 A on N side Thompson Cr., adj. JAMES MATHEWS...granted
to BENJ. JACKSON, 29 Sept 1756...JOHN MATHEWS (✦) (SEAL), Wit: BENJAMIN JACKSON,
ISAAC JOHNSON (X), RICHD. RUSHING (X).

Pp. 100-101: 19 Apr 1763, JAMES McNISH of Anson, to JAMES LYLES of same, for ₺27 proc.
money...land on Long Branch of Jones Creek, 200 A...granted 5 Dec 1760...
JAMES McNISH (SEAL), Wit: ISAAC FALKENBURGH (Ɨ), SAML. FLAKE, WM FIELDING.

Page 102: 14 May 1763, JOHN DONOHUE of Cumberland Co., planter, to JOHN CARPENTER, of
Anson, for ₺10 proc. money...100 A granted to DONOHUE 22 Apr 1763 on Cabbin
Cr....JOHN DONOHUE (/) (SEAL), Wit: JOHN JEFFERY, JOHN SMITH.

Pp. 103-104: 27 July 1762, THOMAS TALLANT of Anson, to LEONARD HIGDON of same, planter
for ₺30 proc. money...land granted to JOSEPH WHITE & FRANCIS McELWEAN 13
Apr 1749, & conveyed to THOMAS BERRY 18 July 1752, to NICHOLAS BROADAWAY, __ Oct 1755,
& to THOMAS TALLANT 24 Sept 1757, on Smith Cr...150 A....THOMAS TALLANT (SEAL), Wit:
BENJN. MARTIN, ISAAC FALKENBURGH (Ɨ).

Page 105: 10 Nov 1763, JAMES GOOLSBE of Anson, to JOSEPH ATTAWAY of same, for Ł20
        proc. money...100 A gr. to WILLIAM STONE 26 May 1757, & sold to GOOLSBE...
JAMES GOOLSBE (SEAL) (J), Wit: ABNER BOUSHEP (A), WILLIAM BATTAN ALLAWAY (X).

Page 106: 10 Dec 1763, THOMAS BINGHAM to JOHN PURKINS, for Ł100...200 A on W side
        Brown Creek, by side of old Catawba Path...THOMAS BINGHAM (SEAL), Wit:
WILLIAM TERRY, BENJAJIN JACKSON.

Page 107: Blank.

Page 108: 4 Nov 1763, THOMAS SUGG & wf MARY of Anson, to WILLIAM SPENCER of same, for
        Ł35 proc. money...100 A granted to sd. SUGGS 1 July 1758, adj. THOS. RANDAL...
THOMAS SUGG (SEAL), MARY SUGG (SEAL), Wit: JAMES ATTAWAY, ROSHA SUGG (X).

Pp. 109-110: 8 Dec 1763, JAMES DENSON of Anson, to JAMES SHEPARD of same, for Ł20
        proc. money...part of a grant to JAMES DENSON 22 Nov 1746, conveyed to
JAMES DENSON JUR. 26 July 1756, on NE side Pee Dee, 150 A...JAMES DENSON (SEAL)
Wit: DORSEY PENTECOST, CHARLES ROBINSON.

Page 111: 10 May 1761, JAMES PICKETT of Anson, to WILLIAM PICKETT, for Ł100 proc.
        money...land on S side Pee Dee, at mouth of turky cock creek, whereon
ISAAC NORMAN formerly lived, 100A & 200 A whereon HENRY FALKENBURG formerly lived...
JAMES PICKETT (SEAL), Wit: CHARITY REGNEY (X), THOS. DIXON.

Pp. 112-113: 27 Jan 1763, WILLIAM LITTLE of Anson, yeoman, to MORGAN BROWN, of same,
        for Ł25 proc. money...100 A granted to THOMAS SHEPPARD, 27 Sept 1750 &
conveyed to sd. LITTLE...WILLIAM LITTLE (SEAL), Wit: EDMD FANNING, JNO. HAMER, WM
TEMPLE COLESSE.

Page 115: 29 Dec 1763, NATHANIEL HILLEN SR. of Anson, to NATHANIEL HILLEN, JR. for
        Ł60 proc. money...200 A, 1/2 of 400 A on N side Pee Dee...NATHL. HILLEN
(SEAL), HEZEA HILLIN (X) (SEAL), Wit: LUKE ROBINSON (X), DORSEY PENTECOST.

Pp. 116-117: 9 June 1762, GEORGE FOULDS, planter, to DAVID BRUTON, planter, of Anson,
        for Ł24 proc. money...100 A on N side Densons fork of Little River, granted
to sd. FOULD 5 Dec 1760...GEORGE FOULDS (SEAL), Wit: JOHN PATE (X), SAML. PARSONS.

Pp. 118-119: 14 Oct 1763, JACOB UNDERWOOD of Edgecomb Co., NC, carpenter to MORGAN
        BROWN JUR. of Anson, for Ł50 proc. money...100 A on N side Pee Dee,
adj. MATHEW CREED, WM COKERHAM, granted to THOMAS UNDERWOOD 25 May 1757, and at his
death became property to sd. JACOB as heir in law...JACOB UNDERWOOD (SEAL), Wit:
JOHN WEBB, NICHL. WHITE (X), GEO. TERRY.

Pp. 119-120: 9 Feb 1764, WILLIAM CRITTENDEN of Anson, planter, to JOSEPH WILLKIE,
        for Ł30...100 A on bank of Little River...lower part of grant to ROBT.
MILLS, conveyed from sd. MILLS 2 Aug 1758...later states conveyed by MILLS to
CRITTENDEN 8 Aug 1748 & then to WM STONE, then to HUMPHRIES & from heirs to sd.
CRITTENDEN...WILLIAM CRITTENDEN (SEAL), Wit: JOHN SMITH, SAML RATLIFF, DOWNS.

Pp. 121-122: 9 Feb 1764, WILLIAM CRITTENDEN to JOSEPH WILLKINS, for Ł30...land on
        N side Pee Dee, on NE side Little River, adj. DAVID MILLS upper survey...
granted to sd. CRITTENDEN 25 May 1757, 75 A...WILLIAM CRITTINDEN (SEAL), Wit: JOHN
SMITH, SAML. RATLIFF, DOWNS.

Pp. 123-124; 8 Feb 1764, ZACHARY PHILLIPS & wf MARY of Anson, to JULUS (JULY) HOLLEY
of same, for ₺50 Va. money...land on W side Cains Cr., part of a grant
to JOSEPH PHILLIPS 1756, 150 A...ZACHARY PHILLIPS (Z) (SEAL), MARY PHILLIPS (P)
(SEAL), Wit: WM. PHILLIPS, WM HOLLY, NATHL. HOLLY (H).

Pp. 124-125: 20 Mar 1764, GEDION JONES of Anson, to THOMAS FANNING of same, for ₺40
proc. money...100 A on NE side Pee Dee, on N side Silver Run, a branch
of N fork Mountain Creek, granted 24 Apr 1762, to THOMAS HARRINGTON & conveyed to
sd. JONES...GIDEON JONES (SEAL), Wit: HENRY TIPPENS (H), JAMES BRUTON (‡).

Pp. 126-127: 16 Feb 1764, NICHOLAS BOND & wf ALCE of Anson, to THOMAS BOLDWIN of same,
for ₺20 proc. money...land granted to GEORGE CLEMONS 4 Apr 1750, on W
side Little River of PD, adj. CHARLES ROBINSON, 100 A...NICHOLAS BOND (SEAL),
ALCE BOND (A) (SEAL), Wit: SAML. DAVIS, JR. (S),DANIEL DAVID (D).

Pp. 127-128: 13 Nov 1763, JOHN CRAWFORD of Anson, for ₺20 proc. money, to JAMES REED
of Craven Co., ...50 A granted to sd. CRAWFORD 20 Apr 1763, adj. JOHN
McBRIDE, near WM GORDON called Davis folly...JOHN CRAWFORD (SEAL), Wit: JOHN MULCASTER
GEOR. PENNINGTON, ANNE CRAWFORD.

Page 129:3 Mar 1764, GEORGE TERRY of Anson, to WILLIAM COLE, for ₺30 proc. money...
land on N side Pee Dee, near mouth of Cole Cr., 200 A granted to SAML DAVIS
24 Dec 1754...GEORGE TERRY (SEAL), Wit: JOHN COLE, JOHN TERRY, JOSEPH BRETT.

Page 130: 2 Jan 1764, ALEX. GORDON of Anson, to ANDREW INGRAM of same, for ₺20 proc.
money...land on N side Pee Dee, S side Marks Creek, crossing a reedy br.
of Whites Creek, 200 A...ALEXANDER GORDEN (SEAL), Wit: WM. TEMPLE COLE, WILLIAM COLE.

Page 131: 24 Apr 1764, CHARLES MEDLOCK of Anson, to SOLOMON SNEAD of same, planter, fo
₺12 proc. money...land on NE side Pee Dee, on Solomons Cr., adj. land surveyed for JAMES MECKELROY, 200 A granted to WM LANGFORD, 6 Dec 1760...CHAS. MEDLOCK
(SEAL), Wit: SAML. SNEAD, JOSEPH ALLAWAY.

Page 132: Blank.

Pp. 133-134: 12 Apr 1764, WILLIAM CRITTENDEN of Anson, to FRANCIS SMITH of same, for
₺50 proc. money...land on S side PD, near ROBERT PARKES on Walkers Island
adj. land sold by WALKER to JAMES ADAMS, decd., 75 A, part of 300 A granted to JOHN
GILES 26 Nov 1746, conveyed to HENRY WALKER, then to AARON SMITH 10 Apr 1758, then
to sd. CRITTENDEN 17 June 1762, & 50 A adj. to sd. tract, granted to AARON SMITH, 5
dec 1760, adj. to DUMAS, HENRY WALKER...WILLIAM CRITTENDEN (SEAL), SARAH CRITTENDEN
(S) (SEAL), Wit: TIREY ROBINSON, RICHD. DIXON (X).

Page 135: 21 Dec 1760, THOMAS HIGHTOWER of Anson, to JOHN MORRIS of same, for ₺12...
150 A on S side PD, Williams Cr., where sd. HIGHTOWER now lives, adj. WM
MORRIS...THOMAS HIGHTOWER (SEAL), Wit: THOMAS WILLIAMSON, WILLIAM MORRIS (W).

Pp. 136-137: 19 Feb 1761, THOMAS ARMSTRONG of Cumberland Co., NC to JOHN SMITH
of same, for ₺30 proc. money...land on NE side PD at the Great Bluff,
SW side Little R., 300 A...THOS ARMSTRONG (SEAL), Wit: WILLIAM ARMSWORTH, DAVID GORDON

Pp. 137-138: 26 July 1764, JOHN CHEEK & wf JANE, to JOHN STEPHENS of Cumberland Co.,
for ___...200 A on Pee Dee above mouth of Brown Cr., at JOHN CLARKs lower
corner...granted to JOHN COLLSON, 26 Nov 1746, conveyed to JOHN CHEEK 28 June 1750...
JOHN CHEEK (SEAL), JANE CHEEK (X) (SEAL), Wit: J. PICKETT, THOS. WILLIAMS.

Page 139: 9 Apr 1764, LEONARD HIGDON of Anson, to CHARLES HIGDON of same, for Ⱡ10
        proc. money...25 A, part of 100 A granted to sd. LEONARD on Buffellow Cr.,
...LEONARD HIGDON (X) (SEAL), Wit: ANTH. HUTCHINS, MARSHALL DEGGE.

Pp. 140-141: 11 July 1764, DAVID HILDRETH & ANNE HILDRETH, EZEKIEL VICKRY, SARAH VICK-
        RY, JAMES VICKRY, THOMAS VICKRY, & EDITH TAYLOR, all of Anson, to JOHN
CLARK of same, for Ⱡ10s10...300 A on Rocky River at mouth of Ugly Cr., in Mr. McCULLOCHS
line...DAVID HILDRETH (SEAL), NANCY HILDRETH (X) (SEAL), EZEKIAH VICKRY (X) (SEAL),
SARAH VICKRY (X) (SEAL), JAMES VICKRY (X)(SEAL), THOMAS VICKRY (X) (SEAL), EDITH
TAYLOR (X) (SEAL), Wit: JOHN GIBSON, ELY S. CLARK.

Pp. 141-142:[no date], RICHARD ODAM & wf ANNE of Anson, to CHARLES HILL of same,
        planter, for Ⱡ16 proc. money...200 A on Finches branch of N fork of
Mountain Cr., granted to sd. ODAM 24 Apr 1762...RICHARD ODAM (R) (SEAL), ANNE ODEM
(A)(SEAL), Wit: JOSEPH DONHAM, JACOB COCKERHAM, PATRICK SANDERS.

Page 143: 10 Mar 1763, CHRISTOPHER HUNT of Anson, to WILLIAM S. SHERLY of same, for
        Ⱡ10 proc. money...100 A granted to sd. HUNT, 24 Apr 1762, on N side Pee
Dee, adj. WILLIAM BLEWETT, dry fork of Cartledge Cr....XTOPHER HUNT (SEAL), CATY
HUNT (C) (SEAL), Wit: GEORGE CARTER, GEORGE MARTIN.

Pp. 144-145: 10 July 1764, BENJAMIN MOORMAN of Anson, to JOHN RYLE of same, for Ⱡ40
        s12 proc. money...200 A on the upper end of tract granted to JOHN HORNBACK,
on S side Indian Camp Creek, adj. JOHN COLSON...granted 25 June 1746, sold to ANDREW
MOORMAN 11 May 1755...BENJAMIN MOORMAN (SEAL), Wit: CHAS. MEDLOCK, SAML. SNEAD, ISHAM
HAILEY.

Page 146: 13 Jan 1764, THOMAS TOMPKINS of Anson, to JOHN FLOWERS of same, for Ⱡ25 proc.
        money...100 A where SAML. TOMPKINS lived, on the old mill creek...THOMAS
TOMPKINS (SEAL), Wit: THOMAS DIXON, PHILLIP HERNDON, M. BROWN.

Page 147: 7 Apr 1764, NICHOLAS BOND of Anson, to WILLIAM BURT Of same, for Ⱡ10 proc.
        money...200 A on W side N fork Mountain Cr., Bonds Br., granted to sd.
BOND 24 Apr 1762...NICHOLAS BOND (SEAL), Wit: M. BROWN, THOS FROHOCK.

Page 148: 3 July 1764, JOHN EDWARDS of Anson, to JOHN ASHLY of same, for Ⱡ30...100 A
        on N side Pee Dee, Cheeks Cr...JOHN EDWARDS (SEAL), Wit: J. PICKETT, SAMUEL
RAY.

Pp. 149-150: 23 Oct 1762, GEO. CARTER & wf SARAH of Anson, to WILLIAM ST. SHERLY of
        same, for Ⱡ21...125 A granted to WILLIAM BLEWETT, 6 May 1769, on N br.
Cartlidges Cr....GEORGE CARTER (C) (SEAL), LETTY CARTER (LC) (SEAL), Wit: JOHN CRAW-
FORD, XTOPHER HUNT.

Pp. 150-151: 25 June 1764, ELIZABETH GRIGG of Anson, to ISAAC BLUYE of Anson, for
        Ⱡ10 proc. money...land on SW side Pee Dee, E side Cedar Cr., Griggs
spring branch...adj. SAMUEL FRENCH...100 A granted to SAML. FRENCH 25 May ____,
& conveyd to sd. ELIZABETH 15 Nov 1758...ELIZABETH GRIGG (+) (SEAL), Wit: BENJM.
VAUGHAN, SAML. FRENCH.

Page 152: 24 Mar 1763, ELIZABETH GOULD Of Barte Co., Extx of her late husband, GEORGE
        GOULD, to JOHN CAMPBELL of same, merchant, for Ⱡ20 paid on 29 Mar 1757...
land in fork of Mountain Creek, 640 A granted 26 Mar 1748...ELIZA GOULD (SEAL), Wit:
ROBT. RAINEY, ALEX. FORD.

Page 153: 30 July 1763, TARRANCE KERRELL of Anson, to THOMAS LEE of same, for ₺10
proc. money...land on NE side PD, S side Naked Creek, 87 A...TARRANCE
KERREL (T) (SEAL), Wit: STEPHEN JACKSON, WILLIAM PHILLIPS.
[This land now in S. C.]

Pp. 154-155: 11 July 1764, JAMES TERRY of Anson Co., to FRANCIS CLARK of same, for
s10 proc. money...1 A on N bank Hitchcock Cr., condemned by order of
court on petition of THOMAS MOORMAN & FRANCIS CLARK, for their mill...part of 300 A
granted to JACOB PAUL & conveyed by deed to TERRY 11 Oct 1764...JAMES TERRY (SEAL),
Wit: WILLIAM MASK, EDWARD SMITH (S), THOMAS MOORMAN.

Page 156: 25 Oct 1764, JOHN CARTRITE of Anson, to JAMES SHEPARD of same, for ₺40
proc. money...100 A on N side Pee Dee, adj. DENSON, JORDAN ASHLEY...
granted to JOHN ASHLEY, conveyed to his son FRANCIS, then to sd. CARTRITE...JOHN
CARTRITE (✝) (SEAL), Wit: JACOB WOMOCK, EDWARD ALMONDS.

Pp. 157-158: 24 Oct 1760, JAMES DENSON of Anson, to SHADRACH DENSON, for ₺40 proc.
money...3 tracts on N side Pee Dee (1) 150 A, part of a grant to JAMES
DENSON, SENR. 22 Nov 1756, being the land where sd. SHADRACH & his mother now live
...(2) land adj. to JOSEPHUS WHITE, granted to sd. JAMES DENSON, SENR, 5 Dec 1763
(3) Land between the lines of JAMES SHEPARD...3 tracts falling to JAMES DENSON, JR.
by heirship by the death of his father, he being the oldest son & the will not
proven for want of evidences...300 A total...JAMES DENSON (SEAL), Wit: ANNE CARTRITE
(S), PRISCILLA DENSON (Ʒ), DORSEY PENTECOST.

Pp. 159-160: 3 Oct 1764, PETER PRESLER of Anson, to OWEN SLAUGHTER of same, for ₺5...
61 A on both sides Mountain Creek including the mill, granted to PRES-
LAR 2 Dec 1761...PETER PRESLAR (X) (SEAL), Wit: WILLIAM BLEWETT, ANDREW PRESLAR.

Pp. 160-161: 4 Aug 1764, BENJAMIN SMITH of Anson to JOSEPH MURPHEY of same, for ₺40
proc. money...100 A granted to sd. SMITH 5 Dec 1760, adj. Youngs Island,
ROBERT PARKE, THOS GEORGE...BENJAMIN SMITH (B) (SEAL),   RUTH SMITH (X)(SEAL),
Wit: WALTER GIBSON, WILLIAM IRBY.

Pp. 161-162: 23 Oct 1764, JOSEPH HALL of Anson, to JOHN HALL of same, for ₺5 proc.
money...50 A on S side Hitchcocks Cr., part of 100 A granted to sd.
JOSEPH 22 Feb 1764...JOSEPH HALL (₤) (SEAL), Wit: JONATHAN LEWELLING, JAMES BOUNDS.

Pp. 163-164: 25 July 1765, ROBERT RAINEY, late of Dobbs Co., merchant to ROBERT BOYD
of London, merchant, for ₺100 sterling...whereas said RAINEY is indebted
to sd. BOYD for goods Bought & Shipped in transacting business in England & Ireland
& for s5...6 tracts (1) 300 A on Goulds fork, once claimed by BENJAMIN DUMAS, but
granted to RAINEY 22 Apr 1765 (2) 200 A granted to RAINEY on Goulds fork, adj. to
GOULDS, ZACHARY PHILLIPS granted 22 Apr 1763 (3) 200 A granted 22 Apr 1763 on Huckleberry Creek, above GEORGE DOBBS (4) 200 A on Goulds fork, nigh to JOHN LEVERITT (5)
300 A on S side Jones Cr., adj. JASON MEADOR, JUNR, BURLINGHAM RUDD, granted 22 Apr
1763 (6) 200 A granted 22 Apr 1763 on head of Murpheys spring branch, nigh HENRY
FORTENBURY where PATRICK McCAPOCK once lived...ROBERT RAINEY (SEAL), Wit: JOHN
DUNN, D. S., SAMUEL SPENCER, JAT. C. SHEPPHERD.

Page 165: 22 Aug 1758, EDMOND IRBY of Anson, carpenter to WILLIAM HAMER for ₺100 proc.
money...200 A granted 6 Oct 1748 to JOHN BERRY.....
"The Ballance of this deed together with twenty four pages
not to be found in the Original Books."

Page 166: Blank.

Page 167: [deed fragmentary]...land granted 5 Dec 1760, conveyed from sd. McNISH
        to JAMES LYLES __ Apr 1762, 200 A...then to sd. WILLIAM WEATHERFORD...
JAMES LYLES (‡) (SEAL), Wit: JOHN HORNBACK (ℱH), WILLIAM FEILDEN.

Pp. 168-169: 11 Jan 1765, WILLIAM PHILLIPS SENR of Anson & wf ANN to ROBERT WHICKER
        for ₺20 proc. money...300 A granted to JOSEPH WHITE SENR. 1756, sold
to WILLIAM PHILLIPS SENR, on E side Lanes Cr....WILLIAM PHILLIPS (SEAL), ANN PHILLIPS
(X) (SEAL), Wit: ROBERT LASITER, JULIUS HOLLEY, WILLIAM HOLLEY.

Pp. 169-170: 17 Sept 1764, JOSEPH & STEPHEN KEMP of Craven Co., SC, planter, to
        BENJAMIN CLARK of Louisa Co., Va., for ₺44 proc. money...200 A on S
side Pee Dee, granted to WILLIAM KEMP 21 June 1746 for 640 A, the 200 A conveyed
by will...JOSEPH KEMP (‡) (SEAL), STEPHEN KEMP (X) (SEAL), Wit: HENRY SNEAD, ZACHARIAH
MOORMAN, ARCHELOUS MOORMAN.

Page 171: 19 June 1765, JOSEPH MURPHEY of Anson, to JOSEPH CHEEK JUR. of same, for
        ₺40...100 A granted to BENJAMIN SMITH 5 Dec 1760 in Youngs Island, adj.
ROBERT PARKS, THOS GEORGE...JOSEPH MURPHEY (SEAL), VOLUNTINE MURPHEY (X-her mark)
(SEAL), Wit: WALTER GIBSON, SHADRACH HOGAN.

Page 172: Blank.

Page 173: 7 Jan 1765, JOHN COLSON of Anson, to JOHN CULPEPPER of same, planter, for
        ₺40 proc. money...200 A on Brown Cr, S side PD....JOHN COLSON (SEAL), Wit:
ELIJAH GIBSON, JOHN PRESLER, CHAS. HARRINGTON.

Page 174: 22 Jan 1764, MICAJAH PICKETT Of Anson to SARAH CHEEK..one mair...MICAJAH
PICKETT (SEAL), Wit: MICHAEL WEEKS (X), MARY WEAKS (X).

Pp. 174-175: 15 Dec 1764, CHARLES SPRADLIN of Anson, to THOMAS WRIGHT of Craven
        Co., SC, for ₺67 s10 proc. money...land on SW side Pee Dee, granted
to JOHN HUSBANDS 5 Dec 1760, conveyed to NICHOLAS BROADAWAY 24 Dec 1760, & to
SPRADLIN 27 Oct 1763, adj. CALEB HOWELL, JOHN GRIGGS, Grassy Island Waggon ford...
CHARLES SPRADLIN (S) (SEAL), Wit: M. BROWN, JOHN WRIGHT, ELIZ. BROWN.

Pp. 176-177: 23 Sept 1762, MATHEW CREED, late of Anson, but now of Craven Co., SC,
        to LAURENCE EASTERWOOD of Anson, for ₺50 proc. money...part of 640 A
surveyed by WILLIAM DENKINS, adj. PHILLIP DILL, PAUL TRAPRER, known as FURBUSHES
lands...MATHEW CREED (SEAL), Wit: THOMAS DICKSON, PHILLIP DILL.

Pp. 178-179: 16 Dec 1764, JOHN LEE of Anson, to HENRY STOKES of same, for ₺ s10...
        50 A on S side Rocky River, beginning at mouth of sd. LEES spring...
part of 180 A granted to LEE 27 Oct 1762...JOHN LEE (‡) (SEAL), Wit: ROBERT LEE (ℛ),
GABRIEL DAVIS (G).

Pp. 179-180: 1 Jan 1765, JAMES SHEPARD of Anson, planter, to WILLIAM MASK of same,
        planter, for ₺ 300 Va. money...3 tracts granted to JAMES DENSON 22
Nov 1746, & one tract granted to JOHN ASHLY 27 Nov 1746, conveyed to FRANCIS ASHLEY,
then to JOHN CARTRITE, then to SHEPHARD, adj. JAMES LONG, JORDAN ASHLEY & 100 A
granted to HENRY DOWNS 26 May 1757...5 tracts in all, 550 A...JAMES SHEPHERD (J)
(SEAL), LUCY SHEPHERD (SEAL), Wit: DENNIS NOLLEN (2), CHAS. ROBINSON.

Pp. 181-182: 1 Jan 1765, JAMES LONG of Anson, carpenter, to WILLIAM MASK for Ŀ110...
          part of a grant to JOHN ASHLY 27 Nov 1746, adj. JORDAN ASHLY, 200 A
on Little River...JAMES LONG (X) (SEAL), ELIZABETH LONG (X) (SEAL), Wit: DENNIS
NOLLEN (2), CHAS. ROBINSON.

Page 183: 24 Jan 1765, WILLIAM IRBY sold to RANDOLPH CHEEK...10 sows...WILLIAM IRBY
          (SEAL), Wit: JAMES HUTCHINS, GABRIAL DAVIS (G).

Pp. 183-184: 22 Jan 1765, SAMUEL SNEAD of Anson, planter, to ISRAEL SNEAD, of same,
          planter, for Ŀ50 proc. money...200 A on HItchcock Cr., adj. JOHN WILES
...JOSEPH HALLS, granted to SNEAD 22 Jan 1765...SAML SNEAD (SEAL), Wit: THOS. DOWNER,
MARSHALL DEGGE, JOSEPH HALL (J).

Pp. 185-186: 26 May 1762, MATHEW CREED, late of Anson, but now of Craven Co., SC, to
          PHILLIP DILL of Anson, for Ŀ80 proc. money...200 A, part of 400 A...
granted to THOMAS THOMPKINS...MATHEW CREED (SEAL), Wit: WM LITTLE, THOMAS DIXON,
LAURANCE EASTERWOOD.

Pp. 186-187: 23 Feb 1765, WILLIAM WITTSHEAR of Anson, to EDWARD ELLERBE of Craven
          Co., SC, for Ŀ75...250 A on S side Hitchcock Cr., adj. JOHN CRAWFORD,
Waltens branch...WILLIAM WITTSHIER (SEAL), MARY WITTSHEER (SEAL), Wit: THOMAS
ELLERBE, JOHN ELLERBE, JOHN MULCASTER.

Page 188: 14 Feb 1765, GEORGE SKIPPER to BARNABA SKIPPER, for Ŀ20...2 strawberry
          Rone Horses, 3 sorrel Do., 3 mares & colts...GEO. SKIPPER (SEAL), Wit:
JOHN CRAWFORD, SAML. SNEAD.

Pp. 189-190: 22 Apr 1765, JOHN GIBSON of Anson, to JOHN RYLE of same, planter, for
          Ŀ40...140 A granted to sd. GIBSON on S side Rockey River, granted
2 Nov 1764...JOHN GIBSON(SEAL), Wit: JOSEPH CULPEPPER, CHARLES HARRINGTON.

Pp. 190-191: 23 Oct 1764, CHARLES HIGDON of Anson, to ELIZABETH TALLANT, for Ŀ4...
          25 A, part of 100 A adj. LEONARD HIGDON, on Buffelow Cr., nigh Mount
Pleasant...granted to LEONARD HIGDON 24 ___ 1762...CHARLES HIGDON (SEAL), Wit: JNO.
PICKETT, MARSHALL DEGGE.

Pp. 192-193: 13 Feb 1765, GEORGE SKIPPER of Anson, planter, to BARNABA SKIPPER, for
          Ŀ20 proc. money...50 A adj. MR. GRIFFUTHS, granted to JOHN CLARK,200
A on N side PD, near mouth of Little Creek, conveyed from CLARK to SKIPPER 1 Feb
1749...GEO. SKIPPER (SEAL), Wit: SAML SNEAD, JOHN CRAWFORD, THOS. MOORMAN
          Recd. Ŀ20 of BARNABA SKIPPER 14 Feb 1765. GEO. SKIPPER (SEAL).

Pp. 193-194: 19 Jan 1765, JOHN VANHOSE, SEN. of Anson, to JOHN HAGLER, of same, for
          Ŀ20 proc. money...150 A on SW side Pee Dee, adj. JOSHUA WEAVER, JOHN
HALL...granted to JOHN DAVIS 25 May 1757 & conveyed to VANHOSE 14 Apr 1760....JOHN
VANHOSER (SEAL), Wit: EDMUND LILLY, SARAH LILLY, JOHAN JACOB [could be VANHOSER,
German signature].

Pp. 195-196: 20 Oct 1764, TILMON HELMS of Anson, to DENNIS NOLLEN of same, for Ŀ15
          proc. money. .150 A granted to HELMS, 27 Nov 1762 on E side Little River
South side Buffellow, adj. GEO. HELMS, CHAS. ROBINSON...TILMON HELMS (T) (SEAL), Wit:
DANIEL McDANIELD (D), CHARLES ROBINSON.

Pp. 196-197: 20 Mar 1765, WILLIAM BROWN of Prov. of Georgia, to SUSANNAH BELL of
Anson, for ₺50 proc. money...100 A on W side Hitchcock Cr., granted
9 Nov 1764 to WILLIAM BROWN of Georgia...WILLIAM BROWN (SEAL), Wit: JOHN CRAWFORD,
JONATHAN LEWELLING, JOHN COLE.

Pp. 197-198: 30 Dec 1759, JOHN NIELLY of Anson, "Doctor of Phisic," to PHILLIP
DILL of Anson, Silver Smith, for ₺160 proc. money...396 A on NE side
Pee Dee, about 9 miles above Great Cherraw, granted to JOHN HICKS 22 May 1741...
JOHN NIELLY (SEAL), Wit: SAMUEL HOLLON, WILLIAM WILLIAMSON.

Page 199: 30 Jan 1765, JOHN PARSONS of Anson, to BENJAMIN HENSON of same, for ₺12
proc. money, 150 A, part of 400 A granted to WILLIAM KEMP, adj. JOHN
FLOWERS & "Hays land" on both sides Old Mill Cr....JOHN PARSONS (SEAL), Wit:
THOMAS DICKSON, JOHN HINSON.

Pp. 200-201: 20 Apr 1765, RICHARD DOWNS of Anson, to JOHN SMITH of same, planter, for
₺20 proc. money...part of 500 A granted to ROBERT MILLS, 22 Nov 1746, &
conveyed to his son NATHAN MILLS, then to HENRY DOWNS, then to RICHARD DOWNS, 100 A
on W side Little River...RICHARD DOWNS (SEAL), Wit: JOHN SMITH (Little River) JOSEPH
WILKINS.

Pp. 202-203: 23 July 1765, THOMAS & ZACHARIAH MOORMAN of Anson, to GEORGE MATHEWS,
of same, for ₺25 gold and silver...part of 640 A granted to SOLOMON
HEWS 22 May 1741 & conveyed to JOHN LEE 27 Aug 1746 & to JOHN HORNBACK, then to
ANDREW MOORMAN, adj. FRANCIS CLARK, 107 A...THOMAS MOORMAN (SEAL), ZACHARIAH MOORMAN
(SEAL), Wit: ISHAM HAILEY, JOHN MATHEWS, ARCHIBALD MOORMAN.

Pp. 203-204: 25 July 1765, JOHN HAMER of Craven Co., SC to WILLIAM HAMER of Anson,
for ₺20 proc. money...100 A granted to JOHN HAMER 25 Feb 1754, adj.
JOHN NEWBERRY, JOHN McCOY...JNO HAMER (SEAL), Wit: SAMUEL SPENCER, ANTHONY HUTCHINS,
MORGAN BROWN.

Page 205: 22 Apr 1765, CHARLES SMITH to HENRY WILLIAMS, for ₺20...100 A granted to
WILLIAM WALTEN 1 July 1758, conveyed to CHARLES SMITH 2 Mar 1761...CHARLES
SMITH (X) (SEAL), Wit: WILLIAM BURT, ROLAND WILLIAMS (R).

Pp. 206-207: 21 Apr 1765, SAMUEL DAVIS of Anson, to EDWARD ALMOND of same, planter,
for ₺12 proc. money...100 A on Mill Cr., N side Pee Dee, granted to
DAVIS 5 Dec 1760...SAML DAVIS (SEAL), Wit: WILLIAM ALMOND, WILLIAM MORRISS, JOHN
PARNALL.

Pp. 207-209: 14 Feb 1763, HENRY McCULLOH, Esqr. of Tomham Green, Middle-sex Co.,
Great Britain & JOSEPH ROBSON & JOSEPH WILLCOCKS, late of Bristol,
appointed by L. W. & T. of JOSHUA WILLCOCKS, late of city of Bristol, merchant, now
decd., to HENRY EUSTICE McCULLOH of Hallifax Co., NC...by grants dated 3 Mar 1745
gave to sd. HENRY McCULLOH, 8 tracts...12,500 A each upon Yadkin or PD River...
for ₺25 Va. money...tract #7....HENRY McCULLOH (SEAL), JOSEPH ROBSON (SEAL), &
JOSEPH WILLCOCKS (SEAL), by JNO. CAMPBELL. Wit: ALIX FORD, AMBROSE KNOX.
Chowan County: 23 Aug 1765, Proven before me, CHARLES BERRY.
[The next several deeds are quite similar and will be abstracted
in a much shorter form.]

Pp. 210-212: 10 Apr 1763, HENRY McCULLOH to HENRY EUSTACE McCULLOH...part of tract
#7, 350 A including mouth of Uhary Creek or River...HENRY McCULLOH
(SEAL), Proven 23 Aug 1765, CHAS. BERRY.

Pp. 213-215: 12 Apr 1763, HENRY McCULLOH to HENRY EUSTACE McCULLOH...part of tract
#7, 600 A on E side Yadkin...Same sign., wit., proving date.

Page 216: Blank.

Pp. 217-219: 9 Apr 1763, HENRY McCULLOH to HENRY EUSTACE McCULLOH, for ₺38 Va. money
...land above JOHN HOPKINS, opp. ENOCH FLOYDS clearing, 430 A on
McClains Cr....same sign., wit., proving date.

Pp. 220-222: 7 Apr 1763, HENRY McCULLOH to HENRY EUSTACE McCULLOH...part of tract
#7, 300 A on N side Pee Dee...same sign., wit., proving date.

Pp. 223-225: 25 Mar 1763, HENRY McCULLOH to HENRY EUSTACE McCULLOH...for ₺12 Va.
money...100 A on Buffelow Bottom...same sign., wit., proving date.

Pp. 226-228: 10 Nov 1763, HENRY McCULLOH to HENRY EUSTACE McCULLOH, for ₺19 s10
Va. money...land on Brushey Bottom...same sign., wit., proving date.

Pp. 229-231: 10 Nov 1763, HENRY McCULLOH to HENRY EUSTACE McCULLOH, for ₺20 Va.
money...land on N side Pee Dee, known as WILLIAM HAMBYS, THOS HARRING-
TONS place, part of tract #7...same sign., wit., proving date.

Pp. 232-234: 9 Apr 1763, HENRY McCULLOH to HENRY EUSTACE McCULLOH, for ₺34 Va. money
...565 A above JAMES SARGENTS improvement...same sign., wit., prov. date.

Pp. 235-236: 2 Apr 1763, HENRY McCULLOH to HENRY EUSTACE McCULLOH, for ₺21 Va. money.
...land on Uhary River, where WM BARNS lived, 246 A...same sign., wit.,
prov. date.

Pp. 237-238: 2 ___ 1765, ANTHONY HUTCHINS of Anson, to SAMUEL SPENCER of same, for
₺20 proc. money...200 A granted to HUTCHINS 22 Feb 1764...ANTHONY
HUTCHINS (SEAL), Wit: JAMES BRUCE, DANIEL GRIGG.
Rec. July Term 1765. THOMAS FROHOCK, Clk.

Page 239: 25 Apr 1765, JOHN CULPEPPER of Anson, to WILLIAM BROOKS of same, for ₺25...
100 A on S side Rocky River, where BROOKS now lives at JOHN LEEs ford, Richardson Cr....JOHN CULPEPPER (SEAL), Wit: HENRY STOKES, THOS. DENARD, JACOB DENARD (X).
Recorded according to law. THOS FROHOCK. Clk.

Page 240: Blank.

Pp. 241-242: 25 Apr 1764, SAMUEL DAVIS of Anson, to THOMAS BOLDIN of same, for ₺11
proc. money...100 A adj. CHARLES ROBINSON, JOHN McCOY...granted to
JOHN EVERITT 27 Sept 1756...SAMUEL DAVIS (SEAL), Wit: CHARLES ROBINSON, CALEB TOUCH-
STONE.   Recorded according to law. THOS FROHOCK, C.C.

Pp. 242-243: 11 Sept 1765, JOSEPH CULPEPPER of Anson, to EDMUND LILLY of same, for
₺40 proc. money...100 A on N side Rockey River, opp. WALTER GIBSON, at
mouth of Spring branch...granted to JOHN PRESLAR, conveyed unto WALTER GIBSON, then
to JOSEPH CULPEPPER, 6 Sept 1760...JOSEPH CULPEPPER (SEAL), Wit: TYRE ROBINSON,
JOHN GIBSON, SHADRACH HOGAN.   Recorded according to law. THOMAS FROHOCK, Clerk of C. (

Page 244: 1 Aug 1765, JOHN CLARK of <u>Macklingburg</u> Co., to SILVESTER WALKER of Anson, for Ł50...195 A granted to <u>CLARK 1746</u>, on S side Pee Dee, Turkey cock Cr....JOHN CLARK (SEAL), Wit: WM. HARRINGTON, JOSEPH WHITE, JOEL PHILLIPS (X). Recorded according to law. THOMAS FROHOCK. Cl. Ct.

Pp. 245-246: 13 Mar 1765, WILLIAM PELLAM, JUNR. of Anson, to ROBT. THORN of same, for Ł20 proc. money...part of 400 A granted to JAMES GOWERS, 137 A on Buffelow Cr....WILLIAM PELLAM (W) (SEAL), Wit: WILLIAM McDANIEL (W), GEORGE THOMAS.   Recorded according to law. THOMAS FROHOCK, Clk.

Pp. 246-247: 10 May 1765, MARY FORMAN of Anson, planter, to WILLIAM ALMONDS of Anson, for Ł20 proc. money...100 A on NE side Pee Dee, adj. JAMES TERRY, SAMUEL DAVIS, granted to MARY FORMAN 24 Apr 1762...MARY FORMAN (O) (SEAL), Wit: VIOLET PRIMROSE, RICHARD JONES (X).   Recorded according to law. THOS. FROHOCK, Clk.

Page 248: 15 Aug 1765, THOMAS DIXON of Anson, to JOHN WRIGHT, Younger, son of JOHN WRIGHT, Merchant of same, for Ł130 proc. money...land on SW side Pee Dee, adj. Huckleberry Cr., THOMAS THOMPKINS...granted to THOMAS JONES...THOMAS DIXON (SEAL), Wit: THOMAS THOMPKINS, THOMAS WRIGHT (T).
Recorded according to law. THOMAS FROHOCK, C. C.

Page 249: 7 Oct 1758, BENJAMIN JACKSON of Anson, to JOHN JACKSON SENR. of same, for Ł5...400 A...BENJ. JACKSON (SEAL), Wit: PHILLIP HERNDON, JOHN JACKSON. Recorded according to law, THOMAS FROHOCK, C. C.

Pp. 250-251: 16 July 1765, WILLIAM NEWBERRY of Anson, to JOSEPH DUNHAM, for Ł40 proc. money...1/2 of 200 A granted to WILLIAM FERRELL 27 Sept 1756, conveyed to sd. NEWBERRY 5 May 1757...land N side PD, on W side N fork of Mountain Cr., on the lower end of land patented to JOSEPH DAYSON , formerly surveyed for WILLIAM COLEMAN...WILLIAM NEWBERRY (W) (SEAL), Wit: SAMUEL WILLIAMS, JOSHUA COLLINS, JOHN CARTRIGHT (I C), Recorded according to law, THOMAS FROHOCK, C. C.

"October Court 1805.
We the committee of the Court appointed to examine the Books have Examined up to this page. WM JOHNSON, JAMES MARSHALL, JAMES DOUGLASS, J. CULPEPPER, J. JACKSON."

Page 252: Blank.

Page 253: 13 Aug 1765, JERDONE GIBSON of Anson, to THOMAS WADE of Craven Co., <u>SC</u>, for Ł30...300 A on N side Hitchcocks Creek, adj. JOHN CRAWFORD, JENNEYs branch, JOSEPH HALL...JERDONE GIBSON (SEAL), Wit: JAMES THURSBY, WILLIAM WILTSHER (W),
Recorded according to law. THOMAS FROHOCK, C. C.

Pp. 254-255: 23 Oct 1765, CORNELIUS ROBINSON & wf ELIZABETH of Anson, planter, to CHARLES ROBINSON, planter, for Ł80 proc. money...part of 600 A granted to <u>CHARLES</u> ROBINSON 22 Nov 1746, & bequeathed to sd. CORNELIUS by L. W. & T. of CHARLES ROBINSON...CORNELIUS ROBINSON (SEAL), ELIZABETH E. ROBINSON (SEAL), Wit: ROBERT THORN (R), WILLIAM MacDANIEL (W), Recorded according to law, THOMAS FROHOCK, C. C.

Page 256: Blank.

Pp. 257-258: 22 Jan 1765, JOSEPH DUNHAM to WILLIAM NEWBERRY, both of Anson, planter, for Ł40 proc. money...part of 600 A granted to MORGAN BROWN 16 Mar 1756, & conveyed to GEORGE PENNINGTON, then to sd. DUNHAM on S side Mountain Creek, adj. GOLDS line...150 A...JOSEPH DUNHAM (SEAL), MARY DUNHAM (M) (SEAL), Wit: SAML. WILLIAMS

JOSHUA COLLINS, JOHN CARTRIGHT (I C). Recorded according to law, THOMAS FROHOCK, C. C.

Pp. 259-260: 7 May 1766, THOMAS BOLDIN of Anson, to ISAAC JOHNSON of same, planter,
for Ł80 proc. money...2 tracts: (1) 100 A adj. CHARLES ROBINSON, on E
side Little River, adj. land surveyed for JOHN McCOY, granted to JOHN AVERITT 27
Sept 1756 (2) 100 A granted to GEORGE COLEMAN, 4 Apr 1750...THOMAS BOLDIN (T) (SEAL),
Wit: SHADRACH DENSON, JACOB SHEPPARD, HENRY FINCH. Recorded according to law,
SAMUEL SPENCER, C. C.

Page 261: Blank.

Pp. 262-263: 18 Feb 1765, HUGH McBRIDE of Anson, planter, to MATTHEW BAILEY of same,
for Ł30 proc. money...200 A on a branch of Jones Cr., laid out for JACOB
PAUL 10 Apr 1761, conveyed to sd. McBRIDE...HUGH McBRIDE (X) (SEAL), MARY McBRIDE (M)
(SEAL), Wit: S. BROWN, DANIEL MURPHEY (D), Recorded according to law, THOMAS FROHOCK, C.

Pp. 264-265: 25 July 1765, JOHN HAMER of Craven Co., SC, merchant, to WILLIAM HAMER
of Anson, yeoman, for Ł20...112 A granted to JOHN HAMER 15 May 1754,
adj. JOHN NEWBERRY...JNO. HAMER (SEAL), Wit: SAML. SPENCER, ANTHO. HUTCHINS, MORGAN
BROWN. Recorded according to law, THOMAS FROHOCK, C. C.

Pp. 266-267: 1 Nov 1763, WILLIAM PICKETT of Anson, planter, to CORNELIUS ROBINSON,
of same, planter, for Ł50 proc. money...300 A on S bank Pee Dee, granted
to WILLIAM PHILLIPS...WILLIAM PICKETT (SEAL), MORNING PICKETT (M) (SEAL), Wit:
J. PICKETT, CHAS. ROBINSON, Recorded according to law. THOMAS FROHOCK, C. C.

Pp. 268-269: 14 June 1764, BENJAMIN MANOR of Anson, to GEORGE COLLINS, for Ł10
proc. money...part of 300 A granted to sd. MANOR 21 Oct 1758, 100 A
...BENJN MANOR (B) (SEAL), Wit: JOHN CUNDALL, CHARLES SPRADLIN (CS), Recorded
according to law. THOS. FROHOCK, C. C.

Pp. 270-271: 30 Oct 1764, WILLIAM DOWNS of Berkley Co., S. C.,to HENRY DOWNS of
Mecklingburg Co., NC, for Ł100...land on W side Little River near
DYSONs line...300 A, part of a grant to ROBERT MILLS 2 Nov 1746...WILLIAM DOWNS
(SEAL), Wit: THOMAS HUSTON, ZEPHANIAH JOHNS, JOHN WILSON. Proven by ZEPHANIAH
JOHNS23 Mar 1765. MAURICE MOORE.

Pp. 272-273: 20 Sept 1764, TILMAN HELMS of Anson, planter, to CHARLES ROBINSON,
planter, for Ł10 proc. money...50 A granted to sd. HELMS 27 Nov 1762...
TILMAN HELMS (T) (SEAL), Wit: ZECHARIAH SMITH, CORNELIUS ROBINSON, THOS. BOLDIN
(T). Recorded according to law. THOMAS FROHOCK, C. C.

Page 274: 21 July 1764, ELISHA PARKER SENR of Anson, to beloved son, ELISHA PARKER,
JR. for natural love & affection...100 A on E side Pee Dee, adj. GOODMAN's
upper corner, Marks Creek, COCHRAN's corner, 300 A granted to SAMUEL GOODMAN 17
June 1746...ELISHA PARKER (P) (SEAL), Wit: MORGAN BROWN, JOHN THOMAS.
Recorded according to law. SAML. SPENCER, C. C.

Page 275: 21 July 1764, ELISHA PARKER to son STEPHEN PARKER, both of Anson, for
natural love & affection...my Manor plantation on N side Pee Dee, Marks
Creek, adj. BRYAN WARD, 300 A granted to WILLIAM COHAN 13 Mar 1756...ELISHA PARKER
(P) (SEAL), Wit: MORGAN BROWN, JOHN THOMAS. Recorded according to law, SAML.
SPENCER, C. C.

Page 276: 20 July 1764, SAMUEL PARSON of Anson, to HADEN MORRIS of same, for Ł30
proc. money...200 A granted to WILLIAM STONE 3 Oct 1755 & conveyed to

sd. PARSONS...on N side Little River...SAMUEL PARSONS (SEAL), RACHEL PARSONS (SEAL), Wit: MATTHEW RAIFORD, WILLIAM QUEEN (X), Recorded according to law, THOMAS FROHOCK, C. C.

Page 277: Blank.

Page 278: 10 Aug 1764, THOMAS DICKSON of Anson, to THOMAS THOMPKINS of same, for Ł10 proc. money...10 A on SW side Pee Dee, adj. THOMPKINS old line...THOMAS DICKSON (SEAL), Wit: JOHN WRIGHT, THOMAS WRIGHT (T). Recorded according to law, SAML. SPENCER, C. C.

Page 279: 20 Sept 1764, DAVID EVANS of Anson, planter, to THOMAS WILLIAMS, for Ł10 proc. money...land on SW side Pee Dee, at mouth of Davids Cr., adj. McCULLOHS line, 140 A...DAVID EVANS (D) (SEAL), Wit: TIERY ROBINSON, EDMD LILLY, JOSEPH MURPHEY (I). Recorded according to law. SAML SPENCER, C. C.

Page 280: Blank.

Pp. 281-282: 20 Sept 1764, THOMAS CRAWFORD of SC, to STEPHEN COLE, of Anson, for Ł 8 proc. money...300 A granted to ENOS THOMAS 1 July 1758, 1/3 or 100 A, conveyed to JAMES DOWNING 10 July 1758, then to sd. CRAWFORD 27 Apr 1759... Cartlidges Creek...THOS. CRAWFORD (SEAL), Wit: WILLIAM ADAMS, JOHN COLE. Recorded accofding to law. THOMAS FROHOCK, C. C.

Pp. 283-284: 29 Jan 1765, WILLIAM PICKETT of Anson, to JOHN STEPHENS, JR. of Cumberland Co., NC, for Ł80 proc. money...land on S side Pee Dee, below the mouth of Brown Cr...260 A & 25 A, part of THOMAS GEORGE's land as pr. deed from ZACHARY PHILLIPS to JOSEPH OATS 5 Sept 1761, and then sold to WILLIAM PICKETT 20 Sept 1763...WILLIAM PICKETT (SEAL), Wit: MORGAN BROWN, WILLIAM TEMPLE COLE, Recorded according to law, THOS. FROHOCK, C. C.

Page 285: Blank.

Page 286: 10 Oct 1765, JOHN JONES of Anson, to JAMES SHORT of same, for Ł20...100 A on N side Jones Creek, adj. JAMES JONES...JOHN JONES (H) (SEAL), Wit: ISHAM HALEY, RANDAL HALEY, MARSHALL DIGGS. Recorded according to law, THOS FROHOCK, C. C.

Page 287: 8 Oct 1765, ZACHERY PHILLIPS of Anson, to WILLIAM PHILLIPS, JUNR. for Ł50... land on Goulds fork, granted to sd. ZACHR. 23 NOv 1764...ZACHR. PHILLIPS (SEAL), Wit: WILLIAM THOMPSON, SAMPSON CULPEPPER (X), JAMES UPTON. Recorded according to law. THOS FROHOCK., C. C.

Page 288: Blank.

Pp. 289-290: 21 Apr 1765, DAVID BRUTON, planter, to WILLIAM PAGE, weaver, for Ł12 proc. money...100 A on N side Densons frk of Little River, granted to GEORGE FELDS 1 Dec 1760...DAVID BRUTON (SEAL), Wit: WILLIAM HOLTON, WILLIAM QUEEN (X), MATTHEW RAIFORD.

Pp. 291-292: 9 May 1765, WILLIAM CRITTENDEN of SC, planter, to JOSEPH WILKINS of Anson, for Ł30 proc. money...35 A adj. DAVID MILES (MILLS), granted to CRITTENDEN 25 May 1757...WILLIAM CRITTENDEN (SEAL), Wit: SAML RATCLIFF, JOHN SMITH. Recorded according to law. THOMAS FROHOCK,C.C.

Pp. 293-294: 9 May 1765, JOSEPH WILKINS of Anson, planter, to CHRISTOPHER CHRISTIAN
            of same, planter, for ₤50 proc. money...100 A on bank of Little River,
granted to ROBERT MILLS 2 Aug 1748, conveyed to WILLIAM STONE, to HUMPHRIES, to
CRITTENDEN, to WILKINS...JOSEPH WILKINS (₤) (SEAL), Wit: H. DOWNS, JOHN POOL (₤),
JACOB SHEPPARD, Recorded according to law, THOMAS FROHOCK, C. C.

Page 295: 4 Oct 1765, JOHN MORRIS of Anson, to JOHN COOK of same, for ₤30 proc.
          money...150 A on Williams Creek where COOK now lives, adj. 100 A where
WILLIAM MORRIS now lives...JOHN MORRIS (∧) (SEAL), ELIZABETH MORRIS (I) (SEAL),
Wit: JOHN BLOODWORTH, WILLIAM LEVERITT. Recorded according to law, SAML. SPENCER, C. C

Pp. 296-297: 2 Feb 1765, WILLIAM PELLAM, JUNR. of Anson, to WILLIAM McDANIEL of same,
            planter, for ₤30 proc. money...land granted to JAMES JEWERS on E side
Little River, Buffaloe Creek, 50 A...WILLIAM PELLAM JUNR (W) (SEAL), Wit: CHARLES
ROBINSON, GEORGE THOMAS. Recorded according to law. THOS. FROHOCK, C. C.

Page 298: 14 Feb 1765, RICHARD CASWELL of Dobbs Co., to THOMAS SWEARINGHAM of Pitt
          Co., for ₤60 proc. money...land on Each side the fork of Cheeks Creek,
called Townsends fork, 600 A granted to sd. CASWELL 7 July 1750...RICHD. CASWELL
(SEAL), Wit: SAMUEL SWEARINGHAM, VAN SWEARINGHAM. Recorded according to law, SAML.
SPENCER, C. C.

Page 299: Blank.

Page 300: 22 July 1765, THOMAS LACY of Anson, planter, to CHARLES MEDLOCK of same, for
          ₤7 s10 proc. money...part of a granted to JAMES MUCELROY 26 ___ 1757, 330 A
on Solomons Creek, adj. SOLOMON HUES, 130 A...THOS LACY(SEAL), Wit: THOMAS FROHOCK,
JOHN COLLSON. Recorded according to law. THOS FROHOCK, C. C.

Page 301: Blank.

Page 302: 24 Sept 1765, WILLIAM MORRIS of Anson, to JOHN COLE, for ₤30...100 A where
sd. MORRIS now lives on Williams Creek...WILLIAM MORRIS (₶) (SEAL), ALLS MORRIS (℞)
(SEAL), Wit: JOHN BLOODWORTH, WILLIAM LEVERITT. Recorded according to law. SAML.
SPENCER, C. C.

Pp. 303-304: 13 Mar 1765, WILLIAM PELLAM JUNR to GEORGE THOMAS, both of Anson, for
            ₤5 proc. money...200 A granted to JAMES JEWERS, on Buffaloe Creek, 12
A adj. McDANIEL...WILLIAM PELLAM (W) (SEAL), Wit: WILLIAM MacDANIEL (X), ROBERT
THORN (X). Proved July Session 1766, SAML. SPENCER, C. C.

Pp. 305-306: 13 Apr 1765, WILLIAM YOUNGBLOOD of Anson, to JACOB HAMMILL of Orange
            Co., NC, for ₤50 proc. money...250 A on Bomporesfork of Little River,
above YOUNGBLOODs first survey...granted to YOUNGBLOOD 26 Nov 1757...WILLIAM YOUNG-
BLOOD (SEAL), Wit: JAS. ATTAWAY, FRANCIS EITHERINGTON (X), WILLIAM ATTAWAY (W).
            Proven July Term 1765, THOS. FROHOCK, C. C.

Pp. 307-308: 23 July 1765, TILMAN HELMS of Anson, to WILLIAM BURT of Cumberland Co., fo
            ₤10...100 A on Buffaloe, granted to JOHN ASHLY 5 Dec 1760 & conveyed to
HELMS 4 May 1762...TILMAN HELMS (T) (SEAL), Wit: THOMAS FROHOCK, HENRY WILLIAMS.
            Proven July Term 1765, THOS FROHOCK, C. C.

Pp. 309-310: 1 July 1765, JOHN CARPENTER of Anson, to SAMUEL PARSON of same, for ₤35
          proc. money...100 A on S side Cedar Creek, granted to JAMES ALLEY & sold
to CARPENTER...JOHN CARPENTER (₤) (SEAL), ELIZAB. CARPENTER (X) (SEAL), Wit: WILLIAM
QUEEN (X), WILLIAM HOLLAN, OBADI THERRELL. Proven July Term 1765, THOS.FROHOCK, C. C.

Page 311: Blank.

Pp. 312-313: 9 May 1765, JOSEPH WILKINS of NC, planter, to CHRISTOPHER CHRISTIAN
          of Anson, planter, for ₤30 proc. money...land on NE side Little River,
adj. DAVID MILLS upper survey. .35 A, part of a tract granted to WILLIAM CRITTENDEN
25 May 1757 & sold to JOSEPH WILKINS...JOSEPH WILKINS (₤) (SEAL), Wit: WILLIAM YOUNG,
JOSEPH FINCHER, J. DOWNS. Proven July Term 1765, THOMAS FROHOCK,C. C.

Pp. 314-315: 24 July 1765, ISAAC BELYEU of Anson, to JOHN HENRY of same, for ₤15
          proc. money...100 A, part of 200 A granted to SAMUEL FRENCH 25 May
1757, conveyed to ELIZABETH GRIGGS, then to sd. BELYEU on Cedar Cr....ISAAC BELYEU
(O) (SEAL), Wit: JAMES POSTON, PETER WATKINS. Recorded July Term 1765, THOMAS
FROHOCK, C.C.

Pp. 316-317: 10 June 1765, JOSEPH DONHAM of Anson, planter, to JOHN CARTRIGHT of
          same, for ₤110 proc. money...350 A on Mountain Cr., adj. NEWBERRY,
granted to MORGAN BROWN 15 Mar 1756, conveyed to GEORGE PENNINGTON 5 Feb 1761,
conveyed to DONHAM 25 Feb ____ ...JOSEPH DONHAM (SEAL), MARY DONHAM (M) (SEAL), Wit:
SAML. WILLIAMS, JOSHUA COLLINS, WILLM NEWBERRY, (W), Recorded July Term 1766, SAML.
SPENCER, C. C.

Page 318: 10 Aug 1765, JOSEPH ATTAWAY & wf GOOLSPRING of Anson, to JOHN SPENCER
          of same, for ₤90 proc. money...200 A on Bupores fork of Little River,
granted to WILLIAM STONE 26 May 1757...JOSEPH ATTAWAY (SEAL), GOOLSRING ATTAWAY (X)
(SEAL), Wit: WILLIAM SPENCER, JOS.PERSONS (J), Recorded July term 1766, SAML.
SPENCER, C. C.

Page 319: Blank.

Pp. 320-322: 25 Oct 1765, CHARLES MEDLOCK, sheriff of Anson, to EDMUND FANNING of
          Orange Co., NC...by an act passed for easy recovery of debts...Inferior
Court...estate of JOHN HERN, recovered in Court by JOHN HAMER...land granted to
FRANCIS CLARK 25 May 1757...sold to HENRY 26 Apr 1758...CHAS.MEDLOCK (SEAL), Wit:
FRANCIS SMITH, HENRY STOKES, JOHN SMITH. Recorded July Ct. 1766, SAML. SPENCER, C.C.

Pp. 323-324: Blank.

Pp. 325-327: 25 Oct 1765, CHARLES MEDLOCK, Sheriff to EDMUND FANNING of Orange Co...
          estate of HENRY TIPPINS confiscated, for case awarded to JOSEPH SCOTT...
100 A...CHAS. MEDLOCK (SEAL), Wit: FRANCIS SMITH, HENRY STOKES, JOHN SMITH. Recorded
July Ct. 1766, SAML. SPENCER, C. C.

Pp. 328-330: Blank.

Page 331: 5 Oct 1765, JERM MILLER of Anson, to WILLIAM RAIFORD of same, for ₤4 proc.
          money...land on Gulds fork, adj. WILLIAM POWELLs...JEROM MILLER (SEAL), Wit:
PICKETT, MARTHA PICKETT. Recorded July Term 1766, SAML. SPENCER, C. C.

Page 332: Blank.

Page 333: 16 Oct 1765, JOHN SHEPPARD of Cartaret Co., NC to MATHEW McKINNE of Anson, for Ƚ20 proc. money...200 A on Browns Cr, including McKINNES improvement... McMANNESS line, granted to SHEPPARD 22 Apr 1765...JOHN SHEPPARD (SEAL), Wit: ZACHARIAH SMITH, JACOB SHEPPARD. Recorded July Ct., 1766, SAML. SPENCER, C. C.

Page 334: Blank.

Pp. 335-336: 19 Oɕt 1765, THOMAS MOORMAN of Anson, planter, to WILLIAM ADAMS of same, Blacksmith, for Ƚ15 proc. money...200 A on a drean of Crooked Creek, part of 400 A granted to MOORMAN 25 May 1757..THOMAS MOORMAN (SEAL), Wit: JOHN WEBB (Ɨ), EDWARD SMITH (2), GEO. WILSON. Recorded Oct Ct., 1766, SAML. SPENCER, C. C.

Page 337: 22 Feb 1765, WALTER GIBSON of Anson, to SHADRACH HOGAN of same, for Ƚ10 proc. money...100 A on SW side Pee Dee, adj. BENJ. MOORMAN, Rockey River, granted to GIBSON 5 Dec 1760...WALTER GIBSON (W) (SEAL), Wit: JOSEPH CULPEPPER, ELIJAH CLARK(X). Recorded July Term 1766, THOS. FROHOCK, C. C.

Page 338: Blank.

Pp. 339-340: 28 Oct 1765, THOMAS TALLENT of Anson, to TIRENCE CARROLL of Craven Co. SC, planter, for Ƚ30 proc. money...land on Smiths Cr., adj. THOMAS BERRY, part of a tract granted to JOSEPH WHITE & FRANCIS McELWAIN 13 Apr 1749, conveyed to THOMAS BERRY 18 July 1752, conveyed to his ɛon CHARLES BERRY __ Oct 1755, conveyed to TALLENT 17 Aug 1760...THOMAS TALLANT (SEAL), Wit: MOSES TALLANT (M), SAML. SPENCER. Recorded July Ct., 1766, SAML. SPENCER, C. C.

Pp. 341-342: 29 Oct 1765, TERENCE CARROLL of Craven Co., SC, planter, to PETER WATKINS of Anson, planter, for Ƚ40...(land in preceding deed)...TIRENCE CARROLL (X) (SEAL), Wit: MOSES TALLANT (M), SAML. SPENCER. Rec. July Ct., 1766, SAML. SPENCER, C. C.

Pp. 343-344: 20 Apr 1765, THOMAS FANNING & wf TABITHA of Rowan Co., to FRANCES LEE of Anson, for Ƚ 8 proc. money...200 A granted to FANNING 24 Apr 1762, on W side Naked Creek...THOS FANNING (T) (SEAL), TABITHA FANNING (X) (SEAL), No Wit. Proven July Ct., 1767 [1765?].

Page 345: 13 Apr 1765, WILLIAM YOUNGBLOOD of Anson, to JACOB HAMMILL of Orange Co., NC, for Ƚ 50 proc. money...240 A granted to sd. YOUNGBLOOD 26 Nov 1757... WILLIAM YOUNGBLOOD (SEAL), Wit: JOS. ATTAWAY, FRONES EITHRINGTON (X), WILLIAM ATTAWAY X. Proven July Term 1765.

Page 346: Blank.

Pp. 347-348: 20 Jan 1766, DAVID DUMAS of Anson, planter, to BENJAMIN DUMAS of same, planter, for Ƚ500 proc. money...1181 A in 4 tracts: (1) 188 A opp. to Rocky River, on PEE DEE, (2) 50 A, these two granted to BENJAMIN DUMAS the elder in his lifetime (3) land on S side Buffaloe Island, formerly belonged to JOHN CLARK 236 A, granted to EDMD LILLY 10 Apr 1763 & (4) 810 A granted to JOHN CLARK 20 June 1746... DAVID DUMAS (SEAL), SARAH DUMAS (X) (SEAL), Wit: FRANCIS SMITH, RICHARD DIXON (X). Proven July Ct., 1766.

Page 349: Blank.

Pp. 350-351: 22 Jan 1766, ROBERT WHICKER of Anson, & wf HANNER of Anson, planter, to
                JULIUS HOLLEY of same, for £20 proc. money...part of 300 A granted 1756
to JOSEPH WHITE, SR. & conveyed to WILLIAM PHILLIPS, SENR. then to ROBERT WHICKER...
150 A on Lains Cr....ROBERT WHICKER (R) (SEAL), HANNER WHICKER (X) (SEAL), Wit: JOSEPH
WHITE, SOLOMON WARD (X), JOSEPH WHITE [again].
                Proven July Term, 1766.

Pp. 352-353: 24 Jan 1766, THOMAS TALLANT of Anson, to JAMES ALMOND of same, for £50
                proc. money...80 A at mouth of Naked Creek, granted to HENRY FALCENBURGH
6 Apr 1750, conveyed to TARRANCE CARROLL, then to JOHN LEETH 15 Oct 1754, then to
TALLANT 2 Mar 1756...THOMAS TALLANT (SEAL), HANNER TALLANT (H) (SEAL), Wit: THOMAS
UPEAY [USERY?], LENARD WIGDON [HIGDON?] (X), MARY WIGDON. Proven Oct. Court [1766?].

Page 354: Blank.

Pp.355-356: _____ 1766, ISAAC JOHNSON of Halifax Co., Va., to JAMES SHEPPARD of Anson,
                for £____...200 A adj. CHAS. ROBINSON, JOHN McCOY...ISAAC JOHNSON (SEAL),
Wit: PETER HUDSON, PETER ROGER, JACOB SHEPPARD.
                Proven Oct. term 1766.

Pp. 357-358: 4 Feb 1766, DAVID DUMAS of Anson, to FRANCIS SMITH of same, for £20 proc.
                money...400 A on S side Great Pee Dee, partly in Walker Island, 2 miles
below the mouth of Rocky River, granted to ROBERT PARKS 1745, & sold to JOHN SPAN
14 Oct 1747, proved 14 Sept 1749, Reg. in Bladen Co., Book C, folio 126, 25 June 1750,
sold to AMBROSE JOSHUA SMITH 22 June 1756, then sold to BENJAMIN DUMAS 7 Aug 1756...
DAVID DUMAS (SEAL), SARAH DUMAS (X) (SEAL), Wit: BENJAMIN DUMAS, RICHD. DIXON (X).
                Proven July Ct. 1766.

Page 359: 3 May 1766, JOHN FLOWER of Anson, planter, to CHARLES HENSON of same, for
                £25 proc. money...100 A, part of 400 A granted to W. KEMP...sold to FLOWER
by THOMAS TOMPKINS...JOHN FLOWER (SEAL), Wit: HEZA. RUSS, JOHN PARSON.
                Proven Oct. Ct. 1766.

Page 360: Blank.

Pp. 361-362: 15 June 1766, THOMAS BLASSINGAME of SC, to JOHN LONG of Anson, for £60
                proc. money...land on S side Cartledge Cr., part of a grant to WILLIAM
BLEWETT, 6 Mar 1759, sold to BLASSINGAME 29 May 1761, 103 A...THOMAS BLASSINGAME (B)
(SEAL), Wit: JOHN COLE, WILLIAM WATKINS. Reg. July Term, 1766, SAML. SPENCER, C. C.

Pp. 363-364: 16 June 1766, THOMAS BLASSINGAME of NC, yeoman, to JOHN LONG, Blacksmith,
                of Anson, for £100 proc. money...200 A on Cartledge Cr., adj. WILLIAM
BLEWETT, granted ___ Apr 1762 to JOHN LONG & conveyed to BLASSINGAME 24 Apr 1762...
THOMAS BLASSINGAME (B) (SEAL), Wit: JOHN COLE, WILLIAM WATKINS. Reg. July Term 1766.

Pp. 365-366: 23 July 1766, JOSEPH WHITE of Anson, planter, to ZECHARIAH SMITH of same,
                Blacksmith, for £20 proc. money...land on N side Pee Dee, adj. DENSON...
JOSEPH WHITE (SEAL), Wit: WILLIAM BROOKS (B), MARSHALL DIGGS. Proven July Court 1766.

Pp. 367-368: 14 July 1766, THOMAS MITCHELL of Anson, to NICHOLAS BROADAWAY of same,
                for £30 proc. money...150 A on N side Jones Cr...THOS MITCHELL(SEAL), Wit:
HENRY FALKENBROUGH (F), WM FIELDEN. Proven July Ct. 1766.

END OF VOLUME 3.

Arrinton William	1
Arrinton Thomas	1
-------- Joseph &	

-------- John	1
Ashley John	1
Altman James	1
Adams Richard	1
Ashley Robert	1
Brown Morgan ⎫	
John Condall & Negroes ⎬	
Aber & Dole ⎭	4
Bound John	1
Bound James	1
Bound James Junr	1
Blassingham Thomas ⎫	
William Moody Negrows ⎬	
Moss and Will ⎭	4
-ennett John	1
-lewet William	1
Burges William &	
Benja. Aivers (?)	2
------- Thomas &	

-ond Nicholas	1
belew Isaac	1
Broadaway Nicholas	1
B------- Robert	-
-------------	-
Bruce (?) James	1
Berrey Thomas	1
Bailey Mathew	1
Benton Margts. Son	1
Bailey Thomas	1
Bruton Samuel	1
Brown William	1
Brown James	1
Boan John & Son	2
Barns William	1
Brooks William Negros ⎫	
Sharper Cesor Quuan Mol ⎬	
& David Snead ⎭	6
Brooks John John Do Junr ⎫	
--------- ⎭	3
Black Edward & Joel Chevers	2
Ballin William & Richd Green	2
Barns Charles & Barnit Do	2
Bright Albert	1
Bishop Abner Constable for ⎫	
William Willson ⎭	1
Barns John	1
Brutain David	1
Blake Archabald	1

Boldin Thomas	1
Coleman Willaim & Negr. Simon	2
Cheak John	1
--------	-
Cannon Joseph	1
Constant William	1
Carpender John & ⎫	
James Gibson ⎭	2
Culpeper Joseph & ⎫	
Adams William ⎭	2
Crittenden William & ⎫	
Sampson Oneal ⎭	2
Culpeper John	1
Culpeper Sampson	1
Culpeper William &	
Culpeper Robert	2
Collson John ⎫	
Charles Harrington ⎪	
Whipmell Harington ⎪	
Negros--- ⎪	
Jack Syphoor Danah ⎬	14
Lindah Dinah Junr ⎪	
Mole Philles ⎪	
William Shewell & ⎪	
John Purkins ⎭	
Cole Mark	3
Clark Frances	3
Coward William & Wm Paul	2
Carter George	1
Cox William	1
Coleman John	1
Clark Christopher Negros ⎫	
Duke & Luie (?) ⎭	3
Cockram William (stricken)	
Cook Abraham	1
Cole John & Negros Diner ⎫	
& John Beard ⎭	3
Cole Stephen & Wm Lewalling	2
Cole William & Nathl Williams	2
Clark Jeremiah	1
Cockerham Jacob	1
Crawford John	-
Jack _____	
------------Abbey	
Tamer & John Glen	
Collock Richard	1
Cockerham Thomas & Thomas	
Lawton (?)	2
Diggs Marshall	1
Downer Thomas	1
Downer John	1
Dickson Thomas & ⎫	
Hezekiah Jones ⎭	-

Dill Phillip & Negro Sambo	-	Gordon Alexander Esqr	2
		Gibson Jordon	4
Dinkins William & Thomas Do	2	Griffeth Zeakel	1
Denson James	1	Gibson Walter Gibson Elijah & Molatah Tom	3
Dennis Nathaniel	1		
Dark Samuel	1	Grotehouse Jacob	1
Dumas David Negros Tom & Nan	-	Griffeth Benjamin	1
Denson Shadrick	-	Giles John Wm Norton Negro Boson Pompy Sippes & Phillis	6
Dicks John	-		
Davis Thomas & Davis Gabril	-	Griggs Daniel	1
		Graves Robert	1
Davis Samuel & Two sons	-	Gibon Thomas	1
		Guin Christopher	1
Deas Arthor	-		
Deas James	2	Harget Henry	1
Dunbar John	1	Hasey Isum	1
Dumas Benjamin Dumas Benjamin Junr Zeakel Patrick Negros Frank, Harrey Will. Cooper hanah Phillis Cape Guine Tib & Thos Enol(?) Overseer	13	Hall Joseph Jons Wm & Son John	3
		Haley William	3
		Hamer John Do John Junr Hamer William John Hern(?) & Negro Hannah	5
Denis John & Do Junr & George Shankle	3	Howell Hopkin	
		Hughs John	2
Evants David	1	Hightower Thomas	1
English Thomas	1	Hightower John	1
Erby William	1	Higdon Leonard	1
Elerbee Edward	4	Hornbuck John	1
Elerbee Thomas	4	Henson Phillip Junr & John Flowers	2
Elerbee John	2		
Elsey Merad	1	Hart Arron	1
Etherington Frances	1	Herndon Phillip Samson Carry & Two Negros	4
Easterwood Laurance & Charles Thompson	2		
		Hawkins William	1
Edwards John	1	Higgins William Higgins James &	3
Frayshear William	1	Higgins _____	
Fu James	1	Halton John	1
Franklin Bentley	1	Higgins John & Higgins James	2
Flake Samuel & Negros Mingo		Higgins William	1
French Samuel	1	Halton William	1
French James	1	Howard James	1
Falkinburg Henry	1	Holms Jonathan	1
Falkinburg Andw & Isaac Do	1	Harrelson Joseph	1
		Helms George	1
Fealdin William Constable		Holms Tilman	1
Franklin Laurance	1	Hillen Nathaniel	1
Floyd Enock	1	Hutchins James	1
Frederick John	1	Hutchins Anthony	4
Falkner James	2	Harbord John Senr	1
		Hogan Shadrick	1
		Hoggins William	1
		Hall Henry	1

Homer Walter	1
Hambey Samuel	1
Hildreth David	1
Hodges William	1
Henderson Rice (?)	1
Howell Lewis	1
Hugberry John	1
Henson Phillip Senr	-
Henson Bartlet	1
Henson Banja.	-
Henson Isum	1
Hickson John & Solr. Snead	2
Hicks William	5
Hardick William	1
Hill Charles	1
Husbands John	1
Ivey James	-
Ingrum Willi--	-

Johnston Henry	-
Jinkins John	4
Johnston Thomas	1
Jiu Joseph	1
Jones John	-
Irvin James	-
James Richard	-
Johnston Isaac	-
Johnston William	-
Jackson Banja.	-
Jackson John Senr.	-
Jackson John Junr	-
Jackson Stephen	1
Jefrey John	1
Jordon Esbell Widow for ⎫ Jordon Frances & ⎬ Jordon Rubin ⎭	-
Jinkins John	-
Johnston Lu--	-
Quin Timothy	1
Quin William Cons ⎫ for John Lackey ⎭	1
Quinn Henson	1
Russ Hezekiah & ⎫ Negroe Sarah ⎭	2
Rus Thomas	1
Rushin William ⎫ Negros Mart & Cofee ⎭	3
------------	1
------------	1

Raford Mathew & ⎫ Negro Mingo ⎭	2
Robinson Cornelius	
Negros Walton & Jingo	3
Ratliff Samuel & 2 Sons	3
Robinson Charles	5
Ray Samuel	1
Rottenbury Richard	1
Ry-- John & Brother	2
-ose Samuel	1
Read William	1
Royal John & Thomas Do	2
Roland John	1
Roland Auguston	1
Robins John	1
Ryals Edmond	1
Raley John	1
Sumaran William	1
Smith William & Son	2
Skipper George Senr	5
Skipper Barnaba	1
Skipper Benjamin	1
Sutten Elisha	1
Shin Cornelus	1
Stoaks Henry	1
Sisco John	1
Smith Benjamin	1
Smith Zachariah ⎫ Terey Robinson & ⎬ Negro Jams ⎭	3
Snead Henly & Negro	2
Snead Israel & Son Wm	
Nann Judey Jenny & Peter	6
Snead Samuel & Negro Tom	2
Sanders Patrick	1
Sanders James	1
Smith Edward	1
Stutley Sherly Wm ⎫ James Martin ⎬ & Two Negros ⎭	4
Snipe Robert	1
Smith John & ⎫ Richard Downs ⎭	2
Sway John & Isaac Do	2
Sheppard James ⎫ Jacob Do Joseph Barnet ⎬ Negro Bess & Agg ⎭	5
Slaughter Owen	1
Smith Zachariah	1
Storor Henry	1
Sugg Rasha	1
Suggs Thomas & ⎫ Suggs Thomas Junr ⎭	2

122

Smith Charles	1
Sugg George	1
Simpson Thomas	1
Simpson Samuel	1
Simpson Gilbert	1
Simmons John	1
Spradlin Charles &	
Wm Rottenbury	2
Short James, Daniel Short & Frederick Temples	3
Travis John	1
Tallant Moses	1
Terrey William James Do Negro Ned	3
Taler John	1
Thurman John	1
Touchstone Caleb	1
Terrell Obediah	1
Toutchstone Daniel Negros Charles & Jud	3
Tow-------	1
Tow-------	1
Toutchstone -----	1
Terrey William	1
Tallant Thomas	1
Tallant Aaron & John Moses	2
Thomas Robert	1
Terrey James Negros Jim, Sue & Easter	4
Terrey George	1
Terrey John	1
Tannor Thomas & Robert Parker	2
Tutchstone Stephen	1
Tomkins Thomas	4
Tho well William	2
Tabour Timothy	1
Towers Mary Widow for Thomas & Wm Do	2
Tippins Henry	1

Vines Benjamin	-
Ussery William	-
Useery John, James	
Osmon & Negros Jane	-
Vanhooser John Junr & John	-
Jacob Do Negro	
Cak Charles & Ann	-
Vickery James	-
Vickery Ezeakel	-
--------------	-
--------------	-

Weake Thomas	2
White David	1
Williams Roland	1
Wats John	1
White Nicholas & William Wright	2
Winneham Frances	1
Weak Thomas	1
Weak William	1
White Joseph Junr	1
Williams Thomas	1
Wright John	1
Wells Robert	1
Wolferd Nicholas	1
Welsh James	1
Wilburn Robert	3
Welshear William	1
Watkins William	1
Wright John	1
Williams Samuel	1
Webb John & Son	2
Williams John	1
Wason Wm & Thos Michaell	-
Wood Thomas	1
Willson John	1
Wilkins Joseph & Ben Burt(?)	2
Wilkins Jonathan	1
Wood John & Benja. Vahan	2
Yarbrough Joel	1
Yarbrough Humphry Yarbrough Jonathan	2

N. C. Archives   C. R. 005.801.1

Page 1: Will of THOMAS SMITH of Anson County...to wife SARAH the hole [sic] of
my estate...she is to give children good learning...the estate be Equally
divided between ANN & ELIZABETH & CHARLES...the two orphan Boys should have their
dues from my Estate...JONATHAN HUNT & SARAH my wife, Exrs....12 Aug 1751....THOMAS
SMITH (SEAL), Wit: ROBERT HOATON, AARON VANDEOVER, MARTHA HOATON (X).

Pp. 2-3: Will of CHARLES McDOWELL of Anson County...wife RACHEL, Exr. and friend
GEORGE CATHEE, her assistant...to wife RACHEL, one third part of Estate,
and desire that she make her home with her daughter HANNAH CALLOE...to son JOHN
McDOWELL, b10 Va. money...to daughter RACHEL EAGAN of Augusta Co., Va., 200 acres
on Broad River in Anson Co., NC...to Brother Josep[h] McDOWELL of Frederick Co.,
Va., one brown broad Cloath Coat & one beaver hat & one pare of Show bootes...
my four daughter ANNE EVANES, ELIZABETH BARNS, MARY McPETERS, & HANNAH CALLOE...
24 Jan 1754...CHARLES McDOWELL (SEAL), Wit: EVAN MORGAN, JOHN DAVIS.
     At court held for Frederick County on Tuesday the 4th Day of June 1754...
EVAN MORGAN and JOHN DAVIS proved will....Test, J. WOOD.

          [The land on Broad River bequeathed to RACHEL EAGAN, was sold by
          RACHEL and her husband BARNABY EAGAN by their attorney JOHN McDOWEL;
          see Mecklenburg Co., NC, Deeds, Vol. II, pp. 471-474. The land was
          granted to CHARLES McDOWELL, 4 April 1751, and is now in Cherokee
          County, South Carolina.]

Page 4: Will of JOHN COBURN of Anson County, sick in body...brother SAMUEL, Exr.
     ...to brother JONATHAN ye least thing that the law will allow him,
shilin _____...to brother SAMUEL, land that I had of my sister JUDAH [JUDITH?]...
unto my sister REBEKAH one Inglish shillings...to my sister MARY one Inglish
shilling...to sister JUDAH, the mear that I had at ye fork...to sister SARAH...to
Brother JACOB, the Black mear...to brother ISAAC, the plantation adj. to my
brother SAMUEL...to SAMUEL COCKENDOL, the sorrel mare & colt...November 26, 1754...
JOHN COBURN (+) (SEAL), Wit: CHARLES BETTY.

Pp. 5-6: Will of RICHARD HOUGH of Anson County, planter, sick and weak in body...
     9 September 1754...to wife MARTHA HOUGH, half of my cows and Dry Cattle
& b100 Pa. money...to son WILLIAM my Dwelling plantation & 300 acres & my Waggon
& furniture & four Houses...to son THOMAS HOUGH, b100 Pa. money & one set of
Plow _____...to daughter HANNAH CROABBE, b150 Pa. money...to daughter ELIZABETH
SHARPE, b5 Pa. money...to daughter in law LETTHY STALL, b5 Pa. money...to son
RICHARD HOUGH, 300 acres joining the ford of Broad River & b200 Pa. money...
wife MARTHA & son WILLIAM, Exrs...RICHD HOUGH (X) (SEAL), Wit: TAMER LOVE, GABREL
BROWN.

Page 7: The Nuncupative Will of JOHN MOORE Deceased who was Killed at the Eakoun
     in the Middle Settlement of the Cherekee Nation of Indians taken by me
PETER KOCKINDOLPH before the said JOHN MOORE dyed...his Brother MOSES's son JOHN
should have the place which he bought of JEREMIAH POTTS...and the remainder to his
own wife MARY....6 August 1760....PETER KUYKENDOL.

Pp. 7-8: Will of ALEXANDER McCONNELL of Anson County...weak in Body...to my
        cousin ANDW McCONELL of Roan County, my case of Pistoles & Black
broad Cloth Jacket & Beaver hat to his son JOHN Mc ONNELL...to my Cousin JOHN
McCONNELL of Roan County, silver stock Buckle and to his son JOHN McCONNELL, JR.
a blue Broad Cloth coat...to my step children THOS & JANE BLACK...my man
ALEX HENDERSON to serve out the rest of his time to my wife CATHERINE McCONNELL
...remainder of estate divided between my wife CATHERINE & daughter AGNESS
McCONNELL...wife & Cousin ANDREW, Exrs...2 June 1760...ALEXANDER McCONNELL (SEAL),
Wit: CHARLES MOORE, JAMES SHARG, CHARLES McPETERS.

Pp. 8-10: Will of JAMES ARMSTRONG of Anson County...to son WILLIAM ARMSTRONG one
        bay mare...to son JOHN ARMSTRONG one cow...son MARTIN, one Gray mare
& Coalt...two sons JAMES & JOSEPH, two tracts of patent land joining where I
now live, 450 A...to my two youngest sons BENJAMIN and MATHEW ARMSTRONG, land
where I now live, 370A...to son JAMES a black mare...to daughter MARY ARMSTRONG
Ł40 & one Sorrel mare...three youngest sons JOS., BENJ., & MATHEW, one years
schooling...son JAMES, daughter MARY, Exrs....JAMES ARMSTRONG (SEAL), Wit: CHARLES
MOORE, JOHN BETTY, JAMES PRICE. Will dated 11 May 1760.

Page 11: Will of DAVID FERGUSON of Anson County...SAMUEL NEALEY, JR., PETER KULP,
        Exrs...to my wife, all that was her own right & property...to sister
MARY FERGUSON, Ł8...to sister Ł2...if my wife has a child...my sister ELISABETH
...sister SARAH...22 Dec 1761....DAVID FERGUSON (+) (SEAL), Wit: ROBERT McCREARY,
ROBERT WALKER.

Pp. 12-13: Will of JOHN HICKS of Anson County...wife OBEDIANCE HICKS, one feather
        bed & furniture...to son WILLIAM HICKS...to son JOHN HICKS...to
daughter FRANCES HICKS...to daughter MARY HICKS...to granddaughter SARAH HICKS...
to son JOHN, one Sorrel Stallion...sons JOHN & WM, Exrs....24 Apr 1760...
JOHN HICKS (SEAL), Wit: ALEXR. GORDON, WM HICKS. Proved May Court, 1761, by
ALEXR GORDON. JOHN FFROHOCK.

Pp. 13-14: Will of JOHN VANHOSER of Anson County...to son JOHN Ł4...to daughter
        YONEKEY [sic]...son VALENTINE...daughter CATHERINE...daughter CHRISTIAN
...daughter MARY...son JACOB...son ABRAM, 150 A, lower part of Tract I now live
on & Ł10...daughter ELIZABETH, tract I bought of JOHN DAVIS...wife [not named]
...21 Jan 1762. JOHN VANHOSER (+) (SEAL), Wit: EDMUND LILLY, JOHN WATTSON (+).
        [The wife was apparently HANNAH VANHOSER, see Returns of Administrations
        and probates of wills in this volume.]

Pp. 14-16: Will of ROBERT LEE of Anson County, sick in body...wife SARAH LEE,
        mare, side saddle & furniture...three children WILLIAM & JUDITH &
RICHARD LEE, negro fellow Jack...son JAMES LEE, 3 cows & calves...son ROBERT
LEE, half of tract I live on & rifle Gun...son JOHN LEE, other half of tract...
to daughter MILLEE, bed & furniture...3 daughters MAY YARBROUGH & MITTRY & ELIZA-
BETH LEE, Ł10...daughter SARAH CRITENDEN, s10...wife SARAH, son ROBERT and
Brother, JOHN, Exrs...29 Nov 1766...ROBERT LEE (SEAL), Wit: JOHN COLSON, SAMUEL
COOPER, MARY COLSON (+).

Pp. 16-17: Will of JASON MEADORS of Anson County...to wife ELIZABETH, plantation
        I now live on...eldest son LEWIS, s5 & also DRUSILLA, MARION, & THOMAS,
s1 sterling....children LEWIS, JASON, JOB, & MARIAH...wife ELIZABETH & sons
LEWIS & JOHN, Exrs...23 Mar 1774....JASON MEADOR (SEAL), Wit: WILLIAM EVISS, JOB
MEADOR, CHARLES BOLT.

Pp. 17-18: Will of JENNET McLEOD of Anson County...nephew NORMAN McLEOD, Gold
          cloth & linen...2 Feb 1772...JENNETT McLEOD (+) (SEAL), JOHN McLEOD.

Page 19: Will of JOHN HUSBANDS of Anson County...wife TABITHA, whole of my
         moveable estate...12 Oct 1773...JOHN HUSBANDS (SEAL), Wit: WILLIAM
BLEWETT, JOSEPH MARTIN, WILLIAM THOMAS. Anson April Court 1774, Proved by
WILLIAM BLEWITT & WM THOMAS, TABITHA HUSBANDS, Exr. qualified. J. AULD Clk.

Page 20: Will of WILLIAM LOVE of Anson County...to my loving and Eaged [sic]
         Father all the Entrys of Land which I have made in my own name...JOHN
CLARK told me that he paid for surveying of four tracts...7 May 1753...WILLIAM
LOVE (SEAL), Wit: ROBERT LOVE (+), BENJAMIN LOVE (+).
         [The "Eaged Father" mentioned in the will is apparently one JAMES
         LOVE whose will is recorded in Charleston, S. C. Wills, Vol. PP, pp.
         291-292. JAMES LOVE names sons THOMAS, JOHN, and JAMES, a daughter
         JEAN and a son in law ADAM McCOOL. The will is dated 8 Apr 1760,
         and executors were qualified 2 May 1760. The tracts granted to
         WILLIAM LOVE are in present Union and Chester Counties, S. C.]

Page 21: Will of JOHN GILES of Anson County...unto PHEREBY POOL alias GILES,
         Daughter of JERE POOL, late of Waccamaw, my Young Negro Wench Bess...
to wife MARY, all estate real & personal...wife MARY & HEZEKIAH RUSS, Exrs...
5 July 1766...JOHN GILES (SEAL), Wit: THOMAS DICKSON, CHARITY DICKSON.

Page 22: Will of CHARLES MORRIS Leatt of Virginia and at present a Residenter [sic]
         of Anson County, am sick in body...to wife ELIZABETH all goods &
Chattels in the province of Virginia and in Carolina...27 Dec 1774...CHARLES
MORRIS (+) (SEAL), Wit: JOHN MORRIS, SAMUEL RUSS, WM LEEY [LECY?] (+).

Page 23: Will of GEORGE INGRAM of Anson County, sick in body...land purchased of
         CORNELIUS ROBERTSON, 300 acres & 180 acres that WILLIAM LEEK is to
make a right to, equaly between my four Children, JOHN INGRAM, TABITHA INGRAM,
JESSE INGRAM, & NANCY INGRAM...the boys to have their part at age 21, the girls
at age 18...JOHN WALTERS [WATTERS?], Exr. and HUMPHREY ROGERS to assist him...
2 Aug 1775. GEORGE INGRAM (+) (SEAL), Wit: JAMES BURN (+), CHARLES TURNER (+),
REBECCA LEYTON (+). Proved by JAMES BURN Oct. Ct. 1775, JOHN AULD, Clk.

Pp. 24-25: Will of SAMUEL SNEAD of Anson County...son ISRAEL SNEAD, land where
          he now lives, to be a Straight line from THOMAS MOORMANs land...son
DAVID SNEAD, 100 A adj. FRANCIS CLARKs land...to son PHILIP BURFORD SNEAD, 100
A adj. my sons ISRAEL & DAVID...to son WILLIAM SNEAD, the land I live on adj.
to ISRAEL, DAVID & PHILIP, adj. JOHN COALES...that DANIEL BURFORD made to him...
son DANIEL SNEAD the Remainder of tract I live on adj. JOHN COALES, JOHN SNEAD,
my fathers & FRANCES CLARKS also my land at Huwarry adj. THOMAS CRESSES land...
to daughter ANN CROSLAND, sl sterling...my three daughters CATY, PATTY & BETTY
SNEAD 500 A called COLEMANs pasture...land on Marks Creek where JOHN LEC [sic]
lives to be sold...to wife TEMPERANCE SNEAD, all the rest of my estate...to
granddaughter TEMPERANCE CROSLAND...DANIEL SNEAD & JAMES COTTON, Exrs...14 Mar
1775. SAMUEL SNEAD (SEAL), Wit: CHARLES MEDLOCK, Jurat, NICHOLAS GREEN (+),
DEMPSE GRANT (+).

Pp. 26-27: Will of WILLIAM RATLIFF of Anson County, planter...wife SUSANNAH RAT-
          LIFF, my manor plantation...14 A purchased of STEPHEN THOMAS to sons
WILLIAM & ZACHARIAH RATLIFF... to son THOMAS RATLIFF, s5...two sons JOHN & JAMES
RATLIFF, 300 A on long branch of Joneses Creek...son ROBERT CLOTHIER RATLIFF, 200
A on Island Creek adj. land formerly taken up by JAMES LILES...unto ELIZABETH

CURTIS, ₤30...friend WILLIAM THOMAS, son of PHILEMON THOMAS & MR. ROBERT THOMAS, Exrs...10 Feb 1777. WILLIAM RATLIFF (+) (SEAL), Wit: THOMAS DICKSON, G. JEFFERSON, SAMUEL CURTIS.

Pp. 28-29: Will of JOHN RYLE of Anson County, weak of body...to my son JAMES, one Negro Mark...to daughter ELIZABETH one Negro Moll...to son JOHN one Negro haney...son WHITMILL...son LARKIN...daughter MARY... to my six children, each one bed & furniture...to son JAMES, shot gun...wife [not named[, Extx... 8 Jan 1777...JOHN RYLE (SEAL), Wit: WM. REMEY, HENRY PLEAR, HANNAH HUTCHINS. Proven by WM REMEY Jan. Ct. 1778.

Pp. 29-31: Will of JOHN PRESLER, SENR. of Anson County, Haberdasher...to wife MARY...daughter ELIZABETH MANGSS, s2...son JOHN PRESLER...daughter MORGAN...daughter ANN NONALS[?]...daughter MARY BLASLEY [?]...daughter SUSANNAH PRESLER...son ANTHONY PRESLER, 150 A on Landes Creek, paying his younger brother WILLIAM ₤50...son ELIAS PRESLER, 150 A on Lanes Creek, paying his younger brother LEVI, ₤50 & letting his mother live on the land...daughter JANE PRESLAR...son WILLIAM PRESLAR...6 Dec 1777. JOHN PRESLER (+) (SEAL), Wit: SAMPSON HOUGH, JOHN PRESLER. Proved by both witnesses, Jan. Ct. 1778, JOHN AULD, Clk.

Pp. 31-32: Will of PRISCILLAH McPHERSON of Anson County...weak in body...son SHADRACH DENSON, all land...granddaughter BETSEY DENSON...son SHADRACH, Exr....23 Mar 1778...PRISCILLAH McPHERSON. A true copy, THOS WADE, Clk.

Pp. 32-33: Will of JOHN HAYMES of Anson County...28 Sept 1779...wife RUTH HAYMES, 8 negroes...Daughter BETTY ANN HAMOCK, 7 negroes...daughter CHARITY THOMAS...to son[?] WILLIAM HAMES, s5...wife RUTH HAMES, friends WILLIAM HAMMOCK & WILLIAM BEST ,Exrs....JOHN HAYMES (+) (SEAL), Wit: DAVID JAMESON, JAMES JAMESON, WM HAMMOCK (+). Proved by DAVID JAMESON Oct ct 1784.

Pp. 33-35: Will of JOHN LEE of Anson County...weak in body...wife ELIZABETH... son RICHARD...son ANTHONY, the lower part of my land...to son JOHN ...daughter ELIZABETH, one note on RICHARD YARBROUGH...RICHARD LEE, Exr....10 Sept 1778...JOHN LEE (+), Wit: ROBERT LEE, RICHARD LEE.

Pp. 35-36: Will of JAMES ROPER of Anson County, being very sick...to daughter MARTHA ROPER, 300 A where I formerly lived on Long Creek, in Montgomery County...daughter LUCY ROPER, 200 A on Long Creek, patented by WILLIAM HOGAN, also 100 A adj. WILLIAM TAYLORs line on Long Creek...to son GREEN ROPER, plantation where I now live,300 A, purchased of COLO. DRY...to daughter MARY ROPER, 200 A on Davids Creek, surveyed by MOSES HALL...to son WILLIAM ROPER, 200 A patented by WILLIAM HILDRETH on Cedar & 200 A on the Ridge surveyed by GEORGE DAVISON, & the mill...to daughter SUSANNAH ROPER, 400 A on Buffelow surveyed by COLO. DAVIDSON...to wife [not named], 50 A of the land where I now live...wife & JOHN LILLY, Exrs...17 Aug 1781. JAMES ROPER (SEAL), Wit: VANN SWEARINGIN (+), JOHN JOHNSON, DENNIS McCLENDON (X).

Pp. 37-38: Will of WILLIAM TERRY of Anson County, being very sick & weak in body...daughter MARTHA PICKETT, one negro & ₤20...daughter MOURNING COLEMAN, one negro...daughter MARGARET SMITH...to ELIZABETH HELLAMS [no relation stated]...wife MARY TERRY...four children MARTHA, JAMES, MOURNING, & MARGARET... son JAMES & wf MARY, Exr...6 Sept 1775...WM TERRY (SEAL), Wit: JOHN COLEMAN, WILLIAM ROBERTS.

Pp. 38-39: Will of MATTHEW CLEMENTS of Anson County, very sick & weak in body...
            wife MARY, Extx...27 Nov 1782...MATTHEW CLEMENTS (+) (SEAL), Wit:
WM MORRISS (+), ROLAND WILLIAMS (+), ELIZABETH MORRIS. Proven April Ct 1783,
MICH AULD, Clk.

Pp. 39-41: Will of GEORGE WILSON of Anson County...sick & weak in body...son
            ROBERT, one negro which I sent to him in Virginia some years ago...
my grandson GEORGE WILSON of my sd. son ROBERT...to son GEORGE WILSON, land on
Jones Creek, 330 A in Two Pattents granted to WM FIELDING...four sons SAMUEL,
SOLOMON, ANDREW & JOHN , all my land I now live on on W side Great Pee Dee, when
they arrive at 21...JOHN BOUND & wf MISANIAH WILSON, Ex....9 Apr 1779, GEORGE
WILSON (SEAL), Wit: JOHN AULD, MORGAN BROWN, JAMES HELMS (+).

Page 42: Will of JOHN STEPHENS of Anson County...land on Carrens [?] Creek, on
            the Cape fear River, 150 A to my two sisters NANCY STEPHENS or CAIN
& SARAH STEPHENS...ROBERT RAIFORD & JOHN CAIN , Exrs...12 July 1781...JOHN
STEPHENS (SEAL), Wit: JAMES TERRY, HARDY HOOKER, ANN TERRY.

Page 43: Will of JAMES AULD of Pee Dee in Anson County, but now of Mecklenburg
            Co., Va....to son JOHN AULD, 3 tracts on S side Pee Dee, known as
Wists, Danil, & Knott tracts, 300 A...remainder of estate to wf ROSANNE...snm
MICHAEL & Daughters ANN, MARY & ELIZABETH....wf, son MICHAEL & HENRY WM HARRING-
TON, Exrs...9 Dec 1780...JAMES AULD (SEAL), Wit: ABRAM MITCHELL, JOHN JONES (+),
H WM HARRINGTON.

Pp. 44-45: Will of JOHN McCLENDON of Anson Co...to eldest daughter ANN, 150 A on
            SW side Pee Dee on NW side of Brown Creek, joining title Premata [?]...
also 100 A on Brown Creek aj. to it, & 150 A in Cumberland Co. on head waters
of Lower Little River above THOMAS WADSWORTHs land...to son DENNIS, 200 A on SW
side Pee Dee river, mouth of Golds fork of Browns Creek, also 100 A at head of
Hogan branch...to my son SAMUEL, 100 A on lower side Pormete adj. Brown Creek,
also 100 A from a 500 A tract now in possession of DENNIS McCLENDON, JUNR on
beech branch...to daughter REBEKAH, 200 A patented by BENJAMIN SMITH on W side
Pee Dee, E side Golds fork...to my son SIMON, 100 A in cumberland County on
lower little River about a mile above Shaddocks Creek, also 100 A above the former
tract...for the raising of my above children...WILLIAM MORRIS & JOSEPH COLSON,
Exrs...9 Apr 1784...JOHN McCLENDON (SEAL), Wit: ISHAM INGRAM, JOSEPH SAUCER [?],
DENNIS McCLENDON (+). July 6, 1784, proved by ISHAM INGRAM & WM MORRIS. Mich
Auld, Clk.

Pp. 46-47: Will of SAMUEL BLACKFORD of Anson County...to wife RACHEL BLACKFORD...
            to my eldest son MANNING BLACKFORD, s 20...to son MATTHEW BLACKFORD
s 20...to daughter KESIAH ANDRES...2 daughters SARAH & RUTH, all my land...wf
RACHEL & MT. DUKE GLEN, Exrs...20 June 1781...SAMUEL BLACKFORD, Wit: THOMAS
DICKSON, JOHN DICKSON, REUBEN BRASWELL. Proved by THOMAS DICKSON, April Court
1785, MICH AULD, Clk.

Page 48: Will of STEPHEN VAUGHAN of Anson County...to son WILLIAM VAUGHAN, sl...
            to son HARMAN VAUGHAN, sl...to daughter SARAH VAUGHN sl... 5 Mar 1785...
STEPHEN VAUGHAN (SEAL), Wit: JEREMIAH LEWIS, THOMAS LEWIS.

Pp. 48-49: Will of JOHN SEAGO...to son WILLIAM 200 A near Mays Mill...to son ROBERT
            SEAGO, my Home plantation...to son JOHN...to grandson JAMES SEAGO, son
of ABRAHAM SEAGO, decd, 100 A adj. GEORGE LINDSEYs...to daughter ANN, third of estate
to daughter ELIZABETH...JOHN SEAGO (+) (SEAL), 6 Dec 1784...Wit: WM BENNETT, CHARLES
BURMINGHAM (+).

Pp. 49-50: Will of JAMES MEREDITH of Anson County...wife ELIZABETH, one third of
tract I live on...to son SANDERS MEREDITH, remainder of estate...my
father JAMES MEREDITH & friend JOHN DESENNET, Exrs...14 Mar 1785...JAMES MEREDITH
(+) (SEAL), Wit: DANIEL PERRYMAN, ARNOLD THOMASON, JAMES MEREDITH, JUNR (+).

Pp. 51-52: Will of CHRISTOPHER DAVIS, weak in body...son ARTHUR DAVIS, 50 head
of hoggs...& a 25 pound Horse Creature which CAPT PATT BOGAN owed
me...to son THOMAS DAVIS, heffer bought of JOSEPH WHITE...to daughter SARAH
BENTON, ₤5...daughter MARY BAKER...daughter DICEY BRAZZILL, ₤5...to son JOHN
plantation I live on...son THOMAS...son ISHAM...son LEWIS DAVI , 200 A on Little
Brown Creek, I bought of ROLAND WILLIAMS, to him after my wifes death...daughter
ELIZABETH DAVIS...wife MARY DAVIS...my youngest children LEWIS, JOHN & ELIZABETH...
JOSEPH WHITE, Exr....5 Nov 1785...CHRISTOPHER DAVIS (+) (SEAL), Wit: Wit: WM.
BOGGAN, MARY PRESLER, JOSEPH WHITE, April 6, 1786, Proven by WM BOGAN.

Pp. 52-54: Will of THOMAS WADE of Anson County, merchant...I have given to my children
my deeds of gift a part of my estate...to children HOLDEN WADE, MARY
VINING, THOMAS WADE, SARAH WADE, & GEORGE WADE, ₤10...to SARAH, 200 A on Long
Branch of Jones Creek now leased to PETER BROWN...wf JANE WADE...wf JANE, son
HOLDEN & friends PATRICK BOGGAN & JAMES BOGGAN, Exrs...2 June 1786...THOMAS WADE
(SEAL), Wit:MORGAN BROWN, ELIZABETH KEOWN [?].

Pp. 54-55: 14 Feb 1785, WILL of THOMAS WHITE of Anson County, being sick & weekly...
to daughter UNITY PURNAL, all estate real & personal to be notified
by JESSE GILBERT, my Exr...MARY PURNAL should have possession of sd. child if
she continued single while sd. child becomes of age...THOMAS WHITE (+) (SEAL),
Wit: HUMY YARBROUGH, WILLA. McCRAKEN (+).

Pp. 56-57: Will of JOSEPH MARTIN of Anson County...to son JESSE MARTIN, all land
I now live on not granted by deed of gift to JOHN HAIL MARTIN, 150 A...
to daughter NANCY MARTIN, at her mothers death...to son JOHN HAIL MARTIN...13 Feb
1787...JOSEPH MARTIN (SEAL), Wit: BUCKNER NANCE, JAMES VANDERFORD (+).

Page 58: July 27, 1786, WILL of WILLIAM JOHNSON...son HUGH JOHNSON & my wife to
settle my estate between MARY AN JOHNSON, WM JOHNSON, DANIEL JOHNSON,
MALCOLM JOHNSON, JAMES JOHNSON, an equal part to all the children...to daughter
KATHARINE KENNEDY, s4 & land purchased of RICHARD ODEM & patented by JAMES NUTS [?]
...JOHN CORMORAN & ARCHIBALD BURT VINION [?], Exrs [?]...WM JOHNSON, Wit: JOHN
McRA, JOHN JOHNSON.

Pp. 59-61: Will of JOSEPH COLSON of Anson County...wife MARY COLSON, house &
plantation...son JOSEPH COLSON 170 and a half acres on SE side Brown
Creek, where he now lives...daughter SUSANNAH...son JOHN COLSON, 1/4 of 310 A
where I now live...until my son THOMAS comes of age of 21...daughter MARY COLSON...
daughter CHARITY...daughter FEREBE...daughter NELLE...son SANDERS COLSON, 1/4
of 310 A...to son JACOB COLSON 1/4 of 310 A...to son THOMAS 1/4 of 310 A...
wf MARY & son JOHN Exrs...8 July 1788...JOSEPH COLSON (+) (SEAL), Wit: WM
THREADGILL, JR., JOHN RYLE, WM HOWELL, JR.

Pp. 61-64: Will of MICHAEL AULD of Anson County...monies due me as clerk of Anson
County...3 sisters, ANN, MARY & ELIZABETH, all my share of my fathers
estate & also my lands on Long Branch of Jones Creek & 110 A I bought of PHILLIP
GUTHING [?], 150 A bought of JESSE GIBBERT, Esqr as sheriff of Anson Co, & sold
by Execution against WM GARRISON & 50 A bought of EDWARD SMITH...to my mamma
ROSANNAH AULD, mare I bought of JOHN HAMER...640 A on waters of Smiths & McCoys

Creeks adj. JUDGE SPENCER, JOHN WEST & WM BLEWETT to be sold...to wife SIDNEY, all lands on Jones Creek, about 500 A bought of Sheriff MILLER, on an Execution agnst. EMORY TARMAN, including where ROBERT TANMAN formerly lived...to son JOHN FIELDS AULD, land I bought of my brother JOHN AULD on Pee Dee, adj. Island Creek & 300 A on redy branch of Cedar Creek, where MATHEW BAILEY formerly lived & 130 A on Savannah Creek I bought of JAMES LIFES [?]...130 A adj. WM RATLIFF, JOHN HAMER, & JOHN AHNDAN on waters of Island Creek & McCoys Creek....If son JOHN AULD should die before 21...HENRY WM HARRINGTON & COL. JOHN STOKES, Exrs...17 Sept 1789. MICH AULD (SEAL), Wit:SMITH FIELDS, BENJAMIN CARTER, R. HARRINGTON.

Page 65: Will of JOHN STEWART of Anson County...land on Carvers Creek on Cape
        fear river...150 A, to sisters NANCY STEWART CAINE & SARAH STEWART...
ROBERT RAIFORD & JOHN CAIN, Exrs...12 July 1781...JOHN STEWART (SEAL), Wit:
JAMES TERRY, HARDY HOOKER, ANN TERRY. Test Mich Auld Clk., Anson Co., July
29, 1783. A true copy.
        [This is almost a verbatim copy of the will of JOHN STEVENS found
        on page 42. Evidently one is in error.]

Pp. 66-67: Will of JOHN JACKSON of Anson County, being sick & weak in body...to
        daughters ELIZABETH, MARY, SARAH, & REBECKAH, s5...daughters PHEBE,
JEMIMAH, & HANAH...STEPHEN JACKSON & JOHN PERKINS, Exrs...15 Apr 1768...JOHN
JACKSON (SEAL), Wit: JOHN MEADOW, JOHN MAY, CHARLES BOOTH, Proven by MEADOWS
& BOOTH Oct. term 1772. JAMES AULD, Clk.

Pp. 68-69: Blank.

Page 70: Will of SAMPSON LANIER...to wife ELIZABETH LANIER...plantation near
        Wadesborough in Anson County...to son JAMES LANIER, 550 A where I now
live & 150 A on Brown Creek, adj. ELISHA KINDRED...if JAMES dies before 21, to
my brothers and sisters...BURWELL LANIER, WILLIAM LANIER, & COLO. JOHN STOKES,
Exrs...7[?] June 1789...SAMPSON LANIER (SEAL), Wit: JOHN JENNINGS, BENJAMIN
SELBY, JAMES B. PORTER.

Pp. 71-79: Blank.

Page 80: Inventory of Estate of WILLIAM LOVE, late of Anson County, planter, decd,
        taken by JAMES LOVE, Admr. 4 Apr 1756. Proven before ADAM McCOOLE, J.P.
16 July 1756.

Page 81: Inventory of Goods of Estate of JAMES ARMSTRONG, Decd, taken July 12,
        1760. JAMES ARMSTRONG (X).

Page 82: Inventory of Goods & Chattles of JAMES HAMER, Esq. decd, Exhibited
        13 July 1774. P JOHN HAMER, Exr.

Page 83: Inventory of the State [sic] of ROBERT LEE...[n. d.] MARGIR LEE (X).

Page 84: Inventory of the Goods & estate of CHARLES MORRIS decd taken 1 Oct 1775.
        6 cattle in Possession of JOHN MORRIS...CHARLES MORRIS.

Pp. 84-85: Inventory of Estate of GEORGE INGRAM...JOHN WALTER, HUMPHREY ROGERS (X).

Page 86: Inventory of Estate of JOHN LEE, decd, JAMES GRAY.

Page 86: A true Inventory of the property belonging to the Estate of JAMES
MEREDITH, decd...Bond of BARREL EVEREE & EDWARD WILLIAMS filed in
Richmond County
bond of DAVID JAMERSON, on demand 30 Sept 1786
bond of JAMES PICKETT, on demand since August 1782, credit for cash paid 30 Aug
1782 & 16 Sept 1782
note on THOMAS CHILES endorsed by JASPER SMITH, on demand since 18 Oct 1784
one specie tickett against THOMAS JENNINGS.
April 17th 1786.   JAMES MEREDITH (+).

Page 87: Inventory of Estate of WILLIAM JOHNSON, decd 13 Oct 1786...HUGH JOHNSON
Ex.
[Apparently notes on] NEAL MORRISON, WM KENADY, ALEXR. SWINTER, HUGH JOHNSON,
DANIEL McINNIS, ALEXR. GRAHAM.

Pp. 88-90: Inventory of Estate of COLONEL THOMAS WADE, decd 10 Dec 1786
4 grants for land in his own name, two on Browns Creek & one on Jones Creek &
the other in SC, St. David's Parish.
A deed from PATT. BOGGAN & wf on Golds fork
A deed from JAMES WILLIAMS on Jones Creek
A deed from HENRY FALCONBERRY on Jones Creek
A deed from JOSEPH BROWN for 4 tracts
A deed from JNO. EDWARDS on Brown Creek
A deed from JNO. WADE IN So Carolina, Island Creek, Pacolet River
A deed from RICHD FARR, in SC, St David's Parish
A deed from RICHD DABBS SPAIGHT for 10 tracts
a deed from CHARLES HARRINGTON on Pee Dee in Richmond County
A grant in the name of JOHN JOHNSON with his bond for titles lying in SC, Craven
County, waters of Broad River
Several tracts in SC

Debts due from: WILLIAM & GUTHERIDGE LYON, ETHELDRED CLARY, ROBT RUSHIN, HARTWELL
AYRES, EDWARD BROWN, BURWELL LANIER, WILLIAM FERRELL, JOHN COUNTRY-
MAN, SAMUEL SPENCER, ELISHA PARKER, JOHN K. HUTCHIN, ANDREW KINSLER, JOHN GRESHAM &
JOHN HELMS, JOHN BRYANT, JOHN COPELAND, WILLIAM HUNTER, EDWARD MOOR, SAMPSON ONEAL,
DANL McCLAREN, JOHN BLACK, BER & ABNER BAUGHN, ROBT CLARY, WM GAINER & JNO BROWN,
JOHN SPEED & WM DAY; DENNIS McCLENDON, to WILLIAM CRAWFORD; GEO. BELLUE & DENNIS
McCLENDON to HENRY LITFOOT; WILLIAM CRAWFORD, HUMPHREY YARBRO to JOHN TOCKS; WM
CARLEE, THOMAS CHILES.

Page 91: Inventory of Estate of EDWARD DAVIDSON October 14th 1777...GEORGE DAVIDSON,
Admrt.

Pp. 91-92: Inventory of JOHN HENRY decd Estate...CATHA HENRY (+) Admx.

Pp. 92-93: Inventory of Estate of WILLIAM COX, decd...MARY COX (+), Extx.

Page 93: Inventory of Estate of HENRY CHAMBERS, Returned Jan. Sessn 1775. SOLOMON
GROSS, Admr.

Page 94: Inventory of Estate of JOHN SPENCER, Apr the 4, 1775.

Page 95: (n.d.), Inventory of estate of WILLIAM PRICE, returned by ELINOR PRICE, THOMAS PRICE.

Page 95: An inventory of the estate of ELISABETH JOHNSON, returned 1774.

Page 96: 14 Jan 1778, Inventory of estate of ALEXR. McPHERSON.

Pp. 96-97: (n.d.), Inventory of estate of JOEL CHEEVERS, by SARAH CHEEVERS.

Page 97: Inventory of estate of BENJAMIN GUARDINER, 1 Jan 1774...Goods taken out of MR. SAMUEL FLAKEs hand...ISAAC FALCONBERRY (+), Admr.

Page 98: 1 Apr 1767, Inventory of WILLIAM WHITE, by JAMIMA WHITE, Admx.

Page 99: 8 July 1775, Inventory of Estate of MALCOM MARTIN.

Page 100: Jan Ct. 1775, Inventory of Estate of FRANCES MOSELEY, by MARGARET MOSELEY.

Page 101: Oct Ct. 1784, Inventory of Estate of JOHN STANFIELD, included carpenter's tools, shoe maker's tools. Test. MICH AULD, Clk.
Inventory of Estate of BENJAMIN INGRAM, 12 July 1774 JS. PICKETT.

Page 102: (n.d.), Inventory of WILLIAM MOODY, by WM BLASSENGEM, Admr.

Page 103: 7 July 1784, Inventory of Estate of AARON BAXLEY, by MARY BAXLEY (+), Admx.
Inventory of Estate of JOSEPH HOUGH, 4 Apr 1775.

Page 104: 1 Oct 1781, Inventoyr of MOODY INGRAM, by MARTHA INGRAM (+).

Page 105: Inventory of SOLOMON TOWNSEND, 25 Jan 1788.

Page 106: 8 Jan 1771, Inventory of Estate of VIOLET PRIMROSE ..goods bequeathed to MARY his wife...MARY PRIMROSE (+).

Page 107: (N.D.), Inventory of STEPHEN THOMAS.

Page 108: __ July 1753, Inventory of Estate of MOSES DICKEY...includes 2 English Bibles, Mr. Rutherfords Letters, Sermon Book, Mr. JOhn Warden on Baptism...
Due sd. estate from : JAMES FANNING, OWEN CARTER, RICHARD REYNOLDS, MATTHEW TOOLE, PRESTON GOFORTH.

Page 110: (n.d.), Inventory of JAMES LONG, by ELIZABETH LONG (L).

Page 111: 20 July 1754, Inventory of JOHN SNODDY, by AGNESS SNODDY (+).

Page 112: (n.d.), Inventory of JOHN BRASFIELD, by ISAAC JACKSON, Exr.

Pp. 113-114: 9 July 1777: Inventory of THOMAS TOMKINS.

Page 115: ____ 1757, Inventory of Estate of ANDREW PICKENS, by ANN PICKENS (+), and WILLIAM DAVIS.

Oct Ct. 1783, Inventory of Estate of JOHN BAILEY by LYDIA BAILEY, 29 Sept 1784, Ordered that perishable estate be sold DAVID HILDRETH or THOMAS BAILEY, SEN. to sell it 28 Sept. S. MILLER, Sheriff.

Page 116: Estate of JAMES PICKETT, SR. Notes & Accounts due estate: STEPHEN BROWN, PRESWOOD to CRAG, GEORGE RENEK, JAMES DAVIS, WM PHILLIPS, JOHN BETTY, JAMES McNISH, JOSEPH CULPEPPER, THOS HARRINGTON, WM HARRINGTON, ROBERT PATRICK, THOS DAVIS. Order from CRAWFORD to PATRICK, LAWRENCE FRANKLIN, DAVID HILDRETH, JOHN DUNN, note from LITTLE to THOMSPON. (n.d.)

Inventory of Estate of JESSE BAILES, decd Oct. Ct.1783, MICH AULD, Clk.

Page 117: (n.d.), Inventory of Estate of JOHN HALL, by ELIZABETH BROOKS (+), Exr.

Page 118: 6 Jan 1758, Inventory of Estate of JOSEPH HOLLINGSWORTH, inhabitant of Broad River, by MARTHA HOLLINGSWORTH, widow of JOSEPH.

Page 119: (n.d.), Inventory of Estate of ISRAEL PICKENS, by MARTHA PICKENS (+), WILLIAM PICKENS.

Page 120: __ Jan 1760, Inventory of PHILIP HENSON, JR. by PENELOPE HENSON (X).

Page 121: (n.d.), Inventory of ANDREW BERRY, by RICHARD BERRY.

Page 122: (n.d.), Inventory of AVINGTON SHERRILL by PIRSHANNA SHERILL, Amx.

Page 123: 23 July 1757, Inventory of ROBERT McCORKALL by JAMES McCORKALL, MARGARET McCORKALL and JAMES LINN, Exr.

Page 124: Inventory of JOHN DAVIDSON, taken 1 Dec 1749, by JAMES McKILWAIN, HILL MORIGAN, Returned 27 Dec 1749.

Page 125: Inventory of Estate of JOSEPH SMITH, Decd. (n.d.).

Page 126: (n.d.), Inventory of CHAS ROBERTSON...decd against CALEB HOWELL, SARAH ROBERTSON, Exr.

Inventory of Estate of JOSEPH WEAVER, by GABRIEL DAVIS (+).

Pp. 126-127: Inventory of Estate of JOSEPH THOMPSON, Oct. 1783.

(n.d.), Inventory of Estate of RICHARD and SARAH TOUCHSTONE, Additional inventory of HENRY TOUCHSTONE.

Page 128: 6 Jan 1783, Inventory of Estate of WILLIAM TERRY, by MARY TERRY, Exr.

Page 129: 7 Oct 1784, Inventory of Estate of JOHN HOWARD, by JAMES HOWARD (+). debt from THOMAS TALLANT.

Inventory of Estate of AARON BAKER, 1 Apr 1782, by D. JAMESON.

Page 130: Oct Ct. 1772, Inventory of JOHN HICKS, by JOHN HUSBANDS, FRANCES HUBSANDS.

Page 131: (n.d.), Inventory of Estate of WILLIAM FEIDLING.

Page 132: (n.d.), Inventory of Estate of RICHARD & SARAH TOUCHSTONE, by HENRY
TOUCHSTONE and FREDERICK TOUCHSTONE.

Page 133: Feb. Ct., 1762, Inventory of Estate of JAMES McMANUS, by MARY Mc-
MANUS, Admr.

Page 134: 28 Mar 1768, Inventory of WILLIAM STEPHENS by JOHN STEEL.

Estate of WILLIAM STEVENS, Decd: Note of hand by SAMUEL WEBSTER
living in Bladen County. In the case of JAMES HUTENS: Note of WILLIAM PICKETT,
28 Jan 1768.

Page 135: (n.d.), Inventory of Estate of JOHN COLSON, JR. by ELIZABETH COLSON.

6 Apr 1768, Inventory of MOSES HARRELL.

Page 136: (n.d.), Inventory of Estate of GOIN MORGAN, by MARY MORGAN.

Inventory of Estate of REUBEN RONE, by SARAH RONE.

Inventory of Estate of LATITIA SHARP.

Page 137: 3 Jan 1783, STEPHEN GARDNER's inventory by VEREBY GARDNER, Admr.
includes one prayer book, 2 Bibles.

Page 138: 1782, Inventory of ROBERT JARMAN.

Page 139: (n.d.), Inventory of JAMES LOWRY by ELIZABETH LOWRY.

Page 140: (n.d.), Inventory of Estate of SAMUEL HAYWARD, by SAML WILSON,
SARAH WILSON, his wife, Admrs.

Page 141: 22 July 1789, Inventory of Estate of ROBT PHILLIPS...debts due
from ROBERT PHILLIPS, JUNR., MARY LEE, TOM RATLIFF, MICH AULD.

Page 142: (n.d.), Inventory of JOSEPH THOMPSON...includes Blacksmith tools,
Test   MICH AULD Clk.

Inventory of Estate of ABRAHAM BELUE, Anson County, July Ct., _____.
The "above killed man's estate" by Sheriff, JONATHAN JACKSON, Test. THOS WADE,
JR., Clk.

Page 143: (n.d.), Inventory of Estate of CHARLES McDOWELL.

Page 144: 18 Aug 1774, Inventory of Estate of PETER ROAN, by EDWARD MOORE.

Page 145: 27 Sept 1782, Inventory of Estate of JAMES ROPER...part of estate
left out of his will...MARY ROPER, Admr.

Page 146: (n.d.), Inventory of Estate of JOHN THURMAN, by MARY THURMAN, ABRAHAM
COOK.

Page 147: (n. d.), Inventory of Estate of SIMON HOOKER.

April 1761, Remaining part of Estate of WILLIAM BLACK.

Page 148: 9 Oct 1758, inventory of Estate of JOHN CARMICHAEL, by WM CARMICHAEL (+), Admr.

Page 149: 8 Nov 1759, Inventory of Estate of JAMES GOODFELLOW by MOSES ALEXANDER, Admr.

July Ct., 1782, Sale of Estate of PETER LEWIS, by Shff. JONATHAN JACKSON, THOMAS WADE, JR., Clk.

Page 150: (n.d.), Inventory of Estate of JULIUS HOLLY, by SARAH HOLLY, Admx. (+).

Page 151: Inventory of MATHEW PATTON, Decd (n.d.), ELIZABETH PATTON (+), JAMES PATTON.

Page 152: 2 Jan 1783, Inventory of Estate of GEORGE WILSON, by MISSANEAH WILSON. MICH AULD, Clk.

Page 153: 29 July 1762, Inventory of Estate of JOHN MILLS, by JOSEPH HARDEN, Esq.

Page 154: (n.d.), Inventory of Estate of SHADRACK DENSON, by PATRICK BOGGAN, JR.

Inventory of Estate of EDWARD TRAVIS 1782.

Page 155: 2 Jan 1782, Inventory of Estate of ISAAC NICHOLS, by HONOR HICHOLS (+).
Debts: WILLIAM BOGGAN, JAMES LITTLE, JAMES GORDAN, THOMAS GADDY, ABRAM STRICKLIN, THOMAS CREEL, WILLIAM STEWART, JOHN MOORE, FREDERICK GORDON.

Page 156: 6 Oct 1771, Inventory of Estate of TIMOTHY MONCEAR...200 A of land... exhibited by THOMAS MOORMAN 11 Oct 1771.

Page 157: 2 Oct 1781, Inventory of Estate of REUBEN PHILLIPS, by STEPHEN MILLER.

8 July 1785, Inventory of Estate of ELIZABETH RYLE, by JAMES RYLE.

Page 158: 8 Jan 1785, Inventory of Estate of JESSE IVEY by MICH AULD, Clk.

1 Jan 1785, by MARY IVEY, JOHN BLOODWORTH, Wit.

Page 159: 10 Apr 1770: Inventory of Estate of THOMAS HUNTER by CATHARINE HUNTER Extx, ANTHO HUTCHINS...includes "money due in Ireland and New Jersey."

Page 160: July Ct. 1783, Inventory of ROBT. KEYS by SOLOMON RUSHING (X).

9 Jan 1782, Inventory of Estate of THOMAS TRULL, by CHARITY TRULL (+).

Page 161: 9 Oct 1783, Inventory of Estate of JOHN BAILEY, by LIDIA BAILEY.

7 Jan 1783, Invnetory of Estate of WIDOW CONNER.

(n.d.), Inventory of Estate of WM McHENRY, by MARY McHENRY (+).

Page 162: (n.d.), Inventory of Estate of DAVID RICH by TIMOTHY RICH, Test, THOMAS WADE, JR. Clk.

Page 163: Jan 1783, Estate of ISAAC BELIEU.

Page 163: (n.d.), Memo of Estate of WILLIAM BIRD, by JOHN SMITH.

8 July 1762, Inventory of Estate of MATTHEW PARKER, by JAMES HOWARD.

(n.d.), Inventory of Estate of LEWIS LOWRY, by ELIZABETH LOWRY.

Page 164: 8 Apr 1783, Inventory of JAMES CHILES by THOMAS CHILES, Admr.
Amended 2 June 1783. Bond due from JOHN MAY with Interest from 15
July 1780; WILLIAM ROBERDS bond; JOSEPH HINDS bond with Interest from 23 June
1780: Collo. EDWARD WILLIAMS Bond; BACON FRANCIS MARTIN bond; EVAN VAUGHAN note.

Page 165: 15 July 1780, Inventory of NATH'L CURTIS, by FRANCS CURTIS, Admr.

Additional Inventory of JOHN MILLER by JONATHAN JACKSON, Admr.

Page 166: 7 Jan 1782, Inventory of Estate of JOHN WILLIAMSON by DAVID JAMESON.

24 July 1777, Inventory of Estate of WILLIAM BENNETT, JR. by THOS
WADE.

Page 167: (n.d.), DEVALT PAFF's inventory of JOHN THOMAS, Admr.

Page 168: Inventory of Estate of WM KEMP...includes 300 A in SC, 427 A left to
the children.

Page 169: Blank.

Pp. 170-75: Inventory of Estate of BENJAMIN DUMAS, by DAVID DUMAS, includes
one Virginia law book.

Page 175: Inventory of Estate of JOHN RYLE, April 1784.

Page 176: 26 June 1787, Inventory of Estate of THOS WHITE, by JESSE BILGER, Exr.

Page 177: (n.d.), Inventory of THOS DINKINS.

26 Jan 1788, Inventory of Estate of JAMES CHILES, by ELIZABETH CHILES
& THOMAS CHILES, Admr.

Page 178: 5 Apr 1783, Estate of WILLIAM HOLLEY...includes 300 A on Richardson
Creek, one grindstone in possession of MR. NATHANIEL HOLLEY; one
very nice rifle gun in possession of JAMES MAXFIELD in McLenburg (sic) County
which he refuses to deliver...Note on REUBEN MATHUS, CHARLES EVANS, THEOPHILUS
HILL, one prayer book.

Page 179: 13 Apr 1789, Inventory of JOSEPH COLSON by MARY COLSON (+).

(n.d.), Inventory of WM DENSON, by WILLIAM BOGGAN, Exr.

Page 180: 15 Jan 1787, Inventory of Estate of JOSEPH MARTIN, by KATHERINE
MARTIN (+) and JOHN MARTIN, Exrs.

(n.d.), Inventory of Estate of CORNELIUS EVANS, by ANN EVANS (+).

Page 181: Remiander of Estate of CORNELIUS EVANS...THOMAS FINNEY ₤29, BARBARY
ROBERTSON & a paper _____ from Pennsylvania.

Inventory of Estate of JOHN HAMER by MARY HAMER.

Page 182: July Ct. 1789, Inventory of Estate of WM DENSON...his part of his
        father JAMES DENSONs estate...Paid SYLVANOUS GIBSON.
        6 Oct 1777, Inventory of Estate of JAMES DENSON, by JAMIMA DENSON,
Admx., "copy made out for WM BOGGAN" M. A. (MICH AULD).

Page 183:July Ct 1782, Inventory of Estate of JOHN MILLER, by THOS WADE, JR, Clk.
        April Ct 1782, Inventory of WILLIAM BENSON.

Page 184: 14 Apr 1758, Inventory of JOSEPH HOLLINGSWORTH, by MARTHA HOLLINGS-
        WORTH. Wit: ADAM McCOOL.
        (JOSEPH HOLLINGSWORTH was a resident of what is now Union
        County, South Carolina.)

Pp. 185-186: 23 Nov 1782, Division of lands of WALTER LEAK:
        to WALTER LEAK, 640 A on N side Pee Dhe & 300 A on head of
Buffelow Creek
        to FRANCES LEAK on S side Pee Dee, 690 A & land in fork of Pee Dee
& Little River & one tract in Pitsilvania Co., Va., on Banister River, 400 A.
        to ELISABETH LEAK, to JUDITH LEAK, to MARY LEAK, SALLY LEAK
(received no land)

Pp. 187-197: Blank.

Page 198: 7 July 1750, Inventory of JOHN DAVIDSON by JOHN BREVARD, ALEX. OZBURN,
        MATT CARRUTH.

Page 200: Blank.

Page 201: 31 Oct 1750, Sale of Estate of JOHN CARMICHAEL by WILLIAM CARMICHAEL.
        Buyers: WILLIAM CARMICAL, ELIZABETH CARMICAL, JOSEPH CARMICAL, JOHN
CLARK, DAVID ADAMS; Cash Recd of JOHN NEWHOUSE, WIDOW GRAHAM, JACOB SMITH.

Pp. 202-203: Inventory of Estate of JACOB RICHARDS, by WM RICHARDS, JOHANNES
        VANHOESE, EDMUND LILLY, 1 May 1761.

Page 204: 31 May 1783, Sales of estate of WILLIAM HOLLEY by SABRAH HOLLEY, JONA-
        THAN JACKSON, Sheriff.
        List of sales of estate of PETER LEWIS by BURWELL LANIER, COL. THOMAS
WADE. 2 Oct 1782, JONATHAN JACKSON, Sheriff.

Page 205: 13 Sept 1783, List of sales of Estate of WM GRIFFIN HOGAN. Buyers:
        ELIZABETH HOGAN, HANNAH HOGAN, WM COOPER, JOHN BEVERLEY, JAMES
McHENRY, SHAD HOGAN, JAMES SHEPARD, WALTER GIPSON, WM HILDREN, JONATHAN JACKSON,
Sheriff.

Page 206: 15 Feb 1783, Sales of Estate of JOHN COLSON. Buyers: ELIZABETH COLSON,
        JONATHAN JACKSON, Sheriff.

        Inventory of estate of MATTHEW TOOLE, by ELENOR TOOLE, Admr.

Page 207: Sales of Estate of WILLIAM McHENRY. Buyers: MARY McHENRY, ARTHUR DAVIS,
        JESSE MILLER, PETER WATTS, JESSE McHENRY, JOHN McCLENDON, JONATHAN
JACKSON, Sheriff.

Page 208: Sale of estate of ROBT JARMAN, 2 Dec 1783, by JONATHAN JACKSON, Shff.
        Buyers: MAYAN JARMAN, JEPTHA VINING, ELIZ. RICE, RICHARD WORTHEN,
WILLIAM GULLEDGE, CARNEY WRIGHT, THOS HUNTLYE, JONATHAN JACKSON.

Pp. 209-210: 5 June 1758, Inventory of Estate of WILLIAM PRICE, by ELEANOR
        PRICE (E), THOS PRICE.

Page 211: Apr Ct 1779, Amount of estate of BENJAMIN SMITH by JOHN SMITH,
        Sandhill, Admr. MICH AULD, Clk.

Page 212: Sale of estate of JOHN WILLIAMSON, decd Buyers: MARY, REBECKAH, PATTY
        WILLIAMSON, RALPH VICKERS, BURWELL LANIER, PATT BOGGAN, JOHN MAY,
JOSHUA MORGAN, DAVID JAMESON, PAT BOGGAN JR., NAT DOBBS, JESSE MILLER, JOHN
LEVERETT, GEO. HAMMONS, JOHN BLOODWORTH, MARY MORGAN, DAVID JAMESON, Admr. (n.d.)

Page 213: 6 Oct 1758, Account of sales of estate of JOHN SNODDY, by AGNESS
        SNODDY (+), Buyers: GIDEON THOMPSON, JESPER SUTTON, JOHN MOOR,
HUGH PARKS, JAMES AUSTIN, SAMUEL WATSON, ROBERT COURTNEY, JAMES DOUGHTERY,
ROBT TINNER, JOSEPH TANNER, SAMUEL GIVENS, WILLIAM SIMS, WILLIAM BARR, WM
COATNEY.

Pp. 214-215: Estate of JAMES ERWIN, decd sold by MARGRAET IRWIN, Admr. 22 Dec
        1761.

Page 215: 29 Jan 1785, Account of sale of Estate of JESSE IVY decd. Buyers:
        WM WOOD, DAVID JAMESON, BURWELL LANIER, WILLIAM YEW, FREDERICK
BASS, MARY IVEY, MARGARETT BELIEU, PHILIP GITHING, STEPHEN MILLER, JOHN THREADGILL,
REBEKAH DODD, PLEASANT MAY, ELENOR WHITE, JOHN IVEY.

Page 216: (n.d.), Sale of estate of JOHN SIMPSON, decd. Buyers: JOHN PARSON,
        CARNEY WRIGHT, THAD HARRIS, JOHN CARRUTH, RICHARD WORTHEN, JOHN
MURDOCK, SAML BLACKFORD, THOS HARRIS, JOHN JACKSON, THOS DICKSON.

Page 217: Account of sales of estate of JOHN MILLER. Buyers: PHEBE MILLER,
        JOHN STANFIELD (n.d.).

Pp. 218-219: (n.d.) Account of sale of estate of ROBERT LEE, Decd. Buyers:
        JOHN POKE, THOS PRESLAR, JESSE GILBERT, JAMES LEE, CHAS MEDLOCK,
JOHN SMITH, SAMPSON CULPEPPER, FRANCIS SMITH, WILLIAM MILLER, MILLI LEE, SARAH
LEE, WILLIAM ARNETT, WALTER GIBSON, HENRY STOKES, JOHN SMITH, JOHN HALE GILBERT,
NEOMI DICKSON, JOHN STEPHENS, ELIJAH CLARK, JOHN COLSON. Certified by CHAS.
MEDLOCK.

Page 220: Sale of Estate of THOS BRIGMAN, decd. Buyers: JOHN BOUNDS, JOSEPH
        HALL, JOHN HATHORNE, ISAAC BRIGMAN, SAMUEL SNEAD, JERE TOUCHBERRY,
WILLIAM BRIGMAN, CHAS MEDLOCK, DUNKIN BURRY, WILLIAM SPEED, NICHOLAS GREEN,
by ISAAC BRIGMAN (n.d.)

Page 221: 4 Nov 1782, Sale of estate of JAMES ROPER, MARY ROPER, buyers. JONATHAN
        JACKSON, Sheriff.

Page 222: 17 May 1774, Account of sales of JOHN HUSBANDS estate. Buyers:
        MR JOHN JAMES, MR. WILLIAM BLEWETT, MR. ROBT WEBB, JOHN WALL, JOHN
COLE, JACOB PAUL, MARK ROLLINS, SAMUEL SNEAD, CHARLES MEDLOCK, WILLIAM JAMES,
HENRY WILLIAMS, EDWARD WILLIAMS, HENRY COVINGTON, WILLIAM LEGETT, JOHN WEBB,
DAVID COLE, SOLOMON SNEAD, DAVID LOVE, BENJAMIN COVINTON. Presented by
JOHN JAMES, TABITHA JAMES, Admrs.

Page 223: 8 Dec 1782, Sale of estate of REUBEN RORIE. Buyers: SARAH RORIE, WILLIAM
        RORIE, JOHN STANFIELD, SOLOMON RUSHING, WILLIAM HILL, THOMAS MIRES.
JONATHAN JACKSON. Sheriff.

Pp. 224-225: (n.d.) Sale of estate of JOHN HARMON decd. Buyers: JOHN HAMON,
        HOPKIN HOWELL, CHAS MEDLOCK, THOMAS SLAY, WILLIAM PICKETT, Shff.

Pp. 226-227: Sale of Estate of ABRAM BELIEU, decd. Buyers: CATHERINE BELIEU.
        30 Aug 1782, JONATHAN JACKSON Sheriff.

Pp. 228-229: 29 June 1784, Sales of persihable estate of JOHN RYLE. Buyers:
        JAMES RYLE, WM RYLE, EDMUND LILLY, JAMES HOGGAN, STEPHEN MILLER,
ROBERT BROADWAY, HENRY PLAYER, JESSE GILBERT, JAMES HOGAN, ROBERT LEE, DRURY
ROBERTSON, JAMES MARSHALL, JAMES SHEPPARD. STEPHEN MILLER, Sheriff.

Page 230: Sale of estate of EDWARD TRAVERS. Buyers: MARY TRAVES, WILLIAM
        MORRIS, JOHN BEAVER. 3 June 1782, JONATHAN JACKSON, Sheriff.

Page 231: 10 Feb 1783, Sale of Estate of THOS CONNER. Buyers: RUTHEY CONNER,
        JAMES HOWARD, JOHN HOWARD, LAWRENCE FRANKLIN, NATHAN FALKNER, JOSEPH
WADE, THOMAS VINING, DAVID JAMESON.

Pp. 232-233: Sale of Estate of JOHN HAMER. Buyers: MARY HAMER, JONATHAN
        JACKSON, 10 Dec 1782.

Pp. 234-235: 7 Dec 1782, Sale of Estate of JAMES LOWRY. Buyers: ELIZABETH,
        WILLIAM,SUSANNAH, NANCY, ROBERT, JOHN, & PETER LOWRY; ELIZABETH
LOW, JACOB RUSHION, NATHAN FALKNER, NATHAN RENFROW. JONATHAN JACKSON Shff.
Additional sales, June 1784. STEPHEN MILLER, Sheriff.

Pp. 236-237: 29 Sept 1752, Inventory of estate of JOHN ELERBEE, appraised by
        E. CARTLIDGE, JOHN HICKS, PHILIP KENNEY.

Page 237: 29 Nov 1783, Sale of estate of JESSE VAILES. Buyers: MARTHA VAILES.
        STEPHEN MILLER, Sheriff.

Pp. 238-239: Sale of Estate of JOHN STANFIELD, 6 Dec 1784. Buyers: MARY
        STANFIELD, FRANK FALKNER, JACOB STANFIELD, WILLIAM WOOD, SAMPSON
STANFIELD, SARAH BOSTWICK, ROBERT HALL, THOMAS JONES, JAMES FARR, WM BENNETT,
JOHN STANFIELD, HENRY STANFIELD. S MILLER, Shff.

Pp. 240-241: 20 Jan 1775. Sale of estate of HENRY CHAMBERS. Buyers: SOLOMON
        GROSS, WM USSERY, JAMES CHILES, JONATHAN JONES, GRIFFIN HAYWOOD,
JOHN SKINNER, DONALD McFERSON, WM PICKETT, JAMES ALLEN, CALEB TOUCHSTONE,
EDWARD CHAMBERS, JERRY MENESCO, WM COLEMAN, ISAAC ARMSTRONG, JAMES PICKET,
JAMES SMITH, MURDOCK McCASKILL, JOHN CHAMBERS, WILLIAM CHAMBERS, BENJ. POWELL,
THOMAS GOWERS, THOS USSERY, DUNCAN McLEOD, JOSEPH TARBUTTON, JOHN SKINNER,
THOAMS ISTES, ROBERT LEVRETT, JACOB BROWN, JAS PICKETT, DUNCAN McNABB, WM
CHAMBERS, JOHN SWAY, SR., JOSHUA GROSS, RICHD DOWNS, JESSE WALTON; WILLIAM
PICKETT, Sheriff.

Page 242: 12 Jan 1788, Sale of estate of CORNELIUS EVANS. Buyers: ANN EVANS, WILLIAM POLK, ISAAC FORD, THOMAS NIGH (?), JOHN MEDFORD, DAVID GRIFFIN, JOEL WARKER, JOHN PARKER, THOMAS PHENEY, ISAAC BRUMLOW, HENRY HARGETT, GEORGE BREWER.

Page 243: 3 June 1783, Sale of estate of WM FIELDING. Buyers: MRS. FIELDING, JAMES FARR, SAMUEL PHILLIPS, JONATHAN JACKSON, Sheriff.

Pp. 244-246: Sale of Estate of FRANCIS MOSELEY, by MARGARET MOSELEY. 24 Oct 1774. Buyers: WILLIAM LEAK, MARGARET MOSLEY, THOMAS MEGERSON (?), JAMES CHILES, THOMAS WADE, JOHN COATNEY, WILLIAM MASK, WILLIAM COLSON, WILLIAM PICKETT, M. MOSLEY, GEORGE WILSON, BENJAMIN POWELL, HAMES HINES, HENRY WILLIAMS, GEORGE HAMMONS, JAMES WINFREW, JAMES AULD, PETER LEWIS, ALEXANDER McCRAW, MR. THOMAS, JOHN LAMBDEN, DANIEL McFERSON, WM LEWIS, GEORGE INGRAM, JAMES MEREDITH, NAT. ASHLEY, JOHN SMITH, CORNELIUS ROBERTSON.

Pp. 246-248: 5 Sept 1774. Sale of estate of DUNCAN SMITH. Buyers: COL. CHAS. MEDLOCK, CATHERINE SMITH, THOMAS CHILES, JOHN WILSON, JOHN SMITH, CHARLES SMITH, MARY SMITH, NEAL SMITH, ROBT. WEBB, MATTHEW WATSON. PETER McCAIN, JOHN BROWN.

Page 249: December ___. Sale of estate of JOHN THURMAN. Buyers: MARY THURMAN, JOHN SUHNAH, JOHN WRITE, ABRAM COOK, WILLIAM LITTLE. CHAS. MEDLCOK.

Pp. 250-251: 25 Oct 1772, Sale of estate of JOHN HENRY. Buyers: ABRAHAM BELYEU, CATHERINE HENRY, GEORGE INGRAM, BENJAMIN INGRAM, JAMES AULD, JOHN BOND, WM BOND, THOMAS WADE, JOSEPH HINES, SHADRACK DENSON, MOSES WHITE, THOMAS TALLENT, THOMAS CONNER, CHARLES BURNIGHAM, GEORGE WILSON, WILLIAM BENNETT, JOHN CHILES.

Pp. 252-253: 25 Aug 1768. Sale of Estate of WM STEPHENS. Buyers: CHAS. MEDLOCK, MATHEW STEPHENS, JOHN STEPHENS, WM COLEMAN, JAMES PICKETT, STEPHEN COLE, JACOB COLE, ROBERT RAIFORD, JOSHUA MORGAN, WILLIAM TERRY, THOS WARD, BENJ. McNATT, ABNER STEPHENS, BENJAMIN DUMAS, DAVID DUMAS.

Page 254: 6 Aug 1774. Estate of STEPHEN THOMAS. Sale report Oct Ct. 1774. Buyers: WILLIAM SPEED, WILLIAM THOMAS, ROBERT THOMAS, JOHN THOMAS, CHARLES MEDLOCK, WILLIAM PRIMROSE, JOSEPH HOWELL, JAMES POSTON, LEWIS THOMAS, GEORGE MATTHEWS, JOHN DONDALSON, JOSEPH RYE, WILLIAM THOMAS, SR., WM PICKETT, Shff. JOHN AULD, Clk.

Page 255: 26 Mar 1758, Inventory of Goods and Chattels of estate of THOMAS LOCKARD sold at publick vendue.

Page 256: (n.d.), Inventory of estate of NATHANIEL DOUGHTERTY by JOHN MERMAN (MOORMAN?), E. CARTLEDGE, JAMES TERRY.

Page 257: 11 May 1750, Estate of JOHN PRICE. Inventory of GEO. RENOX, GEO. CATHEY.

Pp. 258-259: 4 Aug 1789, Sales of estate of ROBT. PHILLIPS by WILLIAM MAY, Shff. Buyers: MARY PHILLIPS, ROBERT PHILLIPS, SIMON CHURCHWELL (?), ROBERT CLARK, MICH AULD, JOHN RICKETT, WM MAY, MORGAN BROWN.

140

Pp. 260-262: 4 Dec 1754, Inventory of estate of MATTHEW PATTON.

Page 262: Estate of WILLIAM HACKNEY...includes cattle remaining on Thompsons
Creek...BENJ. JACKSON (n.d.).

Page 263: 4 Dec 1774, Inventory of Estate of JOHN POTEET by JOB CALLOWAY, DANIEL
BANCKSTON. Includes cash recd of JOHN POTEET, THOMAS RANALS, JOHN
WALSER (?), RICHARD POTEET, JOHN DOSON.

Pp. 264-266: (n.d.), Account of Sale of estate of THOMAS TOMPKINS decd. Buyers:
JOHN PARSONS, STEPHEN PARKER, JOHN HENSON, RICHARD FARR, CHARLES
HENSON, MORGAN BROWN, NATHANIEL CURTIS, ELISHA PARKER, MARY THOMKINS, FRANCIS
TOMKINS, THOMAS TOMKINS, STEPHEN TOMKINS.

Page 266: A list of the sale of WILLIAM GRIFFIN HOGAN, decd July Ct 1783. MICH
AULD Clk.

Page 267: Sale of estate of EDWARD DAVIDSON, decd 25 Oct 1777. Buyers: WM
THREADGILL, GEORGE JEFFERSON, WM HAY.

Page 268: Sales of estate of ROBT KEE, decd. 1 Oct 1783. Buyers: WILLIAM SMITH,
JOHN HILL.

A sale of a negro man of the estate of AARON BAKER to JAMES JAMESON.
28 Jan 1784. S. MILLER, Sheriff.

Page 269: Estate of THOMAS DINKINS (n.d.)

Sales of estate of NATHANIEL MARTIN, decd (n.d.)

Pp. 270-272: 28 Oct 1760, Account of the sale of the estate of JAMES McCORKALL,
Buyers: JANE McCORKALL, ROBT. DAVIS, WM DAVIS, JOHN CROCKET,
JAMES BARNETT, HUGH MONTGOMERY, JAMES GAMBEL, JOHN LINN, SAMUEL TOMSON, ANDREW
PICKENS, JOHN COFFEE, ALPHIUS SPAIN, HUGH McCAIN, THOS DAVIS, JOHN NUTT, MOSES
DAVIS.

Page 273: (n.d.), Estate of JAMES CHILES. Buyers: WM MAY, DAVID JAMESON, ELIZ.
CHILES,JOHN MAY, WM WISDOM, CHARLES VIVION, by D. JAMISON.

Page 274: 10 Sept 1782, Sale of estate of SHADRACK DENSON. Buyers: BURWELL
LANIER, PATT BOGGAN, JONATHAN JACKSON, DAVID JAMESON, JAMES BOGGAN,
WM THREADGILL, JOHN LEVERETT, JOHN ADKINS. JONA. JACKSON, Sheriff.

Pp. 275-276: (n.d.), Sale of estate of PETER RONE. Buyers: HENRY RONE, ADAM RONE,
DAVID SMITH, WILLIAM PICKETT, WILLIAM NOBLE, EDWARD MORE, JOHN
HAGLER, JOHN WALKER, JACOB VANHUSER, HENRY Mc MILLION, WILLIAM PRITCHETT, THOMAS
NOBLE.

Page 276: 27 Jan 1762, Sale of estate of SAMUEL BEASON, Decd, by SOLOMON BEASON,
Admr. Buyers: THOMAS BLACK, SOLOMON BEASON, GEORGE POTTS, THOMAS
ROBERTSON, THOMAS ROBINSON.

Page 277: 13 June 1749, Inventory of Estate of HENRY JOHNSON, by JOHN HANDBY,
and HENRY DOWLAND, before SAMUEL DAVIS, ESQ.

Page 278: (n.d.), Division of estate of McCORKALL. Legatees: WM. JANE, MARY, ANDREW, & JAMES McCORKALL; JANE LOWRY.

Page 279: 25 Nov 1760, Account of the sale of the estate of JOSEPH CLOUD, returned by MARY CLOUD (X), Admx. Buyers: CHARLES McKNIGHT, AARON MOORE, PETER LABOONE, MARY CLOUD, JEREMIAH POTTS (POOTS), HUGH PACKS (PARKS), SAMUEL BICKOSTAF (BIGGERSTAFF), JOHN BOYLS, JAMES AUSTON,STEPHEN POOTS (POTTS), MOSES MOORE, JOHN BAYLE, JAMES HAINS.

Pp. 280-283: (n.d.), Account of sale of estate of MATTHEW TOOLE, decd. Buyers: JOHN ANDERSON, JOHN LEWIS, WILLIAM HAGER, SAMUEL COBUN, JOHN CATHEY, PATRICK ONEEL, WILLIAM TRUNEBERRY, MOSES MOORE, HENRY VERNOR, WILLIAM HOGAN, BENJAMIN HARDIN, ANDREW CATHEY, MICHAEL HOYLE, WILLIAM HAGARTY, JOHN JONES, HENRY SIGHTS, JOHN RICHMOND, RICHARD BERRY, JOHN HANNAH, JOSEPH JONES, HUGH BERRY, JAMES PEELE, ANDREW DOWNS, ELENOR TOOLE, GEORGE RUTLEDGE, JOHN MILLER, JAMES ODEARE, JOHN BEATTY, MICHAEL HOLEY, THOMAS CLARK, WILLIAM DREW, JOSEPH HARDIN, JANE CATHEY, JOHN McCORDE, JOHN THOMAS, WILLIAM FRONE-BERRY. ELENOR TOOLE (X).

Pp. 283-285: Estate of CHARLES BURNETT (n.d.), Buyers: MR. KEERSHA, DAVID KER, ANDREW BURNETT, SAMUEL BURNETT, JOHN BURNETT, by ANN BURNETT, Admx.

Page 285: Estate of MOSES DICKEY (n.d.), by MARGARET DICKEY, Adm . (also name of MARY DICKEY appears.)

Page 286: Sale of estate of THOMAS WHITE, by JESSE GILBERT, Sheriff. 15 Aug 1787.

Pp. 288-291: Estate of MANUAL (EMANUEL) EAKLES by JOSHUA BRADLEY by order of ALEXANDER GORDON, Sheriff. Buyers: DAVID GRIFFITH, JOHN EASTER, BOSTON HAGLER, JOSHUA WRADLEY, JAMES PHILIPS, DAVID MARTIN, MR. PERKINS, WILLIAM CHILDRESS, JAMES ROBERTSON, ISAAC WHITEN, JACOB WHITEN, EDWARD WILLIAMS,JOHN LASTLEY, JOSEPH TAYLOR, JACOB FREE, ROCHINA (?) BRADLEY, HATHORNY FUNDERBURK, ANDREW JONES, DEVALT FINDERBURK, SAMUEL GRAY, JAMES WHITE, CHARLES SPENDER, TITUS LENNY, GEORGE MILLER, WILLIAM BRATTON, PETER ARON, NICHOLAS BECK, JOSEPH SAYLER, ANTHONEY FINDERBURK, SAMUEL WILSON, THOMAS PAGE, VEAST SAYLN, MICHAEL WHETEN, JAMES ROBERTSON.

Page 291: Estate of DAIL HOLLEY, Decd.

Page 292: 20 May 1784, Perishable estate of WM BENSON, by ELIZABETH BENSON. Buyers: JOHN KNOTTS, ELIZABETH BENSON, SAMUEL FLAKE, MICH AULD, JOHN HANDS, BENJAMIN CARTER, THOMAS ELLIS, JOHN WEST.

Page 293: Estate of JAMES CHILDS, decd. 2 June 1783. Buyers: COL. THOMAS CHILES, ELIZABETH CHILES, KINCHEN McKINSEY, NATHAN FALKNER, RICHARD FARR, THOMAS STANFILL, WILLIAM MAY, DAVID JAMESON, JAMES FARR, MALAIPI WATTS, WILLIAM RUSHION, JONATHAN JACKSON Shff.

Page 294: 7 Nov 1783, Perishable estate of JOSEPH THOMPSON, by ELIZABETH THOMPSON. Buyers: ELIZABETH THOMPSON, JOHN SMITH, JOHN W. GRET, THOMAS DAVIS, EDWARD WILSON, THOMAS ELLIS.

Page 294: 29 Jan 1782, Amount of sale of the estate of REUBEN PHILLIPS, returned
          April Ct. 1782, by JONATHAN JACKSON, Sheriff.

Page 295: 10 Nov 1764, List of sale of estate of ROBERT CULPEPPER, Buyers:
          HENRY STOKES, ELIJAH CLARK, THOMAS PRESLER, WILLIAM CULPEPPER.

          Sale of estate of GEON MORGAN 31 Jan 1782. JNO JACKSON, Shff. Returned
April Ct. 1782.

Pp. 296-298: Sale of estate of JOHN HICKS. 6 Nov 1772. Buyers: JOHN HUSBANDS,
          SAMUEL SNEAD, DAVID SNEAD, COLO. MEDLOCK, MATTHEW TERRY, WILLIAM
MORRIS, HENDLEY SNEAD, JOSEPH HOWELL, ALECK MARTIN, JAMES PICKETT, JOHN WATKINS,
ROBERT WEBB, WILLIAM HICKS, JOHN JONES, WILLIAM COLENG, SAMUEL WISE, WILLIAM
HICKS, JOHN HAMER, RICHARD FARR, WILLIAM HAMER. CHARLES MEDLOCK.

Page 298: ISAAC LANIER in account with JAMES LANIER, 27 Jan 1793, as guardian.

Page 299: Estate of ROBERT LEE to JOHN LEE, Admr. Legacies to MINTRY & ELIZABETH
          LEE....Allowed Oct. Ct. 1774. Pd.: JOHN HAMER, JOHN FROHOCK, WILLIAM
BROOKS, JOHN COLSON, MR. MEDLOCK, MR. COLSON, MR. COOPER , MR. SPENCER, JAMES
PICKETT, HUMPHRYE YARBROUGH, MR. COLE, THOMAS PRESSLER, THOMAS LACY, MR. DUNN.
JOHN LEE (+).

Page 300: STEPHEN MILLER to the Estate of REUBIN PHILLIPS, decd. 1792. Pd.:
          CLEMONS PHILLIPS, WILLIAM MAY, POLLY STRICTLIN, Pr. STEPHEN MILLER.

Pp. 301-302: Acct of money expended to the Estate of ANDREW BERRY. Recd by RICHD
          BERRY, Admr. Pd. THOMAS WARE, THOMAS PRICE, NATHANIEL HENDERSON,
CAPTAIN FIER, THOMAS YEATS, ANTHONY HUTCHINS, ANDREW CATHEY, JAMES MILLER,
DANIEL HACKETT, JOHN FROHOCK, JOHN CONBEL, GEORGE ELLIET, ROBERT McCLENACHAN
JOSEPH JONES, JOHN CATHEY, WILLIAM MORRISON, THOMAS ROBINSON, WILLIAM ADAMS,
JOHN JOLTON, JOHN COWEN, DAVID CAVE, JOHN DAVIS, JAMES MORE, DAVID WHITE,
JAMES McCOLOUGH, WILLIAM LEWING, MOSES POTTS, SAMUEL COBOURN, MICHAEL WALLACE,
CHARLES HARRIS, JOHN McCONNELL, GEORGE CATHEY. RICHD BARRY.

Page 302: Jan. Ct. 1772, Account of TIMOTHY TAYLOR, Admr. of estate of JOSHUA
          WEAVER. Pd. 1 Jan 1766, Schooling for two children. Bibles for WM.
& ELIZ. WEAVER. Pd. Widow 1/3.

Page 303: Estate of MATTHEW TOOLE to WILLIAM DREW, __ Feb 1757. Cash of SAMUEL
          COBOURNs acct. March 1757-Feb. 1758.
Rowan County: WILLIAM DREW proved acct 18 Jan 1762. ALEXR. OSBURN, JP.

Page 304: Estate of AMBROSE STILL, decd to wife ANN, Admx. 25 July 1760. Pd.
          NICHOLAS WHITE for going to Charleston. Pd HOPKIN HOWELL for going
to fetch part of estate from Charles Town. JOHN FROHOCK, Clk. Cash recd from
THOMAS JONES, JOHN CRAWFORD, THOMAS TOMKINS, GEORGE DOBBS. Estate of JOHN MOORMAN.
ANN STILL (+).

Page 305: Account of BURWELL GREGG, decd. to ABNER GREGG, of Dinwiddie Co., Va.,
          20 Aug 1756. Cash to my brother, JESSE GREGG. Sworn by ABNER GREGG,
Anson Co., 28 Sept 1756, before ALEXANDER LEWIS. ABNER GREGG (X).

Page 305: 17 Jan 1757, I assigned my whole right to property. Test MATTHEW
          CLEMENTS. ABNER GREGG (X).

Page 306: Account of THOMAS SPRATT, decd, to THOMAS POLK, Admr. (n.d.). Pd.:
          JOHN CLERK, WILLIAM BARNETT, JOHN BARNETT, INFINES (?) NEEL, & THOMAS
POLK, legatees.
          Contra Cr.: GEORGE CRAWFORD, ANDREW BERRY, JOHN PRICE, WILLIAM POLK,
SEN., WILLIAM POLK JUNR., GEORGE DERUMPLE (DALRYMPLE), THOMAS POLK.

Page 307: 26 Sept 1772, Account of JOHN HICKS, decd, 11 Jan 1772. to RICHARD
          DIXON, Admr. Wit: CHAS. MEDLOCK.

Page 308: Estate of JOHN HICKS, decd 25 July 1767-4 July 1772. MORGAN BROWN,
          JOHN AMER.
          1770, JOHN HICKS to SAMUEL SNEAD...
          13 Sept 1784: DANIEL SNEAD, Exr. of L. W. & T. of SAMUEL SNEAD made
oath that the above acct is as it stands in his fathers books. CHARLES MEDLOCK.

Page 309: 1773, Account of CHAS. MEDLOCK, guardian to orphans of JOHN HICKS,
          decd. JOHN HUSBANDS, note. Cash pd.: MRS. KERSHAW, STEPHEN JACKSON,
ELISHA PARKER, WILLIAM SPEED, WILLIAM HICKS, MORGAN BROWN, ROBERT THOMAS,
HUNT & TANNEY (?), WILLIAM HALEY, WM PICKETT, Sheriff. ANDR. GIBSON. Vouchers
all destroyed by "British and Toryes." MICHAEL AULD, Clk.

Page 310: JOHN HICKS, decd to ROBERT THOMAS, Child's coffin, coffin for self,
          4 Apr 1774. Wit: JAMES COTTEN (COLLON?). Final Settlement of Estate of
JOHN HICKS. Money pd. to ALEXR. BIGGAM, JOHN HUSBANS. 1788 Jan. Ct.

Page 311: 7 Jan 1783, Estate of PETER LEWIS to BURWELL LANIER, 1779. STEPHEN
          MILLER, JP.

          Estate of REUBEN PHILLIPS, decd to CLEMENT PHILLIPS 18 Mar 1782. Pd.
THOMAS GADDY, TIMOTHY HANEY, JERRY GULLEDGE, NATHANIEL DOBBS, ABRAHAM STRICKLAND.

(There are two pages numbered 312 and 313 each, they are abstracted in the order
 they occur in the original.)

Page 312: 7 July 1783, Account of JAMES ROPER's estate with JOHN LILLY. To:
          PETER RANDLE, MR. KENDLE, CHARLES RAY, JOSEPH McALLISTER, MRS. ROPER.
Contra: GEO. GOODWIN.

Page 313: Estate of WILLIAM BENSON to ELIZABETH BENSON, Admr. 28 Apr 1784. Settled
          1 Apr 1785. Paid: ARCHER LAYNS, JOHN HAND "for bringing the children
from South Carolina" to JOHN & JOSEPH PLEDGER, WIDOW FAUTENBERRY, Paid Grannys fee
for a child born before the death of WILLIAM BENSON...MICH AULD, Clk.

Page 312: Estate of WILLIAM BENSON to ARCHER LAYNE 1780. Attested to 8 Sept 1784.
          JOHN AULD, JP.

Page 313: 26 July 1758, Account of estate of JOHN CARMICHAEL to WM. CARMICHAEL...
          "to the carriage of his goods from Pensylvania to Dann River...to
carriage of sd. goods from Dann to Rockey River...Pd. JAMES HARRIS, CHARLES
HART, NATHANIEL ALEXANDER. WILLIAM CARMICHAEL (X).

144

Page 314: Account of estate of BURWELL GRIGGS, to PRESTON GOFORTH, Nov. 1752-1756. Cash pd. by RICHD. WALLICE.

Estate of ROBT McCORKELL to JAMES LINN, (n.d.). Pd. MARGARETT McCORKELL, THOMAS McELHINEY.

Page 315: PRESTON GOFORTH proves account on estate of BURWELL GRIGGS, 3 Feb 1757. Estate of MATTHEW TOOL to ELENOR TOOL. Pd: JOHN DUNN, WILLIAM DREW, JOHN CARTHY, GEORGE CARTHY.

Pp. 316-317: 1767, Estate of JAMES McMANUS, decd to MARY McMANUS, Admx. Pd.: WILLIAM RUSHIONS, WILLIAM & GEORGE LITTLE, JAMES GROVES, JOHN EDWARDS, JOSHUA BRADLEY, GEORGE CATHEY, THOMAS PAGE, GEORGE PARKS, DAVID ADAMS, GEORGE KIST, BOSTON HAGGLER, JAMES PHILLIPS, JOHN SILLS, MARTIN PHIFER, PHILIP HERNDON, SAMUEL YOUNG, GEORGE RENNIX, ISAAC WIDNOR, HENERY WHITE, JAMES PICKETT, EDWARD BLACK, MATHEW ARDIS, ANTHONY FUNDER BURY, SAMUEL WILSON, TITUS LANEY, EPHRAIM CANNER, HUGH MONTGOMERY; NICHOLAS COONE Bond, JOHN PICKENS, JR., Bond.

Page 318: 1759, Estate of JOHN MORMAN, decd, to THOMAS MORMAN, Admr. Pd.: JOHN COLE, SAMUEL BRUTON, JOHN JONES, CHARLES CLERK, JOHN DOWING, CHARLES MORMAN, RICHARD YARBOROUGH, WM HARRINGTON, ALEX McKOY, CHARLES HILL.

Pp. 319-320: 1763, Estate of JAS IRWIN, to MARGARETT IRWIN, Admx. Pd.: SARAH WILSON alias POTTS, JAMES TANNER (TAMER?), MOSES ALEXR., ANDW NEEL, WILLIAM STAIRET, COL NATHL. ALEXR., JOS. KERSHAW, BENJM. ALEXR., WILLIAM WILLIAMSON, JOHN GILMORE, SAMUEL PICKENS, DANIEL ALEXR., MOSES FERGUSON, HUGH ERWIN, ANDW. ALEXR., WILLIAM MILLIKIN, JNO PENNY, JOS JONES, CHARLES MOORE, JNO STALFINGER, WM SMALL, ARTHUR IRWIN, CHARLES HARRIS, WIDOW ROSS, JAMES MARTIN, COL. FROHOCK, MATTHEW IRWIN, THOMAS POLK, FRANCES ROSS.

Page 320: (n.d.), Estate of DAVID LOGAN, decd. Pd: WILLIAM STARRAL, THOMAS DAVIS. MARY CARRADINE (+).

Page 321: (n.d.), Estate of AVINGTON SHERRILL to PERSHANNA WILLIAMS, Admx. Pd: JOHN PATTAN, DANL WAMOCK, MR. DUNN, GEO TUMELSON, ROBT McCLENACH; PERSHANNA WILLIAMS.
(PERSHANNA WILLIAMS was the widow of AVINGTON SHERRILL and had apparently remarried.)

Pp. 322-323: Estate of JOHN KELLER, Pd.: THOMAS JOANS, MOSES ALEXANDER, WILLIAM MOORE, MICHAEL HOYL, JOHN PATTAN (?), HUGH BERRY, PATRICK ONEAL, ALEXANDER DAVIS, JOHANNA HUMPHREYS, CHARLES MOOR, MARTIN PHIFER, EDWARD GIVENS, THOMAS JONES, PETER KIRKINDALE, GEORGE DENNY, JOHN KENNY, MATHEW McCLURE, BENJAMIN HARDING, GEORGE CATHEY, CATHARINE McCONNEL, JOHN ARMSTRONG, GEORGE RUTLEDGE, JOHN MOORE, JOHN WALKER. Recd. of MR. MOTTE for JOHN KELLER, service in Provincial troops...Recd. of JAMES ORMOND...HANNAH MILLER, Admx. (n.d.)

Page 323: JOHN THOMAS Claim agnst estate of STEPHEN THOMAS decd. (n.d.)

Page 324: Estate of PHILLIP CHITTAM to WILLIAM HENRY. 26 July 1758. Note from WILLIAM McKELHONEY & MALCAM ALLEN; note of JAMES McCORD; Pd.: J. THOMAS, DAVID STANLEY. ₤2 s1 WILLIAM HENRY delivered to the mother of the orphans.

Page 325: Estate of MATTHEW TOOLE to JOHN HILL 20 Jan 1761. Estate of PETER HOYLE decd to MICHAEL HOYL...to JACOB HOYLE.(n.d.)

Page 326: JOHN GIFFORD's estate to THOMAS BURNS, 1755. Pd: ANDREW PICKENS.

19 July 1779, Recd of CHARLES MEDLOCK for guardian for orphans of
JOHN HICKS. FRANCIS HICKS (X-her mark). 25 Mar 1778, Recd of CHARLES MEDLOCK
for tax on HICKS estate...23 Jan 1779, Recd of CHAS MEDLOCK, for tax on HICKS
estate. WILL HARRINGTON.

Page 327: Estate of CHARLES BURNETT (n.d.), Pd: STEPHEN WHITE, SAMUEL BURNETT,
            CHARLES SMITH, ALEXR. NESBITT, JAMES JOHNSON, JOHN BAXLEY.
        Recd 8 July 1774 of CHARLES MEDLOCK on acct. of JOHN HICKS for ELY
KERSHAW & COMPANY. JOHN CONALSON.
        I promise to pay CHARLES MEDIOCK for 2 lots in Rockingham #10 & #44.
22 Oct 1787. JOHN HUSBANDS.

Page 328: 16 June 1781, REUBIN PHILLIPS to WILLIAM MAY proven 2 Sept 1782.
            STEPHEN MILLER, JP. Recd 8 July 1783, WILLIAM MAY.

        1780, MR HACKFORD to Estate of CORNELIUS EVANS, decd. Pd.: JOHN
GRIFFEN, SENR. BRITAN BRASWELL, JOHN RAY, JOHN WALLIS JUNR., THOMAS DUNN,
WIDOW OLIVEHEAD, WILLIAM MEDCALF.

Page 329: Estate of SHACT LONG. July Ct. 1772-Dec 1774. Proven Jan Ct. 1775.
            JOHN AULD Clk.

Page 330: 8 July 1783, Estate of JOHN WILLIAMSON to DAVID JAMESON. Akcts: JOHN
            BLOODWORTH, MATTHEW WILLIAMSON, MARY WILLIAMSON, LAMUEL WILLIAMSON,
BURWELL LANIER, PATRICK BOGGAN, REBECKAH WILLIAMSON, widow of sd. JOHN. Proven
July Term 1783. MICH AULD Clk.

Page 331: 1783. BENJAMIN PHILLIPS to the Estate of WILLIAM FIELDING...wifes right
            to 1/3 of estate....4 Aug 1791 JOHN HINNIGS, WILLIAM WOOD, WILLIAM JOHN-
SON , Commissioners.

Pp. 332-336: WILLIAM LEAKS estate of WILLIAM THOMAS 22 Dec 1778-Nov 1780. Pd:
            JEREMIAH TERRAIL, JOHN CHILES, NOAH AGEE, GEORGE JEFFERSON, JOSEPH
CHAPLIN, JAMES MEREDITH, ELIZABETH LEAK, FRANCIS LEAK, MR. HARDEAWAY, JEREMIAH
NENHS, WALTER LEAK, to Virginia & back; MR. MASK, DAVID RITCH, THOMAS DOCKROY,
JOHN COLEMAN, JANE INGRAM, JAMES GORDON George Town, JOHN LONG, JOHN NEWTON,
THOMAS WADE, JOHN COVINGTON, DAVID FERGISON, ISRAEL SNEED, BENJAMIN POISEL;
            Recd of THOMAS WADE, WILLIAM PICKETT, JOHN WALTERS, DANIEL McDANIEL,
GEORGE CHILES, NOAH AGEE, THOS PICKETT. April Ct. 1783. MICH AULD, Clk.

Page 336: 17 May 1784, Account of JOHN COVINGTON, SR., with estate of WILLIAM
            LEAK for 1783.

Page 337: Estate of WILLIAM GRIFFIN HOGAN 4 Oct 1784, to FORD DEJARNETT, Shff of
            Montgomery County; CHARLES HARRINGTON, note; RICHARD YARBROUGH, proven
acct; EDMOND LILLY, proven acct; MARY ROPER, note; HENRY PLAYER, proven acct;
JAMES FLETCHER, pr. Judgemt.
            29 June 1784, Recd of MSSRS HANNAH, JESSE GILBERT, HOGAN.
                                                    HENRY PLAYER.

Page 338: 17 Apr 1765, Recd of MARY McMANUS, Admx. of Estate of JAMES McMANUS, decd....HUGH MONTGOMERY.
2 Oct 1765, Recd of MARY McMANUS....FRANKLIN (sic).
7 Apr 1762, Recd of MARY McMANUS ....GEORGE PARKS.

6 July 1784, Recd of MRS. HANNAH HOGAN, Admx. of WILLIAM G. HOGAN part of a judgement obtained by SHADRACK HOGAN agnst. WM. G. HOGAN by me FORD DEJARNETT, Shff of Montgomery Co.

Page 339: Recd 24 May 1793, of GEORGE LITTLE of Chowan County...for McNEALS admn. against JAMES McMANUS. SAMUEL JOHNSON Clk.

Recd of MARY McMANUS...deposition taken by JOHN OGLETHORP, ESQ. 26 Apr 1766, CARL BRENT.

CHARLES BENCE vs. JAS McMANUS--Rowan Inferior Court 1761...Execution Docket #37, JOHN FROWHOCK, Clk.

Pp. 340-341: WILLIAM ROBERTS in acct with JAMES TERRY (estate?)....
4 Oct 1774---tending Cumberland Court.20 Jan 1775, 1 Jan 1776, 9 Sept 1776, 2 Feb 1777, Account returned July CT. 1777. JOHN AULD, Clk.

Page 342: Blank.

Page 343: JOHN STANFIELD, Decd 22 July 1795, DANIEL YOUNG, JOHN LOWRY, MALACHI WATTS. Anson Court, July Session 1795.

Page 344: SAMUEL PHILLIPS, decd, Report. By order of April Ct 1795, Debts of sd. estate discharged...EZRAH BOSTWIC, WILLIAM HENRY, CHAS. VIVION. Returned July Ct. 1795.

(END)

WILLS FROM SECRETARY OF STATE'S PAPERS

Vol. I, p. 74: Will of JOHN ASHLEY of Anson County...to son JOHN ASHLEY, sl
            to son FRANCES ASHLEY, sl...to daughter MARY ANN FRANCES, sl
...to daughter EALINER SUTTON, sl...to daughter ROSE TOUCHSTONE, sl...to son
WILLIAM ASHLEY, 100 A I now live on & 100 A on Bare Creek...to daughter SARAH
ASHLEY 100 A, the remainder of WILLIAMS ASHLEYs on Bare Creek...to son JURDEN
ASHLEY, my young Blaz faced mare...wife MARY ASHLEY, Exr...19 Feb 1759...
JOHN ASHLEY (2) (SEAL), Wit: RICHD YARBROUGH, FREDRICK TOUCHSTEN, CHRISTOPHER
TOUCHSTONE.
            [The above named ROSE TOUCHSTONE was the wife of FREDERICK
            TOUCHSTONE, see Anson County Deeds, Vol. 3, pp. 60-61.]

Vol. VI, p. 66: Will of WILLIAM COLEMAN of Anson County...1 May 1750...three
            eldest sons WILLIAM, THOMAS and JOHN COLEMAN, the plantation
where I now live, to be divided as they arrive to the years of 21...my two
youngest sons JAMES & SAMUEL COLEMAN, the plantation on Mountain Creek, 300
A, as they arrive at 21...to all my 5 children, my breeding mares...wife
ELIZABETH...wife & JOSEPH WHITE, Exrs...WILLIAM COLEMAN (SEAL), Wit: MARY
COLEMAN (M), ANTHONY HUTCHINS, JNO. HAMER.
            Letters issued 10 July 1750.
At court held 4th Tuesday in June 1750. Justices: JAMES McLEWEAN, JOSEPH
WHITE, CHARLES ROBINSON, EDMD CARTLEDGE, SAML. DAVIS, ALEXR OSBORN, will
was proved by all three witnesses...ELIZABETH qualified as Extx...THOMAS
JONES Clk. C:

Vol. XVII, p. 24: Will of WILLIAM KEMP of Anson County, 20 April 1750...
            to wife, one grey horse, one strawberry roan horse...
five sons, JOHN, WILLIAM, THOMAS, JOSEPH, & STEPHEN KEMP...daughter SARAH
KEMP and orphan committed to my care namely SARAH WALBROOK...two tracts of
land in Craven County, South Carolina on Black Mingo Creek...land over the
river bought of JOHN STAFFORD, to son WILLIAM...wife ELIZABETH, Extx...WILL-
IAM KEMP (K) (SEAL), Wit: ANDREW MOREMAN (A), Jurat, JO [JNO?] STAFFORD,
ANTHONY HUTCHINS. Proven by ANDREW MOREMAN & ANTHONY HUTCHINS, 3rd Tuesday
in October 1750. Also mentions land bought of SOLOMON HUGHES, 214 A on
Pee Dee, adj. ANDREW MOREMAN.

Vol. XVIII, p. 22: Will of JOHN LEETH of Anson County...21 July 1757...to
            JOSIAH LEETH, son of GEORGE LEETH...unto MARY WHITE,
daughter of JOSEPH WHITE...friend ANTHONY HUTCHINS, Exr...J. LEETH (SEAL),
Wit: JOHN THOMASON (+), SAMUEL SMART (+), ANTHO. HUTCHINS, MARY THURMAN.

XVIII, p. 50: Will of JOHN LITTLE of Anson County, being now advanced unto
            old age and gray hairs & Long sickness...to son THOMAS LITTLE
of Rowan County, Ł5 (if ye Ł28 s9 now in dispute between JOHN BETTY & me
be recovered)...to son WILLIAM LITTLE...to son JOHN LITTLE...to grandson
THOMAS LITTLE...to son ACHD LITTLE...to daughter MARTHA, wife of JNO. REED...
to wife (not named)...to son JAMES...to daughter MARGRET... to son ALEXR, one
cow bought at KALLYs vendue...to two youngest sons sd. JAMES & ALEXANDER, ye
plantation where I now live...son JOHN & neighbor JOHN CATHEY, Exr... 8
Dec 1755...JOHN LITTLE (SEAL), Wit: CHARLES MOORE, HENRY JOHNSTON, MARY RENICK.
            [The WILLIAM LITTLE named in the above will has a will
            which was probated in Tryon County, N. C.; filed in
            N. C. Archives with Lincoln County Wills.]

Vol. XIX, p. 38: Will of ROBERT McCORKEL of Anson County...to children
ARCHABL McCORKEL & ROBERT McCORKEL ye plantation I now
live upon also a tract on ye East side Cataba adj. ANDREW NOTT [sic],
when of age... to wife [not named]...200 A on watters of Cain Creek...JAMES
McCORKEL, MARGRET McCORKEL & JAMES LINN, Exrs...___ Aprill _____...ROBERT
McCORKEL (SEAL), Wit: JOHN CROCKETT, _____ WHITE.

Vol. XXIV, p. 42: Will of ANDREW PICKENS...WILLIAM DAVIS & my wife NANCY,
Exrs...plantation I now live on, 551 A, 300 A to son
ANDREW, & rest to son JOSEPH ...to son JOHN PICKENS, ₤10 after five years...
to son JOHN, a meare...to daughter JEAN, a black mear...4 Nov 1756...
ANDW PICKENS (SEAL), Wit: ROBERT McCLENACHAN, JOHN PICKENS.

Vol. XXVI, p 17: ___Nov 1750, WILL of JOSEPH REED, being very sick...to wife
one riding horse...to son WILLIAM REED, 400 A near Cutawba
River...my plantation I now live on to my wife...JOHN BRANDON & JOHN NESBET,
Exrs...JOSEPH REED (O), Wit: JOHN ARLEDGE, JOSEPH CATE, JOHN RAILY. Proved
July Ct 1751. Letters granted 6 April 1752.

Vol. XXVI, p.74: Will of CHARLES ROBINSON of Anson County, being very sick...
29 Dec 1754...son CORNELIUS as soon as he shall arrive at
full age to make title to land already sold to ADAM READEN in Virginia &
received the money in trust for his mother...two daughters SARAH & ELIZABETH
300 A known as Island tract...2 sons TOWNSEND & CHARLES and daughter CATHERN
MOORMAN, tract known as DISONs tract...to wife SARAH ROBINSON, plantation
where I now dwell...wife SARAH, CHARLES, & TOWNSEND ROBINSON, Exrs...
CHARLES ROBINSON (SEAL), Wit: WM. DOWNS, JOHN SLOAN (Htt), JAMES DENSON (J).

Vol. XXX, p. 7: Will of THOMAS SPROT of Anson County, weak in body...my son
JOHN CLARK, s5...to daughter MARY BARNET s5...to daughter
ANN BARNETT... to daughter JEAN NEEL, s5...to daughter SUSANNAH POLK, s5...
to my only son THOMAS, plantation on Twelve Mile Creek...to daughter MARTHA,
plantation on Sugar Creek...wife [not named]...ANDREW SPROT & THOMAS POLK,
Exrs...15 Jan 1751...THOMAS SPROT (O), Wit: WILLIAM BARNET, JAMES SPROT,
JAS: CAMPBELL.

S. S. 1 [No county given] Estate of JAMES ALEXANDER 8 Oct 1754; ANN
     ALEXANDER, JAS. CARTER, JOHN LUCKIE. Before CHARLES COGDELL
JUNR.
     [This was determined to be a bond from Anson County, by deeds
     from JAMES ALEXANDER & wf ANN; See Anson County Deed Book B,
     pp. 314-316.]

S. S. 5 Anson County Estate of NATHANIEL DAUGHTERTY 28 July 1757;
     PHEBE DAUGHERTY, FRANCIS DEVENPORT, SAMUEL DAVIS Before
JOHN FROHOCK, WILLIAM DAVIES.

S. S. 6 Anson County Estate of WILLIAM FORGUSON 22 Jan 1759; ALEXANDER
     FORGUSON (FERGUSON), GEORGE RENNIX, JAMES BARNETT. Before JOHN
FROHOCK, ROBT McCLENACHAN.

S. S. 7 Anson County Estate of BURRIL GRIGGS 26 Jan 1756;   ALEXANDER
     LEWIS, JAMES PICKIT, JOHN PRICE. Before JOHN FROHOCK, JAS. ROBIN-
SON.

S. S. 9 Anson County Estate of JOSEPH HOLLINGSWORTH 24 Jan 1758;
     MARTHA HOLLINGSWORTH, ISAAC COX, ISAAC COOK. Before JOHN
FROHOCK, ROBT McCLENACHAN.

S. S. 11 Anson County At Court 3rd Tuesday in April 1753... JAMES KILL-
     PATRICK petitioned for letters of administration on the estate
of WILLIAM LEECH...Security RICHARD HILLIAR, WM LINN. JOHN DUNN, Clk Ct.

S. S. 11 Anson County Estate of JOHN LITTLE 28 July 1756; JANNET LITTLE,
     JOHN CATHEY, JAMES ARMOUR Before JOHN FROHOCK.

S. S. 11 Anson County Estate of THOMAS LOCKARD 24 Jan 1758; NATHANIEL
     ALEXANDER, LEVINOUS HUSTON, JAMES ALEXANDER, WILLIAM ALEXANDER.
Before JOHN FROHOCK, JONATHAN DOWNS.

S. S. 12 Anson County Estate of JOHN MORMAN 26 Apr 1758; THOMAS MORMAN,
     THOMAS UNDERWOOD, FRANCIS CLARK. Before JOHN FROHOCK, WILL
CUMMING.

S. S. 13 Anson County Estate of WILLIAM McKEE 27 Apr 1757; JANE (JEAN)
     McKEE, ALEXANDER LEWIS, ROBERT McCLANNAHAN. Before JOHN FROHOCK.

S. S. 14 Anson County Estate of DAVOLT PAFF (PATF) 22 Jan 1756; JOHN
     THOMAS, ESQ, ROBERT McCLANNAHAN, GEO RENNIX. Before JOHN
FROHOCK, JNO. HAMER.

S. S. 14 Anson County Estate of JOHN PRICE 4th Tuesday in March 1750.
     RACHELL PRICE, widow of JOHN PRICE...ALEXD OSBORN, ESQ; JOHN
BREVARD, ESQ.

S. S. 15 Anson County FREDERICK VALEER ROACHMET 24 Oct 1757; GEORG
          BARRINGER [German signature], MICHAEL MOYER (MYERS) [German
signature]; PAUL BARRINGER, HEINRICH (HENRY) FURR [German signature].
Before JOHN FROHOCK, WM DOWNS.

S. S. 16 Anson County Estate of AVINGTON SHERRILL 25 Apr 1759; PERSHANNA
          SHERRILL, JAMES ROBINSON, JOHN THOMAS. [No wit. or Clk. sign.]

S. S. 16 Anson County Estate of WILLIAM SMITH 27 Apr 1757; JOHN SMITH,
          CHARLES ROBINSON, WILLIAM STONE. Before ANTHO HUTCHINS, JOHN
FROHOCK.

S. S. 17 Anson County Estate of JOHN SNODDY 26 July 1758: AGNISS SNODDY,
          HENRY HENDRY, ALEXANDER LEWIS. [No wit. or Clk. sign.]

S. S. 18 Anson County Estate of SARAH TOUCHSTONE 29 Jan 1758; FREDERICK
          TOUCHSTONE, HENRY TOUCHSTONE, HENRY DOWNS, JAMES PICKETT, ESQ.
Before JOHN FROHOCK, JONATHAN DOWNS.

S. S. 20 Anson County Estate of WILLIAM WILSON 24 Jan 1758; SARAH WILSON,
          WILLIAM SHARPE, JAMES FANNEN [No wit. or Clk. sign.].

          Inventories from Secretary of State's papers
Archives S. S. 887; S. S. 892; S. S. 894; S. S. 897.

S. S. 887, pp. 2-4: Inventory of JOHN DAVISON, decd 1 Dec 1749/50, by
          WILLIAM MORRISON, Admr. before JAMES MACKILWEAN. Anson Court
Dec. 1749/50. Inventory filed Feb 1749/50. JANE DAVISON was Admx, now
Admr. is WILLIAM MORRISON, sd. JANE's present husband. JOHN DUNN Clk Ct.

S. S. 892: Inventory of JOHN DAVISON, 1 Dec 1749/50, by WILLIAM MORRISON.

S. S. 894: Anson County: Inventory of goods & Chattles of BURILL GRIGG, Decd.
          Includes 500 A on ye South fork Catawba. Notes on: NATHAN
ORR, JOSEPH REES, SAMUEL COBOURN, ROBT BRANKS, JOSEPH CLARK, THOS KELLY,
RICHARD RUNELS, JOHN McCLANE, JAS JONES, MATHEW ERWIN, EDWARD CONNOWAY,
WILLM REES, WILLM WILKINS, MATHS CLEMENTS, MARGT ROSS, AVINGTON SHERRILL,
JOHN PICKENS, WILLM GREEN, THOS LEONARD, JOSEPH CURRY, JAS KILLPATRICK,
THOS BETTY, WATSON FERILI, SAML OXFORD, WILIM RFFORD, ROBT McCLANAGHAN,
THOS REYNOLDS, JOHN LARGE, RICHD PERKINS, JACOB COUBOURN, ROBT GUTRY, THOS
HUSTON, JNO MOORE, ADAM SHERRILL, ALEXR. REYNOLDS, THOS WELGH, ELISHA
PERKINS, PHILIP SHEVER, WILLM WELCH, BLENY MILLS, SAML HOWARD, JOSEPH
GREEN, JAS. ROBINSON, JOHN ANDERSON, SAML BRASON. PRESTON GOFORTH (X), Admr.
Anson Court October 28, 1756. JOHN FROHOCK, Clk.

S. S. 897: Inventory of Estate of JOHN LITTLE by JENNET LITTLE, Admx. 17
          Aug 1756. Returned 10 Oct 1756. ALEXR. LEWIS.

                                    151

Archives S. S. 883

Returns of Probates of Wills and Administrations Granted Anson County 1766-1772

"No letters of Administration or Letters Testamentary, granted for the County of Anson, in the year from July Term 176_ or at any Time Since. Certified 25 Day of October, 1766. Saml Spencer, C. C."

"No Letters of Administration or Testamentary Granted for the County of Anson in the Year 1769. Certified 20 November 1769, Saml. Spencer, C.C. "

Date of Letters	To Whom Granted	Whose Estate	Names of Securities	Bond	What Court
27 Jan 1767	Robt John & Sarah Lee	Robert Lee	Last Will & Test.		January 1767
27 Jan 1767	Hezh Russ & Mary Giles	John Giles	Last Will & Test.		January 1767
30 Jan 1767	Jemima White	William White	Antho. Hutchins &) Nicholas Broadway)	₤50	January 1767
28 Apr 1767	Elizabeth Long	James Long	Last Will & Test.		April 1767
30 Apr 1767	Samuel Spencer	Charles Cox	James Hutchins &) Charles Medlock)	₤100	April 1767
		Certified the 25th of October 1767, SAML SPENCER.			
27 Jan 1768	Isaac Jackson	John Brasfield	Robert Broadway &) Sabray Stone)	₤40	January 1768
27 July 1768	John Stevens	William Stevens	Joseph White &) Charles Medlock)	₤300	July 1768
		Certified the 25th Day of October, SAML SPENCER.			
10 Jan 1770	Anthony Hutchins & Katherine Hunter	Thomas Hunter			January 1770
11 Oct 1770	Hannah Vanhooser	John Vanhooser			October 1770
12 Oct 1770	Mary Primrose	Violet Primrose			October 1770
		Certified this 23d Day of November 1770, SAML. SPENCER.			
	Sarah Holley	Julius Holley	William Holley &) John Jackson)	₤1500	July Term 1771
	Frans Hicks	John Hicks	Charles Medlock &) Samuel Snead)	₤1000	July Term 1772
	Catherine Little	Wm Little	Chas Medlock &) Saml Snead)	₤500	July Term 1772
	Catherine Henry	John Henry	Shadrach Denson &	₤500	October 1772

152

Index Prepared by Mary Elizabeth Phillips, Fort Worth, Texas

158

Hall (cont'd)
 Henry 121
 John 11,15,28,36,66,82,87,
 108,110,121,133
 Joseph 5,8,27,32,38,44,69,
 77,84,85,86,88,108,110,113,
 121,138
 Moses 127
 Robert 139
 William 51,121
Hallams, William 21
Halles, James 94
Haltman, James 65
Halton, John 69,121
 William 121
Hambey, Samuel 122
 see also Hamby
Hambright, Frederick 14,45,56
 Sarah 14,71
Hamby, William 112
 see also Hambey
Hamelton, John 34
Hamer, James 130
 John 3,6,7,8,17,18,23,24,
 25,36,43,52,54,56,61,78,
 80,85,90,99,100,105,111,
 114,117,121,129,130,136,
 139,143,144,148,150
 John Jr. 102,121
 Mary 136,139
 William 19,108,111,114,121,
 143
 see also Haimer
Hammill, Jacob 116,118
Hammock, Betty Ann 127
 William 127
Hammon, George 138,140
 William 69
Hamon, John 139
Hampton, Adam 102
 Andrew 2,6,41,97
Handby, John 141
Hands, John 142,144
Haney, Timothy 144
Hanna(h), Mr. ___ 23
 James 75
 John 86,142
Hansure, James 34
Harbor, John Sr. 121
Hardeaway, Mr. ___ 146
Hardan, Henry 9,10,12
Harden, Benj. 14,18,55,56,60,
 97,99,102
 Catherine 97
 John 60,77
 Joseph 135,142
 see also Hardin
Hardick, William 122
Hardin, Benj. 142,145
 Benj. Jr. 62
 Benj. Sr. 62
 Jean 56
 Joseph 14,42,56,60,77,99
 see Hardan, Harden
Harding, John 18
Harford, Nicholas 29
Harget(t), Frederick Jr. 67
 Henry 121,140
Harmon, John 139
Harrell, Moses 134
Harrelson, Joseph 121
Harrington, Agnes 5
 Charles 109,110,120,131,
 146
 Elizabeth 5
 Henry Wm. 128,130
 John 5

Harrington (cont'd)
 R. 130
 Thomas 2,4,5,6,8,14,23,24,
 34,36,41,53,59,63,66,67,80,
 88,90,103,106,114,133
 Whipmell 120
 Whitmill 5
 Widow ___ 27
 William 18,75,113,133,145,
 146
Harris, Charles 86,143,145
 Hugh 76
 James 29,44,71,74,144
 Nathaniel 29
 Robert 52,61,74,75,86
 Robert Jr. 19,57,74,75,76,
 100,102
 Robert Sr. 76
 Samuel 71,74
 Thad 138
 Thomas 138
 Tyree, 4,21,85
 Will 52
 William 86
Harrison, William 4,18,23,24,
 29,50,54
Hart, Aaron 104,121
 Charles 144
Harvey, John 12,72
 Mary 72
Hasell, James 10,89
Hasey, Isum 121
Haslep, Andrew 70
Hataway, Joseph 53
Hathorne , John 138
Hawkins, ___ 121
Hay, Abraham 90
 David Jr. 76
 David Sr. 76
 William 141
Hayes, Gilbert 22
 John 91
 see Hays
Hayle, Peter 41
Haymes, John 127
 Ruth 127
 William 127
Hays, ___ 111
 see also Hayes
Hayward, Samuel 22,46,134
Haywood, Griffin 139
Henker, George 41
 Margaret 41
 William 41
Heker, George 51
Hellams, Elizabeth 127
Hellan, Elijah 83
Hellier, Richard 21
Helms, George 59,70,90,98,100,
 110,121
 James 128
 John 59,131
 Jonathan 5,49,50,68,98,99,
 121
 Thomas 101
 Tilman 49,100,110,118
 T. 116,120
Henderson, Alex. 125
 James 15
 Mathew 55
 Nathaniel 143
 Rice 122
Henric, Frederick 92,93,94
Hendry, Frederick 60,62
 Henry 13,25,26,27,29,31,32,
 33,37,38,40,42,43,45,48,52,
 61,151

Henly, Peter 9,13,14,15,89
Henn, John 102
Henry, Catharine 131,140,152
 Izabella 42,58
 John 94,117,131,140,152
 William 42,45,58,64,145,147
Henson, Bartlet 122
 Benj. 111,122
 Charles 119,141
 Isum 122
 John 111,141
 Penelope 133
 Philip 4,7,18,35
 Philip Jr. 121,133
 Philip Sr. 122
Hern, John 117,121
Herndon, Philip 2,16,92,101,
 102,107,113,121,145
Herrington, Widow 7
Hews, Solomon 1,3,6,7,18
Hicks, Frances 125,146,152
 John 1,3,101,111,125,133,
 137,143,144,146,152
 John Jr. 85
 Mary 125
 Obediance 125
 Sarah 125
 William 1,3,17,85,100,122,
 125,143,144
Hickson, John 122
Higdon, Charles 107,110
 Leonard 103,104,107,110,119,
 121
Higgins, James 121
 John 121
 William 121
Hightower, Kindness 103
 John 121
 Thomas 103,106,121
 Widow ___ 103
Hildren, William 137
Hildreth, Anne 107
 David 11,50,56,89,107,122,
 133
 James 11,88
 Nancy 107
 William 127
Hill, Charles 107,122,145
 John 18,67,93,141,145
 Theophilus 136
 William 139
 see also Hills
Hillen, Hezea 105
 Nathaniel 2,5,8
 Nathaniel Jr. 65,97,105
 Nathaniel Sr. 65,105,121
Hillhouse, William 9
Hilliar, Richard 150
Hilliens, George 90
Hills, Durham 19,39
 see also Hill
Hinds, Joseph 136
Hines, Hames 140
 Joseph 140
Hinnings, John 146
Hinson, Philip 1
Hitchcock, John 5,6,8,9,10,12,
 27,38
Hoatan, Martha 124
 Robert 124
Hocker, William 19
Hodgen, Leonard 38
Hodges, William 122
Hogan, ___ 146
 Edward 16
 Elizabeth 137
 Hannah 137,147

164

166

Sheppherd, Jat. C. 108
Sherif, William 22
Sherly, Wm. Stutley 99,107,122
Sherrill, Abbenton (Avington) 7,12
  Adam 151
  Avington 133,145,151
  Pershanna 87,133,145,151
  Shana 12
  William 7,8,25,84,102
Shever, Philip 151
Shewell, William 120
Shin, Cornelius 122
Shite, Joseph 57
Shoefoot, George 47
Short, Daniel 59,65,123
  James 59,65,69,100,115,123
Sights, Adam 53
  Henry 142
Sigle, Elizabeth 41
  John 41
Sills, John 145
Simerman, Jacob 51
  see also Simmerman
Simm, William 76
Simmerman, Jacob 70
  Peter 70
  see also Simerman
Simmons, John 64,123
Simonson, Magnus 86
Simonston, Margaret 79
  Robert 79
Simpson, Gilbert 123
  John 138
  Samuel 123
  Thomas 123
Sims, William 78,138
Simson, Thomas 58
Sinior, George 85
  see also Senior
Sisco, John 122
Skinner, John 139
Skipper, Arthor 25
  Barnaba 110,122
  Benjamin 122
  George 7,110,122
  Thomas 102
Slaughter, Owen 108,122
Slay, Thomas 139
Sliger, Elizabeth 16
  Gasper 16
  George 20
Sloan, John 76,149
  Joseph 48
  Robert 65
Small, William 145
Smart, Humphrey 31
  Samuel 148
Smith, Aaron 60,76,87,90,98, 106
  A.F. 27
  Ambrose Joshua 16,18,90,119
  Ann 124
  Benjamin 23,30,49,59,60,103 108,109,122,128,138
  Catherine 140
  Charles 59,111,123,124,140, 146
  David 141
  Duncan 140
  Edward 69,98,106,118,122
  Elizabeth 124
  Francis 16,76,106,117,118, 119,138
  Jacob 137
  James 139
  Jasper 69,131

Smith (cont'd)
  John 4,10,13,14,22,23,24, 28,56,59,63,69,98,103,104, 106,111,115,117,122,136, 138,140,142,151
  Joseph 133
  Margaret 127
  Mary 140
  Neal 140
  Nicholas 2,3,5,8,28,31,50, 52,65,66,97
  Peter 43
  Ruth 108
  Sarah 124
  Thomas 124
  Thomas Jr. 69,98
  W. 47
  William 23,25,35,58,90,92, 101,122,141,151
  Zachariah 65,67,69,114,118, 119,122
  Zechariah 10,11,14
Snapp, Lawrance 53
Snead, Betty 126
  Caty 126
  Coger 68
  Daniel 126,144
  David 126,143
  Hendley 143
  Henley 69,122
  Henry 85,109
  Israel 69,77,86,88,110,112, 126,146
  John 126
  Patty 126
  Philip 126
  Philip Burford 126
  Samuel 98,106,107,110,122, 126,138,143,144,152
  Solomon 106,122,139
  Temperance 126
Sneed, David 57,75,120
Snider, Adam 40,42,71
  Hance Adam 71,84,86
  Sarah 71,84,86
Snipe, Robert 122
Snoddy, Agness 132,138,151
  John 132,138,151
Snody, John 33
Snow, James 75
Snuggs, Richard 60
  William 60
  see also Suggs
Sommerlin, Henry 1,23
  see also Summerlin
Spaden, Charles 95
Spaight, Richard 131
  Richard Dabbs 131
Spain, Alphius 141
Span(n), John 16,18,90,119
Speadling, Charles 19
Speed, John 131
  William 138,144
Spencer, Mr. ___ 143
  John 117,131
  Judge ___ 130
  Samuel 78,79,108,111,112, 131,152
  William 101,105,117
Spender, Charles 142
Spike, David 72
Spite, Richard 62
Spradlin, Charles 102,109,114, 123
Sprat(t), Jas. 12
  Samuel 17
  Thomas 21
  see also Sprot

Sprot, Andrew 149
  James 149
  Martha 149
  Thomas 149
Stafford, ___ 89
  Jo. 2
  John 7,39,148
Stairet, William 145
Stalfinger, Jno. 145
Stall, Letthy 124
Stanfield, Henry 139
  Jacob 139
  John 132,138,139,147
  Mary 139
  Sampson 139
Stanfill, Thomas 142
Stanley, David 60,97,145
Starral, William 145
Steel(e), John 77,134
  Joseph 93
  Thomas 77,11
  see also Stille
Stephen, Mr. ___ 62
  John 64,106
Stephens, Abner 140
  John 128,130,138,140
  John Jr. 115
  Mathew 140
  Nancy 128
  Sarah 128
  William 134,140
Steven, William 13
Steveright, John 16
Stewart, James 8
  John 82,130
  Nancy 130
  Sarah 130
  William 135
  see also Stuart
Still(e), Ambrose 6,14,15,18, 27,31,34,50,143
  Ann 143
  Stokes, Henry 15,28,36,67,82, 97,109,112,117,138,142
  Col. John 130
  Marcus 12
  Micajah 15
  Marcus 9
Stone, John 23,27,31,59
  John Jr. 63,66
  Sabray 152
  William 2,6,10,15,16,22,24 38,44,52,53,65,68,77,88, 105,113,120,121,151
Storey, George 37
Storor, Henry 122
Storry, James 92
Street, Richard 53
Stricklin, Abram 135,144
  Polly 143
Strode, George 86
Strowd, Joshua 3
Stuart, John 37
  see also Stewart
Stunkey, William 99
Sugg, George 63,123
  Mary 63,64,105
  Rosha 105,122
  Thomas 63,64,105,122
  Thomas Jr. 101,122
  Thomas Sr. 101
  see also Snugg
Suhnah, John 140
Sumaral(1), Henry 101,102
  Jacob 32
Summaral(1), Henry 3,49
  Jesse 95

167

Wilson (cont'd)
   Samuel 14,40,55,61,76,87,
     128,134,142,145
   Sarah 134,145,151
   Solomon 128
   William 151
   see also Willson
Winfrew, James 140
Winneham, Francis 123
Wisdom, William 141
Wise, Samuel 143
Wiser, Philip 72
Withrow, John 46,57,92
   Mary 57
Wittsheer, Mary 90
   William 90,113
Wodson, John 7
Wolford, Nicholas 93,123
Womack, Jacob 108
Wood, John 57,79,123
   Thomas 123
   William 138,139,146
   see also Woods
Woodmason, Charles 75
Woods, Curtis 39
   John 41
   see also Wood
Woodson, Donald 8
Worthen, Richard 138
Wradley, Joshua 142
Wright, Carney 138
   John 100,109,113,115,123
   Thomas 33,100,109,113,115
   William 123
Write, John 140
Wynsect, Richard 29

Yarbrough, Aille (Eliee) 68,
   69
   Hum. 57,80,89
   Humphrey 123,129,131,143
   Joel 15,80,123
   Jonathan 123
   Mary 125
   Richard 15,16,22,28,53,57,
     59,64,67,68,80,90,93,127,
     145,146,148
Yearly, William 59,60
Yeats, Thomas 143
Yew, William 138
Yost, Francis 67
Young, ___ 59,60
   Daniel 147
   James 72
   Mathew 72
   Robert 18
   Samuel 18,32,36,37,39,40,
     46,51,57,58,70,76,77,85,89,
     92
   William 117
Youngblood, William 116,118

Zeiklag, Samuel 48
Zickleg, Jean 87
   Samuel 87

www.ingramcontent.com/pod-product-compliance
Lightning Source LLC
Chambersburg PA
CBHW061740270326
41928CB00011B/2314

* 9 780806 308715 *